COLLECTING PAPER MONEY
for PLEASURE
& PROFIT
A comprehensive guide and handbook
for collectors and investors

BARRY KRAUSE

BETTERWAY BOOKS
Cincinnati, Ohio

Other books by Barry Krause:

Advanced Stamp Collecting
Collecting Coins for Pleasure & Profit
Collecting Stamps for Pleasure & Profit
Stamp Collecting

Photographs by Barry Krause
Prepress Services by Studio 500 Associates

Currency catalog numbers of Albert Pick's *Standard Catalog of World Paper Money*, Volumes I and II, are 1990 copyrighted and used here with permission of Krause Publications, Iola, WI.

Author's article, "Collecting Paper Money Errors," originally appeared in the copyrighted October 1991 issue of *The Numismatist*, official publication of the American Numismatic Association, Colorado Springs, CO. Reprinted here with permission.

Excerpts from *MRI Bankers' Guide to Foreign Currency*, copyright 1991 by Monetary Research International, Houston, TX. Used by permission.

U.S. currency price quotes copyrighted December 1991 by *The Currency Dealer newsletter*, Torrance, CA. Used by permission.

Official photographs copyrighted and courtesy of agencies cited. Unless otherwise credited, all photographs are by the author, of currency in his present or former collections.

97 96 95 94 93   5 4 3 2 1

Library of Congress Cataloging-in-Publication Data

Krause, Barry.
    Collecting paper money for pleasure & profit : a comprehensive guide and handbook for collectors and investors / Barry Krause.
        p. cm.
    Includes bibliographical references and index.
    ISBN 1-55870-256-3 : $17.95
    1. Paper money—Collectors and collecting—United States.
2. Paper money—Collectors and collecting. I. Title.
HG353.K73 1992
 769.5'5'075—dc20   92-18100
                                                               CIP

Acknowledgments

Jay Tell (Company President) of Americana Stamp and Coin Company, Inc. of Tarzana, CA — for generously allowing me to handle and photograph his stock of choice U.S. paper money, for use as illustrations in this book.

Krause Publications, Inc. of Iola, WI — for providing review copies of their books, for permission to reproduce covers of their publications, and for permission to use catalog numbers from Pick's *Standard Catalog of World Paper Money*. Special thanks to company editors Colin R. Bruce II and Arlyn Sieber.

Currency Auctions of America, Inc. — for permission to reproduce photos from their auction catalogs. Special thanks to Allen Mincho (Company Vice President) of Cedar Park, TX.

Lyn F. Knight, Inc. of Overland Park, KS — for permission to reproduce photos from their auction catalogs. Special thanks to Lyn F. Knight.

Stanley Morycz of Englewood, OH — for permission to reproduce photos from his company catalog.

R.M. Smythe & Company, Inc. of New York City — for permission to reproduce photos from their auction catalogs. Special thanks to Bruce R. Hagen (Company Vice President-Sales).

The currency dealers in Chapter 17 — for providing me with information about their companies, sample catalogs, and personal replies to my questions. Namely: Allen's Coin Shop, Inc.; Americana Stamp & Coin Company, Inc.; Bowers and Merena Galleries, Inc.; Corbet Cache; Terry Cox; Currency Auctions of America, Inc.; Denly's of Boston; Early American Numismatics; Gene Elliott; Steve Eyer; Hickman Auctions, Inc.; Richard T. Hoober, Jr.; Lyn F. Knight, Inc.; Gene F. Mack; Mid American Currency; Stanley Morycz; Old Dominion Paper Collectibles; Larry Parker; Ponterio & Associates, Inc.; Hugh Shull; R.M. Smythe & Company, Inc.; Stack's Coin Galleries; Mel Steinberg & Son; Superior Stamp & Coin Company, Inc.; Weymouth National; Jeffrey Hoare Auctions, Inc.; Olmstead Currency; InterCol London; Colin Narbeth and Son Ltd.; Spink & Son Ltd.

Currency dealer organizations — for providing information for Chapter 17. Namely: American Numismatic Association of Colorado Springs, CO; Professional Currency Dealers Association of Milwaukee, WI; Professional Numismatists Guild of Van Nuys, CA; Canadian Association of Numismatic Dealers of Ottawa; and British Numismatic Trade Association of Coventry.

The American Numismatic Association of Colorado Springs, CO — for permission to reprint my article on paper money errors, which appeared in the October 1991 issue of *The Numismatist*.

The currency literature dealers in the Bibliography — for providing price lists and catalogs of currency literature. Namely: Charles Davis of Morristown, NJ; Sanford J. Durst of Long Island City, NY; Lawrence Falater of Allen, MI; Orville J. Grady of Omaha, NE; George Frederick Kolbe of Crestline, CA; Marlcourt Books of Willowdale, Ontario; Numismatic Arts of Santa Fe, NM; and BNR Press of Port Clinton, OH.

The dealers in checks, stocks, souvenir cards, etc., in Chapter 6 — for providing catalogs and information about their companies. Namely: M.S. Kazanjian of Barrington, RI;

Scott J. Winslow Associates, Inc. of Nashua, NH; U.S. Bureau of Engraving and Printing of Washington, DC; American Bank Note Commemoratives of Huntington, NY; and Ken Barr Numismatics of San Jose, CA (for those not already mentioned for Chapter 17 dealers above).

Monetary Research International of Houston, TX — for permission to reprint a passage from their publication, *MRI Bankers' Guide to Foreign Currency*, in Chapter 11. Special thanks to Arnoldo Efron (Company Director).

Capital Plastics, Inc. of Massillon, OH — for providing information for Chapter 7.

Ron Downing (Company President) of *The Currency Dealer newsletter* of Torrance, CA — for providing information on his publications for Chapter 19, and for permission to reprint price quotes from the *Greensheet*.

House of Collectibles of New York City — for permission to reproduce the cover of their publication, *The Official 1992 Blackbook Price Guide of United States Paper Money*.

Atwater Kent Museum of Philadelphia — for providing photo and permission to reproduce same, of a *Fractional Currency Shield* in the museum's collection. Special thanks to Robert Eskind (Curator of Exhibits).

Western Union Financial Services of Upper Saddle River, NJ — for providing company information, photo, and permission to reproduce same. Special thanks to Warren R. Bechtel (Corporate Communications Director).

The United States Secret Service, U.S. Department of the Treasury — for providing photos and information on counterfeiting for use in Chapter 21. Special thanks to Robert R. Snow, Assistant Director, Office of Government Liaison and Public Affairs, U.S. Secret Service.

The United States Bureau of Engraving and Printing, U.S. Department of the Treasury — for providing photos and information for use in this book. Special thanks to the staff of the Office of External Affairs, U.S. Bureau of Engraving and Printing.

The United States Federal Bureau of Investigation, U.S. Department of Justice — for providing information on bank robbery for use in Chapter 4. Special thanks to Thomas F. Jones, Inspector in Charge, Office of Public Affairs, U.S. Federal Bureau of Investigation.

The United States Customs Service, U.S. Department of the Treasury — for information on laws regarding international currency transport. Special thanks to Jeff Casey, Director of Financial Investigation Division, U.S. Customs Service.

Society of Paper Money Collectors, St. Louis, MO — for providing information about the Society, and for permission to reproduce a cover of *Paper Money*. Special thanks to Society members Ron Horstman and Gene Hessler.

International Bank Note Society — for providing information about the Society, and for permission to reproduce a cover of the *IBNS Journal*. Special thanks to Milan Alusic (General Secretary) and Clyde M. Reedy (First Vice President).

ANA Library, ANA Resource Center, American numismatic Association of Colorado Springs, CO — for loan of research materials for this book. Special thanks to Lynn Chen (Librarian).

The staffs of Santa Monica Public Library, Santa Monica, CA, and Los Angeles Public Library, Los Angeles, CA — for helping me with research.

Long Beach Numismatic, Philatelic and Baseball Card Exposition, Inc. of Long Beach, CA — for information on the Exposition and for photo of bourse floor and permission to reproduce same. Special thanks to Teresa Darling.

The currency show promoters and societies of Chapter 18 — for providing information on their shows.

The currency/numismatic periodicals in Chapter 22 — for providing me with up-to-date information for this book.

The corresponding secretaries of the paper money societies in Chapter 23 — for providing detailed information about their organizations.

The museums of Chapter 24, whose staffs provided detailed information about their organizations. Special thanks to Robert W. Hoge, Curator of the ANA Museum; and to Elvira Clain Stefanelli, Executive Director of the National Numismatic Collection, Smithsonian Institution.

The Board of Governors of the Federal Reserve System — for providing information for this book. Special thanks to the staff members of the Los Angeles branch of the San Francisco District Federal Reserve Bank.

George Alevizos of Santa Monica, CA — for allowing me to use the currency reference books in his company's library.

The authors and publishers of the currency books listed in the Bibliography — books that refreshed my memory on many things I discuss in this book.

Special thanks to *Confederate Currency* experts who gave me personal advice on Chapter 3. Namely: Col. Grover C. Criswell of Salt Springs, FL; Hugh Shull of Leesville, SC; and the staff of the National Museum of American History, Smithsonian Institution, Washington, DC.

Richard Photo Lab of Los Angeles, CA — for film processing and print preparation of this book's photos.

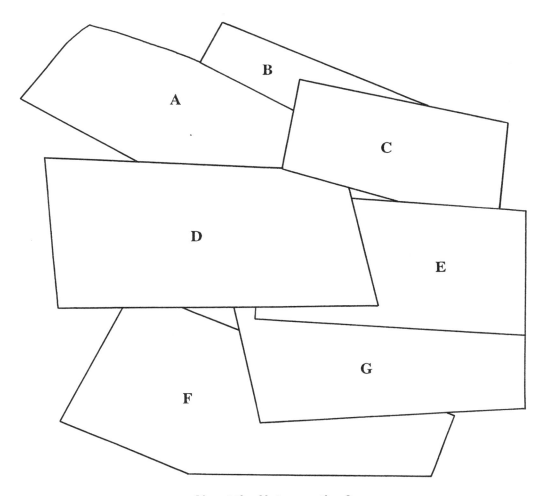

About the Notes on the Cover

All notes pictured are from the author's collection.

A. *Japanese Military Issue* of 5 *Yen*, used in occupied China. No date (but 1938). (Pick # M25)

B. Cuban 5 *Pesos* note of *El Banco Español de la Isla de Cuba* (The Spanish Bank of the Island of Cuba), issued at Havana, 15 May, 1896. (Pick # 48b)

C. World War I French emergency money, issued for use as small change due to a shortage of circulating coins. 15 *Centimes* note dated 31 October, 1915.

D. £5 *Special Voucher* of the British Armed Forces, "Second Series," no date (but 1950). Issued to British troops for use in their canteens. Invalid today. (Pick # M23)

E. Israeli 5 *Pounds* note of 1968. With engraving of physicist Albert Einstein at right. (Pick # 34a)

F. 10 *Kronen* note of Austria, 1915. "Boy" vignette. Issued by the *Oesterreichisch-Ungarische Bank* (Austro-Hungarian Bank). (Pick # 19)

G. German occupation note for Bohemia and Moravia Protectorate, World War II. 20 *Korun* note of 1944. When Germany lost the war in 1945, Bohemia and Moravia provinces reverted to their original country of Czechoslovakia. (Pick # 9s)

1. Detail of *Republic of Hawaii* $20 *Silver Certificate of Deposit*, issued in 1896 per Act of 1895; souvenir card impression. Entitled "Little Family," this vignette was engraved by Charles Schlecht. Printed by the American Bank Note Company of New York City. (Pick # 13)

Contents

Introduction 9

1. The Origins and History of Paper Money 11

2. History of U.S. Paper Money 23

3. Confederate States of America Notes 45

4. Making Modern U.S. Paper Money 55

5. Collecting Specialties of Paper Money 71

6. Collateral Fiscal Paper 81

7. Handling and Preserving Notes 91

8. Condition and Grading 101

9. Popular U.S. Notes 113

10. Rare U.S. Notes 121

11. Popular Foreign Notes 127

12. Foreign Inflationary Notes 137

13. War Notes, "Distress" Notes, and Money of Necessity 143

14. Rare Foreign Notes 153

15. Buying Notes 155

16. Selling Notes 165

17. Paper Money Dealers 173

18. Paper Money Shows 183

19. Currency Investing 189

20. Error Notes 199

21. Forgeries, Counterfeits, and Fantasy Notes 205

22. Currency Periodicals 219

23. Paper Money Societies 223

24. Museums 227

Glossary 233

Bibliography 241

Index 249

Introduction

Take a piece of PAPER MONEY out of your wallet or pocket. Stretch this NOTE in front of your eyes, with your left and right fingertips grasping opposite ends.

Look at the *face* (front side, "obverse") and notice the *portrait* — a visage of a famous person, frozen in waterproof ink rendered elegantly in graceful lines, the finished product of the master engraver's art.

Read the *legend* (inscription, lettering) on this NOTE — is it *legal tender* (lawful money)? Find the official *signatures* — is one of them the *hectographic* (printed facsimile) autograph of the nation's Treasurer? Glance at the *date* — are you sure that this NOTE was made during that year?

Turn this PAPER CURRENCY over and inspect the *back* ("reverse" side): What *shade(s)* would you call its *color(s)* of ink? Is this NOTE's *paper* really white (or is it ivory or buff or light yellow or cream)? Is the *vignette* (major pictorial part of the NOTE's *design*) simple or complex? Realistic or abstract? Historical or allegorical? Are there hidden secrets embedded in the *scrollwork* (ornate border design)? Are there *watermarks, silk fibers*, or *security threads*?

Move your finger along the PAPER MONEY's *edge* — is it smooth or frayed? Tilt this CURRENCY in front of a strong light source, and gaze across its flat *surfaces* — are there any *creases, folds, pinholes*, color *fading, scrapes, tears, thins*, or other signs of wear and damage?

What is the *denomination* (face value) of this NOTE? Is it (or was it) *convertible* (redeemable, legally exchangeable) into gold or silver? Was this piece of PAPER CURRENCY issued by a government or by a private bank?

Can you tell if this NOTE is *counterfeit* (fraudulently made)?

If the NOTE seems to be *Uncirculated* (UNC, "New"), gently fold it once in half *vertically* (up and down the NOTE's "height" or "width" — for conventionally oriented NOTE designs) through the *center* of its *body* (main portion of the paper) ... so that a *fold* ("light" paper bend) is permanently visible. Your NOTE now grades *About Uncirculated* (AU) at best!

Fold it two more times: once *horizontally* (along the NOTE's *length*), and maybe once *diagonally* (from one corner to the *opposite* corner), and press down on these folds, so that three major *creases* ("deep" paper bends) are permanently visible. Your NOTE now grades *Very Fine* (VF) at best!

Why collect PAPER MONEY?

Because it is more than mere "cash" to save or spend. PAPER CURRENCY collections chart the rise and fall of peoples and empires, the booms and busts of economic cycles, and the hopes and dreams of human beings — all symbolically etched, for the whole world to observe, in these little bits of decorated paper.

PAPER MONEY is beautiful, interesting, fun, and often valuable. Politicians *authorize* it. Skillful artists *design* it. Master craftsmen *print* it. Security crews *transport* it. Banks *distribute* it. Workers *earn* it. Businesses and charities *solicit* it. Governments *tax* it. Investors *save* it. Misers *hoard* it. Gamblers *squander* it. Thieves *steal* it. Counterfeiters *fake* it. Collectors *collect* it. Notaphilic numismatists *research* and *study* it. "Everyone" (almost!) *wants, needs*, and *thinks* about it.

Chinese Ming Dynasty NOTES on mulberry bark, Tibetan NOTES on rice paper, French Canadian *Playing Card Money*, *Bank of England* NOTES, American *Colonial* and *Continental Currency*, French *assignats*, *Confederate Currency*, NOTES of Mexican *Bancos*, *Fractionals* (*"Shinplasters"*), *"Broken Bank Notes,"* *Siege Notes of Khartoum*, Russian *Revolutionary Notes*, German *notgeld*, *Provisional Notes* of Brazil, *spurious* and *counterfeit*, *cancelled* and *reissued*, *essays* and *proofs*, *specimens* and *topicals* (NOTES with common themes, such as animals or sailing ships or lofty mountains or peaceful lagoons in their *vignettes*) — these are the paper wonders and glories in the imaginations and in the albums of *notaphilists* or *syngraphists* (PAPER MONEY collectors).

This book explores the beauties and mysteries of PAPER CURRENCY, both U.S. and foreign, both *current* (presently circulating) and *obsolete* (non-circulating), *redeemable* (exchangeable for lawful money at a bank or government agency) and *invalid* (worth only "collector" value).

The romance of early and primitively fashioned NOTES, the history behind specific NOTES of fame and obscurity, and the financial evolution of certain national CURRENCIES are all part of this story of PAPER MONEY.

Tips on buying, selling, collecting, preserving, and researching your NOTES are in this book. CURRENCY manufacturing, grading, and classifying are explained in detail. Rare U.S. and foreign NOTES, popular U.S. and foreign NOTES, CURRENCY periodicals, societies, museums, dealers, errors, investing, shows, and literature — each of these has a separate chapter in this book.

Pause and look again at the piece of PAPER MONEY in your hands. Admire this delicate paper-and-ink work of art, this ingenious fiscal creation, this "two-dimensional" economic mediator in the survival of individuals and nations, this splendid and universally recognized ephemeral concentration of power and value.

PAPER MONEY? As with anything that is small and remarkable and precious — the more you look at it, the more you see in it.

1

"When to the sessions of sweet silent thought I summon up
remembrance of things past ..."
William Shakespeare (1564-1616)
Sonnet 30

The Origins and History of Paper Money

The invention of paper is sometimes credited to Tsai Lun of the Han Dynasty in China, circa 105 A.D., but a paper-like material called *papyrus* was made from the papyrus plant (*Cyperus papyrus*) in ancient Egypt over 3,000 years ago. The word "paper" thus originally comes from an Egyptian word, which was transliterated into the Greek *papyros* ... to Latin *papyrus* to Old French *papier* to Middle English *papir* to modern English *paper*.

Barter was the original method of commerce, antedating the invention of coinage (which occurred in Lydia and Ionia in Asia Minor — what is now Turkey — in the 7th century B.C.). Coins were the first practical medium of financial exchange; i.e., a recognized standard unit of wealth freely transferable from person to person. Gold, silver, and bronze coins quickly became the money of the ancient world, and all wealth was tabulated as "so many pieces" of this or that type of coin.

The word *Money* is from the Latin *moneta* (from *moneo*, "to warn"). Juno was the Roman goddess of warning and guardian of finances, and as such she was known as *Juno Moneta*. *Currency* comes from the Latin *currens* ("to run or flow"); i.e., a constant movement (of money) from person to person.

Paper Money is any type of currency printed on paper. Besides the traditional wood pulp and cloth rags (with silk fibers, etc., added), "paper" money has been fashioned out of tree bark, leather, silk cloth, and other materials. So the term *Paper Money* must be broadly defined to include currencies made from the various raw materials that have served as paper substrates and surrogates down through the ages.

Notaphily (from the linguistic hybrid fusion of the Latin *nota* ["note"] with the Greek *philos* ["love"]; hence, "love of [paper] notes"), pronounced no-TA-fil-y, and *Syngraphics* (from the Greek roots syn ["together" or "with"] and *graphos* ["to write"], pronounced sin-GRAF-iks; i.e., "writing together" or "a written document signed by everyone legally bound to it") are both terms used for "the study and collection of paper money." The terms *Notaphilist* (pronounced no-TA-fil-ist), *Syngraphist* (pronounced SIN-graf-ist), and *Rag Picker* (slang term) are all used for "paper money collector."

A *Bank Note* (also written: *Banknote*) is, technically, a piece of paper money issued by a bank (public or private). But in common notaphilic communications, collectors and dealers use the term *Bank Note* for any paper money, whether or not it came from a bank (government or private).

In this book, I generally use the terms *Paper Money, Paper Currency, Currency, Bank Note*, and *Note* interchangeably because they are so used by many paper money collectors and dealers. Whenever I use one of these terms restrictively, I make that clear, although I try not to use *Bank Note* for non-bank issues. I sometimes include *coins* under the heading of *Currency*.

Legal Tender means "lawful money," and governments from earliest times have declared their circulating currencies to be *legal tender*, i.e., subject to compulsory acceptance by their citizens. Paper money itself has no *intrinsic value* (it is not gold or silver, you don't eat it or wear it, etc.). But paper money may be *convertible* (exchangeable into a valuable material, like gold or silver), also called *redeemable* (although the word *redeemable* is also used to mean that a particular piece of paper money is still "honored" by its issuing authority [or institutional descendant]; it is exchangeable for other money of some kind, including more bank notes). *Fiat Money* (also called *Fiduciary Money*) is not "backed" by anything materially valuable (not redeemable in precious metals, etc.). In the past, fiat paper money was often issued because (1) of government greed, (2) of general inflationary pressures, and/or (3) the royal treasuries were low on *specie* (precious metal, like gold or silver, *after* it has been minted into coinage).

We use fiat money in the United States today: our currency is inconvertible (but it is still "worth something," despite the fanatical ravings of "hard money" advocates who, sincerely or for effect, say that paper money unbacked by specie is hardly worth touching).

ORIGINS OF BANKS

Embryonic banking functions existed in ancient Mesopotamia, then Greece, then Rome. People called *money changers* and *money lenders* set up business by (a) helping other people exchange their foreign coinage for local legal tender money, (b) making loans at interest, and (c) issuing *letters of credit* (on papyrus or whatever). Money changing, interest-bearing deposits, loans, and letters of credit were well established by Roman times (services that are still offered by your neighborhood bank today). Ancient financiers were useful for "transferring" credit to distant places in an era when real money consisted of heavy metallic coins, which were impractical to move long distances. Hence the popularity of *letters of credit* in ancient Rome, carried by Roman travelers to a financier in the destination town where the credit was made good into actual coins.

The word *Bank* is derived from the Italian *banca*, meaning "bench." The moneychanger's bench or table was set up in the marketplace to serve customers who needed currency exchanges. *Bank Deposit Receipts* from Italian banks in the Renaissance circulated as money, as they were guaranteed for stated sums to the original depositors — a direct fiscal evolutionary stage to legal tender paper money. When the Bank of Barcelona opened in 1401, its financial affairs were "guaranteed" by the city government.

The First Bank Notes

Sweden is considered the first European country to have issued true *Bank Notes* (i.e., the first bank-issued paper money, payable on demand, freely transferable, and non-interest-bearing). Johan Palmstruch proposed circulating *Banckbrieflein* ("small bank letters") in 1652, which had standardized stated sums, and were transferable by endorsement by the holder. Palmstruch is therefore honored as being the "inventor" of true Bank Notes, and he founded the *Stockholms Banco*, which actually issued these notes on July 16, 1661 as *Kreditiv-Sedlar* (credit notes), with letterpress inscriptions and handwritten dates, signatures, and numbers. These were the first true Bank Notes in Europe where, therefore, Sweden has the longest paper money history (in the contemporary sense). None of these notes dated 1661 has survived, but museums own several 1662 and 1663 examples.

Some European banks are older, such as the Bank of Amsterdam, founded in 1609. And the Bank of England, which started in 1694, is the oldest European bank to have issued Bank Notes without interruption.

Central versus Commercial Banks

Central Banks are run by the nation's central government, while *Commercial Banks* are privately owned and operated (albeit under government charter). In modern times, Central Banks issue the country's paper money and coins, and assist commercial banks, which, in turn, offer financial services to the ordinary citizens of that country. Central Banks negotiate international trade between governments and manipulate (encouraging or discouraging) the convertibility of the "home" country's currency into other national currencies. Although its operation is not rigidly controlled by the government (as in many other countries), the "Central Bank" of the modern United States is the Federal Reserve System, with cooperative coordination with the U.S. Department of the Treasury.

LEATHER MONEY

Leather "money" (of a sort) was used in pre-Christian times in Greece, Rome, Carthage, and China, also in England and Russia circa 1000 A.D. Some notaphilists, such as Kenneth R. Lake (see Bibliography), prefer to classify this leather currency as "debased coinage" rather than paper money proper. If you want to use loose definitions, then this *leather money* could be called "paper" money, as could *letters of credit* carried by Roman travelers, moneylenders' *deposit certificates*, etc. But most notaphilists don't like to define "paper money" so casually.

FIRST TRUE PAPER MONEY: CHINESE NOTES

The world's first true paper money originated in China, but scholars debate the particulars. There are those who say that *fei'-ch'ien* ("flying money" — referring to the ease in transporting it, in contrast with heavy coins) from the T'ang Dynasty, perhaps as early as 650 A.D., was the first paper money. These 7th century A.D. notes were illustrated in old Chinese manuscripts, but none of the notes has survived to our own time. Chinese notes from the T'ang Dynasty in the 9th century A.D. have been discovered, so paper money may well go back to 9th century China, if not earlier. But other scholars argue that the *fei'-ch'ien* should be considered a *merchants' draft* rather than true paper money.

Chinese merchants in the 11th century A.D. issued *Jiao Zi*, a kind of paper money, depending on the definition. *Jiao Zi* circulated, and could be redeemed for metal, but it wasn't government-issued until the year 1024 A.D. (the Song Dynasty). The Song authorities set up a government paper mill in 1168, where grayish-green mulberry bark paper was made for currency. Early Chinese government notes were printed from copper plates, which replaced the wood plates of the merchants' money. Paper money devaluations and counterfeiting damaged public confidence in the notes. In 1223, Jin Dynasty printers made paper money on silk.

Marco Polo's Description of Chinese Paper Money

In 1277, the Yuan Dynasty Mongol Emperor, Kublai Khan, declared that paper money was the only legal currency in his Empire, and he abolished circulating metallic money. When the Venetian Marco Polo visited the court of Kublai Khan in the late 13th century, he was astonished to see "paper money" in use:

All these pieces of paper are issued with as much solemnity and authority as if they were of pure gold or silver; and on every piece a variety of officials, whose duty it is, have to write their names, and put their seals ... and the Khan causes every year to be made such a vast quantity of this money, which costs him nothing, that it must be equal in amount to all the treasure in the world.

Ming Dynasty Notes

Chinese paper money of the Ming Dynasty (1368-1644 A.D.) was printed from 1368 to about 1450, when paper money was abolished in China. Counterfeiting of notes persisted, despite the warning printed thereon: "To counterfeit is death." Ming notes of the 14th century are the earliest paper money that collectors can reasonably hope to obtain, with notes occasionally appearing at auction at $1,000+. Ming notes are also among the largest paper monies ever issued: about 9 x 13 inches, in vertical format.

Government abuse of its currency-making powers led to overissue of paper money in China, with the inevitable inflation and depreciation following. Paper money experience in China was so disastrous that no new notes were issued by the government for four centuries, from about 1450 to 1853.

EARLY CANADIAN NOTES

Canada has a wonderful history of paper money, which can be divided into "note categories" and time periods as follows:

1.   *Playing Card Money* (1685-1719) — first issued in June 1685 to pay the troops in New France (Canada). Lack of coin forced the Intendant of New France to create his own money by writing on the backs of playing cards. This first paper money of Canada had several issues, all of which are extremely rare today because they were redeemed for silver, then burned. Few Canadian soldiers in 1700 could afford to "collect" and hoard their *Playing Card Money*, which was declared worthless after a redemption period.

2.   *Card Money* (1729-1757) — pieces of plain white cardboard, with handwritten denominations, year of issue, and the signatures of the Governor and Intendant of New France. With a number of issues from 1729 through 1757, this *Card Money* evolved from *Playing Card Money* (above) and was issued for the same reason: coin shortage. This *Card Money* was exchangeable for *Bills of Exchange*, which, in turn, were redeemable for silver from France. Canadian *Card Money* circulated far into the 18th century but was banned by the British military authorities in Quebec in the 1790s.

3.   *Ordonnances* (*Treasury Notes*) (1753-1760) — printed notes with handwritten serial numbers, amounts, dates, and signatures, issued for military expenses. Never as popular as the simultaneously circulating *Card Money*, these *Treasury*

Notes were issued in inflationary quantities, and were redeemed at only 25% of face value after Canada was ceded to Great Britain. Like the *Card Money*, the *Ordonnances* are rare today.

4.   *Army Bills* (1813-1815) — issued by Canada to finance her resistance against America in the War of 1812. *Army Bills* were redeemable in specie in London, and because almost all were converted, they are rare. Considered by some experts to be the first true paper money of Canada.

5.   *Provincial Issues* (1763-1920) — paper money of Canadian "Provincial" Treasuries; e.g., Newfoundland, Nova Scotia, Prince Edward Island.

6.   *Municipal Issues* (mid-1800s) — notes of counties, towns, etc.

7.   *Private* and *Chartered Bank Notes* (19th and 20th centuries).

8.   *Spurious and Expired Banks* (*Notes*) (19th century; some overlap with above issues).

9.   *Dominion of Canada Notes* (1870-1925).

10.   *Bank of Canada Notes* (1935 to date) — produced by the British American Bank Note Company Ltd. and the Canadian Bank Note Company Ltd. for the government of Canada.

PAPER MONEY REPLACES COINS

The history of paper money, in every country where it appeared, has been the story of its struggle to replace coinage as the primary circulating money. Compared to heavy, bulky coins, paper money is easier and cheaper to make, store, and use. True, a coin may circulate for twenty-five years or more, while a bank note may get worn or severely damaged in a matter of months, but the public prefers a pocketful (walletful, purseful) of paper over coins, especially since the late 1960s when silver coins disappeared from the world's circulating money, and notwithstanding the efforts of national governments to eliminate low denomination bank notes in lieu of $1 coins, £1 coins, etc. For most of the world's countries with long-established, financially sophisticated cultures, 18th century paper money experiments led to 19th century gradual public acceptance and to 20th century virtual dominance of paper money as the main circulating cash medium.

HISTORY OF THE BANK OF ENGLAND

Let's look at some highlights in the history of the most famous national "Central Bank" of all time: the Bank of England, whose paper money history is well-documented. All Bank of England Bank Notes, from the first ones made in 1694, are still redeemable in London, making every one of them worth at least face value and leading to the oft-repeated adage: "As safe as the Bank of England."

Early London Goldsmiths

Before the Bank of England was created in 1694, London goldsmiths served many functions that bankers do. They had secure vaults for storage of bullion and coin; they paid *drawn notes* (similar to modern checks) on their customers' deposits; they took deposits at interest; and they issued *deposit receipts* for coin and bullion deposited by their customers (similar to pawn shop loan tickets). These goldsmiths' *deposit receipts* were payable on demand to the bearer's affixed name, and as such were the forerunners of Bank Notes. These *deposit receipts* evolved into *promissory notes* of 17th century London goldsmiths. *Promissory notes* were documents that promised to pay a specified sum to a specific person or "bearer." All paper money can be called *promissory notes* and because these notes from London goldsmiths circulated at par value, they can be considered, in effect, a type of paper money, perhaps the first "British" paper money for wide circulation (provided the *promissory notes* were recognized for what they were!). Of course, there was also the risk that a given goldsmith was a crook; i.e., issued de facto "fiduciary" notes (fiat money) without the backing (redeemability) of precious metal or other material security.

Founding of the Bank of England

In the summer of 1694, over a thousand prominent citizens, including the King and Queen, subscribed to stock (capital) in a new business venture, the Bank of England (BofE). Total capital amounted to £1,500,000. The Bank was founded partly to keep the national and City of London finances sound, it being generally agreed that goldsmiths and private financiers were too limited and unreliable to handle the growing financial needs of a great nation. The first deposits in the BofE were used specifically to support the British Army and Navy in the war against France; thus another major reason the Bank was created was to finance warfare.

In 1694, the first "paper money" of the BofE was produced: handwritten *promissory notes* and *certificates of deposit*. Partly printed notes were issued in 1696, with the sums filled in by hand as a security measure. In the 1690s, *specie notes* were issued by the Bank to lure badly needed silver in from depositors, who were given these notes in exchange, payable in silver on demand.

On May 6, 1696, the first serious "run" on the Bank occurred when nervous depositors demanded bullion (due in part to general fear of competition from other new banks), and the Bank partially suspended specie payment. There was no dividend for the Bank's Proprietors (investors) in 1696.

Bank of England in the 18th Century

The first forty years (1694-1734) of the BofE were spent in its facilities at Grocer's Hall in London. In 1724, Daniel Defoe praised the Bank's efficiency: "No place in the world has so much business done with so much ease."

Early Bank Notes of the BofE include *Cashier's Notes* or *Running-Cash Notes* — originally with handwritten dates, serial numbers, and amounts; but in 1725, some notes bore printed amounts (in denominations of £20, £30, £40, £50, and £100 … all substantial sums for that era and with moderate purchasing power even today!). The 1725 printing of fixed sum notes (from copper plates) was made possible by the invention of Henry Portal of a harder and more durable paper with better watermark definition. (The Portals still make the paper for BofE notes today.) Forgeries were a problem, and the forgers and the BofE were always trying to outguess each other in the ever-changing Bank Note production technology.

In 1734, the BofE moved into premises on Threadneedle Street, where it expanded and absorbed adjacent properties over the years to arrive at its present size and arrangement of buildings.

In 1743, the "sum block" became part of the BofE note design (with the amount printed in white gothic letters on black background), a characteristic of British Bank Notes into the mid-20th century, introduced to make the notes recognizable and as an anti-forgery device.

In 1745, all BofE notes had *fixed denominations* printed in "round figures" from £20 to £1,000. In 1759, the BofE printed £10 and £15 notes to help finance the Seven Years' War. The first £10 notes thus appeared in 1759; the first £25 notes in 1765.

Various large and small scandals infected BofE employees from time to time, such as Charles Clutterbuck's stealing blank Bank Notes, filling in the amounts, and forging the signatures. After cashing a number of these notes, he escaped to France in the early 1780s, where he was tried and condemned "to the Gallies for life." When William Guest stole gold filings from the Bank, he was convicted and hanged on October 14, 1767.

An assault on the Bank's premises by rioters in 1780 led to official demolition of adjacent St. Christopher's Church, which posed a potential attack point for Bank assailants.

A run on the BofE in 1793, when France declared war on England, resulted in bankruptcies of persons and smaller banks and a scarcity of circulating paper money. So the Bank, with the guidance of Prime Minister and Chancellor of the Exchequer, William Pitt the Younger, issued £5 notes for the first time, restoring public confidence in the Bank. Panic in 1797, caused by bullion drain from the Bank and fear of an immediate French invasion, made the BofE suspend specie payment; and the public was appeased only when London's top merchants openly declared they would accept BofE Bank Notes for any purchases. £1 and £2 notes were printed in 1797 and were widely forged, so they were replaced with a new note variety in 1798. By the end of the 18th century, £13,500,000 in BofE notes were in circulation.

Bank of England in the 19th Century

The Bank of England was the world's most powerful bank

in the 19th century, and its legendary power and security awed and reassured both nobility and commoner alike, in and out of England. In 1821, with £26,000,000 in BofE notes in circulation, and after the Napoleonic Wars with France were successfully concluded, the Bank resumed specie payments. In the early 1800s, over 30,000 Bank Notes were being made each day for the Bank.

Starting in 1826, the BofE opened branch banks outside of London. Check books with blank checks were created in 1830. Directly because of the ease with which Deputy Chief Cashier Robert Aslett embezzled £500,000 from the Bank in the early 1800s, the BofE created its "dual control" procedure, whereby valuable paper items could only be accessed by two or more employees, each with separate drawer keys, etc.

In 1855, the Bank's notes were redesigned, and the paper and watermark improved. BofE note designs remained, however, quite similar throughout the 19th and the first half of the 20th centuries. These notes are collected by *signatories*, i.e., the names of the Chief Cashiers who "signed" them (signatures have been *printed* on BofE notes since 1798). Many private banks in England went broke or were absorbed into the BofE. The BofE was the first London financial house to hire women clerks (in 1894), who were assigned to sort and count Bank Notes.

Bank of England in the 20th Century

During World War I, the BofE facilitated England's financing of her part in the War with government borrowings such as *War Loans* and *War Bonds*. From 1925 to 1939, the Bank's buildings were torn down and rebuilt to increase work space. On September 21, 1931, gold specie payments were suspended again, and Britain went off the "gold standard" as the worldwide Depression deepened.

As World War II approached, the Bank's main printing operations were transferred to the village of Overton where over two billion Bank Notes were made (over half the wartime output), including £1 and 10-*Shillings* notes printed by offset lithography (instead of the more complex engraving method). In 1945, notes above £5 in denomination were recalled by the Bank to thwart tax evaders and black market currency dealers. By 1973, over £3 billion in BofE Bank Notes were circulating.

Today the Bank of England is the only paper money-issuing bank for England and Wales, handles government loans for the National Debt, and, as the "Central Bank" of Britain, negotiates with other nations' Central Banks in intergovernmental commerce.

PRIVATE BRITISH BANKS

At the same time that the Bank of England was issuing notes, private British banks issued their own paper money from the mid-18th century into the 20th century. Hundreds of these banks issued notes in the 19th century; many of these banks either went broke or were consolidated into larger banks. If any private British bank is extant, its notes are still redeemable,

no matter how long ago they were issued (provided they aren't cancelled — rendered invalid due to redemption already).

BRITISH TREASURY NOTES

When World War I broke out in 1914, the British Treasury issued its own 10 *Shillings* and 1 *Pound Treasury Notes* to move gold coin from circulation to the British Treasury. Sometimes called the *Bradburys* for the facsimile signature of Permanent Secretary of the Treasury John Bradbury, which appeared on them, these *Treasury Notes* appeared in several subsequent issues and circulated simultaneously with the currency of the Bank of England.

SCOTTISH BANK NOTES

The Bank of Scotland was founded in 1695, and its 1696 notes consisted of £5, £10, £20, £50, and £100 denominations. Its first £1 notes were issued in 1704. The *Royal Bank of Scotland* was created in 1727, and issued its own notes. A number of 18th century Scottish banks, such as the *British Linen Company*, were founded and issued their own paper money, their descendants surviving into the 20th century. The Commercial Bank of Scotland dates from 1810, the National Bank of Scotland from 1825, and both issued notes in their first year of business. Many private banks in Scotland were founded in the first half of the 19th century, and either were absorbed by other banks or went insolvent, resulting in a few banks (like the Bank of Scotland, Clydesdale Bank PLC, etc.) surviving into the late 20th century.

IRISH PAPER MONEY

About 100 private banks in Ireland circulated their own notes in the early 19th century, and the *Irish Republic's Promissory Bonds* (of 1866-1867) passed as currency. Over a dozen major Irish banks issued notes in the late 19th/early 20th centuries.

The island of Ireland was part of the United Kingdom of Great Britain and Ireland from 1800 until December 6, 1921, when the island was partitioned into the Irish Free State ("Republic" of Ireland) in the south, with Northern Ireland remaining part of the United Kingdom in the north. Private bank notes continued to circulate throughout Ireland until 1928, when *Irish Free State Currency Commission* notes were introduced (in the south), although the private bank notes remained in the north. The Central Bank of Ireland (which continues to issue notes today for the south) issued its first notes in 1943, and the Irish Free State left the Commonwealth completely on April 18, 1949, when it became a republic. Northern Ireland, still an embattled part of the United Kingdom, continues to issue its own distinctive notes.

PAPER MONEY OF INDIA

British-India local banks issued notes during the first part of the 19th century, but all of these private bank notes were eliminated by 1862 when *Government of India* British Colonial notes (begun in 1861) were the common currency. The late 19th/early 20th century *Government of India* notes are interesting for their multi-language panels. On August 15, 1947, India was partitioned into two self-governing dominions, India and Pakistan, and India became a republic in 1950. As an independent state, India has issued her own paper money, often without dates.

EARLY PAPER MONEY OF FRANCE

French paper money can be classified by historical types as follows:

1. *Billets de Monoye* (1701-1710) — considered the first French paper money by many authorities. Issued in denominations from 25 to 10,000 *Livres*.

2. *Billets de l'Estat* (1716) — with amounts of 30 to 1,000 *Livres*.

3. *La Banque Générale* (1716-1718) — notes of John Law, a Scottish "economist" (?!) who invented "assignats" (land-backed paper money), which he explained in his treatise entitled, *Money and Trade Considered with a Proposal for Supplying the Nation with Money.* Law convinced the French government to let him issue paper money at will, and he was made *Comptroller General* of France. He issued money in inflationary quantities to support stock in his company, and when the value of the notes and stock collapsed, he fled from the country. *La Banque Royale* (see below) notes were officially declared invalid on October 10, 1720, and "all" of Law's bank notes and stock shares were burned, making them rare today. So many French people were financially ruined that the country didn't experiment with paper money again on a wide scale until the end of the century.

4. *La Banque Royale* (1719-1720) — notes of John Law.

5. *Caisse d'Escompte* notes (1776-1793).

6. *Billets de Confiance* (1790-1793) — issued to relieve a coin shortage during the French Revolution. These notes were supposed to be destroyed in 1793, so most are scarce today. Of special interest are the French *Playing Card Notes* of this issue.

7. *Assignats* (1789-1795) — French Revolutionary notes, supposedly backed by land confiscated from the Church. John Law's *assignat* monetary theory was finally put into effect in France (although it was tried earlier in Russia), with devastating consequences because the non-convertible (i.e., "fiat") French *assignats* were printed in inflationary quantities, and their real value was discounted drastically. When the government note printers went on strike in Paris in 1795, they refused to accept their own depreciated paper money, going back to work only when they were paid in bread!

8. *Siege of Lyon* notes (1793) — make lovely additions to any collection. In 1793, the city of Lyon was besieged by anti-revolutionaries, and simply designed notes were printed to serve as money. Most of them bear the legend "SIEGE DE LYON."

9. *Private French Bank Notes* — issued by 19th century French banks (examples: those at Bordeaux, Nantes, and Rouen, all of which were chartered in 1818). These banks were absorbed by the *Banque de France* (which has issued notes from the early 19th century to the present time).

FIRST JAPANESE IMPERIAL NOTES

Although some accounts indicate that the first paper money in Japan was issued as early as 1335, the first successful circulation of large quantities of government paper money began in 1868, following a proposal by councillor of state Hachiro Mioka in his January 29, 1868 speech before the *Imperial Household*. He later described his speech:

> *When my turn came, I proposed and discussed at some length the necessity and benefit of the issue of a paper money. My statements created great excitement among those assembled, and an excited discussion of the problem, pro and con, ensued. The final result of the debate was the order that my proposition be accepted, and I was authorized to make preparation for the issue of paper money at once.*

There was still some opposition to paper money from certain classes of people who sent "many assassins" to try to kill Mioka, who recalled:

> *I did not care so much for my life as for the plans of the government, for if I fell under the dagger of an assassin, the work we had undertaken might never be accomplished ... and we worked day and night, until most of the required amount was prepared.*

FIRST BANK NOTES OF SELECTED COUNTRIES

Here is a list of the years when the "first" paper money was issued in these countries. I had a few problems in compiling this list; e.g., how do we define "paper money" and how do we define "country"? Is temporary scrip from a local merchant paper money? Are unissued notes from dubious "banks" paper money? Are "emergency notes" (such as siege money) paper money? Does paper money have to be issued by a bank? And what is a *country*? A town that issued notes in the 18th century? A province or region whose politically shifting borders have moved it from nation to nation?

I have decided to use all these terms very loosely, without rigid meanings. Here is a list that some notaphilists might consider the first paper money (Bank Notes?) issue dates for certain parts of the world:

1661 — SWEDEN

1690 — "AMERICA" — Colony of Massachusetts notes (see next chapter)

1694 — ENGLAND

1695 — SCOTLAND — Bank of Scotland notes, £5 to £100

1695 — NORWAY — issued by private merchant, Jorgen thor Mohlen, under royal decree; denominations from 10 to 100 *Rixdaler Croner*

1701 — FRANCE — *Billets de Monoye*

1706 — GERMANY — Principality issues. I didn't count the cardboard emergency coinage of Leyden and Middelburg of 1574, which romantic optimists call "paper money."

1713 — DENMARK

1746 — ITALY — Italian States: *Regie Finanze* issues

1759 — AUSTRIA — *Wiener Stadt Banco-Zettel* notes

1769 — RUSSIA — Czarist Empire *State Assignats*: 25, 50, 75, and 100 *Rubles*. These *assignats* (notes backed by land), from the Imperial Assignat Banks of Moscow and St. Petersburg, were issued under Catherine the Great and were redeemable in copper until 1777, but still circulated in the mid-1780s.

1771 — BRAZIL — Colonial issue, from the Administracão Geral Dos Diamantes (Royal Diamond Administration) — drafts issued to pay diamond prospectors, redeemable in coin; printed in Lisbon, Portugal

1783 — SPAIN — the *cedulas*, royal notes issued by the Banco de San Carlos

1790 — FINLAND — issued under Swedish influence by the Kongl. General Krigs Commissariatet (King's General War Commissioner)

1794 — POLAND — the *Bilet Skarbowy* (Treasury Note) issues by General Thaddeus Kosciusko, Polish patriot, issued during the Polish revolution of 1794; first issue (dated 8 June, 1794) was in denominations from 5 to 1,000 *Zloty*. Also called: *Kosciuszko's Insurrection Notes*.

1803 — GREENLAND

1814 — NETHERLANDS — by Netherlands National Bank, the predecessor to the Nederlandsche Bank, which is the sole note-issuing authority in the Netherlands today

1819 — AUSTRALIA — notes of the Bank of New South Wales (in Sydney). Earlier notes can be argued, but this issue is undeniable.

1820 — ARGENTINA — Province of Buenos Aires *Customs Notes*

1822 — GREECE — Provisional Administration "bonds," which circulated as money; issued in Corinth and Nauplion. Feel free to disagree with me if you think another Greek issue has a better claim to the country's first paper money.

1822 — PERU — the Banco de la Emancipación "miniature" notes of José San Martin during the revolution

1823 — MEXICO — El Imperio Mexicano (the Mexican Empire) issues of Emperor Agustin de Iturbide; in 1, 2, and 10 *Pesos*

1825 — SWITZERLAND — notes of the Deposito-Cassa der Stadt Bern (in Bern)

1827 — HAITI

1840 — TURKEY — Ottoman Empire issues of Abdul Mejid; denominations from 50 to 100 *Kurus*

1840 — NEW ZEALAND — notes drawn on the Wellington branch of the Union Bank of Australia (which continued to issue New Zealand notes from 1840 to 1923). Other banks issued notes in 19th century New Zealand. The Bank of New Zealand, established in 1861, issued notes until 1934, when the first notes of the Reserve Bank of New Zealand appeared.

1847 — HUNGARY — notes signed by Lajos Kossuth, Hungarian patriot in the 1848-1849 Independence War

1852 — PHILIPPINES — Spanish Colonial notes of the Banco Español Filipino de Isabel 2a; issued in 10, 25, and 50 *Pesos*

1853 — SIAM (THAILAND) — issued under King Rama IV

1856 — LUXEMBOURG — issued by Die Internationale Bank in Luxembourg

1857 — CUBA — Spanish Colonial notes (of 50 to 1,000 *Pesos*) of El Banco Español de la Habana

1866 — JAPAN — notes of foreign banks in Japan, followed in 1867 by vertical format *Hansatsu* notes, which travelers to Japan had a habit of bringing home to use as souvenir bookmarks

1885 — ICELAND — issues of Landssjodur Islands and Rikissjodur Islands (although 18th century notes of Denmark were overprinted with an inscription meaning "For Circulation in Iceland")

1890 — IRAN — Imperial Bank of Persia notes in denominations 1 to 1,000 *Tomans*

1893 — KOREA — *Treasury Department (Hojo) Convertible Notes*

1946 — NORTH VIETNAM (DEMOCRATIC REPUBLIC OF VIETNAM)

1947 — PAKISTAN

1948 — ISRAEL

1955 — SOUTH VIETNAM (REPUBLIC OF VIETNAM)

2.   French *Assignat* of 10 *Sous*, dated 23 May, 1793, with watermark and official embossed "seals." Although purportedly "backed" by land, *Assignats* were quickly discredited in public eyes due to: (1) inflationary printing of them, (2) counterfeiting of them, and (3) their non-convertibility into specie (precious metallic coinage). (Pick # A70b)

3.   5 *Pesos* note of Paraguay, no date (but 19th century). National coat-of-arms at center, man with two burros at upper left. This note was cut from a "counterfoil" at left (i.e., a "receipt sheet" having identical Serial Number and signatures as the note). Lower center has this warning: "La ley perseguirá á los falsificadores y sus cómplices." (The law persecutes counterfeiters and their accomplices.") (Pick # A25)

4.   1 *Sol* note of *El Banco de Tacna* in Peru, 19th century. Unissued, unsigned "remainder." Girls' heads at upper left and lower right; railroad train on rural bridge at center. (Pick # S382)

5.   Uniface (printed on one side) $1 *Hungarian Fund* note issued in New York in 1852 by Lajos Kossuth to finance his Hungarian War of Independence. With Kossuth's printed signature at bottom. An engraving of him at left(!), and of "Liberty" at right. (Pick # S136)

6.   Detail of *Hungarian Fund* $1 note of 1852, showing "Hungaria" over fallen figure with crown. Printed by Danforth, Bald & Company of New York City. (Pick # S136)

7.   Local Argentine bank note: 4 *Reales* of *El Banco Oxandaburu y Garbino*, 1869. Dog portrait at center! Unissued unsigned "remainder." Printed by the American Bank Note Company of New York City. (Pick # S1781)

8. 100 *Mark* note of the "German State" *Sächsische Bank* (Bank of Saxony), 1911. (Pick # S952b)

9. Miniature 2 *Pfennig* German *notgeld* (emergency town money) of Baldenburg (to-day located in Poland). No date, but circa World War I.

10. 50 *Pfennig* German *notgeld* (emergency town money) of 1921 from Ohrdruf, a town in Thuringia. Shows Saint Boniface on one of his three visits to Pope Gregory II in Rome. Boniface was an 8th century English monk who brought Christianity to Germany.

11. *Bank of England* 10 *Shillings* note, signed by K.O. (Kenneth Oswald) Peppiatt, Chief Cashier from 1934 to 1949. This note is a "post-war" issue of 1948, as per included metal security thread (visible running vertically through the letter "B" of "Bank") and prefix coding 74J ("number, number, letter") of the Serial Number. Notice adhesive tape repair on left and right edges — virtually ruining the note's collector market value. Printed at St. Luke's Works, London.

12.	£1 note of New Zealand, type with R.N. Fleming (Chief Cashier) signature, issued 1956-1967. Captain James Cook, English naval officer and explorer, at right; watermark of Maori head at left white oval. (Pick # 159d)

13.	£1 note of Gibraltar, 1965. Vertical security thread is visible, running through the "O" of the word "ONE" at center. (Pick # 18a)

14.	Detail of the bottom reverse of £1 Gibraltar note of Photo 13. Thomas de la Rue & Company has been a London-based security printer for over a century. (Pick # 18a)

15.	£1 note of Ireland (Republic), 1983. Queen Medb at right, and watermark at upper left. (Pick # 70c)

"I know of no country, indeed, where the love of money has
taken stronger hold on the affections of men ..."
Alexis de Tocqueville (1805-1859)
Democracy in America

2

History of U.S. Paper Money

In the earliest Colonial days, there was no locally produced money in America. Permanent settlements of transplanted Europeans began to be established along the Atlantic seaboard of what is now the United States in the early 1600s. Colonial governments derived their just powers from the mother countries in Europe: the French in the north (Canada), the English in the central region (New England through the Carolinas and Georgia), and the Spanish in the south (Florida and the Caribbean and into Mexico and beyond).

The first coins to circulate in the New World were British, Spanish, and French. We speak English in the United States because the British settled what is now our eastern seaboard, and their culture spread westward as the nation grew. Eastern Canada, especially Québec, still has a strong French influence. And, of course, Spanish is the native tongue of inhabitants of most areas in the Western Hemisphere south of the United States, with Portuguese-speaking Brazil the prime exception.

The European governments were opposed to supplying their colonies with coins (and later, with paper money). The philosophy of mercantilism ran rampant in the courts of Europe as medieval feudalism declined and as the Age of Exploration flowered in the 15th and 16th centuries. Mercantilism held that a mother country's economic interest is best served by fostering strong home-based industries protected by tariffs, monopolies, and exploitation of Colonial natural resources to tilt the balance of trade always in the direction of the mother country, with the resultant amassing of huge quantities of precious metal bullion in the royal treasuries. In other words, the American Colonies (French, English, and Spanish) existed solely for their mother countries' benefit. Colonial settlers were supposed to produce raw materials, such as lumber, metal bullion, furs, and spices, which were shipped to Europe in exchange for manufactured goods like furniture and farm tools.

BARTER

Barter was the method of commerce in the early American Colonies, not by choice of the Colonists, but by default. The Colonial governments in Europe were afraid to give coins or paper money to their Colonists because the Colonists could thereby become more independent financially. No mints were established by Britain in her American Colonies, and any coins that the American Colonists happened to come by were quickly sent back to Europe to pay for manufactured goods, taxes, and "hard currency" debts.

Barter (commodity swapping) was commonly used in Colonial America, where beaver skins, tobacco, and Indian wampum (strings of shell beads) were the most prevalent money substitutes. In 1631, Massachusetts declared corn legal tender. In 1642, tobacco was declared legal currency in Virginia; tobacco was also used in extensive bartering in the Carolinas. Counterfeiting of wampum and inferior quality tobacco plagued the Colonies, which had to set up special commissions to verify the "value" of the commodity money — evidence of "currency" depreciation even before real currency existed. Wampum was still legal tender in New York until 1701.

COLONIAL CURRENCY

In paper money collecting, *Colonial Currency* is pre-Revolution American paper money. American *Colonial Currency* was made out of desperation because of chronic severe coin shortages caused, in large part, by Britain's refusal to allow her Colonies to coin their own money. Foreign coins (especially *Spanish Milled Dollars* from Spanish Colonial America) circulated in the British Colonies in America, and John Hull (a Boston silversmith) made illegal silver coins for Massachusetts Bay Colony. But the rising population and increasing commerce within and between the British American Colonies pushed them to issue their own paper money out of necessity.

The First American Paper Money

In 1690, Massachusetts Bay Colony printed *Bills of Credit* to pay military expenses for the soldiers sent to Canada to fight in "King William's War" against the French Colonists. These *Bills of Credit* bore fixed amounts of value, from 5 *Shillings* to 5 *Pounds* — for the December 1690 "issue" — and were quickly imitated by cash-short assemblies (legislatures) in other Colonies. From *Bills of Credit* (the most popular form of paper money in pre-Revolutionary Colonial America), we get the slang term "bill" — a piece of American paper money (also used for Canadian money).

South Carolina was the second British American Colony (of the original thirteen American states) to produce paper money — on May 8, 1703 — which was used to finance her military forces fighting in Florida against the Indians and Spanish soldiers. So the first two official indigenous American paper money issues were produced to pay for military expeditions.

In 1709, four more Colonies (New York, New Jersey, Connecticut, and New Hampshire) followed the convenient money-generating example set by Massachusetts and South Carolina when they issued their first paper money. Colonial "brush wars" had to be fought and paid for, and what better way to do it than by printing pieces of paper currency? Supposedly this *Colonial Currency* was backed by something, ideally convertible into bullion (gold or silver) upon demand, but in actuality this paper money circulated on public faith that the issuing authorities would honor it for its face value (or fear that they wouldn't; holders of *Colonial Currency* preferred to spend it for material goods, rather than try to redeem it for bullion — and find out what it was really worth).

Then, in succession, *Colonial Currency* was first issued by Rhode Island in 1710, North Carolina in 1712, Pennsylvania in 1723, Delaware in 1729, Maryland in 1733, Georgia in 1735, Virginia (finally!) in 1755, and Vermont in 1781.

Vermont, of course, was carved out of New Hampshire during the closing period of the Revolutionary War, and was not one of the original thirteen state signatories to the Declaration of Independence. Vermont's *Colonial Currency* notes of February, 1781 are classified as *Colonial* rather than *Continental* issues because they were authorized by the local colonial government of Vermont, rather than the Continental Congress (the nominal "central government" of the "United States" at that time); and these notes are called *Colonial*

instead of state notes because Vermont became a state on March 4, 1781, just days after the February notes were printed. Vermont *Colonial Currency* of this February 1781 issue is rare and costly, so be sure it is genuine if you buy it.

Arguments for Colonial Currency

The first *Bills of Credit* were issued by Pennsylvania on January 17, 1723, followed by several more "issues" in the following years. In 1729, 23-year-old Benjamin Franklin, recently arrived in Philadelphia, published his anonymous pamphlet entitled, *A Modest Inquiry into the Nature and Necessity of Paper Money*, in which he forcefully argued in favor of more paper money for Pennsylvania. Franklin was later employed by the Pennsylvania Assembly to print notes (dated January 1, 1756 through June 18, 1764), which he describes in his *Autobiography* as "a very profitable job and a great help to me."

A chronic coin shortage, in an era when coinage was the traditional medium of exchange as circulating money, and a lack of mother country-supplied paper currency made the production of *Colonial Currency* paper issues inevitable. Paper money was easy to manufacture, easy to store or hide, and convenient to carry when shopping or traveling. The heavily worn and folded examples of much *Colonial Currency* is paper testimony to the fact that it did circulate and was accepted by a cash-starved populace, although not always to beneficial effects. *Colonial Currency* notes were issued when the government had local debts to pay; thus the paper money "expanded" or "contracted" as financial necessity dictated, in war and in peace. And any denomination could be issued, unlike coinage, which had standard weights, when you could get coins at all.

Arguments Against Colonial Currency

Colonial Currency had three severe liabilities: (1) no specie backing (i.e., not generally convertible into gold or silver, encouraging overissue, and causing inflation and currency depreciation), (2) limited circulation (used mainly within the colony of issue), and (3) easily counterfeited.

Cash-strapped colonial assemblies were too often tempted into overissuing paper money to pay local expenses (taxes to the Crown and payments to merchants overseas still had to be paid in specie because overseas creditors didn't recognize the validity of American *Colonial Currency*). The ensuing ruinous inflation and currency depreciation were welcomed by debtors (who always benefit during times of heavy inflation). John Adams said, in 1775, "Half of the nation if not more are debtors." And the politically influential American debtor class most definitely encouraged the issuance of more and more paper money. This "printing press" mentality for paper money "solutions" to financing expenses led to repeated financial ruin of creditors and money hoarders whose handfuls of *Colonial Currency* became worth less and less. For example, in Rhode Island in 1740, some *Bills of Credit* circulated at only 4% of their face value (compared with British sterling parity). A nation's currency is stable when all citizens, including (especially) the merchants and creditors, have confidence in its relatively constant value over time.

Limited circulation of *Colonial Currency* made inter-Colonial business a constant headache. Imagine traveling from Baltimore to New York City by horse, a distance of only 200 miles, but having to cross four Colonial borders (Delaware, Pennsylvania, New Jersey, and New York), hoping that your money would be accepted in each Colony (as, in fact, it sometimes was, in the case of adjacent Colonies with frequent business with each other). But, then again, when you arrived in New York, would New York inns and taverns recognize your Maryland money? Or would they discount it, accepting it at less than face value? As a rule, the farther away from its issuing Colony, the less likely money was to be accepted.

Counterfeiting of *Colonial Currency* was epidemic (see Chapter 21). The notes were of simple designs and easily counterfeited. Some counterfeits looked better than the genuine notes; and to a largely illiterate population, they looked the same. Few people were executed for counterfeiting in Colonial America (in contrast to England at that time, where capital sentences were routinely carried out for counterfeiters), but the disruption of orderly currency management made counterfeiters a constant threat to the integrity of paper money in the Colonies.

Another problem with Colonial notes was the many different "odd" or fractional denominations. If all you had was a 1s3d (1 *Shilling*, 3 *Pence*) note from Georgia, and wanted to buy something for 6 *Pence*, and the other seller didn't have "change," what would you do? The standardization of currency denominations in convenient increments is a 19th century phenomenon, which was unknown to many people living in the 1700s.

In 1729, the same year that Franklin wrote his pro-paper money pamphlet, another Philadelphian, James Logan, had a different opinion on the newly-embraced American habit of using paper currency:

> *I dare not speak one word against it [paper money]. The popular phrensy will never stop till their credit will be as bad as they are in New England, where an ounce of silver is worth twenty shillings of their paper. They already talk of making more, and no man dares appear to stem the fury of the popular rage.*

Parliamentary Prohibition of Colonial Currency

In 1763-1764, the British Parliament decided to prohibit the American Colonies from issuing *Bills of Credit*, but this was to no avail, as the Colonies continued to issue paper money at will, especially during the years from 1775 to 1781 (when the Colonies didn't recognize British authority anyway).

CONTINENTAL CURRENCY

Continental Currency is U.S. paper money issued by the Continental Congress. *Continental Currency* was issued to finance the American Revolution, because Congress then had no power to tax, and the individual Colonies refused to contribute to the Congressional Treasury.

When I was in elementary school in the 1950s, we were taught that "everybody" in America wanted the Revolution. In fact, only about a third of the American Colonists wanted Revolution; another third (the "loyalists") wanted to remain a Colonial dependency of Great Britain; and about another third were neutral or undecided. At the start of the American Revolution in 1775-1776, with a Colonial population totaling about 2$\frac{1}{2}$ million, the currency in circulation in America has been estimated at from 12 to 22 million dollars, with maybe half of that in paper (much of it counterfeit) and half in coins (mostly foreign mintages, such as *Spanish Milled Dollars*).

The Issues of Continental Currency

Eleven different dated issues of *Continental Currency* were authorized by the Continental Congress, starting on May 10, 1775, with $1 through $30 denominations, and bearing the legend, "The United Colonies." *Continental Currency* actually began circulating in earnest during the second half of 1776, when it started depreciating as it drove gold and silver coins out of circulation (due to hoarding by nervous citizens) — a perfect textbook example of "Gresham's Law" in action. Gresham's Law states that when two monies of equal face value are simultaneously circulating, the money with less intrinsic value will drive the more precious (hence, more desirable) money out of circulation.

Our country's name on the *Continental Currency* was changed with the issue effective May 20, 1777, when all the notes now had "The United States" on them. The final outcome of our Revolution was very much in doubt during 1777, a year that saw the ebb and flow in the fortunes of war, with American defeats at Brandywine and Germantown and victories at Trenton and Princeton. General Washington wintered with his ragged army, much of it sick and frostbitten, in the snows at Valley Forge, as 1777 became 1778, all the while writing pleading letters to a financially fickle Congress, which seemed to hesitate forever, while debating whether or not to send assistance to Washington's army. No *Continental Currency* was approved for almost a year, from May 10, 1777 to the April 11, 1778 issue. Then more appeared, dated September 26, 1778.

Ever the optimist as far as American paper money was concerned, Benjamin Franklin commented on this *Continental Currency* as the Revolutionary War itself was raging at his doorstep: "The currency as we manage it is a wonderful machine ... it pays and clothes troops, and provides victuals and ammunition; and when we are obliged to issue a quantity excessive, it pays itself off by depreciation."

Although the Revolutionary War would drag on until 1783, the final issue of *Continental Currency* was dated January 14, 1779, and bore a name change for our country: "The United States of North America."

Continental Currency: Inflation and Depreciation

Over $240 million in *Continentals* (as this currency was called) was in circulation by 1779. The occupying British Army was well paid in coin, which the British soldiers ironically spent to buy things in American towns, much to the financial delight of American merchants who were loyal to the Crown or loyal to coinage. The American "bluecoats" meanwhile found themselves paid with handfuls of paper Continentals, which underwent disastrous inflation and depreciation due to excessive issue by Congress. Almost $500 million face value in the combined total printings of paper money issued by the Continental Congress and individual "state" governments was created during the American Revolution.

Continental Currency counterfeiting added to inflationary pressures, and some Americans were not beyond making a "quick buck" one way or another. Continental "bill" counterfeiting was encouraged in New York, for example, when it was under English occupation.

In 1780, Continental notes were worth 2$1/2$¢ on the dollar, giving birth to the saying, "not worth a *Continental*" — meaning anything that is essentially valueless. Patriotic Americans found their life savings wiped out, their stashes of *Continentals* fit only to stoke a fireplace, or (as a number of barbers did) to paper their shop walls as decoration! American soldiers stuffed their boots with *Continentals* to keep their feet warm.

In May 1781, Congress had the audacity to recommend that the states revoke the legal tender status of *Continental Currency*, which they did! At the end of the War, the once-noble *Continentals* were redeemed at one cent on the dollar, a memory that stayed in the minds of many people long after the Revolution drifted into past history, and instilled an "anti-paper money" attitude in large segments of American public opinion for many years to come. Benjamin Franklin's adage of "a penny saved is a penny earned" applied, of course, to money whose value could be depended upon.

MONEY IN THE NEW NATION

In 1784, a year after the American Revolution ended, Thomas Jefferson proposed a decimal monetary system for our young nation to replace the cumbersome *Pounds/Shillings/Pence* British system, in use since the first English settlers came to the New World. Although all *Continental Currency*, and much of the Revolutionary War state currency, was denominated in *dollars*, most business accounts in America continued to be kept in *pounds* sterling, while most specie payments were done with transfers of silver *Spanish Milled Dollars*. Decimalization officially started in the United States in 1792, when one *dollar* became equal to 100 *cents*, and when the first "United

States of America" coins were struck under authority of the newly established U.S. Mint, as per Act of Congress of April 6, 1792.

Shays' Rebellion

Shays' Rebellion, led by Daniel Shays in western Massachusetts in 1786-1787, was a violent protest against high land taxes, but was due, in part, to the legislature's repeal of paper money's legal tender status, insisting that farmers' debts to the government be paid in scarce specie (gold or silver coin). The Rebellion was defeated, but the desire for paper money, at least among the debtor class, was not.

The United States Treasury Seal

The U.S. Treasury traces its history back to the paper money-flush Continental Congress. The Treasury Seal, which appears on all federally-issued U.S. currency since 1862, was authorized in 1778, and is known on documents from 1782. The "balance scales" represent Justice, while the Seal's "key" symbolizes the functions of the state. In the "old style" U.S. Treasury Seal, the inscription around its edge reads: THESAUR. AMER. SEPTENT. SIGIL. (abbreviations for: THESAURI AMERICAE SEPTENTRIONALIS SIGILLUM, meaning "The Seal of the Treasury of North America").

In 1968, the Treasury Seal was changed, including removal of the Latin and replacement with the English legend: THE DEPARTMENT OF THE TREASURY. Thus, U.S. paper money made since 1968 bears the new version of the Treasury Seal. The new Seal was first used on $100 *U.S. Notes*, *Series* 1966 (but issued 1968). All U.S. currency of *Series* 1969 or later bears the new Seal.

Alexander Hamilton

Alexander Hamilton, the first U.S. Secretary of the Treasury (1789-1795), insisted that American Revolutionary War debts (both to foreign and domestic creditors, both Confederational and state) be paid off in sound money, which did much to establish the good credit of the new nation. Such debts were paid off, at a time when fiat money, deficit spending, and the national debt were looked on as unacceptable government fiscal policy.

Hamilton, who ironically is now on our heavily circulated $10 "bill," was against the issuing of paper money, either by state or federal government, and he undoubtedly was thinking of the recent fiasco of *Continental Currency* when he said this about paper money:

> *In times of tranquillity it might have no ill consequence; it might even perhaps be arranged in a way to be productive of good; but in great and trying emergencies, there is almost a moral certainty of its being mischievous.*

AMERICAN COLONIAL CURRENCY (Issues of the Individual Colonies)		
COLONY	DATE OF FIRST KNOWN ISSUES	DATE OF LAST KNOWN ISSUES
Massachusetts	February 3, 1690	1781 (handwritten)
South Carolina	May 8, 1703	1788
New York	May 31, 1709	February 8, 1788
New Jersey	July 1, 1709	May 17, 1786
Connecticut	July 12, 1709	July 1, 1780
New Hampshire	1709	April 29, 1780
Rhode Island	August 16, 1710	May 1786
North Carolina	1712	December 29, 1785
Pennsylvania	January 17, 1723	March 16, 1785
Delaware	1729	May 1, 1777
Maryland	1733	August 8, 1781
Georgia	1735	October 16, 1786
Virginia	June 1755	May 7, 1781
Vermont	February 1781	no further issues

AMERICAN CONTINENTAL CURRENCY (Issues of the Continental Congress)	
ISSUE DATE	DENOMINATION RANGE
May 10, 1775	$1 to $30
November 29, 1775	$1 to $8
February 17, 1776	$¹/₆ ("one-sixth" of a *dollar*) to $8
May 9, 1776	$1 to $8
July 22, 1776	$2 to $8
November 2, 1776	$2 to $30
February 26, 1777	$2 to $30
May 20, 1777	$2 to $30
April 11, 1778	$4 to $40 (notice the inflation)
September 26, 1778	$5 to $60
January 14, 1779	$1 to $80

(FIRST) BANK OF THE UNITED STATES

Because there was a "Second" Bank later on, in retrospect we call it the (First) Bank of the United States, chartered by Congress for twenty years, as per the Act of February 25, 1791. This Bank was organized by Alexander Hamilton and was highly successful from the beginning. (At the outset, its stock was oversubscribed, especially by English investors! "Foreign control" of American assets is hardly a recent innovation.) The Bank of the United States was capitalized for $10,000,000, and it issued bank notes, which were well regarded and redeemable in specie (precious metal coinage). The Bank paid high dividends to its stockholders and was the talk of Philadelphia (where it was located). Hamilton transferred U.S. Treasury funds to this Bank, which, in turn, loaned out the money at interest to finance domestic and foreign trade. Bowing to pressure from "hard money" advocates (people who favored specie over paper currency), Congress failed (by one vote) to renew the charter for the (First) Bank of the United States, so it liquidated in 1811 on the eve of the War of 1812, leaving the country to be flooded with paper money from private, state-chartered banks.

(Bank Notes from the "First" and "Second" Bank of the U.S. have collector value only because both of these banks went insolvent, and no longer exist to redeem their paper money.)

Early 19th Century State-Chartered Banks

The young United States was growing rapidly in population: 4.2 million in 1792 when U.S. finances were organized, 5.2 million in 1800, and 7.2 million by 1810. State-chartered private banks served the banking needs of much of the citizenry, but there was no guarantee that private bank paper money would be redeemable (exchangeable for coinage) on demand. In the whole country, there were 28 of these state-chartered banks in 1800, 89 in 1811, 208 in 1815, 307 in 1820, 330 in 1830, and 704 in 1835 (a surge due to the demise of the [Second] Bank of the United States, thanks to President Jackson's opposition to it).

Basically, anybody could open a bank in America, and "anybody" often did. Private banks routinely overissued their own paper money, causing local inflation of excess paper currency, leading to currency-holder panic and a "run" on banks suspected of not having enough specie to cover their bank notes. For example, about $100 million in paper currency from state-chartered banks was in circulation in America in 1815, three years into the War of 1812 and four years after the end of the (First) Bank of the United States. Following a private bank currency collapse in 1819 (with associated bank insolvencies and merchant bankruptcies), in 1820 the private bank notes in circulation amounted to $41 million. Some notes undoubtedly had been redeemed for specie, but the net effect was that over half of the paper money in the country was wiped out.

How a Bank Goes Broke

There are individual differences, but here is a general scenario of how a bank goes broke:

1.   Bad management, bad luck, bad loans, regional or national economic recession or depression, embezzlement, theft, war, paying excess interest, or overissue of paper money — all these mean trouble for a bank (at least in early 19th century America).

2.   Liabilities greatly exceed assets, leading to:

3.   Insolvency declaration by the bank's management, and then:

4.   Door closure (effectively "freezing" any remaining bank assets), followed by:

5.   Liquidation of available assets, as per court-ordered sales. Then:

6.   Partial settlements with creditors, as per court-ordered distribution rates. Imagine working your whole life on your farm, and converting your life savings into paper money from the neighborhood bank, then hearing the judge announce: "Well, your paper money from Farmers & Mechanics Mutual Bank is worth five cents on the dollar. Everybody line up to cash in your paper!"

Paper Money Debate in Pre-Civil War America

Americans had a love-hate affair with paper money in the early years of our country. Debates, which now seem quaint and silly, raged constantly during the first half of the 19th century, regarding whether or not paper money was a sensible thing.

On the "paper side," orators enumerated the reasons favoring paper currency: (a) a general lack of circulating coinage, (b) increasing population, (c) increasing commerce, (d) the inconvenience of moving large amounts of specie, and (e) the security risks of storing specie at home.

On the "hard money side," coinage advocates discussed: (a) the frequent insolvency of paper money-issuing banks, (b) the routine depreciation of paper currency and its daily fluctuations in value, (c) the ease of counterfeiting paper money, and (d) the lack of a uniformly recognized stable paper currency of national circulation. "Hard money" people tried desperately to draw the population away from the "novelty of worthless paper cash" towards the time-proven "security of solid gold and silver."

Bank embezzlement was common in early 19th century America. In his 1833 book, *The Curse of Paper-Money and Banking*, William M. Gouge described the City Bank of Baltimore:

> *It had what was called a "solid" capital of 800,000 or 900,000 dollars, and its credit was good. But, about the time Mr. McCulloh was removed from the cashiership of the United States branch, the Cashier of the City Bank found it necessary to resign. An investigation was then made by a committee of the stockholders, and it was found that all the persons employed in the Bank, with the exception of one clerk and the porter, had made free with its funds.*

John F. Watson, Cashier of the Bank of Germantown (northwest Philadelphia), in his *Annals of Philadelphia* described how personal and business bankruptcies were rare before the Revolutionary War, but for Philadelphia of 1826-1829, he says that things ...

> *... are so changed, that a certain number of bankruptcies and insolvencies in the course of a year, are regarded as being as much within the order of nature as a certain number of deaths. Periodical redundancies and scarcities of money are looked for as naturally as cold in winter or heat in summer.*

(SECOND) BANK OF THE UNITED STATES

In January 1817, the (Second) Bank of the United States opened its doors in Philadelphia, as per Act of Congress of April 10, 1816. This bank was soundly managed, and its bank notes were accepted readily, being a uniform paper currency throughout the country in the 1820s (although contemporarily coincident with private bank notes).

This "new" Bank of the United States: (a) handled the fiscal affairs of the federal government, (b) had branches in major U.S. cities, (c) loaned money for frontier economic development, (d) collected customs receipts, and (e) served as creditor of state banks by accumulating state bank notes, which the Bank of the U.S. could redeem for specie (thus, if desired, reducing the amount of paper currency in circulation, a function similar to that of the U.S. Federal Reserve System today).

When the public complained about the shortage of circulating money in 1828, the President of the Bank of the U.S. responded, in an essay that appeared in the *National Gazette* of April 10, 1828:

> *The currency of the United States consists of coin, and Bank Notes promising to pay coin ... The constant tendency of Banks is ... to lend too much, and to put too many notes in circulation ... When, therefore, you buy from foreigners more than they buy from you, as they cannot take the paper part of your currency, they must take the coin part. If this is done to a considerable extent, the danger is that the Banks will be obliged to pay so much of their coin for their notes as not to leave them a sufficient quantity to answer the demand for it, in which case the Banks fail, and the community is defrauded. To prevent this, a prudent Bank, the moment it perceives an unusual demand for its notes, and has reason to fear a drain on its vaults, should immediately diminish the amount of its notes, and call in part of its debts.*

Despite its domestic and international successes, the (Second) Bank of the U.S. was hated by "easy money" people who thought the Bank was too conservative by hoarding money and restricting credit. And the Bank was despised by "hard money" fanatics who were against all banks, especially those that issued paper currency.

Andrew Jackson Destroys the Bank

Andrew Jackson was one of these hard money promoters, and his election to the U.S. Presidency in 1828 (serving from 1829-1837) guaranteed the doom of the (Second) Bank of the U.S. In 1833, Jackson stopped depositing from the federal Treasury into the Bank, which cut off the main source of the Bank's funds. The Bank was forced to liquidate in 1836, but rechartered itself under Pennsylvania law, finally going insol-

vent after the Panic of 1837. After the failure of the (Second) Bank of the United States (in Philadelphia), the financial center of America passed from Philadelphia to New York City, where it has remained, more or less, to the present day. New York City's population tripled, from 390,000 in 1840 to 1,200,000 in 1860 on the eve of the Civil War. Largely due to the failure of the (Second) Bank of the U.S., by 1861 there were 1,601 private U.S. banks circulating a total of $207 million in bank notes. Pre-Civil War U.S. Treasury "notes" were issued (in 1815, 1843, and 1847), but these are not of great importance to the "mainstream history" of American paper money.

PANIC OF 1837

The Panic of 1837, and the nationwide economic Depression that followed, resulted directly from: (a) the death of the (Second) Bank of the United States in 1836, (b) disastrous U.S. Treasury policies (such as the "Specie Circular" of 1836, which decreed that only gold and silver could be paid for public lands), and (c) overissue of private bank notes. Other contributing factors were: crop failures, overspeculation in business, withdrawal of credit from England, and (in consequence) private U.S. banks' suspension of specie payment in May 1837 (with $149 million in circulating bank notes).

"BROKEN BANK NOTES"

Broken Bank Notes are paper money issued by private (state-chartered) U.S. banks that became insolvent, especially referring to pre-Civil War issues, particularly those made worthless by the late 1830s financial turmoil. Over 600 banks went broke in the American Depression of the late 1830s. Over 10,000 major varieties of U.S. *Broken Bank Notes* (*BBNs*) are known, from over 1,600 banks, from thirty-four states, with issue dates from 1780 to 1861. Many *BBNs* are exquisitely engraved in beautiful colors, and most are inexpensive to buy for collecting today. Post-Civil War state bank notes are often called *Broken Bank Notes* also, if their issuing authorities became insolvent, even though these were issued by state government banks.

Private bank notes served the paper money needs of America from the end of the Revolutionary War to the outbreak of the Civil War. It is surprising these notes were accepted as well as they were, considering the disastrous ruin of *Continental Currency*, still in the memories of aging citizens.

Nineteenth century private bank notes made interstate commerce difficult. The establishment of a universal national currency during the Civil War greatly eliminated much business suspicion about the legitimacy of paper money. Pre-Civil War American newspapers published tables listing the varying discounts off face value for local private bank notes.

Publications known as *Counterfeit Detectors* and *Bank Note Reporters* arose in the United States in the first half of the 19th century to help bankers and merchants identify counterfeit bank notes (which were epidemic), notes of insolvent banks, and notes of fictitious banks (banks that never existed). *Heath's Detector* was the most popular of these publications.

"Wildcat Banks"

Although sometimes used synonymously for *Broken Banks*, *Wildcat Banks* were shady operations that issued notes without proper backing in specie. Such banks in Canada were also called *Wildcat Banks* (including those that issued *Phantom Notes*). They were so named because they were set up in hard-to-find locations (where "wildcats" roamed) so that their bank notes couldn't easily be redeemed for specie, or because these banks were predatory and dangerous and impulsive (like wildcats), or because some of them had issued notes that pictured "wildcats"! Strictly defined, *Wildcat Banks* are types of *Broken Banks*, which are types of *Obsolete Banks*, but many paper money collectors and dealers use these terms interchangeably.

A banker should look as safe as the vault — no unstable personality, no bizarre clothing or wild hairstyles. But what can protect the citizen from authentic-looking *bank notes* whose issuing authorities are crooks? Gouge, in his prophetic 1833 book, *The Curse of Paper-Money and Banking*, warns against the illusion of ever-increasing wealth and rising prices caused by the proliferation of more and more quantities of inconvertible (non-redeemable for specie) paper money, as was the case in early 19th century America. The gold-silver ratio varied between 1:15 and 1:16 (i.e., if an ounce of silver = $1, then an ounce of gold = $15), but this was irrelevant if your banker refused to give you gold and silver for notes drawn on his own bank.

THE CIVIL WAR — UNION MONETARY PROBLEMS

In 1860, over 1,600 private American banks in 34 states were issuing over 10,000 basic note types, and over 5,000 counterfeit types were circulating. In December 1861, state banks suspended specie payments, and their bank notes immediately depreciated. The federal government did likewise and issued unbacked paper money (the *Demand Notes* or *Greenbacks* of 1861) because the Union authorities couldn't sell bonds to a nervous public, and they didn't want to tax excessively for fear of creating a Southern-sympathetic backlash among Northern citizens.

Financing the Civil War was a major problem for both North and South (see Chapter 3 for the Confederate story). The War dragged on seemingly with no end in sight, and the public hoarded specie. Inflation occurred in both North and South, due to huge government expenditures to prosecute the war, price gouging by merchants loyal to their own profits, actual wartime shortages of goods, with high demand for same, and continued issuance of federal inconvertible paper money that depreciated in the hands of frightened citizens.

In the North, for the first three years (1861-1864) of the Civil War, there was currency depreciation (money worth less and less, helping debtors, hurting creditors) because of overall Union defeats, but during the last year (1864-1865), there was currency appreciation (money worth more and more, helping creditors, hurting debtors) because of Union victories. Civil War business was therefore stressful and uncertain, and the time when you incurred or discharged a debt greatly influenced how much "real money" it actually cost you. American writers, such as Alexander Del Mar (in his pamphlet, *A Warning to the People: The Paper Bubble*, published in New York in 1864), introduced the public to a new word: "inflation," at least as it is used in the now-understood monetary sense.

TYPES OF UNION PAPER CURRENCY — CIVIL WAR

Six kinds of Union (Northern) federal paper money were issued during the Civil War: *Demand Notes, Interest-Bearing Notes, Legal Tender Notes, Compound Interest Treasury Notes, National Bank Notes*, and *Fractional Currency*, all of which are still legal tender today. And, except for the "odd-sized" *Fractional Currency*, all of these issues are classified as U.S. *Large Size Notes*.

Demand Notes

Demand Notes, of 1861, were the first official U.S. government paper currency as we know it today. These notes are also called *Greenbacks* for the green ink used to print their reverses to discourage photographic counterfeiting (which could only be done in black and white at that time). To this day, "greenbacks" is a slang term meaning "U.S. paper money."

These *Demand Notes* were authorized per Acts of Congress of July 17 and August 5, 1861. These notes all bear the legend, "Act of July 17, 1861." as well as the issue date of "August 10th, 1861," when they were supposedly first released.

These *Demand Notes* are the only federal U.S. currency, 1861 to date, that (a) has no Treasury Seal, (b) has a single Serial Number set, and (c) is found without the real names of the U.S. Treasurer and Register (now the Secretary of the Treasury), being hand-signed by clerks' names. Later on, the signatures on U.S. currency were printed directly from the plates, but these early hand-signed notes are sought by collectors.

Sixty million dollars worth of U.S. *Demand Notes* were authorized and were issued in $5, $10, and $20 denominations. Before the U.S. Treasury suspended specie payments on December 21, 1861, *Demand Notes* were actually redeemable in silver coins.

Interest-Bearing Notes

Interest-Bearing Notes were produced in several issues, starting as per Congressional Act of March 2, 1861. Some of these notes paid interest at $7^3/_{10}\%$ — the highest rate paid by the U.S. government at that time. *Three Year Interest-Bearing Notes* had five detachable coupons for collecting interest at six-month intervals, and these *Three Year* notes were made payable to a specific person (the note's "holder") rather than to the usual anonymous "bearer." Few of these *Interest-Bearing Notes* have survived, because most people turned them in to collect accrued interest.

Legal Tender Notes

Legal Tender Notes (also called *United States Notes*) were first issued in 1862 and were accepted by the public even though such notes weren't redeemable in specie. The actual daily "value" of these notes varied at a discount off face value, as the tides of the Civil War ran for or against the Union armies. The Legal Tender Act of March 12, 1862 made the *Demand Notes* (see above) legal tender, but the federal government insisted that customs duties and interest on the public debt be paid in gold — our government wouldn't accept its own paper money for these payments!

"First Obligation" *Legal Tender Notes* of 1862 were exchangeable for bonds at 6% interest (perhaps in gold coin), a fact that made them somewhat desirable during the general currency depreciation during the Civil War.

Legal Tender Notes were first issued in $5 to $1,000 denominations, later in $1 to $10,000 denominations.

Compound Interest Treasury Notes

Compound Interest Treasury Notes were authorized per Congressional Acts of March 3, 1863 and June 30, 1864 by a U.S. Congress desperate for funds as the bloody Civil War dragged on. Denominations of $10 through $1,000 were issued, and all bore interest at the rate of 6% a year, compounded semi-annually, but only redeemable for the accrued interest after three years (for example: at 6% compound interest, a $10 note would be worth $11.94, including face value "principal," after three years).

The holder of *Compound Interest Treasury Notes* had to redeem the notes to collect the interest, and this was done almost always, making these notes extremely rare today. But this interest-generating aspect of the *Compound Interest Treasury Notes* lasted only until maturity (three years), so, although they do have a redemption value in excess of face value today (but a vastly higher "collector" value), these notes haven't been earning interest since the Civil War.

The fronts of these notes were overprinted with "COMPOUND INTEREST TREASURY NOTE" and the denomination in numerals in (unfortunately) corrosive gold ink, so that surviving examples may have paper damage from the overprint ink's chemistry.

National Bank Notes

National Bank Notes were created by Acts of Congress of February 25, 1863 and June 3, 1864. Member banks were required to buy U.S. bonds, then deposit these bonds in the U.S. Treasury for a reserve (against which they issued their own *National Bank Notes* with a total face value up to 90% of their bond deposit). National Banks had to be capitalized with $50,000 minimum, of which $30,000 or more had to be bond deposits. But banks with capital exceeding $3,000,000 could maintain no more than 60% of their capital in U.S. bonds.

National Banks were chartered for twenty years, with option to renew. The number of National Banks spread rapidly in the United States: from none in 1862, to 638 at the end of 1863, to 1,648 by the end of 1866. State-chartered private bank notes were taxed 10% by Act of Congress of March 3, 1865, effectively driving these notes out of existence. The *National Bank Notes* established a uniform currency in America and gradually eliminated state banks. When the Civil War ended in April 1865, almost $100 million in *National Bank Notes* circulated (and almost $433 million in *U.S. Notes* were circulating). The National Bank system outlived the Civil War, indeed lasting through the 1920s, and all *National Bank Notes* were (and still are) legal tender throughout the United States.

National Bank Notes had the same basic designs, with beautiful engravings from American historic scenes (such as "Landing of the Pilgrims," "DeSoto Discovering the Mississippi," and "Baptism of Pocahontas"). The individual *National Bank Notes* were printed with the bank's name, bank signatures, state coat of arms, and bank charter number. *National Bank Notes* are considered to be the most aesthetically pleasing note designs ever issued by the U.S. government.

U.S. Fractional Currency

When coins disappeared from circulation during the Civil War due to public hoarding, a severe shortage of small change developed. This was only partly alleviated by small denomination (less than $1) U.S. postage stamps, which were used at face value to make change at merchants' stores. *Encased Postage Stamps* (brass and mica-enclosed mint stamps) quickly evolved from the loose stamps that easily became dirty and torn as they circulated in lieu of coinage.

Congress authorized the issuance of *Postage Currency* (notes that had facsimiles of then-current U.S. postage stamps of 3¢, 10¢, 25¢, and 50¢ denominations, with the 25¢ and 50¢ notes bearing impressions of five 5¢ stamps and five 10¢ stamps, respectively) by Act of July 17, 1862. This was the first federal U.S. *Fractional Currency*, although this Postage Currency was not officially legal until the Act of March 3, 1863. *Postage Currency* is called the "First Issue" of U.S. *Fractional Currency*.

The U.S. *Fractional Currency* initiated during the Civil War continued to be produced with four post-war issues until 1876. *Fractional Currency* ranged in denomination from 3¢ to 50¢ face value, and like all U.S. federal currency from the Civil War to date, is still legal tender. *Fractional Currency* is defined as: money that is less in face (stated) value than a single standard monetary unit of the issuing nation. In America, this means any paper money less than $1 face value.

Ten years after the Civil War's guns fell silent, the need for *Fractional Currency* in America was greatly reduced due to increasing coinage output from the U.S. Mints. By the mid-1870s, U.S. *Fractional Currency* was becoming inefficient because (a) the U.S. Treasury found it expensive to redeem, sort, and reissue these notes, (b) the notes wore out fast, and (c) the public kept losing them. As per the Acts of Congress of January 14, 1875 and April 17, 1876, U.S. *Fractional Currency* was authorized redeemable in silver coin, and less than $2 million of it is extant today.

THE ROMANCE OF CIVIL WAR NOTES

As a genuine material and personal link to the American Civil War, any paper money used at that time has a romantic historical appeal. U.S. troops spent U.S. currency in the South; much Civil War paper money is worn and ragged (if it exists at all), evidence that it circulated heavily in the towns and villages of the time. At the War's end, some Confederate troops insisted on being paid in U.S. rather than Confederate paper money!

To hold in your hand a bank note that might have been touched by Abraham Lincoln's children, playing with their father's wallet on the White House floor, or that could have been pressed against the heart of the wife of a Union infantryman, freshly removed from the mailing envelope in which he sent it home from his meager Army salary, is to feel the emotional power of paper money, which goes beyond a simple cold analysis of Congressional fiscal legislation and currency printing statistics.

UNION PAPER MONEY VALUE FLUCTUATIONS

Union paper money fluctuated in actual commercial value with the latest success or failure of the Union Armies. This was especially true for the *U.S. Notes* and *Demand Notes* ("Greenbacks"), which were unredeemable in specie and carried no interest-paying provisions. As examples, the following table shows how much "money" Union currency was worth, compared with $100 in gold, at various times during the final two years of the Civil War.

LATER 19TH CENTURY U.S. CURRENCY

American paper money flourished in ever-increasing amounts from the end of the Civil War in 1865 to the year 1900. Total U.S. currency in circulation was $775 million in 1870, $973 million in 1880, and $1,429,000,000 by 1890. National Banks grew in number from 1,648 in 1866, to 2,052 in 1880, to 3,326 in 1890, and continued to issue the most "colorful" U.S. paper money — the ubiquitous *National Bank Notes* with their reassuring "hometown" bank names, *Large Size* "real-looking money" bank note format (of 7³/₈ by 3¹/₈ inches), and intricately engraved allegories and historical scenes.

THE FLUCTUATION IN "MARKET VALUE" OF UNION PAPER MONEY	
COMMERCIAL "VALUE" OF $100 OF U.S. PAPER MONEY, WHEN COMPARED TO $100 IN GOLD	PERIOD OF CIVIL WAR HISTORY
$64.62	After the May 1863 Union defeat at Chancellorsville, Virginia.
$72.46	After the July 1863 Union victory at Gettysburg, Pennsylvania.
$75.47	After Grant's capture of Vicksburg, Mississippi, a week after the Union victory at Gettysburg; July 1863.
$35.08	In July 1864, after six months of Union losses.
$68.49	After Lee's surrender at Appomattox Court House, Virginia, on April 9, 1865.
$60.61	When news broke of President Lincoln's assassination of April 14, 1865.

Notice that ordinary U.S. paper money was always worth less than its "face value" during the national trauma of the Civil War!

NATIONAL GOLD BANK NOTES

National Bank Notes should not be confused with the National Gold Bank Notes of California, which were authorized by Act of Congress of July 12, 1870 and circulated in lieu of gold coin in specie-oriented California. Although the California Gold Rush of 1848-1849 and the early years of statehood in the 1850s were long past, the continued use of coinage instead of paper money was still common in California and other western states/territories. Handling and storing gold coin was tedious, so nine banks in California (and one in Boston) became "Gold Banks" in addition to being "National Banks," and their gold coin-redeemable National Gold Bank Notes readily circulated from 1870 to 1875, as can be seen from their usually worn appearance, if they can be found today at all. These National Gold Bank Notes were gradually withdrawn and redeemed for gold coin, adding to their rarity today.

POST-CIVIL WAR MONETARY CONCERNS

Reconstruction of the shattered Southern economy was a proclaimed goal of post-Civil War America, although it was not always carried out to the benefit of financially ruined Southerners. The worst thing that happened to the South was that they lost the War; the second worst thing was Lincoln's assassination. If President Lincoln had lived, historians are convinced the South would have been treated with more dignity and benevolence by the victorious Northerners. Carpetbaggers from the North invaded the South like so many fiscal vultures, and profits were made but not always for the right reasons. U.S. paper money and U.S.-compatible banks had to replace the Confederate monetary system. People everywhere, both North and South, went to work rebuilding their lives, which required increased paper money issues from the proper authorities.

An economic depression occurred in 1873-1875, but the U.S. government resumed specie payments finally in 1879 (from the December 1861 suspension). A "Greenback-Labor Party" had a brief appearance in American politics of the late 1870s, advocating fiat paper money over hard currency (gold or silver); i.e., the Greenbackers were against the nation's silver interest and the gold standard. The Greenbackers wanted paper money, without backing, as the only official U.S. currency.

Congress forbade the portrayal of living persons on U.S. bank notes as per the Act of April 7, 1866. All U.S. currency after that date has vignettes of deceased historical persons (and sometimes allegorical figures, also).

"Bimetallism" in the Late 1800s

Bimetallism (the "backing" of paper money with gold and silver; the use of silver, as well as gold, in the nation's currency and monetary policy) was a popular economic theory in America in the late 1800s. Bimetallists favored the unlimited coinage of U.S. *Silver Dollar* coins, and they coerced Congress to pass the Bland-Allison Act of February 28, 1878 authorizing the "unlimited" production of U.S. *Silver Dollars* from $2 million to $4 million worth of silver bullion to be purchased every month by the U.S. government. But these *Silver Dollars* didn't circulate, merely piling up in government vaults, as the commodity market bullion value of a U.S. *Silver Dollar* dropped from 89¢ in 1878, to 72¢ in 1889, to 48¢ in 1900.

The Sherman Silver Purchase Act of July 14, 1890 forced the U.S. Treasury to buy $4^1/_2$ million ounces of silver per month and to issue *Treasury Notes* for these silver "deposits," but these notes were redeemable in gold! Inflation raged, and a jittery American public redeemed their *Treasury Notes* for gold. U.S. Treasury gold reserves sank from $190 million in 1890 to under $100 million by April 1893, as people hoarded gold. In the summer of 1893, the "Panic of 1893" began, and the general national economic depression that followed (along with bank failures and unemployment) was in part caused by the overproduction of U.S. silver coins and rejection of silver by international trade.

GOLD CERTIFICATES

Gold Certificates — U.S. paper money redeemable in gold coin — were issued from 1865 to 1875 (the first three "issues") for internal use by banks and clearing houses. The Fourth Issue of *Gold Certificates* was authorized for general circulation, as per Act of Congress of July 12, 1882. $20, $50, $100, $500, $1,000, $5,000, and $10,000 *Gold Certificates* were issued in 1882 (and for some subsequent years), but only denominations below $1,000 of the 1882 notes are usually seen today. Most U.S. *Gold Certificates* have been redeemed for gold coin or exchanged for other types of money.

TREASURY NOTES (COIN NOTES)

The U.S. *Treasury Notes* (also called *Coin Notes* because they were redeemable in silver or gold coin, at the Treasury's option) were authorized by the Legal Tender Act of July 14, 1890. *Treasury Note* denominations ranged from $1 to $1,000, and the $20, $50, $500, and $1,000 notes are rare today. Six of the *Treasury Notes* featured portraits of Union Generals, such as James McPherson (hero of the Battle of Vicksburg) and George Meade (Union commander at Gettysburg). While no longer redeemable in silver, as of June 24, 1968 by Act of Congress, the *Treasury Notes* are avidly collected, and are all worth over face value to collectors today.

William Jennings Bryan was a "free silver" advocate, favoring bimetallism, and was against the gold standard. His "Cross of Gold" speech during the U.S. Presidential campaign of 1896 wasn't enough to sway the majority of American voters, and Republican William McKinley won the election, defeating Bryan and bimetallism "forever." The Gold Standard Act of Congress of March 14, 1900 declared the gold dollar to be the "standard unit of value." *Gold Certificate* issues increased, and silver, as a purported economic panacea in America, was dead.

REFUNDING CERTIFICATES

U.S. *Refunding Certificates*, bearing interest at 4% per year, were authorized by Congressional Act of February 26, 1879. Printed only in $10 denominations, with Benjamin Franklin's portrait on the upper left of the note's face, they are rare today because most holders cashed them in for their interest, the accrual of which ceased on July 1, 1907. Redemption value of these $10 *Refunding Certificates* is thus $21.30 per note, over double face value. But collector value is much more.

SILVER CERTIFICATES

There were four 19th century issues of U.S. *Silver Certificates* (paper money redeemable in silver) from 1878 to 1899, as per Congressional Acts of February 28, 1878 and August 4, 1886. Various denominations were issued, from $1 to $1,000, with many notes of $10 and up being rare.

FEDERAL RESERVE SYSTEM (FRS)

Although America's economy grew and prospered in many ways in the first few years of the 20th century (for example, *Gold Certificates* in circulation increased from $201 million in 1900 to $803 million in 1910), our country was still plagued by "inelastic" currency, immobile reserves, boom and bust cycles (the Panic of 1907 resulted in a hoarding of, and shortage of, cash), and periodic bank failures.

From the inspiration of Virginia's Representative Carter Glass and economic advisor H. Parker Willis, the Federal Reserve System was born when President Woodrow Wilson signed the Federal Reserve Act on December 23, 1913, over the objections of conservative Wall Street bankers, and with reservations by "progressives" who feared that this Act might give big bankers too much control over the nation's currency.

As it became reality, the Federal Reserve Act set up twelve District Federal Reserve Banks in major U.S. cities scattered around the country, with a politically semi-insulated Board of Governors who were appointed by the President (with Senate confirmation) for ten-year terms (later extended to fourteen years). All National Banks were required to join their District Federal Reserve Bank. State banks could join voluntarily. Member banks had to buy stock in their District Federal Reserve Bank equal to 6% of their capital and surplus, and each member bank had to have a minimum capital of $4 million. Bankers were not permitted to serve on the Federal Reserve Board of Governors. And the Federal Reserve System was empowered to issue its own currency.

Federal Reserve Bank Notes

Federal Reserve Bank Notes (*FRBNs*) were issued in two Series: 1915 and 1918, by the individual District Banks of the Federal Reserve System. Almost $762 million in these notes were issued, of which slightly more than $2 million is still outstanding (lost, accidentally destroyed, hoarded, or in collections). *Federal Reserve Bank Notes* were not redeemable for "anything" besides other bank notes by the public holders of them, although in theory they were "secured" by U.S. bonds, gold notes, etc. *FRBNs* appeared in $1, $2, $5, $10, $20, and $50 denominations.

Federal Reserve Notes

Not to be confused with *Federal Reserve Bank Notes* (above), the *Federal Reserve Notes* (*FRNs*) were issued by the Federal Reserve System itself, and not by the individual District Banks of this System. Thus, these *Federal Reserve Notes* are not secured with government bonds, precious metal, or any other specific security (nor are they today). *Federal Reserve Notes* are the only type of paper money produced in the U.S. today. *Large Size FRNs* in $5, $10, $20, $50, and $100 values were issued in 1914; and $500, $1,000, $5,000, and $10,000 notes in 1918.

Federal Reserve Notes quickly became the dominant U.S. currency in circulation: $507 million in 1917; $1.7 billion in 1918; $3 billion in 1920 (the majority of U.S. bank notes that year, in total cash value).

Federal Reserve System Functions

There are four basic functions of the U.S. Federal Reserve System (FRS):

1. **Services to the U.S. Treasury.** The FRS serves as "banker" and "fiscal agent" of the U.S. government. Examples: Incoming federal revenues are credited to the U.S. Treasury at FRBs. FRBs auction government securities and supervise U.S. Savings Bond sales. FRBs move U.S. paper money and coin in and out of circulation, as needed.

2. **Services to Depository Institutions.** Examples: Accepting and safeguarding deposits, transferring funds (via check collections and electronic funds transfers), cash services (providing notes or coin, removing excess bank cash, replacing damaged money), and short-term loans.

3. **Supervision of Banks.** Examination and regulation of commercial banks to ensure compliance with banking laws.

4. **Monetary Policy.** The FRS partially influences U.S. monetary policy in regulating the amount of currency in circulation by: (a) open market operations (e.g., buying or selling securities), (b) varying the discount rate (loan rate charged member institutions, (c) changing reserve requirements of depository institutions, (d) setting the margin requirements (cash down payment percentage of total purchase price) for specified stocks and bonds, and (e) foreign exchange operations (buying or selling foreign currencies) for international balance of payments strategy.

Federal Reserve System Organization

Of the 12,600 commercial banks in the United States, 5,300 are members of the Federal Reserve System. About 25,000 other financial institutions (non-member commercial banks, savings banks, savings and loan associations, and credit unions) have access to FRS payments services. The FRS is a "non-profit" organization: any surplus revenues earned from its service charges to depository institutions are turned over to the U.S. Treasury (over $20 billion per year). The FRS Board of Governors in Washington, DC sets the general policies for the whole FRS, with the major District FRBs delegated lesser decision-making powers for each FRS District office in Boston, New York City, Philadelphia, Cleveland, Richmond, Atlanta, Chicago, St. Louis, Minneapolis, Kansas City, Dallas, and San Francisco.

"SMALL SIZE" U.S. NOTES

On July 10, 1929, U.S. paper money was reduced in dimensions from 7³/₈ by 3¹/₈ inches (*Large Size Notes*, nicknamed "horse blankets") to 6 ³/₁₆ by 2⁵/₈ (*Small Size Notes*) to save paper cost to the government. *Large Size Notes* were produced for 68 years, from 1861 to 1929. *Small Size Notes* have been produced from 1929 to date.

To American citizens using currency in the summer of 1929, the physical "shrinkage" of our paper money was either hated (due to loss of tradition) or philosophically tolerated (as an obvious convenience in handling and storing smaller size currency in wallets, cash drawers, etc.). Newspaper cartoons either ridiculed the new *Small Size Notes*, with comments such as, "At last the size of our money reflects its reduced purchasing power" or praised the new notes for their more convenient folding into wallets and change purses.

Types of Small Size Notes

Like their *Large Size* predecessors, *Small Size Notes* were issued under different authorizations; i.e., different "backings" and bank/government affiliations:

1.   *Legal Tender Notes* (*U.S. Notes*) — issued in $1, $2, $5, and $100 denominations, with some of them (especially the $2 *Series* 1953-1963 notes) still sometimes seen in circulation. All *Small Size U.S. Notes* have red Treasury Seals.

2.   *Silver Certificates* — $1, $5, and $10 notes issued, all with blue Treasury Seals, all originally redeemable in silver. The quantity of *Silver Certificates* quickly increased in circulation after abandonment of the "gold standard" (U.S. payments in gold specie) in 1933: from $361 million in 1933, to $705 million in 1935, to $1,230,000,000 in 1938. *Silver Certificates* became the most common low denomination U.S. paper money; and after a heavy "run" on the silver stocks of the U.S. Treasury, the government stopped redeeming *Silver Certificates* for silver bullion on June 24, 1968. *Silver Certificates* are still legal tender in the U.S. and have been hoarded in huge quantities, but most are not worth much more than face value, except for certain collectible varieties.

3.   *Gold Certificates* — issued in $10, $20, $50, $100, $500, $1,000, $5,000, $10,000, and $100,000 denominations. The $100,000 *Gold Certificate* of 1934 is the highest denomination U.S. bank note ever issued (42,000 printed), but as none were released into general circulation (serving only for banking accounting purposes), they are unobtainable and illegal to own.

U.S. *Gold Certificates* were redeemable in gold until President Franklin D. Roosevelt's Gold Reserve Act of March 9, 1933 took effect, prohibiting gold hoarding by the public and requiring *Gold Certificates* to be delivered for exchange at a bank by May 1, 1933, after which Roosevelt immediately raised the official price of gold, forever making himself hated by "hard money" advocates who maintain that citizens should prefer precious metal coinage over "worthless" paper currency. It is numismatically fortunate that many people in America disobeyed (intentionally or accidentally) Roosevelt's gold confiscation order, or we wouldn't have the wonderful selection of old gold coins and *Gold Certificates* that we do today. The U.S. Treasury lifted the restriction on holding *Gold Certificates* on April 24, 1964, and they can now legally be owned by private citizens and are legal tender but no longer redeemable in gold (or in anything else beside more paper money or cheap copper-nickel coinage).

4.   *National Bank Notes* — issued from July 1929 to May 1935, after which they were gradually removed from circulation by the Treasury. The bonds securing the *National Bank Notes* were called in by the government in May 1935. *National Bank Notes* in circulation went from $902 million in 1934 to $186 million by 1939. Today, they don't circulate at all, but collectors enthusiastically seek them (by state, by town, or by individual bank). Many circulated specimens can be bought for double face value or less, while rare bank charters may command huge collector premiums.

About $17 billion in the combined issues of *Large Size* and *Small Size* U.S. *National Bank Notes* were issued from 1863 to 1935, and about $50 million of this is still outstanding (lost, destroyed, hoarded, or collected).

5.   *Federal Reserve Bank Notes* (*FRBNs*) — $5, $10, $20, $50, and $100 notes issued, all *Series* 1929, all authorized March 9, 1933, to provide a quick cash injection into the national economy. *FRBNs* were actually a "temporary currency" for stimulating the depressed national economy, as shown by their circulating totals: $142 million in 1934, only $26 million in 1939.

6.   *Federal Reserve Notes* (*FRNs*) — issued 1929 (*Series* 1928) to date, this is the only type of U.S. paper money presently being made. *Small Size* U.S. *FRNs* were issued in $1, $2, $5, $10, $20, $50, $100, $500, $1,000, $5,000, and $10,000 denominations, but no *FRNs* higher than $100 have

been made since 1945, and since 1969, all U.S. paper money of $500 or over face value has been destroyed as it is acquired by Federal Reserve Banks. Only *FRNs* up to $100 are made today, and to combat drug dealing and other illegal uses, there is a continual debate about whether or not we should eliminate the $100 denomination as well (thus making it harder to count and transfer vast sums of cash).

THE GREAT DEPRESSION

After a recession in the United States in 1920-1921, and almost carefree prosperity from 1922-1928, the Great Depression began with the New York Stock Exchange crash of October 1929. Overspeculation in business and greed were two causes.

Some results were: "runs" on U.S. banks by domestic and foreign depositors demanding gold in exchange for their paper currency; "bank holidays" declared, whereby banks would close their doors rather than risk immediate insolvency; 2,294 U.S. bank failures in 1931; another 1,456 bank failures in 1933; over 5,000 more banks liquidated after Franklin D. Roosevelt became President of the United States on March 4, 1933; and 25% national unemployment.

Roosevelt's restructuring of U.S. banking regulations gradually increased public confidence in American banks, especially with legislation such as that creating the Federal Deposit Insurance Corporation on January 1, 1934. No funds under the insurance limits in an FDIC-insured bank account have ever been "lost" to depositors; disregarding, of course, the taxpayer "bailouts" of the insured financial institution liquidations in the 1990s.

Roosevelt's "New Deal" programs and the coming economic stimulus of World War II revived the American economy, which, on and off, has made impressive accomplishments in the last half of the 20th century, notwithstanding inflation and periodic recessions. Circulating U.S. currency went from about $6 billion in September 1939 (when Hitler invaded Poland, "officially" starting World War II) to $29 billion in 1945, but with consumer price increases of only 33% during those six years of wartime national economy, due to government price controls, rationing of goods, and heavy economic production.

"MISSING" MONEY IN U.S.A.

A 1985 Federal Reserve System study concluded that about 75% of circulating U.S. money (coins and paper currency) cannot be located — amounting to $154 billion. Possibilities include: illegal drug deals, tax-evading cash transfers, and foreign hoarding of U.S. money. Numismatic "collectors" have very little of it.

TOTAL CASH (PAPER MONEY AND COIN) IN CIRCULATION IN THE UNITED STATES From Treasury Department data		
DATE	AMOUNT IN CIRCULATION	AMOUNT PER CAPITA
June 30, 1910	$3,148,700,000	$34.07
June 30, 1920	5,698,214,612	53.18
June 30, 1930	4,521,987,962	36.74
June 30, 1940	7,847,501,324	59.40
June 30, 1950	27,156,290,042	179.03
June 30, 1960	32,064,619,064	177.47
June 30, 1970	54,350,971,661	265.39
June 30, 1980	127,097,192,148	570.51
June 30, 1990	266,902,367,798	1,062.86

16.   *Colonial Currency* from a recent auction catalog of Lyn F. Knight, Inc. of Overland Park, Kansas. Reproduced with company permission.

17.   19th century $10 *Hagerstown Bank* (Maryland) note, unsigned and unissued. Printed by Danforth, Underwood & Company of New York City.

18.   19th century $2 note of *The West River Bank* of Jamaica, Vermont, unsigned and unissued. Central vignette shows two cherubs fighting over two contemporary U.S. *Silver Dollar* coins.

19. $50 note of *Citizens' Bank of Louisiana* (at Shreveport), 19th century, unsigned and unissued, *Obsolete Currency*. Author's photo, from the stock of Americana Stamp and Coin Company, Inc. of Tarzana, California.

20.   Detail of $100 note of *Canal & Banking Company* of New Orleans, 19th century, unissued. Author's photo, from the stock of Americana Stamp and Coin Company, Inc. of Tarzana, California.

21. $5 note of the *Columbia Bank* of Washington, DC, 1852. Fully issued: with handwritten signatures, date, and Serial Number.

22. Detail of 19th century $2 note of the *Tallahassee Rail Road Company* (Florida). Author's photo, from the stock of Americana Stamp and Coin Company, Inc. of Tarzana, California.

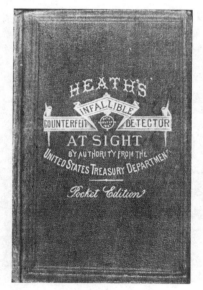

23. *Heath's Counterfeit Detector* — a popular 19th century reference book for identifying counterfeit currency in America. From a recent auction catalog of Currency Auctions of America, Inc. Reproduced with company permission.

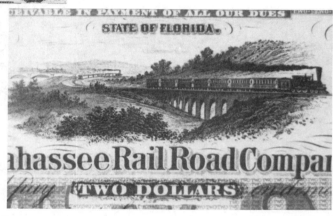

24. *Large Size* U.S. $10 *Demand Note* of 1861, with Abraham Lincoln, who had recently been inaugurated as the 16th U.S. President; eagle and draped shield at center; and female allegory "Art" at right. Margins all around. Author's photo, from the stock of Americana Stamp and Coin Company, Inc. of Tarzana, California.

25. Reverse of U.S. $10 *Demand Note* of 1861 (from Photo 24). The original *Greenback.* Author's photo, from the stock of Americana Stamp and Coin Company, Inc. of Tarzana, California.

26.   *Large Size* U.S. $1 *Legal Tender Note* (also called *United States Note*) of 1862, with low Serial Number (700). Portrait of Salmon P. Chase, U.S. Secretary of the Treasury, 1861-1864. Author's photo, from the stock of Americana Stamp and Coin Company, Inc. of Tarzana, California.

27.   Reverse of 1862 U.S. $1 *Legal Tender Note* (from Photo 26), with clause denying its validity for "DUTIES ON IMPORTS AND INTEREST ON THE PUBLIC DEBT"! Author's photo, from the stock of Americana Stamp and Coin Company, Inc. of Tarzana, California.

28.   *Large Size* U.S. $20 *Legal Tender Note* (*U.S. Note*) of 1862. Female allegory of "Liberty" holding sword and shield, appropriate for a nation engaged in Civil War. Folded and worn, but design completely discernible. Author's photo, from the stock of Americana Stamp and Coin Company, Inc. of Tarzana, California.

29. $1.75(!) note of the *Bank of the Commonwealth*, Richmond, Virginia, 1862. Signed, but no Serial Number. Issued concurrently with "federal" official *Confederate Currency*.

30.   25¢(!) *Indian Head Bank* note of Nashua, New Hampshire, 1862. "Fully issued"—with handwritten Serial Number and signature.

31.   50¢ *Florida "State" currency*, issued at Tallahassee, February 2, 1863. Supposedly "backed" by the "public lands," shall we classify this note as an "American State Fractional Assignat"?! Author's photo, from the stock of Americana Stamp and Coin Company, Inc. of Tarzana, California.

32.   10¢(!) *State of North Carolina* fractional note of 1863, issued at Raleigh, concurrently with federal *Confederate Currency* proper. Severe coin shortage both North and South led to fractional issues during the Civil War. Printed by J.T. Paterson & Company of Augusta, Georgia. Notice hornet's nest at center.

33.   *Large Size* U.S. $20 *Interest Bearing Note*, issued per Congressional Act of March 3, 1863, and paying interest at 5%. Female allegory "Victory" at left, military mortar at bottom center, President Lincoln at right (it was still legal to portray living persons on U.S. currency). Trimmed margins, but rare in any condition. Author's photo, from the stock of Americana Stamp and Coin Company, Inc. of Tarzana, California.

34.   Reverse of Civil War era U.S. $20 *Interest Bearing Note* (from Photo 33). About 20 known of this type. Author's photo, from the stock of Americana Stamp and Coin Company, Inc. of Tarzana, California.

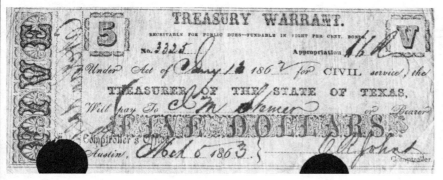

35.   *Treasury Warrant* of the *State of Texas*, with cut out cancels (COC) at bottom, indicating redemption. Issued often in mid-19th century Texas, in lieu of cash.

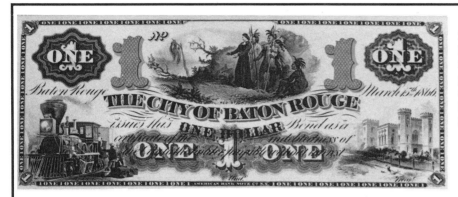

36. $1 municipal note of *Baton Rouge*, Louisiana, 1866. Center vignette shows "Baton Rouge" (the "Red Stick"), which was placed in the ground by war-seeking Indians during the Creek War of 1812-1814. Printed by the American Bank Note Company of New York City. Souvenir card impression.

37.   50¢ U.S. *Fractional Currency*, "Fourth Issue" (1869-1875), with bust of Samuel Dexter, U.S. Secretary of the Treasury in 1801. Printed signatures of John Allison (Register) and F.E. Spinner (Treasurer) — U.S. Treasury officials when this note was issued. Author's photo, from the stock of Americana Stamp and Coin Company, Inc. of Tarzana, California.

38.   "General Francis Marion's Sweet Potato Dinner" as the central vignette on this *State of South Carolina* $5 note of 1872. General Thomas Sumter at left, General William Moultrie at right. Printed by the American Bank Note Company of New York City.

39.   Souvenir card impression of *Large Size* $10,000 *United States Note* (*Legal Tender Note*), Series 1878. 4,000 of the original notes were produced, but all have been redeemed. Andrew Jackson at left.

40.   *Large Size* $20 U.S. *Silver Certificate*, Series 1880, showing Stephen Decatur, War of 1812 naval hero. Author's photo, from the stock of Americana Stamp and Coin Company, Inc. of Tarzana, California.

41.　Reverse of $20 U.S. *Silver Certificate*, Series 1880, from Photo 40. Author's photo, from the stock of Americana Stamp and Coin Company, Inc. of Tarzana, California.

42.　Souvenir card impression of *Large Size* U.S. $500 *Gold Certificate*, Series 1882. Abraham Lincoln at left. Original notes are scarce in high grade, somewhat more available in low grade.

43.　Reverse of *Large Size* U.S. $500 *Gold Certificate*, Series 1882. Souvenir card impression.

44.　Detail of souvenir card impression of *Large Size* U.S. $10 *National Currency*, "Second Charter" period, Series 1882. Vignette is entitled "Franklin and Electricity 1752."

45.　*Large Size* U.S. $2 *Treasury Note* (also called *Coin Note*), Series 1891, portraying the "Hero of Vicksburg," Union General James McPherson. Author's photo, from the stock of Americana Stamp and Coin Company, Inc. of Tarzana, California.

46.   Reverse of $2 U.S. *Treasury Note*, Series 1891, from Photo 45. Author's photo, from the stock of Americana Stamp and Coin Company, Inc. of Tarzana, California.

47.   Souvenir card impression of *Large Size* U.S. $5 *Silver Certificate*, Series 1896 (the celebrated $5 *Educational Note*). Considered by some to be the most beautiful U.S. note ever issued. Central winged allegorical figure of "Electricity Presenting Light to the World." "Jupiter," with horses and thunderbolts, at left; "Fame," with a trumpet, at lower center; and "Peace," with a dove, at right. Vignette design by Walter Shirlaw, border features designed by Thomas F. Morris, engraved by G.F.C. Smillie.

48.   Reverse of U.S. $5 *Silver Certificate*, Series 1896, from photo "face" in Photo 47, but this is a genuine note. Notice silk fibers running vertically through the note. Union Civil War Generals Ulysses S. Grant (left) and Philip H. Sheridan (right). Author's photo, from the stock of Americana Stamp and Coin Company, Inc. of Tarzana, California.

49.   "Spider" printing press. Old Bureau of Engraving and Printing photo, courtesy of the U.S. Department of the Treasury.

50.   Detail of souvenir card impression of *Large Size* $10 *United States Note* (*Legal Tender Note*), Series 1901. The famous *Bison Note*. Charles R. Knight made the original bison drawing, from which Ostrander Smith prepared the design, from which Marcus W. Baldwin engraved this timeless animal of American paper money history.

51.   *Large Size* U.S. $20 *Federal Reserve Note*, Series 1914. Portrait of Grover Cleveland. Author's photo, from the stock of Americana Stamp and Coin Company, Inc. of Tarzana, California.

52.   *Large Size* U.S. $50 *Gold Certificate*, Series 1922. Ulysses S. Grant. Author's photo, from the stock of Americana Stamp and Coin Company, Inc. of Tarzana, California.

53.   *Small Size* U.S. *Federal Reserve Note*, Series 1934. Philadelphia District (3-C).

54.   U.S. currency today is the best known paper money in the world. Western Union, based in the United States, has been in the business of "wiring" money by telegraph for over a century. More than $3 billion per year in Western Union "money transfers" are made worldwide, an especially safe method of transferring currency to foreign countries in economic or political turmoil, where the local postal or banking systems may be inefficient or corrupt. Official company photo, courtesy Western Union Financial Services, Inc.

55.   Reverse of *Small Size* $1000 *Federal Reserve Note*, Series 1934. U.S. note denominations above $100 have not been printed since 1945. Photo courtesy U.S. Bureau of Engraving and Printing.

3

"All we ask is to be left alone."
Jefferson Davis (1809-1889)
In his 1861 inaugural address
as President of the Confederacy

Confederate States of America Notes

When South Carolina seceded from the United States on December 20, 1860, there were about 5.6 million white people and 3.5 million black slaves living in the eleven states that would eventually comprise the Confederate States of America (Alabama, Arkansas, Florida, Georgia, Louisiana, Mississippi, North Carolina, South Carolina, Tennessee, Texas, and Virginia), in contrast with the 22.3 million Northern states' population.

THE NORTH'S ADVANTAGES

Although the agricultural strength of the South (including the cotton culture) has been emphasized by chroniclers of the American Civil War, the North actually had almost twice the cultivated farmland — 105 million acres compared with 57 million acres in the South. Other advantages of the North were 22,000 miles of well-linked railroads over which was transported troops and much war materiel, while the South had 9,000 miles of poorly-linked (i.e., localized) railroads. In factories, the North had an awesome 1,300,000 industrial workers; the South, 110,000. Because of its greater population, the North could field more soldiers, and of the over 2,300,000 men who served in the Union and Confederate armies combined, 1,500,000 were Union, and 800,000 were Confederate (and of these 2.3 million men, 25% died in the war, over half from disease and infection).

A long-established political and business infrastructure was in place in the Northern cities: (1) the federal government in Washington, DC; (2) the business nerve-centers in New York and other eastern cities; (3) the Northern industrial power centers with which many foreign merchants and foreign

governments were accustomed to doing business, etc. (The U.S.A. was a recognized nation-state; the C.S.A. had to struggle for international diplomatic and commercial acknowledgment. Many prominent and influential foreigners were afraid to do open business with the Confederacy, for fear of offending their lucrative Northern contacts.) And, of course, the Union had a functional Navy, which quickly blockaded the Southern ports and controlled ship access to the American coast.

THE SOUTH'S ADVANTAGES

So, while the Union might, at first glance, appear to have had overwhelming advantages in the Civil War, including perhaps the best man imaginable as President (Abraham Lincoln), the war dragged on for four bloody years, during which there were many times when the ultimate Union victory was very much in doubt, due to certain Southern advantages:

1. The South was fighting for its homeland and states' rights. Southerners were convinced that their cause was just. How many Union soldiers were eager to die to keep the Southern states in the Union, or to abolish slavery for that matter? How may Union towns and farms were destroyed in the war?

2. Southerners were fighting on familiar territory. They knew their land, its traditions, and its climate. And they knew their neighbors who lost their property, and maybe their lives, when a regiment of Union infantry marched down a local road.

3. As a rule, the South had better trained soldiers than the North.

4.   The South had better officers overall, including a few military geniuses whose exploits, fighting for the Confederacy, are standard textbook lessons for soldiers even today.

5.   Southerners gave nearly universal popular support for the Confederate cause. Slave revolts were not that common, and many black slaves labored (under compulsion, in many cases) to help the Confederate army, although slave mistreatment by various slave owners made a debatable number of slaves welcome their freedom. Many Northerners were against the war (for example, in New York City in 1861, an area seething with Southern sympathizers), a fact not always made clear in patriotic U.S. history books. Many Northerners voted against Lincoln in the elections of 1860 and 1864. Many Northerners, especially early in the war, openly and secretly aided the Confederacy. Confederate spies and saboteurs were always suspected and feared in the North.

6.   The South expected diplomatic recognition and assistance from England, which was thought to be permanently dependent on Southern cotton as the raw material for British textile mills. In 1860, the South produced 80% of the world's cotton supply.

7.   The Confederate Army took the initiative early in the war. The first two years of the Civil War were in the South's favor, keeping military morale high, despite increasing shortages of military supplies. According to Napoleon, the morale of an army is to its materiel as three is to one.

Confederate Financial Problems

Four urgent problems afflicted Confederate government finances at the very beginning of their organization:

1.   No treasury.

2.   No national monetary policy, including reluctance to tax.

3.   No national currency. Individual Southern states and towns issued their own paper money before and during the war, but an indigenous national Confederate States of America currency had to be established for the same reasons that the North needed a national currency:

• public convenience

• centralized governmental control

• universal national recognition of a uniform money

• anti-counterfeiting coordination

• providing a standardized accounting currency unit (the Confederate Dollar) for the whole Confederacy

• financing the war effort (by paper money inflation, if necessary — see the rest of this chapter)

4.   Extreme shortage of specie (precious metal coinage). In an era when people expected paper money to be redeemable for gold or silver coins, the issuance of unbacked notes guaranteed the fragile financial structure on which the entire Confederate governmental monetary policy had to be based. Little wonder that Confederate money was racked with brutal inflation and depreciation.

Confederate Currency Depreciation-Inflation Cycle

In charitable retrospect, you have to admire the romantically naive patriotic altruism of Confederate citizens who willingly gave their life savings of gold and silver coins to the Confederate government Treasury in exchange for a handful of upstart paper currency and bonds that were proudly hoarded, underneath the floorboards, in hopeful anticipation for the indefinite day when their "country" would emerge victorious from the Civil War of rebellion against the parent United States of America. If the South had won the Civil War and stayed intact as a political entity, Lincoln and Grant might have been hanged as traitors to the principles of states' rights (or at least demoted to less meddlesome jobs), and all *Confederate Notes* might still be legal tender (in the South, anyway!).

The reckless printing of unbacked paper money to finance their war of secession was too tempting to pass up by the Confederate government, which issued over $2 billion in *Confederate Notes*. Theoretically, you might say that cotton, rather than specie, backed the *C.S.A. Currency*, but nobody found that argument very convincing, and as the war lingered on, wrecking the Southern way of life, Confederate paper money depreciated rapidly, causing rising prices by Southern merchants who knew what was happening. Stressed to pay the rising costs for the war, the Confederate government's solution was to print more money. And the more it was printed, the more it "inflated"; the more it inflated, the more it depreciated, and the more it was printed. Thousands of people lost their life savings by holding *Confederate Currency* and *Bonds* until the South lost the war.

Confederate paper money inflation was caused by:

• severe material shortages in the South

• lack of money, causing the Confederate government to print huge amounts of it

• lack of specie, leading to unbacked money

• expensive war effort

• depreciation of Confederate currency due to public distrust of it

• Confederate Army battle defeats as the war went on

• the length of the war

After four years of misery, heartbreak, and homeland devastation, few Southerners were smiling when they put on their gray uniforms. At the end of the war, some Confederate soldiers refused to accept their pay in Confederate money, insisting on being paid in Union currency!

CONFEDERATE CURRENCY PRINTING

Quality and Problems of Supply

The Confederate Treasury, in its production of paper money, faced three logistical problems: lack of skilled engravers; lack of bank note printing facilities; and a shortage of quality bank note paper as the war went on. The Union blockade made foreign supply sources uncertain, so self-reliant Southern-based bank note production was given some priority. Still, most *Confederate Notes* are crudely printed compared with their Northern counterparts.

Northern Printings

Before actual fighting in the war, the first *Confederate Notes* were made in New York City because: New York had the best engravers and printers at that time; it was heavily pro-South and anti-Lincoln in sentiment; and many New York bankers and merchants stood to lose money in accounts receivable from Southern customers, so they wanted to support the South as much as was expedient. Some of this New York-printed Confederate money slipped through the Union blockade; other batches were confiscated by Union agents. Also, the Northern firms were receptive to making Confederate money because private bank note companies have traditionally been more interested in getting business from any source — and less concerned about "politically correct" customers — than have many other types of manufacturers.

Private Northern printers made quantities of faked *Confederate Notes*, generally for sale as souvenirs, but so many of these notes found their way South to be passed as counterfeit *Confederate Currency* that the Confederacy proclaimed the death penalty for Northerners caught passing Confederate counterfeits in the South.

Confederate Currency Condition from the Collector's Viewpoint

After the first printings, the quality of *Confederate Notes* deteriorated, especially by 1864. Many different papers were used, watermarked and unwatermarked, depending on what could be obtained. Because of: (a) the uniface format (printed only on one side) of many *Confederate Notes*, (b) inferior printing quality for many issues, and (c) the fact that the Confederacy lost the war, and their money is no longer legal tender, some collectors shy away from Confederate collecting, preferring to concentrate on well-made, but more expensive, U.S. currency of that period.

Confederate Currency is over 125 years old. Like all paper money, it has suffered the effects of time and aging. Much of it was manufactured under less than ideal conditions, and where it circulated (the warm, humid South) is not the best climate for the preservation of fragile paper. The collector of *Confederate Currency* should expect minor defects in much of what is encountered for collecting purposes: paper and ink fading, foxing, faint folds in high grade notes, some soiling, and even minute surface scrapes are normal for these issues. Uneven hand-trimmed margins, edge tears, pinholes, stray pencil marks, and various stains may detract from the appearance and market price of a *Confederate Note*, but that doesn't make it completely uncollectible. On the other hand, a pristine note in immaculate condition will command a premium price.

VIGNETTES ON CONFEDERATE NOTES

The 1861 *Confederate Note* vignettes were freely borrowed from those used for state bank notes. For example, the 1861 $500 *Montgomery* note's "Cattle, brook, and train" vignette was copied from the 1861 $1 note of the *North Western Bank* of Warren, Pennsylvania. It was common practice in the 19th century for private bank note companies to use vignettes interchangeably for note designs for different customers.

Besides portraits of Confederate politicians, *Confederate Notes* also bore pictures of famous Americans from history — at least those with Southern associations. John C. Calhoun (from South Carolina) and Andrew Jackson (from Tennessee) appeared together on the 1861 $1,000 *Montgomery* note, the highest paper money denomination issued by the Confederacy. Conveniently ignored was Jackson's (who had been dead since 1845) famous toast: "Our Federal Union: It must be preserved!" It is notaphilically ironic that Jackson, who fought to preserve the Union, was honored on the first bank notes of the Confederacy, which sought to destroy the Union. George Washington, the most famous Virginian in American history, graced the $50 *Richmond* notes of 1861.

Allegorical female representations of human endeavors were popular on early *Confederate Notes*. For example, the $20 *Hoyer & Ludwig* printing of September 2, 1861 shows a central vignette of three women ("Ceres seated between Commerce and Navigation") and, on the left side of this note, a standing female "Liberty." The most quaint and manifestly appropriate vignettes include: "Negroes hoeing cotton," "Horses pulling cannon," and a bust of Jefferson Davis. Some collectors specialize in *Confederate Notes* according to vignette theme.

PUBLIC ACCEPTANCE OF CONFEDERATE MONEY

Except for a few non-circulating "patterns" that were struck on a trial basis, no Confederate coinage as such was made. A few days after Louisiana seceded from the Union in January 1861, the South seized the New Orleans branch of the U.S. Mint, along with the Mint's bullion, to which was added specie from Southern banks, which quickly suspended specie payments, giving their specie to the Confederate Treasury.

The romantic 1861 New Orleans U.S. *Half Dollar* was minted at New Orleans from the same dies under three different governments: (1) the United States, (2) the state of Louisiana after secession, (3) as Confederate States' "coinage" (although not changed in design). More than 2½ million of these *Half Dollars* were minted, but generally they cannot be distinguished as to one of the three issuing authorities.

Because the Confederacy didn't have bullion to make their own coins in quantity, it was decided to make paper money instead. The Southern public accepted this *Confederate* paper *Currency* because there was no other choice, despite the unbacked nature of the money and its increasing inflation and depreciation. About $1,000,000,000 worth of the last issue (the February 17, 1864 issue) of *Confederate Currency* was printed, and even this money circulated extensively, as can be seen from the many notes of this issue that are completely worn and ragged in poor condition.

THE END OF CONFEDERATE MONEY

Confederate Notes of later years were nicknamed *Bluebacks* for their blue ink reverses. In 1864, the Confederate Treasury recalled all notes higher than $5 for exchange into 20-year bonds; $100 *Confederate Notes* were taxed at 33½%, with 10% added for every month's delay in redemption. Confederate paper money was put into Confederate soldiers' boots to help keep their feet warm during the winter of 1864-1865. With the end in sight, the Confederates blew up their Richmond arsenal and evacuated.

Confederate Currency circulated in the South until hostilities ceased in the various localities. It is a tribute to their patriotic optimism that the Southerners still used their inflated depreciated money until the very last moment (many of them, anyway). The Confederate paper *dollar* was worth 95¢ in gold during the first paper money issue in 1861. The Confederate *dollar* was worth 1.6¢ in gold on April 9, 1865, when Lee surrendered to Grant at Appomattox Court House, Virginia. On May 1, 1865, the last day that Confederate money was traded in the official currency markets, the Confederate *dollar* was worth 0.00083¢ in gold!

When Confederate President Jefferson Davis was captured in May 1865, he and his compatriots were guarding what was left of the Confederate Treasury: $700,000 in paper money, $85,000 in gold, $36,000 in silver, and $35,000 in silver coin (specie).

After the War

After the war, all *Confederate Notes* and *Bonds* were invalid and worthless, which led to the still-repeated half serious/half funny joke, "Keep your Confederate money, boys. The South shall rise again!"

Vast stocks of *Confederate Currency* were recovered after the war, some to be burned, some to be saved (by Northerners and Southerners alike) as war souvenirs, some to be studied and collected by eccentric people known as "paper money collectors." Until just a few years ago, most Confederate money was so plentiful and so cheap that many collectors didn't even bother to collect it.

Although Confederate money itself was worthless after the war, the U.S. Supreme Court ruled that wartime debts made in Confederate dollars had to repaid in an equal amount of U.S. dollars. This ruling was designed to help reorganize the Southern economy during reconstruction.

COLLECTING CONFEDERATE CURRENCY

All types are believed to be known, so you can confidently plan a long-term strategy in assembling a *Confederate Currency* collection, with the knowledge of approximately how much you'll have to spend to get a "complete set."

Condition Considerations

(Refer to Chapter 8 before reading this section.)

UNC, of course, is the condition of choice, but a rather nice *Confederate Note* set in AU, or even EF condition, could be collected by a budget-minded hobbyist. The scarcer notes in "problem-free" AU or EF condition are certainly desirable and saleable, at an appropriate price. Any Confederate paper money dealer in the country would be happy to buy a nice EF-AU 1861 type set of even the cheaper varieties.

My advice is to buy notes that look "nice" — regardless of grade. An AU note with bright color and large even margins might be worth more than a UNC note with much fading and lousy margins, a fact not always appreciated by novice collectors. If you can, browse through a lot of *Confederate Notes* in the stocks of different dealers, before you lay out serious money for Confederate additions to your collection. Get to know what's rare and what isn't, by condition as well as by type. Handsome notes, carefully purchased one at a time, will soon grow into a wonderful collection. Be patient: buy quality rather than quantity. The cheap 1864 notes are easy to obtain, but wait until you find premium condition.

"Matched Color Set"

"Some collectors like pale shades, others prefer bright red notes," said the paper money dealer at the Long Beach, California show I was visiting. "Don't buy any old note. Buy notes that will give you a 'matched color set.' Personally, I must confess that I like the bright red color," he continued, spreading out on his glass-topped bourse table an impressive selection of 1864 issue *Confederate Currency*. Deep red $500 notes (the "Stonewall" Jackson issue) of this series are exceptionally beautiful, provided, of course, that they aren't counterfeit.

Ways to Collect Confederate Currency

Confederate paper money can be collected by:

1. *Issue*. There were seven printed issues, 1861-1864, with the rarest being the FIRST ISSUE (the *Montgomery* printings of 1861, actually made by the National Bank Note

Company of New York City, and smuggled past the Union blockade; and the *Richmond* printings of the FIRST ISSUE, printed by the Southern Bank Note Company, actually the New Orleans office of New York's American Bank Note Company). The SEVENTH ISSUE (1864) is the most common, and all of the 1864 notes of $10 through $500 denominations can still be purchased at less than face value for reasonably nice AU or better notes. Many collectors start with the cheaper 1864 notes and work backward.

2. *Denomination.* All $1 notes, or all $10 notes, etc.

3. *Type.* Major note designs are the most popular way to collect any paper money, including Confederates. See charts for a Confederate Type Set.

4. *Variety.* Same basic type note, but with different design elements, different papers, different printings, etc. Boring and expensive for many beginning collectors, fascinating and addicting for advanced specialists.

5. *Engraver.* Collecting the notes of a specific engraving company, such as Keatinge & Ball of Richmond and Columbia, South Carolina.

6. *Vignette.* Collecting by types of vignette: portraits, buildings, allegorical figures, Southern scenes, etc.

7. *Contemporary Counterfeits.* Fraudulent notes that were made to deceive and circulate as money alongside their genuine versions in the Confederacy. These counterfeits are legal to own because (a) they were made before the Hobby Protection Act of November 29, 1973, and (b) Confederate money is not legal tender.

COUNTERFEIT, BOGUS, AND FACSIMILE CONFEDERATE NOTES

Contemporary counterfeits are notes that were made to pass as money while their genuine versions were circulating. Such counterfeits were often made outside of the South (such as in the North, or in Cuba, e.g., the famous *Havana counterfeit* $100 note of 1864), then smuggled into the Confederacy. When identified by Confederate Treasury employees, such counterfeits were withdrawn from circulation and marked "Counterfeit" either by handstamp or with handwritten ink. Contemporary counterfeit *Confederate Currency* is very collectible, selling for more or less the cost of the genuine.

Collector counterfeits are notes made to defraud paper money collectors. The crude printing of many *Confederate Notes* lends well to counterfeiting. Comparison to a genuine note is the first test of a counterfeit; Confederate counterfeits often have: (a) wrong paper type, (b) wrong size paper, (c) wrong size design elements, (d) printed black signatures rather than written signatures in brown ink (on notes so issued), (e) wrong paper color, and/or (f) poor design definition. Not all counterfeits are marked "Counterfeit," and some have circulated extensively, so they look authentic.

Bogus (fantasy) notes were never officially issued in their designs. *Bogus notes* may have been made for attempts at circulation or for souvenirs in the North; many are worn, showing that they often did circulate in the South. The $20 "Female Riding Deer" *bogus note* with printed signatures, dated July 25, 1861, is the most famous Confederate *bogus note*, and because it is often seen worn, it undoubtedly had some actual circulation in the South.

Facsimile notes are those made for souvenirs or commercial advertising. *Facsimiles* were never intended to pass as counterfeit money. Confederate *facsimiles* can be *contemporary*, such as those by the infamous "forger" of *Confederate Notes*, Samuel C. Upham (of Philadelphia), who himself admitted that during 1862 and 1863 he made over 1.5 million *Confederate Note facsimiles*. *Facsimiles* can also be of post-war or modern manufacture, and may or may not have the *facsimile* printer's name along the bottom margin (such names are often trimmed off, to make the note seem more legitimate). Many *Confederate Note facsimiles* were made as advertising promotions in the 1950s and 1960s, and are essentially worthless: they all have black printed signatures (instead of the genuine brown ink handwritten signatures) and are on paper that looks too new or that is that hideous artificial brown parchment, making a collector cringe when seen.

SOUTHERN STATE CURRENCY

Individual Southern states issued state government and local bank/town currency during the Civil War. Many of these *State Notes* are of great beauty and historical interest, and come in all price ranges for today's collector who wants notes in addition to federal *Confederate currency*. See Criswell's *Confederate and Southern States Currency* in the Bibliography.

CONFEDERATE CURRENCY "TYPE SET"

Absolutely essential for the serious collector of Confederate paper money are the two popular collector reference books: Criswell's *Confederate and Southern States Currency* and Slabaugh's *Confederate States Paper Money* (see Bibliography). By custom, everybody in the hobby uses Criswell's catalog numbers when referring to *Confederate Note* types. Criswell's book is also indispensable for evaluating collectible varieties of major types, such as paper variations, different *Serial Letters*, and minor engraving alterations between printings (many of which have different scarcities and market prices, as mentioned in the book).

Here are the various *Confederate Notes* that would constitute a basic "type set" in my opinion. Refer to the Criswell and Slabaugh references for more information on these notes.

CONFEDERATE PAPER MONEY TYPE SET

ISSUE	AUTHORIZATION DATE (Acts of Confederate Congress)	DATES ON NOTES	DENOMINATIONS	ENGRAVING COMPANY
First Issue	March 9, 1861	various handwritten dates	$50, $100, $500, $1,000 *"Montgomery Issue"*	National Bank Note Company (New York City)
			$50, $100 *"Richmond Issue"*	Southern Bank Note Company (New Orleans)
Second Issue	May 16, 1861 and July 24, 1861	July 25, 1861	$5	J. Manouvrier (New Orleans)
			$5, $10, $20, $50, $100	Hoyer & Ludwig (Richmond)
Third Issue	August 19, 1861 and December 24, 1861 and April 18, 1862	September 2, 1861 (all)	$5, $10, $20, $50, $100	Hoyer & Ludwig (Richmond)
			$5, $10, $20	J.T. Paterson (Columbia, South Carolina)
			$5, $10, $20, $50	Southern Bank Note Company (New Orleans)
			$2, $5, $10 (two types), $20	B. Duncan (Richmond and Columbia, South Carolina)
			$5 (three types), $10 (four types), $20, $50	Keatinge & Ball (Richmond)

CONFEDERATE PAPER MONEY TYPE SET, CONT.

ISSUE	AUTHORIZATION DATE (Acts of Confederate Congress)	DATES ON NOTES	DENOMINATIONS	ENGRAVING COMPANY
Fourth Issue	April 7, 1862	various handwritten dates	$100	Hoyer & Ludwig (Richmond)
			$100 (two types)	J.T. Paterson (Columbia, South Carolina)
			$100	Keatinge & Ball (Columbia, South Carolina)
		June 2, 1862	$1 (two types) $2 (two types)	B. Duncan (Columbia, South Carolina)
Fifth Issue	October 13, 1862	December 2, 1862	$1, $2, $5, $10, $20, $50, $100	Keatinge & Ball (Columbia, South Carolina)
				(various printers, however, after engraving was done)
Sixth Issue	March 23, 1863	April 6, 1863	50¢	Archer & Daly (Richmond)
			$1, $2, $5, $10, $20, $50, $100	Keatinge & Ball (Columbia, South Carolina)
Seventh Issue	February 17, 1864	February 17, 1864	50¢	Archer & Halpin (Richmond)
			$1, $2, $5, $10, $20, $50, $100, $500	Keatinge & Ball (Columbia, South Carolina)

CONFEDERATE CURRENCY DEALERS

Here are a few dealers who specialize in buying and selling *Confederate Currency*, among other things. Call or send a self-addressed stamped envelope for the cost and information on their latest retail catalog (listing *Confederate Notes* by Criswell numbers — see Bibliography):

GENE ELLIOTT
1429 Clairmont Road
Decatur, GA 30033 (404) 329-0811

GENE F. MACK
P.O. Box 60991
Jacksonville, FL 32236 (904) 771-4796

OLD DOMINION PAPER COLLECTIBLES (Dorsey A. Howard)
P.O. Box 418
Chesterfield, VA 23832 (804) 748-9189

HUGH SHULL
P.O. Box 712
Leesville, SC 29070 (803) 532-6747

"THE CONFEDERATE NOTE" — "THE LOST CAUSE"

Although we may never know the truth, this is the accepted version: Shortly after the Civil War ended, a friend asked Confederate Major S.A. Jonas, of Aberdeen, Mississippi, to write a "compliment or sentiment" on the back of a *Confederate Note*. Major Jonas wrote a poem, usually referred to as "The Lost Cause" or (especially among currency collectors) "The Confederate Note":

Representing nothing on God's earth now,
And naught in the waters below it,
As the pledge of a nation that's dead and gone,
Keep it, dear friend, and show it.
Show it to those who will lend an ear
To the tale that this paper can tell
Of liberty born of the patriot's dream,
Of a storm-cradled nation that fell.

Too poor to possess the precious ores,
And too much of a stranger to borrow,
We issued to-day our promise to pay,
And hoped to redeem on the morrow.
But days flew by, weeks became years,
Our coffers were empty still;
Coin was so scarce our treasury'd quake
If a dollar would drop in the till.

We knew it had scarcely a value in gold,
Yet as gold the soldiers received it;
It looked in our eyes a promise to pay,
And each patriot believed it.
But the faith that was in us was strong indeed,
And our poverty well we discerned;
And these little checks represented the pay
That our suffering veterans earned.

But our boys thought little of prize or pay,
Or of bills that were over due;
We knew if it bought us our bread to-day
T'was the best our poor country could do.
Keep it, it tells our history over
From the birth of the dream to the last;
Modest and born of the Angel Hope,
Like our hope of success it passed.

Richmond, Va., June 2, 1865

56. $20 *Confederate Note* of September 2, 1861 ("Third Issue"). "Sailor" at left, "Sailing Ship" at center. Engraved by Hoyer & Ludwig of Richmond.

57.   Genuine $20 *Confederate Note* of September 2, 1861 ("Third Issue"). Alexander H. Stephens, Confederate Vice President, at left; Stephens was against secession, but joined the Southern cause anyway. Allegorical "Industry" seated between Cupid and a beehive at center. "Hope" with an anchor at right. Engraved by B. Duncan of Richmond.

58.   Counterfeit $20 *Confederate Note* of September 2, 1861 (see genuine version in Photo 57). A "contemporary counterfeit" (made when the genuine circulated), fully "issued" (with handwritten signatures and Serial Numbers).

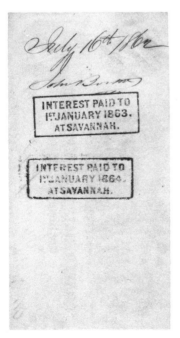

59. $100 interest-bearing *Confederate Note* of 1862 ("Fourth Issue") — "with Interest at two cents per day" — Milkmaid at left, railroad train at center. Engraved by J.T. Paterson of Columbia, South Carolina.

60.   Reverse of $100 *Confederate Note* from Photo 59. Many Confederate issues had unprinted reverses. This one was signed by the "bearer" when issued in July 1862, and has two "INTEREST PAID" handstamps in black ink (both of which have bled through to the face of the note — see Photo 59).

61. $10 *Confederate Note* of 1863 ("Sixth Issue"), "cut cancelled" (CC). State Capitol building at Columbia, South Carolina; portrait of R.M.T. Hunter, Confederate cabinet member. When redeemed or exchanged *Confederate Currency* was invalidated by some type of cancellation; in this case cut cancels (CC). Patterned slits are made, but no paper is removed. Worth less than an uncanceled note.

62.   50¢ *Confederate Fractional Currency* of 1864 ("Seventh Issue"). Profile of Jefferson Davis, Confederate President. This note and its 1863 forerunner are the only officially issued *Confederate Notes* with printed, rather than handwritten, signatures. Engraved by Archer & Halpin of Richmond.

63. $10 *Confederate Note* of 1864 ("Seventh Issue"). Central vignette of "Field Artillery" also called "Horses Pulling Cannon." Notice the irregular margins — *Confederate Currency* sheets were cut apart by hand after being printed. Notes with large and even margins command premiums when sold today. Over 9 million issued, it is the most common genuine *Confederate Note*.

64. $20 *Confederate Note* of 1864 ("Seventh Issue"). Capitol building at Nashville, Tennessee and Alexander H. Stephens, Confederate Vice President. Engraved by Keatinge & Ball of Columbia, South Carolina. Most collectors start with the "cheap" and easily obtainable 1864 *Confederate Notes*, and work their way backward chronologically if they become addicted to *Confederate Currency*!

65.   "Lucy Pickens" $100 *Confederate Note* of 1864 ("Seventh Issue"). It was long thought that Mrs. Jefferson Davis was portrayed on this note; but it is now believed to be Lucy H. Pickens, wife of Governor F.W. Pickens of South Carolina. George W. Randolph, Confederate Secretary of War in 1862, at right. 896,644 of these notes were issued. Engraved by Keatinge & Ball of Columbia, South Carolina. Thin, but "full" (not cutting into printed design) margins all around.

"The almighty dollar, that great object of devotion
throughout our land ..."
Washington Irving (1783-1859)

4

Making Modern U.S. Paper Money

Using modern U.S. paper money production procedures as examples, this chapter explains how paper currency is made — from artists' sketches to finished product in your neighborhood bank vault. Discussed are security measures, authoritative approval, artwork, engraving, printing, distribution, accounting procedures, acceptance by the public, and official destruction of worn notes. The "anatomy" of a bank note's parts, both obvious and hidden; the Federal Reserve System's role in our currency; and some data on bank robbery round out this chapter. Finally, I give the reasons I think paper money will be necessary in the future.

CHARACTERISTICS OF PAPER MONEY

The paper money of any nation, in any era, issued for any purposes, should have these characteristics:

1. Cheap to manufacture. Paper money replaced coinage in world history for several reason, including: (a) it is easier to make, (b) it is convenient to use, and (c) it is cheap to make.

2. Easily recognized. Money must have national symbols and slogans, easy-to-read denominations, and recognizable vignettes, and not be changed in design too frequently, so the public doesn't get confused about what "real money" looks like.

3. Durable. Must be strong enough to withstand repeated handling, folding, washing, and wear.

4. Hard to counterfeit. As has been shown many times in history, paper money's value becomes questionable when it is extensively counterfeited. Hence, special papers, elaborate

designs, and engraving developed as time-honored anti-counterfeiting measures. The notes of modern nation-states may also have security strips, microprinting, holograms, watermarks, invisible inking (detectable with ultraviolet light, etc.), and special security papers and inks, which are treated to show alterations and other tampering.

5. Readily accepted by the public. If this doesn't happen, all else is futile.

PARTS OF A U.S. BANK NOTE'S PRINTED DESIGN

These are the parts of a modern U.S. Bank Note's printed design; i.e., the presently circulating *Federal Reserve Notes*. Not all of these parts appeared on U.S. paper money from past eras, and not all of these parts (of course) are found on foreign notes.

1. National Identification — the issuing country's name. On U.S. notes, this is "The United States of America" (at the top of the note, on both sides).

2. Denomination — the face value of the note, appearing both in lettering (e.g., "One Dollar") and in numerals (1, etc.) on both sides of the note.

3. Portrait — the picture of the famous American in the central oval on the face (front, obverse) side of modern U.S. notes.

4. Vignette — scene portrayed on the note; the central design (building, etc.) on the back (reverse) side; the portrait on the front side.

5. Signatures — the written names of authorizing officials. All modern U.S. (and most world) currency has hectographic ("printed") signatures, which should be identical from note to note for the same signatory (person who signed the note). Pre-20th century notes of various nations often have manuscript (actually hand-signed in ink) signatures. The signatories of modern U.S. notes are the Secretary of the Treasury and the Treasurer of the United States.

6. Serial Numbers — the official set of numerals and letters that designate the individual number of a note; printed twice in green ink on modern *Federal Reserve Notes*: in the upper right and lower left on the face. Serial Numbers have five purposes:

- to keep count of quantities printed
- to identify specific press runs for internal quality control and to combat employee or other theft
- to inhibit counterfeiting (every counterfeit note needs a Serial Number, helping the Secret Service to identify such)
- to "track" notes geographically after issuance
- to keep count of specific notes redeemed, confiscated from criminals, destroyed, or repatriated from foreign countries (if this information is desired)

7. Series — the year when the note's design was adopted; not necessarily the year that the note was printed. When a minor design change occurs (e.g., change in signatory), a letter is found after the date, e.g., 1988A (then, 1988B for another minor change, etc.). On the face.

8. Treasury Seal — the printed Seal of the U.S. Department of the Treasury, in green ink on the note's face.

9. Federal Reserve Seal — Federal Reserve District Bank city and letter, in seal format, in black on the face.

10. Federal Reserve Number — the number of the Federal Reserve District of the note; corresponds with the alphabet letter inside the Federal Reserve Seal (e.g., 1=A, 2=B, etc.). On the face.

11. Type of Note — issuing status, or redeemability, of the note. For current U.S. money, this is "FEDERAL RESERVE NOTE," in white letters (outlined with black ink), at the top of the face side.

12. Check Letter, Face Plate Letter, Quadrant Number — black ink designations on the face, used to identify the printing plates and plate positions of the note.

13. Back Plate Number — small green number on reverse side, used to identify printing plate; in same shade of green ink as the entire reverse design.

14. Legal Tender Clause — wording that declares the money lawful. Modern U.S. notes have, in black ink on the face: "THIS NOTE IS LEGAL TENDER FOR ALL DEBTS, PUBLIC AND PRIVATE." (Anti-counterfeiting clauses have been used on American and foreign money in the past; not, however, on current U.S. notes or on most modern world notes.)

15. Motto — "IN GOD WE TRUST" — first printed in 1955 on U.S. *Silver Certificates, Series* 1935G. Has appeared on all U.S. paper money of *Series* 1963B or later.

16. "Fort Worth" Letters — "FW" letters, appearing before the Check Letter and Face Plate Number (lower right face) on notes made at the new Fort Worth, Texas Bureau of Engraving and Printing plant, for notes produced there, starting January 1991. The Back Plate Numbers of Fort Worth notes are slightly larger than those of Washington, DC notes made at the Bureau's original headquarters.

17. Scrollwork — elaborate designs along the borders of the note, done to discourage counterfeiting. Many paper money collectors use these definitions: Border — the outer limits of the printed design of a note. Edge — the outer limits of the note's paper. Margin — the unprinted area between the border and the edge. However, all of these are often used interchangeably, to add unintentionally to our confusion.

18. Inscribed Security Thread — a clear polyester thread embedded in the note's paper, with "USA" and the denomination printed on it, visible when held up to a backlight, first used on $50 and $100 notes of *Series* 1990 (but first released into circulation during the last half of 1991) as an anti-counterfeiting measure. The repeated patterns of "USA 100 USA 100" OR "USA 50 USA 50" (the denomination spelled out on denominations lower than $50; e.g., "USA TWENTY USA TWENTY") on the security thread cannot be reproduced by modern color copying machines.

19. Microprinting — the lettering "UNITED STATES OF AMERICA" printed repeatedly along the outside of the portrait oval, visibly decipherable only with magnification; introduced concurrently with the new security thread (described above) in *Series* 1990 (issued 1991) $50 and $100 *Federal Reserve Notes* as an anti-counterfeiting device that cannot be reproduced by contemporary color copying machines.

OBSOLETE DESIGN ELEMENTS OF U.S. CURRENCY

No longer found on circulating U.S. currency, but formerly used on certain issues, were:

1. Convertibility Clause — names the material for which the note is redeemable; e.g., specie (gold or silver), government bonds, interest payments, etc. No paper money in the world today is convertible into specie (precious metal coinage).

2. Engraver's or Printer's Name — the name of the company that prepared the printing plates and/or printed the notes. Not used on modern U.S. currency, which is made entirely by the Bureau of Engraving and Printing.

3. National Bank Name and Charter Number.

4. Anti-Counterfeiting Clause.

5. Allegorical Personages (such as "Liberty" or "Justice" in a female representation).

6. Surcharges and other Specialized Overprints (e.g., on *Compound Interest Treasury Notes, Fractional Currency*, the "HAWAII" overprints on World War II notes, etc.).

7. Congressional Authorization Act Dates.

HOW SERIAL NUMBERS ARE DETERMINED

The Serial Number appears in two places on the face side of modern U.S. currency: in the upper right and lower left portions. Serial Numbers on modern U.S. notes are always eight digits long, plus a prefix letter and a suffix letter (except for *Star Notes* — Replacement Notes — with a "Star" [or Asterisk] in place of one letter: the prefix letter on *U.S. Notes*, the suffix letter on *Federal Reserve Notes*). The letters, however, are considered part of the whole Serial Number.

The first note of any denomination in a new *Series* will have the Serial Number A00000001A, and the second note will be A00000002A, and so on. The notes are numbered in lots of 100,000,000. But because the numbering system has eight numerals, a "Star" note is substituted for the 100,000,000th note.

On *Federal Reserve Notes*, the prefix letter is the same as the letter in the Federal Reserve Bank District Seal (printed in black on the note). Each lot of 100,000,000 notes carries a distinctive suffix letter beginning with A and following in alphabetical order through Z, omitting the O because of its similarity to the numeral zero.

No two notes of the same kind, denomination, and *Series* have the same Serial Number, a fact that can be important in detecting counterfeit notes, since counterfeiters usually make large batches of a particular note with the same Serial Number.

STAGES IN BANK NOTE PRODUCTION

In order for United States paper currency to reach the public, these official steps are taken:

1. Design Request (in whole or in part, for a given note) by the Secretary of the Treasury.

2. Original Artist's Sketches of proposed design changes. After these are approved, the next step is:

3. Master Die Engraving — the design elements of the note are hand-engraved on a piece of soft steel known as the Master Die, executed by master craftsmen who have spent years developing their skills. The Master Die is cut into, using special instruments called *gravers*. Different craftsmen specialize in different aspects of the note's design: the portrait, the vignette, the numerals, the lettering, the script (printed "hand-writing" with the letters connected, as in the note's signatures), and the scrollwork. The portrait especially is given great attention, as a slight alteration in the breadth, spacing, or depth of line (by a counterfeiter) will cause a perceptible facial change. A quality bank note portrait is lifelike, with penetrating eyes and crisp features. The Master Die is engraved in reverse; i.e., with the design elements in a mirror image to what they will appear in the finished note. The engraving is done with fine lines, dots, and dashes that vary in size and shape, as can be seen if you magnify a portion of an engraved bank note. The engraver, using a magnifying lens, etches the design line by line, using pointed steel tools harder than the Master Die's steel. Master Die designs are indented (or "recessed") below the flat plane of the Die's surface.

4. *Siderography* is the process by which multiple images of the hand-engraved Master Die are transferred to a printing plate. The Master Die is hardened, and an impression in relief (raised image; the design elements are above the plane of the device) is taken from the Master Die, in plastic (in the old days, metal). Multiple plastic images of the various components (scrollwork, lettering, etc.) of the note's design are made, fitted, and welded into the printing plate configuration consisting of 32 notes. Master Dies are greased, wrapped, and stored indefinitely at the Bureau of Engraving's vaults; these dies can be taken out and used again and again to make printing plates at any time in the future. For example, the Lincoln portrait on the current $5 note was originally engraved in 1869, but it can still be used today to prepare printing plates for our currency.

5. Printing Plate Making — The modern printing plate for U.S. currency consists of a configuration of 32 notes (also called "subjects") — four across by eight lengthwise but with reversed images, as in the original Master Die. A group of plates (called a "series") is prepared from the Master Die and then inspected by an engraver. If the plate passes inspection, it gets chromium coated and is then ready for placing on the printing press.

6. Printing is done on high-speed, sheet-fed rotary presses. A single printing press uses four plates of 32 notes each, and is capable of printing 8,000 to 9,000 sheets per hour. Each sheet is forced under heavy pressure (estimated at 20 tons) into the finely recessed lines of the plate to pick up the ink. This kind of printing is called *intaglio* or *line-engraved recess printing*, and is the most difficult printing technique to imitate by counterfeiters.

Each of these dry sheet printing presses has an intaglio plate cylinder, an impression cylinder, an ink fountain, and an automatic sheet-feeding mechanism. The sheet automatically moves between the plate cylinder and the impression cylinder, and picks up the inked lines from the steel printing plates under pressure, finally being ejected and stacked up, sheet on top of sheet, all mechanically. The "printed side" of the paper feels slightly raised, due to the adhering ink lines — while the opposite side of the paper feels slightly indented. The backs of U.S. currency are printed first (the "First Print") with green ink, which is allowed to dry for 24 to 48 hours. Then the faces are printed (the "Second Print") with black ink, allowed to dry, and inspected for errors. (See Step No. 8, below, for the Overprinting of the Seals, etc.)

Bank Note Paper

U.S. paper money is printed on special paper composed of 75% cotton and 25% linen (rag-content paper as opposed to cheap wood pulp papers). Bank note paper is chemically sized, or treated, to give it the characteristic "crackle" found only in such papers. Crane and Company (of Dalton, Massachusetts) has supplied currency papers to the Bureau since 1879 and is the exclusive supplier today. U.S. currency paper is cream-colored, with tiny red and blue silk fibers scattered through it (not printed on it), and is produced by Crane and Company in sheets about 22 by 25 inches (large enough for the standard "sheet" of 32 notes). About $2^1/_2$ pounds of paper makes 1,000 notes. American notes are made to endure about 8,000 folds, and are unwatermarked to increase durability. European countries tend to like using watermarked paper for currency. Watermarking (impressing a design in the paper, which shows up as a thin area) weakens the paper's strength. Quality bond papers supplied commercially are usually watermarked. If a piece of current U.S. currency is watermarked, it is counterfeit.

Bank Note Printing Inks

Inks used to print U.S. currency are manufactured at the Bureau from dry pigments, oils, and extenders of the best quality. A printing ink is made by dissolving the dry pigment in a fluid "carrier." It is thoroughly ground and blended for uniform consistency. Bank note ink must be:

- Durable — shouldn't rub off too easily (although the inks on U.S. currency will rub off a little under pressure).

- Insoluble — shouldn't dissolve in water (rain, skin perspiration, clothes washing, spilled drinks, etc.).

- Color Fast — doesn't fade with moderate handling and normal exposure to light.

- Color Consistent — should be the same (or nearly the same) shade in any batch.

- Hard to Get — to discourage counterfeiting.

- Non-Toxic — relatively harmless when handled, touched to the mouth, etc. Otherwise, workers who handle money all day long (bank tellers, cash register clerks, theater box office clerks, casino employees, etc.) would be poisoned. Babies and adults may sometimes put paper money in their mouths, and must be protected from harmful effects.

- Strong Adherence to Paper (especially when stressed by repeated handling and folding, washing, etc.) but not deep penetration of paper (so that it doesn't "bleed through" to the other side).

- Ability to maintain consistency in very fine lines and dots of print.

- Secret Formulae — so that counterfeiters cannot make it.

- Fast Drying — must dry quickly to avoid "offset" impressions on freshly printed stacked sheets. Must dry even more "thoroughly" in 24 to 48 hours, so that subsequent printing may be done on the paper.

7.   Sheet Cutting and Inspection — after front and back side are printed, the 32-subject sheet is cut in half into two 16-subject sheets (two notes across by eight notes down), and both sides are inspected for defects. If the sheets pass inspection, they are ready for numbering and processing:

8.   Overprinting and Processing — The Bureau's Currency Overprinting and Processing Equipment (COPE) performs several functions. The Treasury Seal and Serial Numbers are overprinted on the face of the 16-note sheets in green ink (of a different shade than the reverse side color). The Federal Reserve District Seal and District Numbers are overprinted on the face in black ink. This overprinting is called the "Third Print"; i.e., after the note's back (First Print) and front (Second Print). After overprinting, COPE accumulates the 16-note sheets into units of 100 sheets, and conveys them to guillotine cutting knives that slice the sheets into 2-subject (i.e., 2-note) units (100 sheets at a time), and then into single stacks of 100 notes per stack. Units of 100 notes each are banded and packaged into "bricks" containing 40 units per brick — each brick contains 4,000 individual notes, and weighs about $8^1/_2$ pounds.

Star Notes

If a finished note is found to be defective after overprinting, it is replaced with a *Star* note. In design, the star notes are exactly like the note they replace, but they carry an independent series of Serial Numbers, with a "star" (asterisk) appearing after the numerals instead of a suffix letter on *Federal Reserve Notes*. The Serial Number of the imperfect note that was replaced is not used again in the same numbering sequence. *Star notes* are *replacement notes* in the U.S. currency and are sought by specialist collectors.

9.   Wrapping the finished notes — after the COPE operations and a final examination, the 4,000 note "bricks" are compressed and banded, then plastic shrink-wrapped and placed in pouches or boxes for shipment to one of the twelve District Federal Reserve Banks.

10.   Shipment to Banks — The U.S. Treasury ships newly printed currency "bricks" to the twelve District Federal Reserve Banks, which are also designated by numbers and corresponding alphabet letters:

Federal Reserve Districts
  1   A. — Boston
  2   B. — New York
  3   C. — Philadelphia

4   D. — Cleveland
5   E. — Richmond
6   F. — Atlanta
7   G. — Chicago
8   H. — St. Louis
9   I. — Minneapolis
10   J. — Kansas City
11   K. — Dallas
12   L. — San Francisco

Most of the Federal Reserve District Banks also have branches in other large cities in their District (which has interstate extended boundaries). The cash is stored at a Federal Reserve Bank until requested by a depository institution (for example, a member bank), and the currency is then shipped to the local bank by armored car. And that's how paper money gets to your local bank teller's window.

ESSAYS

An *essay* is a rejected bank note design. *Essays* may differ from the final issued notes in minor respects, including color and design elements. As a rule, *Bureau essays* for U.S. paper money should not be in the possession of collectors; but, in the past, *essays* sometimes escaped from official archives of the government/engraver/printer and/or bank where they were stored; hence, "collectible" *essays* (legal or illegal).

PROOFS

Proofs are printed impressions of the design (in whole or in part) of the bank note as finally issued. *Proofs* are usually taken ("lifted" or "pulled" in production terminology) on special *Proof* paper stock (often thicker, more like cardboard, than the final bank note paper) and are uniface (printed on one side), in contrast to the final bank notes, which are printed on both sides (if so issued, as is the case with Bureau U.S. currency). *Proofs* are lifted from the Master Die, either in an unfinished state (*Progressive Proof*) or finished; and are usually (but not always) printed in the shade of ink used for the final circulating note. No *Proofs* of current U.S. currency from the Bureau should be in private collections, as none have been legally released to the public. *Proofs* are taken, of course, from the Master Die to inspect its printing quality, before printing plates are made from it for mass-produced bank notes.

SOME U.S. PAPER MONEY STATISTICS

Until July 1929, *Large Size* U.S. currency was 7.42 inches by 3.13 inches. U.S. general circulation paper money (not *Military Payment Certificates*, etc.) printed since 1929 measures 6.14 inches by 2.61 inches, and the "thickness" of a single note is 0.0043 inches. Two hundred thirty-three new notes can be stacked up to a height of one inch, and 490 notes weigh one pound. A million notes weigh about a ton and occupy approximately 42 cubic feet of space (with moderate pressure).

Seventy billion dollars in face value of U.S. notes are produced by the Bureau every year, but only $240 billion is estimated to be in circulation worldwide (meaning that U.S. currency is often replaced with new notes).

Life Expectancy of U.S. Currency

Currency is strong and durable, but it does wear out with handling and damage. At that point, the Federal Reserve Banks remove it from circulation, and it is destroyed. Life expectancy varies with the denomination: $1 notes circulate for about 1 1/2 years; 2 years for $5 notes; 3 years for $10 notes; 4 years for $20 notes; and 9 years for $50 or $100 notes. (No denomination above $100 has been printed in the U.S. since 1945; and since 1969, all notes of $500 or over have been destroyed upon redemption at a Federal Reserve Bank.)

Redemption of Worn-Out Notes

The U.S. Department of the Treasury asks local banks to send old, worn, torn, or soiled notes to a Federal Reserve Bank (a "branch" bank is fine; e.g., the Los Angeles Branch of the San Francisco District Bank) to be exchanged for new notes. As the Federal Reserve Banks receive currency from commercial banks, they count it and determine if it is "fit" or "unfit." Fit (reusable) money is stored in the Federal Reserve vaults until it goes out again through the commercial banking system as it is needed. Currency (and coin) that is unfit (not reusable) is "retired," then destroyed. Damaged and worn coins are returned to the U.S. Treasury for replacement by the U.S. Mints.

Redemption of Mutilated U.S. Paper Money

U.S. paper money that has been mutilated or partially destroyed may in some cases be redeemed at full face value. Until January 1, 1971, a mutilated note could be redeemed at full face value only if clearly more than 3/5 of its original area remained intact. Portions clearly larger than 2/5 but less than 3/5 of the original were redeemable at half their face value. Prior to 1889, mutilated paper money was sometimes redeemed at discounts of 10%, 20%, etc., depending on the fragment size. Redemption of mutilated paper money is now handled by Federal Reserve Banks if clearly more than half of the original currency surface remains intact. Seriously damaged currency must be sent to the U.S. Treasury for redemption.

U.S. Treasury "Rules" for Mutilated Currency Redemption

The Department of the Treasury, Bureau of Engraving and Printing, redeems partially destroyed or badly damaged U.S. paper money as a free public service. Every year, the U.S. Treasury handles approximately 30,000 claims and redeems mutilated currency valued at over $30 million. The Office of Currency Standards, located in the Bureau of Engraving and Printing, uses experts to examine mutilated currency and will approve the issuance of a Treasury check for the value of the currency determined to be redeemable.

The U.S. Treasury defines mutilated currency as notes that are: (a) not clearly more than ¹/₂ of the original note size and/or (b) in such condition that the value is questionable and special examination is required to determine its value. The most common causes of mutilated currency are: fire; water; chemicals; explosives; animal, insect, or rodent damage; and petrification or deterioration by burying.

Under regulations issued by the Department of the Treasury, mutilated U.S. currency may be exchanged at face value if: (1) more than 50% of a note identifiable as U.S. currency is present; or: (2) 50% or less of a note is identifiable as U.S. currency is present, and the method of mutilation and supporting evidence demonstrate to the satisfaction of the Treasury that the missing portions have been totally destroyed.

What is Not "Mutilated Currency"

U.S. Department of the Treasury guidelines state that the following is not mutilated currency: any badly soiled, dirty, defaced, disintegrated, limp, torn, worn-out currency note that is *clearly more* than ¹/₂ of the original note, and does not require special examination to determine its value. These notes should be exchanged through your local bank and processed by the Federal Reserve Bank.

Shipment of Mutilated Currency to the U.S. Treasury

Mutilated currency may be mailed or personally delivered to the Bureau of Engraving and Printing. When mutilated currency is submitted, a letter should be included, stating the estimated value of the currency and an explanation of how the currency became mutilated. Each case is carefully examined by an experienced mutilated currency examiner, and the Director of the Bureau of Engraving and Printing has the final authority for the settlement of claims.

Mutilated Currency Packing Procedures

Careful packaging is necessary to prevent additional damage. These are the suggested procedures, as advised by the Bureau of Engraving and Printing:

1. Regardless of the condition of the currency, do not disturb the fragments any more than is absolutely necessary.

2. If the currency is brittle or inclined to fall apart, pack it carefully in plastic and cotton without disturbing the fragments, and place the package in a secure container.

3. If the currency was mutilated in a purse, box, or other container, it should be left in the container.

4. If it is absolutely necessary to remove the fragments from the container, send the container along with the currency and any other contents that may have currency fragments attached.

5. If the currency was flat when mutilated, do not roll or fold the notes.

6. If the currency was in a roll when mutilated, do not attempt to unroll or straighten it out.

7. If coin or any metal is mixed with the currency, carefully remove it. Any fused, melted, or otherwise mutilated coins should be sent to the Superintendent, U.S. Mint, P.O. Box 400, Philadelphia, PA 19105 for evaluation.

Mailing Address for Shipping Mutilated Currency

All mutilated currency should be sent Registered Mail, Return Receipt Requested. Insuring the shipment is the responsibility of the sender. For cases that are expected to take longer than four weeks to process, the Bureau of Engraving and Printing will issue a written confirmation of receipt.

Department of the Treasury, Bureau of Engraving and Printing, Office of Currency Standards, P.O. Box 37048, Washington, DC 20013.

Personal Delivery Address for Mutilated Currency

Personal deliveries of mutilated currency to the Bureau of Engraving and Printing are accepted between the hours of 8:00 A.M. and 2:00 P.M., Monday through Friday, except holidays. Just walk right in with your damaged currency, to this address: Bureau of Engraving and Printing, Office of Currency Standards, 14th and C Streets, Washington, DC 20228.

THE LOS ANGELES BRANCH OF THE FEDERAL RESERVE BANK

As an example of perhaps the busiest branch Bank in the Federal Reserve System, the Los Angeles branch of the Federal Reserve Bank (at the corner of Olympic Boulevard and Grand Avenue, Los Angeles, California) is a branch of the District 12 Federal Reserve Bank of San Francisco. Seven hundred employees work in the L.A. branch, and on an average business day, they process 2.8 million checks, ship $500,000 in coin, electronically transfer $2.95 billion, and destroy $31 million in old and counterfeit notes.

Vault employees of the L.A. branch of the Federal Reserve Bank, who work where $5 billion (or more!) in cash is stored, have a "line of sight rule" whereby they must keep each other in sight at all times. To guard against employee theft, no one is permitted to work alone in the vault. In the vault, notes are bundled in rubber-banded packets of 100, then put in clear plastic bags of 10 packets per bag, then put in clear plastic bins of 360 to 420 bags per bin.

At this L.A. branch Federal Reserve Bank, 30 to 50 counterfeit notes are discovered every day — mostly $20 or $100 notes, with $20 being the most common.

Over $5,000,000,000 ($5 billion) in cash rests on an average day in the Los Angeles Federal Reserve Bank because of several factors: (a) the large population in southern California (over 15 million people), (b) a busy multi-faceted southern California economy, (c) the influx of many recent immigrants (from many countries) who use cash by custom and default, and (d) substantial "money laundering" from the illegal drug rackets, which have been shifting from Florida to California.

WORN-OUT CURRENCY PROCESSING AND DESTRUCTION

Responsibility for maintaining the physical quality of circulating U.S. paper currency is shared by the Federal Reserve Banks and the U.S. Department of the Treasury.

Each day, millions of dollars in deposits made by depository institutions (local banks, etc.) into Federal Reserve Banks are carefully scrutinized, and worn and mutilated notes are removed from circulation and destroyed. Only Federal Reserve Banks (including their branches), and in certain cases the U.S. Treasury, are permitted to destroy currency. Counterfeit notes that are detected are forwarded to the U.S. Secret Service.

Between the mid-1960s and the end of 1989, about $474 billion in paper money was deemed unfit for circulation and destroyed. Each year, more than 6 billion *Federal Reserve Notes*, with a face value over $60 billion and weighing about 7,000 tons, are destroyed by the twelve District Federal Reserve Banks and their twenty-five branches. After automatic separating, counting, and verification, the Federal Reserve Banks destroy worn and mutilated paper money by one of three methods:

1.   Burning — in an incinerator where temperatures up to 1,800 degrees Fahrenheit reduce the currency to a whitish ash similar to talcum powder.

2.   Shredding — in a macerator, which cuts the notes into tiny scraps of paper, in the form of little strips.

3.   Compacting — done after shredding of the notes; then pressing the shredded strips by machine into compressed 400-pound bales; then depositing the bales in landfill sites. One bale made up of shredded $20 bills contains about $4 million in face value.

EARLY HISTORY OF THE U.S. BUREAU OF ENGRAVING AND PRINTING

The beginning of an establishment for the engraving and printing of United States paper money can be traced as far back as August 29, 1862 to a single room in the main U.S. Treasury building in Washington, DC, where four women and two men began to separate (by cutting from sheets), seal, and sign (for the Treasury officials) $1 and $2 notes that had been printed for the U.S. by private bank note companies. These functions were later embodied in what was known as the First Division of the National Currency Bureau, which began printing U.S. currency sometime in November 1862 through January 1863, depending on which original source is correct. In 1864, it was

recommended to the Secretary of the Treasury that "The Engraving and Printing Bureau of the Treasury Department" be established, but this Bureau was not recognized as a distinct entity within the Treasury Department until Act of Congress of March 3, 1869. As the years progressed, the Engraving and Printing Bureau gradually absorbed the functions performed by the private bank note companies, and by October 1, 1877, all United States paper money was printed in this Bureau.

The first Bureau of Engraving and Printing (BEP) building was occupied in the summer of 1880, the red brick building that today is north of the main building.

U.S. paper money was actually washed by currency washing machines at the Bureau from 1912 to 1918, a practice abandoned because it changed the feel and appearance of the notes.

A new structure, the Main Bureau building, was completed and occupied on March 19, 1914, south of the original building. The Bureau Annex, across the street from the Main building, was completed May 16, 1938 and is connected with the Main building by a tunnel under 14th Street.

The Bureau's Western Currency Facility was opened April 1991 in Fort Worth, Texas to print the first federal U.S. currency outside of Washington, DC since 1862.

Today the Bureau of Engraving and Printing is the world's largest security manufacturing establishment. It employs 2,300 people and operates 24 hours a day — designing, engraving, and printing U.S. currency, Savings Bonds, Treasury notes, U.S. postage and revenue stamps, White House invitations, federal government identification cards, etc. The combined floor space of the two large buildings is about 25 acres.

Paper Money Printing Security

Security at the BEP is very stringent, to prevent outside as well as employee theft. On rare occasions, an employee has attempted to steal money. On January 4, 1954, two packages of $160,000 in $20 *Federal Reserve Notes* were found missing at the BEP, with two "dummy packages" substituted. The employee thief was apprehended, and the U.S. government recovered all but $26,000 of these notes.

Some countries — like Russia, Pakistan, and India — have had their bank note-making employees strip naked and walk down a corridor (even being made to jump, naked, over a two-foot high bar!) under inspector observation, before putting on special one-piece pocketless uniforms for work, and reversing the procedure at the end of their shifts, to discourage theft, substitution of counterfeits for genuine notes, etc.

Tours of the Bureau of Engraving and Printing

Visitors are welcome to take a self-guided tour of the Bureau, featuring currency production. You can see the production steps in making U.S. paper money, and tour guides are available to answer questions. The tour ends in the Bureau's Visitors' Center where exhibits are on display and where you can buy uncut sheets of currency, engraved prints, small bags of shredded currency, and souvenir cards.

The tour takes about 20 minutes, and may be taken Monday through Friday, 9:00 A.M. to 2:00 P.M., except for federal holidays and the week between and including Christmas and New Year's. No reservations are required, but March through September is the heavy tourist season, when the tour line is cut off sometimes as early as noon to ensure that the last visitor in line can enter the tour gallery by 2:00 P.M., and when the average wait in line can be 1¹/₂ hours. There is no parking or restaurant for the public at the Bureau, and smoking and taking photographs are prohibited.

Bureau of Engraving and Printing (Main Building) 14th and C Streets, S.W. Washington, DC 20228 24-Hour Information Numbers: (202) 447-9709 or 447-9916

Buying Uncut Sheets of U.S. Currency

The Bureau of Engraving and Printing sells uncut sheets of current $1 and $2 *Federal Reserve Notes* in sheets of 4, 16, and 32 notes at a moderate premium over face value. These sheets can be purchased in person at the BEP Visitor's Center at Raoul Wallenberg Place S.W., between Independence and Main Avenues S.W., Washington, DC or by mail. The BEP also sells souvenir cards (see Chapter 6), and engraved and lithographed prints. To be put on the mailing list for BEP products for sale, write or call:

Office of Public Affairs, Room 533W U.S. Bureau of Engraving and Printing 14th and C Streets S.W. Washington, DC 20228 (202) 447-0193

BANK ROBBERY IN THE UNITED STATES

According to legend (but maybe not fact), when asked why he robbed banks, famous bank robber Willie Sutton replied: "Because that's where the money is!"

About 8,000 bank robberies happen every year in the United States — about 800 of these in Los Angeles, the bank robbery capital of America. L.A., with a little over 1% of the nation's population, has about 10% of the nation's bank robberies, perhaps due to the nice weather, numerous banks, and spread-out city geography with many good streets and freeways for plenty of getaway options.

Here is a typical (statistically speaking) bank robbery in the United States: The robber is a white male adult, commits the crime between 1:00 and 3:00 P.M. on Friday, uses a robbery demand note at a teller's counter, either shows a weapon or threatens to show a weapon, gets about $6,550 in

cash, doesn't create violence, doesn't take hostages, and robs a Los Angeles bank.

FBI Investigations of Bank Robbery

The Federal Bureau of Investigation (FBI) of the U.S. Department of Justice investigates bank robbery under three violations: (1) Violations of the federal bank robbery and incidental crimes statute, Title 18, United States Code, Section 2113; (2) Bank extortion violations, which are investigated under the federal bank robbery and incidental crimes statute; and (3) Violations involving armored carriers investigated under the Hobbs Act, Title 18, United States Code, Section 1951.

THE PERSISTENCE OF PAPER MONEY

We are far from being the completely cashless society that is predicted by those who say that coins and paper money will soon be extinct. Checks, money orders, credit cards, and electronic funds transfers are used for most large financial transactions in the United States (with illegal money transfers being the prime exception), but cash, including paper currency, still has a vital role to play in the daily business lives of our citizens, for these reasons:

1. Cash is always in style. If you're traveling where nobody knows you; if you're selling things to strangers; if you're in a foreign country, nobody questions cash.

2. Cash is practical for small purchases. Bus fares, pay telephones, toll roads, vending machines, newsstands, and candy counters take cash.

3. Service employees often take cash. Waiters and waitresses, cab drivers, and parking lot attendants are tipped in cash.

4. Paper money saves time. As fast as they can take your currency, they can process your purchase; no credit checks, no identification necessary.

5. Some situations only call for cash. How many parents pay their children's allowances by check? Does the neighborhood kids' sidewalk lemonade stand accept credit cards? Roadside fruit vendors? Hot dog stands? Laundromats? Subway trains?

6. "Impulse" purchases are often done with cash, and smart retailers know this.

7. "Real" paper money provides security to some people. They swear that they sleep better with some cash under the mattress.

PORTRAITS AND BACK DESIGNS OF CURRENT U.S. CURRENCY (Circulating *Small Size* FEDERAL RESERVE NOTES)		
DENOMINATION	PORTRAIT	BACK DESIGN
$1	Washington	Obverse and Reverse of the Great Seal of the U.S.
$2	Jefferson	Signing of the Declaration of Independence (Series 1976)
$5	Lincoln	Lincoln Memorial building
$10	Hamilton	U.S. Treasury building
$20	Jackson	White House
$50	Grant	U.S. Capitol building
$100	Franklin	Independence Hall
$500	McKinley	(Ornate) FIVE HUNDRED DOLLARS
$1,000	Cleveland	(Ornate) ONE THOUSAND DOLLARS
$5,000	Madison	(Ornate) FIVE THOUSAND DOLLARS
$10,000	Chase	(Ornate) TEN THOUSAND DOLLARS

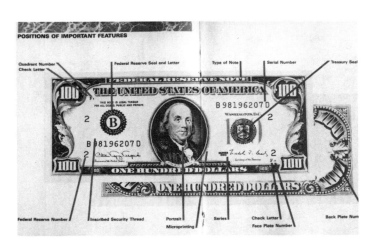

66. "Currency Features" pages from the booklet, "Know Your Money," produced by the U.S. Secret Service, U.S. Department of the Treasury.

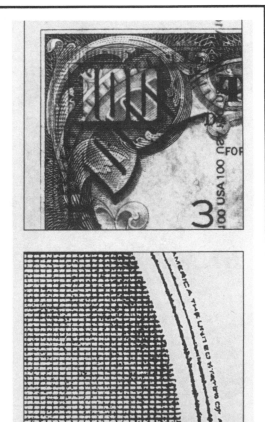

67. Top: A clear polyester security thread, inscribed with "USA" and the denomination repeated, has been incorporated into higher denomination U.S. currency since 1991. Common in many foreign countries. Bottom: Microprinting of "THE UNITED STATES OF AMERICA" appears outside of the portrait border lines of newly issued U.S. notes ($50 and $100, starting in 1991). Cannot be reproduced by current office copying machines. Photos courtesy U.S. Secret Service.

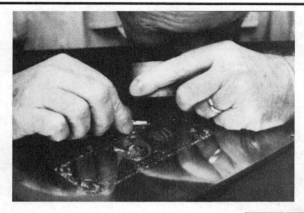

68. A master craftsman hand-engraves a plate. Photo courtesy U.S. Bureau of Engraving and Printing.

69. Intaglio printing plate. Photo courtesy U.S. Bureau of Engraving and Printing.

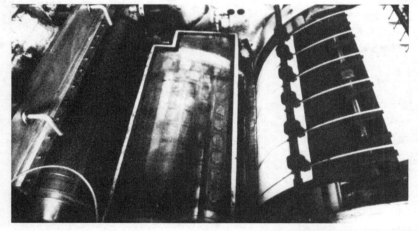

70. Modern currency printing press. Photo courtesy U.S. Bureau of Engraving and Printing.

71. Freshly printed currency sheets coming off the press. Photo courtesy U.S. Bureau of Engraving and Printing.

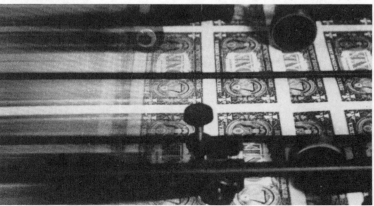

72.   New currency is examined for defects by BEP employees. Photo courtesy U.S. Bureau of Engraving and Printing.

73.   Overprinting new U.S. notes. Photo courtesy U.S. Bureau of Engraving and Printing.

74.   New notes, after slicing into individual stacks. Photo courtesy U.S. Bureau of Engraving and Printing.

75.   Newly cut notes are banded in "units" of 100 notes, then packaged into "bricks" of 4,000 notes. Photo courtesy U.S. Bureau of Engraving and Printing.

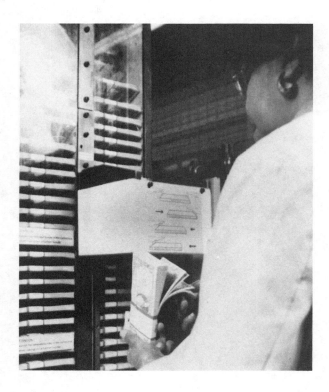

76. A banded stack ("unit") of 100 newly made notes is examined. Photo courtesy U.S. Bureau of Engraving and Printing.

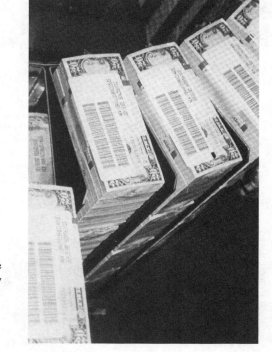

77. Stacks of banded $20 notes ready to be labeled and shrink-wrapped. Photo courtesy U.S. Bureau of Engraving and Printing.

78. Reverse of current *Small Size* U.S. $10 *Federal Reserve Note*, showing the U.S. Treasury building in Washington, DC. The "car" in the foreground is a composite of several different manufacturers. Photo courtesy U.S. Bureau of Engraving and Printing.

79. Reverse of current *Small Size* U.S. $50 *Federal Reserve Note*, showing the U.S. Capitol building in Washington, DC. Photo courtesy U.S. Bureau of Engraving and Printing.

80.   A selection of current *Small Size* U.S. $100 *Federal Reserve Notes* from various Districts. Author's photo of currency at his bank.

81.   When U.S. currency is partially destroyed, the U.S. Department of the Treasury will replace it if clearly more than half of the original note remains. Photo courtesy U.S. Secret Service.

82.   Currency chemically damaged. Photo courtesy U.S. Department of the Treasury.

83.   Mutilated currency, as received at the Bureau of Engraving and Printing for "redemption." Photo courtesy U.S. Department of the Treasury.

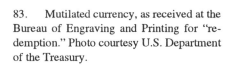

84.   Buried currency. Photo courtesy U.S. Department of the Treasury.

85.   Burned currency. Photo courtesy U.S. Department of the Treasury.

86.   Currency mutilated by explosives. Photo courtesy U.S. Department of the Treasury.

87.   Liquid-damaged currency. Photo courtesy U.S. Department of the Treasury.

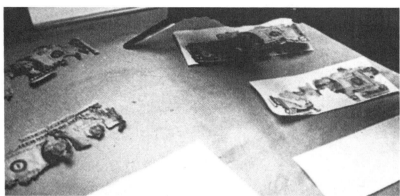

88.   Currency damaged by rodents/insects. Photo courtesy U.S. Department of the Treasury.

89.   The Los Angeles branch of the San Francisco District Federal Reserve Bank, located at Olympic and Grand in downtown Los Angeles. On an average day, $5 billion or so, in cash, rests in the vaults here! Security, of course, is great. Author's photo.

ORIGINAL HOME
1862–1880

90.   The Main U.S. Treasury building (built before the Civil War, with later additions), located on 15th Street next to the White House in Washington, DC, was the first home of the Bureau of Engraving and Printing, from 1862 to 1880. Official engraving, U.S. Bureau of Engraving and Printing.

91.   Completed July 1, 1880, the U.S. BEP got its own building at 14th Street and Independence Avenue, where it resided from 1880 to 1914. This first exclusively BEP building still stands, north of the Main BEP building. Official engraving, U.S. Bureau of Engraving and Printing.

FIRST BUILDING
1880–1914

MAIN BUILDING
1914

92.   The Main BEP building, completed March 19, 1914, is located at 14th and "C" Streets, just south of the first building (see Photo 91). This Main building is where you go (1) for tours of the Bureau, (2) to buy BEP products, and (3) to redeem mutilated currency. Official engraving, U.S. Bureau of Engraving and Printing.

93.   The Bureau Annex, across the street (east) from the Main BEP building, was completed May 16, 1938, and is connected with the Main building by a tunnel under 14th Street. Official engraving, U.S. Bureau of Engraving and Printing.

BUREAU OF ENGRAVING AND PRINTING ANNEX
1938

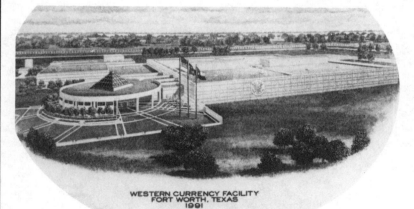

WESTERN CURRENCY FACILITY
FORT WORTH, TEXAS
1991

94.   The Western Currency Facility of the Bureau of Engraving and Printing opened in April 1991 in Fort Worth, Texas, and began printing $100 notes — the first federal U.S. currency printed outside of Washington, DC since 1862. Official engraving, U.S. Bureau of Engraving and Printing.

95.   U.S. *Savings Bonds* are among the many printed items, besides currency, that are produced by the BEP. Photo courtesy U.S. Bureau of Engraving and Printing.

5

"Money, which represents the prose of life, and which is hardly spoken of in parlors without an apology, is, in its effects and laws, as beautiful as roses."
Ralph Waldo Emerson (1803-1882)
Essays

Collecting Specialties of Paper Money

Compared to coin, manuscript, and fine art collecting (all of which predate the Christian era), the collection of paper money is a relatively recent hobby because: (a) people in the past looked on paper money as something to spend or to invest, not something to admire aesthetically; (b) past generations couldn't afford to save their hard-earned paper currency by idly "collecting" it; (c) in the past, paper money was often quickly "redeemed" back to the banks that issued it because nervous citizens were afraid that the issuing banks would, at any unpredictable moment, "suspend specie payment" (stop giving out gold or silver in exchange for their own supposedly bullion-backed bank notes); and (d) for most parts of the world, paper money as we know it has only been in general use for a few hundred years.

The purchasing power of the 19th century (and earlier) bank notes was so much greater than that of today's currency that few people could afford to "hoard" any paper money at all, much less be crazy enough to boast about "collecting" it. Hoarding would only result in effective loss of potential investment interest dividends. And the frequent inflationary depreciation of idle hoarded bank notes, not to mention the well-known habit of banks becoming insolvent (with the consequent invalidation of their paper money issues), precluded the collecting hobby until recently.

Dr. Joshua I. Cohen is known to have assembled a collection of American Revolutionary currency in the 1820s. Rare coin and curio dealers sometimes offered old paper money for sale from the mid-19th century on, in the United States. By the 1880s, American *Colonial* and *Continental* paper items were already a century old, and the earliest American Civil War money originated a generation ago. It was nothing to get excited about, as it was still available in vast quantities but was nevertheless increasing in age and romance as the time and circumstances of issue kept slowly receding further into the legendary past ... in the case of *Colonial Notes*, beyond the memories of living people.

Little collector demand was shown for paper money during the first half of the 20th century, and when the fabulous Albert A. Grinnell Collection of United States Paper Money was auctioned off in the mid-1940s, many incredibly rare notes brought hammer prices a little over face value! Even the Society of Paper Money Collectors and the International Bank Note Society trace their beginnings to the recent year of 1961.

When Norris McWhirter (notaphilist and co-editor of the *Guinness Book of Records*) opened the paper money exhibition held by Stanley Gibbons Currency Ltd. in London in January 1971, he remarked that paper currency is "the most difficult thing to collect except perhaps hailstones." What he meant was that published information on paper money was often as hard to find as the notes themselves. That situation has changed a bit since 1971, and every year now brings new published information on paper currency specialties.

The 1970s saw a collecting boom in paper money in the United States, with notes that went begging at $100 each in 1970 having frantic bidding competition at around $1,000 or more in 1980, when the speculative rage in many collectibles (stamps, coins, etc.) was reaching a fever pitch.

WHY COLLECT PAPER MONEY?

We collect, study, and admire paper money because it has:

1. Beauty. Many bank notes are masterpieces of the engraver's art. Even little children will look at a bank note for many minutes, absorbed mentally in the subtle scrollwork and

interplay of portrait and background lines in the note's design. A finely made bank note is a work of art, every bit as majestic and harmonious in its two-dimensional graphics as an ancient Greek marble sculpture is in its three-dimensional stony splendor.

2. History. The rise and fall of people and empires is chronicled on these paper documents we call bank notes. Human struggles and accomplishments during war and peace are subjects for currency vignettes. The "Founding of Buenos Aires" appears on the back of a recent Argentine note. George Washington and Abraham Lincoln, America's most beloved Presidents, are on our paper money still.

3. Legendary Romance. Like a Shakespearean drama, the story of currency forever reminds us that human nature is the same in all ages and in all states. Paper money, while a momentary creation of human beings, is also timeless and universal in its themes and emotional impact. Hold an 1800 *Banque de France* note in your hand — perhaps the same note that Napoleon himself touched before paying a soldier with it. Let your eyes fall kindly on a frayed *Confederate States of America Lucy Pickens* note — the same note that once had other eyes glance at it, eyes that are now dust but that once were bright and hopeful with the dreams of the glorious Southern cause!

It has been said that the past is like a mirror: if you look carefully, you will see your own reflection.

4. Government approval. Bank notes have the actual or implied approval of official governments, and therefore "speak" to us with an authority derived from important societal institutions. If a scrap of paper comes from a Cheapside pub, it has a certain connotation; if it comes from the Bank of England, it has another meaning.

5. Value. Currency has value, both its original denominational worth and its collector appeal. When you tell someone that you collect seashells or buttons, you evoke amused smiles among your listeners. When you say that you collect $100 United States or £50 British bank notes, and that you prefer them in Crisp Uncirculated condition and over 50 years old, you generate a slightly different spectator response; and when you produce some obsolete high denomination notes from your pocket, the crowd stops smiling.

6. Camaraderie. Friendships, or what passes for them in this restless world, are sometimes earned by collecting things. Fellow collectors and currency dealers will get to know you if you correspond and do business with them. I've met some nice people in the currency hobby; maybe you will, too!

The first issue of the *Currency Dealer* newsletter (the *Greensheet* — see Chapter 19) appeared in September 1980. Every month since then it has helped to publicize the evolving market action in U.S. paper money, especially *Large* and *Small Size Notes*.

7. Universal Appeal. "Everyone" likes money. Even hermits and religious ascetics will occasionally appreciate a cash donation to their favorite charitable endeavor. Paper money has universal value, public acceptance (more or less!), and cross-cultural recognition. Drop a piece of paper money, any money, from any country, on any sidewalk anywhere there is constant walking traffic, and count the seconds until someone picks it up. Even rich people will stoop and put their hands on the ground to retrieve a lowly bank note. What power in a tiny scrap of paper!

WHAT WE CALL OURSELVES

Notaphily is the study and collecting of paper money. British philatelic and numismatic writer Kenneth R. Lake created the term Notaphily about 1970 when he joined the Latin root *nota* ("note") with the Greek *philos* ("love"); hence a Notaphilist is a "lover of (paper) notes," or, simply, a paper money collector.

The Notaphilic (pronounced *no-ta-FIL-ik*) hobby actually became very popular only since about 1970, with an explosion in collecting interest and in note market prices. Notaphily is a branch of numismatics (the study of coins, medals, paper money, and related items).

Syngraphics is an older term for "paper money collecting," derived from the Greek roots *syn* ("together" or "with") and *graphos* ("to write") … hence, meaning "writing together" ("a written document signed by everyone legally bound to it"). A Syngraphist thus, is another name for "paper money collector."

Rag Picker is an affectionate (but crude, in my opinion) slang term for "paper money collector."

MISTAKES OF BEGINNING COLLECTORS

Common mistakes made by novices in paper money collecting include:

1. Quantity versus quality. I've collected many different things during my life (stamps, coins, rocks, shells, books, autographs, military souvenirs, paper money, etc.), and I've noticed that there is one trait that inevitably separates the "beginners" from the more advanced collectors: beginners choose quantity instead of quality. They would rather have a large collection than a rare collection. You can learn a lot from a boxful of cheap notes. But you will rarely regret buying an expensive note (provided, of course, that you don't overpay).

2. Overpaying by not knowing the market.

3. Buying overgraded notes (see Chapter 8).

4. Buying without preliminary research. Read paper money books (see Bibliography), dealer price lists (Chapter 17), currency periodicals (Chapter 22), and society journals (Chapter 23). The informed buyers sure do.

5. Unnecessary duplication. Variety spreads "risks."

6.   Haphazard accumulation without a coherent theme. Do you specialize, or do you collect any note you happen to see?

7.   Believing bad advice. How can you judge whether or not you've just received good advice, if you only get advice from one person? Smart collectors talk with many dealers and fellow collectors, and synthesize their own opinions based on those of many people.

8.   Buying "unpopular" notes, then wondering why they're hard to sell. There's probably a reason the notes are cheap. Could it be that they have little demand? And if everybody has them, to whom do you sell?

9.   Buying severely damaged notes. Of course, you can buy a scarce note cheaply if it is all cut up and taped together. But do you really want it? And does anybody else?

10.   Impatience. Do you need to complete your collection in one month? Fortune may favor the bold, but fools sometimes rush in where angels fear to tread.

KEEPING AN INVENTORY

Keep an inventory of your collection, either on index cards or on a computer. Bank Note Ledger®, a computerized software program sold by MSL Software (see below), has fields for entry of the following data for each of your bank notes: Country, Series, Type, Denomination, Condition, Album and Page (Location), Currency Value, Purchase Price, Purchase Date, Price Sold, Date Sold, Inventory (How Many Multiples), and Description. You can mess around with this data on handwritten index cards, so at least you know what is in your collection. Or you can write to this company, especially if your collection becomes huge, and ask for their brochure and latest prices ($39.95 as of this writing) for their *Bank Note Ledger* programs (and include a self-addressed stamped envelope):

MSL Software
P.O. Box 11170
Pittsburgh, PA 15237
(412) 366-7195

Collection inventory is also needed for insurance or security purposes. Hide a copy of your inventory away from where you store your collection (e.g., at home if your collection is in a bank box), so that you can describe missing notes to an insurance agent or a police detective who investigates a loss, and to identify stolen notes that are recovered.

"COMMON, SCARCE, RARE, AND UNIQUE"

Based on how difficult it is to find certain notes, notaphilists classify paper money as COMMON, SCARCE, RARE, and UNIQUE:

1.   COMMON — easily obtainable note, although it may be priced beyond your collecting budget! Many dealers have this note in stock or can get it for you, without much trouble, as per your "want list."

2.   SCARCE — infrequently seen note, or an infrequently encountered grade in a relatively "common" note design. Scarce notes are missing from most routine collections and perhaps lacking in most dealer stocks. A scarce note will be seen (hopefully!) at major paper money shows/bourses. The retail price of a scarce note should sting a bit when you finger your wallet or checkbook as you stare at the note's price tag. Scarcity, of course, is a state of mind as well as an objective fact of the material world, and many people call something "scarce" when it is actually quite common.

3.   RARE — a note offered for sale maybe only a few times a year, at auction or retail. Selling price is commensurate with condition and demand. *California National Gold Bank Notes* of the 1870s are scarce in any condition, and true rarities in Extremely Fine to About Uncirculated condition. The word "RARE" is overused by zealous retailers. How rare is it? If it is so rare, why is there a "limit" of twenty notes per customer?!

4.   VERY RARE — sometimes used as a superlative, indicating a note that might appear on the market only once in a number of years.

5.   UNIQUE — only one example known (in or out of museums, and government archives, etc.).

"Semi-unique" is a poorly chosen term, often used hyperbolically in advertisements, referring to notes of which several specimens are known. "Semi-unique" is like saying you're "semi-alone" when you're eating with "only" two other people at your table! Like saints and other one-of-a-kind personalities, a piece of paper money is either unique or it isn't.

COLLECTION COMPLETENESS

"Completeness" is a personal opinion, not an immutable command in the realm of notaphilic collections. A "single note signed by a family member stationed at a remote foreign military outpost" may be a "complete" collection from the owner's viewpoint. A "Serial Number study of common low denomination notes extracted from current circulation" may never be complete in the sense that more and more examples will continually be found from time to time for the rest of your life.

A collection too easily "finished" is, for many people, as unsatisfying as a collection that can never be "finished." The availability of the notes you seek and the amount of money that you can spend on your collection will determine the total quantity of notes in your collection.

Following the crowd, collecting what everybody else collects, has value. So does going it alone. As with many aspects of life, a middle ground may be the wisest place on which to stand. So, why not specialize in a group of notes that will challenge but not exhaust your patience, budget, curiosity, acquisitiveness, and sanity?

And who says that you have to have one collection forever? I've formed and sold many collections. The formative stages are filled with excitement and magic as I explore a whole new world ... the "maturing middle period" of my latest collection showers knowledge and surprises on me, and my confidence in comprehending the collection grows as each new piece fills a gap in the collection's "story." Then I mourn after my cherished collection has been sold and dispersed beyond recall, the funds that it generates being used to start another specialized collection — the rebirth of the collector instinct in all its glory!

SPECIALIZED COLLECTIONS OF PAPER MONEY

Rather than collect "everything" (as if that were even possible in a "completeness-seeking" sense), most collectors soon learn to specialize in a limited range of note types, (major designs) and varieties (slight differences within a major type note category). And the wise specialist will pay at least some attention to potential resale value of a particular specialty, before huge sums of money are sunk into an esoteric notaphilic sideline that "nobody" wants to buy when the collector wants to sell it.

Collecting Several Specialties Simultaneously

It is good to have three or four specialty collections at the same time, preferably very different from each other: (a) for variety — you can go from one collection to another at will; (b) to combat collector boredom and "burn-out"; (c) to meet different dealers and collectors; (d) so you can acquire "something" for one specialty collection when the others stagnate; and (e) so you can buy or sell in one specialty (including liquidating the entire specialty collection if necessary) without necessarily affecting your other collections.

Types of Specialized Paper Money Collections

There are many ways to collect paper money, some of them overlapping each other as you tailor your specialized collection to fit your unique needs:

1. U.S. vs. foreign notes.

2. Obsolete vs. current (i.e., no longer circulating vs. presently circulating).

3. Chronologically — by time period. Examples: World War II currency; notes made during the year you were born; 19th century notes.

4. Single country. Example: Bahamas currency.

5. Single state (or province) within a country. Examples: Mississippi notes; Québec notes; Bavarian notes.

6. Single bank. Examples: Bank of England; the Erie & Kalamazoo Bank of Adrian, Michigan.

7. Single town. Example: notes issued in New Orleans, Louisiana.

8. Overseas possessions, either as a group of colonies or individually. Examples: the notes of all French overseas territories; the notes of British Fiji. Collectors with adequate budgets sometimes collect the "mother country's" notes along with her possessions, past or present.

9. Printing company. Examples: the notes made by the American Bank Note Company of New York City; Thomas de la Rue Ltd. of Basingstoke, England.

10. Obsolete "countries." Examples: Notes of the Confederate States of America; Danzig; Newfoundland (as an independent entity).

11. Types. Major note designs.

12. Varieties. Minor design variations.

13. Errors. Notes that are production mistakes. Not to be confused with constant plate varieties.

14. Multilingual. Notes having more than one language printed on them. Examples: Canadian notes 1937 to date (with English and French bilingual inscriptions), Hong Kong (Chinese and English), Belgium (French and Flemish), recent Swiss notes (with three or four languages), and certain Indian notes (eight languages panels, etc.).

15. Topicals. Collecting by design vignette theme. Examples: ships, animals, railroad trains, flowers, allegorical figures. Called *thematics* in British collecting terminology. A popular specialty in currency collecting these days, especially for collectors who collect the notes of many countries.

16. Multicolored. Notes with many colors.

17. Unicolored. Notes with one color ink. Example: 19th century "broken bank" notes in basic black.

18. Denomination. Examples: Just $1 notes; only £1 notes.

19. Series. Example: 1935 *U.S. Silver Certificates.*

20. Hand-signed. Scarce, the closer we get to the present day, because most modern currency has printed signatures.

21. Signatures. Collecting by specific signatories (the people who signed the notes). Popular with affluent collectors of U.S. and British notes.

22. *Counterfeits, facsimiles, bogus,* and *fantasies* (see Chapter 21). Of course, you want to limit yourself to items that can be legally owned, as per current national laws.

23. *Replacement Notes.* Issued when the first printing run gets damaged. Examples: the "Star" (Asterisk) notes of the United States and Canada.

24. Uncut sheets. Either as issued or from printing company stocks and remainders, etc. May be a partial sheet, reduced from the original sheet size.

25.   *Inflation Notes* (see Chapter 12).

26.   *Military Currency* (see Chapter 13).

27.   *Prison, Concentration Camp Notes*, etc. (see Chapter 13).

28.   Cancellations. A cancellation is a mark showing that a bank note, check, bond, etc., has been redeemed (paid) by its issuing authority. Cancellations may be (a) handstamped in ink; (b) machine-stamped in ink; (c) handwritten ("PAID" or "CANCELLED" etc., in manuscript ink); (d) mechanically cut (perforated, punched, cut, or embossed). Perforated means small holes cut out, usually to form lettering. Punched means large holes removed, often through the signatures or Serial Numbers. Cut usually means a straight line or "X" shaped design slit through the paper, with or without paper removal — if no paper is removed, it is called rouletted. Embossed cancels are designs impressed into the paper, concave on one side, and convex on the other side, without breaking all the way through the paper.

29.   Unissued remainders. Notes that are identical to their issued versions but lacking signatures and Serial Numbers (usually) and available to collectors because of one of these reasons: bank failure, note design change, demonetization, deliberate sale to collectors by the issuing authority, or outright theft from the printing company's archives (a crime for which the collector of such notes may not be criminally liable, for a variety of reasons). Remaindered notes are common with many 19th century U.S. *Broken Bank Notes*, and are usually cheaper to buy (and less desirable) than comparable "fully issued" notes in the same condition of preservation. Because of rarity, some notes are only available to collectors in the form of "unissued remainders."

30.   *Essays*. A rejected design for a note. May be similar to issued design but in a different color.

31.   *Proofs*. A trial printing of a note in its design as finally issued, in whole or in part, either in black ink or in the issued colors. Usually printed on one side only, on special proof paper that differs from bank note paper, which distinguishes *Proofs* from "unissued remainders." *Proofs* are sometimes defined as "uniface unissued notes of the issued designs"; i.e., one-sided printed impressions (on special "proof" paper stock) of a note, without the signatures or Serial Numbers but otherwise identical to notes issued for circulation (but maybe in a different color, i.e., black-inked *Proofs*). Modern souvenir cards (see Chapter 6) have *Proof* impressions of bank notes.

32.   *Specimen Notes*. Invalidated or sample notes, overprinted or perforated with the word "SPECIMEN" or other legend to indicate such. In this book, when I use a capital "S" for the word *Specimen*, I mean one of these official *Specimen Notes*. When I use a lower case "s" for specimen, I am using the word in its generic sense, meaning an example or an item in a collection.

Specimen Notes, often not signed or Serial Numbered, have been issued for distribution to central banks throughout the world for currency recognition; lately for sale to collectors to get the collectors' money. Because a *Specimen Note* is not legal tender, the issuing country makes almost pure profit by selling them to collectors (after deducting printing, advertising, and distribution costs). A modern *Specimen Note* can often be purchased for less than face value, as it should, considering it is worthless outside of the notaphilic collector world.

Novice collectors sometimes think they're getting a bargain when they buy a foreign note, only to discover that they actually bought a non-negotiable *Specimen Note*, which is collectible in its own right but often of less market value than the issued version. For example, "MUESTRA" is Spanish for "Specimen" and "MUSTER" is German for "Specimen" — a reason to get a foreign language dictionary if you intend to collect the notes of a country whose language you do not understand.

33.   Vignettes. The exquisitely engraved cameo scenes on paper money. Some collectors specialize in any vignettes showing George Washington. Some fanatical vignette addicts (don't laugh; I was one once!) try to find their favorite vignettes in every form possible: *Essays, Proofs*, on every bank note where they once appeared, even on bonds, company billheads, or other fiscal paper. In the 19th century, especially, vignettes were freely "borrowed" for multiple uses. Popular vignettes, such as the "Indian Princess" or "dog guarding safe" were used over and over again on fiscal paper issued by banks all over the country. Some of the identical vignettes even were used on Northern and Confederate currency at the same time during the Civil War!

Obsolete currency vignettes from the master die storage vaults of the U.S. Bureau of Engraving and Printing and the American Bank Note Company are often put back in service in designing modern souvenir cards (see Chapter 6). A wonderful collection of great beauty can be assembled with historical currency vignettes, on or off the actual bank notes, and at a cost to suit any collecting budget.

34.   Graffiti on notes. Example: A 1935 U.S. *Silver Certificate* signed by the crew of a World War II bomber and dated "Paris, December, 1944" has a certain value to collectors.

When an American fan of Pablo Picasso asked the famous artist, "What's it like to be Picasso?", the artist responded by asking his questioner for a U.S. $1 bill, scribbled some sketches on it, signed it, and handed it back, saying, "Now your dollar is worth five hundred dollars. That's what it is like to be Picasso."

96.   20,000 *Zlotych* note of Poland, 1989, featuring Marie Curie, the only person ever to win two Nobel science prizes. (Pick # 152)

97.   1 *Cruzeiro* note of Brazil, no date (but 1943), hand-signed across the note's face! (Pick # 132)

98.   20 *Cedis* note of Ghana, 1982. Miner at right. Ghana was the British colony of Gold Coast until becoming the first black African colony to achieve independence (on March 6, 1957). The monetary unit, *Cedi*, comes from "sedie" (cowrie) — the shell money of West African coastal tribes. (Pick # 21)

99.   "Pre-Revolutionary" 5 *Pesos* note of *El Banco de Guerrero* (Mexico), issued 1906-1914. Unissued remainder (unsigned, undated). Perforated with the stylized word "AMORTIZADO" (i.e., "redeemed" or "paid off" — invalidated). (Pick # S298c)

100.   Detail of central vignette, "Female with Fruit Basket," of *El Banco de Guerrero* (Mexico) 5 *Pesos* note of 1906-1914 (see Photo 99). (Pick # S298c)

101. $1 note of Guyana, no date (but 1983), with Kaieteur Falls at right. Printed by Thomas de la Rue & Company, Ltd. (Pick # 21b)

102.   100 *Drachmai* note of Greece, dated 8 December, 1978. Athena at left, watermarked classical head at right. (Pick # 200)

103.   50 *Leke* SPECIMEN (overprinted in red) note of Albania, 1976. Marching soldiers —perhaps for a "military topical" collection? (Pick # 45s)

104. 100 *Francs* note of Rwanda, 1978. Nice animal topical, featuring native zebras. Formerly a United Nations trusteeship territory administered by Belgium, Rwanda became independent on July 1, 1962. (Pick # 12)

105. Detail of reverse of *Large Size* U.S. $50 *Federal Reserve Note*, Series 1914. Female allegory of "Panama" between two oceans and two ships. From souvenir card impression.

106. $5 SPECIMEN note (with red overprint on each side) of Bermuda, 1978, with invalidating punch holes through the Serial Numbers. Britain's Queen Elizabeth II. (Pick # 23as)

107. Reverse of 50 *Riels* note of Kampuchea (formerly Cambodia), 1979, featuring the fabulous ancient Khmer temple of Angkor Wat. (Pick # 32)

108.   Reverse of *Large Size* U.S. $2 *Silver Certificate*, Series 1896 (the celebrated $2 *Educational Note*). The ornately engraved designs, including the portraits of inventors Robert Fulton (steamboat) and Samuel Morse (telegraph), are a bank note collector's dream, but a counterfeiter's nightmare. Souvenir card impression.

109.   1991 note from the author's mother, enclosed with a group of $2 *Federal Reserve Notes*, Series 1976.

Dear Barry,

The enclosed 2.00 bills are just as I received them uncirculated in 1976 — 15 years ago. The Sanka Coffee Co. offered the 2.00 bill in a special promotion for the Bi-centennial. I think a person had to send in a couple of coffee labels for each 2.00 bill. Are they a collectible? You can have them.

Love,

"Mom"

The History of the U.S. $2.00 Bill

No American currency could be more appropriately issued to honor the Bicentennial than the new $2.00 bill. This denomination is as old as America itself and as rich in heritage.

The $2.00 bill originated on June 25, 1776 when the Continental Congress authorized its issuance in the form of "... bills of credit

for the defense of America." During the Civil War, Congress authorized the $2.00 denomination as U.S. currency. It reappeared subsequently as over-size Notes, Silver Certificates and Treasury Notes with various portraits appearing on these different versions including Alexander Hamilton's.

(continued on back)

110.   *Small Size* $2 *Federal Reserve Note*, Series 1976, in descriptive envelope as received by the author from his mother in 1991. Since folded.

6

> "Nobody asks how you got your money,
> but merely what its total is."
> Seneca (circa 4 B.C.-64 A.D.)

Collateral Fiscal Paper

Besides paper money proper, many collectors like to collect related fiscal paper items, such as: bank checks, stock certificates, bonds, bills of exchange, letters of credit, municipal and private scrip, bank-related billheads, money orders, bank history books, bank photos, bank postal correspondence, credit cards, souvenir cards (especially with vignettes from currency), lottery tickets (old and new), business ledgers, bills of lading, cash receipts, bank and express company drafts, currency legislation documents, pay vouchers, exposition ("world's fair") admission tickets, currency-making memorabilia (including original design sketches, engraving tools, dies, printing plates, essays, proofs), and books (bank and express company histories, counterfeiting tales, eyewitness accounts of "Central Bank" employees, histories of national currencies, monetary theory books, etc.).

While not absolutely necessary to enjoy paper money, such "collateral fiscal paper" gives historical depth and human interest to a currency collection, although you may find yourself spending lots of money on these sidelines themselves! On the other hand, there are cheaper things available in these collateral collecting specialties for those who seek.

BANK CHECKS

A *Bank Check* is a written order instructing a bank to pay funds out of the check-writer's account. A form of checks was invented by the Romans in pre-Christian times. Fifteenth century Italians and 16th century Dutch used checks drawn on specie deposits of customers.

Checks are known from America at least as early as 1681, and checks have been written by every U.S. President; in fact, Presidential signatures are avidly sought on checks.

Checks were first used with frequency in America in the 1830s, and their use skyrocketed after 1850 due to increasing U.S. population, increasing economic prosperity, and long-distance business. Banks originally employed messengers to carry checks back and forth between banks, until the checks ended up at their bank of origin. This check-routing by runners was inefficient, leading to the invention of clearing houses—official financial buildings where checks from every bank in town (and elsewhere) were "settled" against each other's balances. The first New York City clearing house opened its doors in 1853; the first Boston clearing house, in 1856.

The Appeal of Checks to Collectors

Checks reduce the amount of paper money in circulation, so, in a sense, checks could be considered an "enemy" of paper money collectors. In reality, though, many currency collectors enjoy check collecting because of: (a) the intimate fiscal relationship between checks and real money; (b) the history behind old checks; (c) the beauty of old checks (many 19th century U.S. checks look like bank notes, with elaborate engravings and ornate vignettes); (d) the romance of owning a check written by a famous person; and (e) many checks are cheap to buy, compared with paper money of similar scarcity.

Check Collecting Specialties

It is amazing how many checks have survived the ravages of time. Somehow, the cancelled (redeemed) check accumulations of banks get released to the public, and, of course, most checks have been ultimately returned to their signers, so when a famous person dies, his or her estate may liquidate a hoard of cancelled checks.

Here are some popular check collecting specialties:

1. By bank. Example: Bank of England checks.

2. By company. Example: 19th century Wells, Fargo Express Company checks drawn on western U.S. banks.

3. Chronologically (by time period). You might collect checks from the American Civil War, or those issued during the year you were born.

4. By vignette (the handsomely engraved "picture"). U.S. checks issued from 1850 to 1900 often have beautiful vignettes; some collectors specialize in one type: animals, sailing ships, Indians, railroad trains, mining scenes, street scenes, bank buildings, eagles, or allegorical personages (e.g., female representations of Columbia or Liberty). A common vignette on 19th century U.S. private bank paper money and checks is a dog guarding a safe.

5. By signature: movie stars (living and dead), politicians (especially U.S. Presidents, or signers of the Declaration of Independence), sports heroes, artists, musicians, military generals (especially famous ones), writers, scientists, and anybody who was infamous or controversial — like robbers (Jesse James, John Dillinger) or dictators (Napoleon, Hitler, Stalin) — if they can be found on checks!

6. With revenue stamps affixed. As per Act of Congress of July 1862, checks drawn on U.S. banks were required to have a 2¢ revenue stamp attached (later, the stamp could be "printed" as part of the check's design). This was a government fundraiser for Civil War revenue but, like many taxes, it outlived its original purpose because for the rest of the 19th century, U.S. checks can be found with revenue stamps stuck on. These stamps often make the checks beautiful.

7. By town. Hometown bank checks are beloved by check collectors. Have you ever seen a 75-year-old check from your hometown bank?

8. By amount payable. Check collectors have been known to seek only those checks payable for 1¢ each! Or for huge sums (perhaps over $10,000 per check). Or for specified payment type (such as: a 19th century check endorsed "payable in silver or gold coin").

Check Conditions

You can grade checks just like paper money, but checks tend to be in better condition than paper money because checks usually don't circulate as legal tender currency. Pre-20th century checks often have spindle holes in their centers; personally, I don't like checks with such holes, but they don't bother some collectors.

Check Variations

You can even specialize in check variations, such as:

1. Cashier's checks. These are self-drawn bank checks (i.e., payable from a bank's own funds), and are duly signed by a bank official.

2. Certified checks. These are checks guaranteed for the stated sums by the issuing banks.

3. Traveler's checks. American Express® or other company or bank checks marked "Traveler's Check."

Prices of Collectible Checks

Most checks, including 19th century ones, sell for between $1 and $20 retail. Checks priced at $50 to $100 are very expensive, but "autograph value" checks of famous people (like Thomas Jefferson or Marilyn Monroe) can reach hundreds or even thousands of dollars.

Check Collectors' Society

The American Society of Check Collectors (ASCC) has a quarterly publication, *The Check Collector*, which has information about checks and how to obtain them. For a membership application to ASCC, send a self-addressed stamped envelope to:

ASCC Secretary
P.O. Box 71892
Madison Heights, MI 48071

Check Dealers

Bank Note Reporter (see Chapter 22) may have ads by check dealers. Here are two dealers in checks and other fiscal paper, who publish price lists of such:

RICHARD T. HOOBER, JR.
P.O. Box 106
Newfoundland, PA 18445

M.S. KAZANJIAN
25 King Philip Avenue
Barrington, RI 02806

STOCK CERTIFICATES

A *Stock Certificate* is a paper document denoting a "share" in the ownership of a corporation, as a proportionate amount of capital invested. Obsolete stock certificates (no longer redeemable) are collected for their handsomely engraved vignettes and historical interest. Late 19th and early 20th century U.S. stock certificates are the ones most commonly collected, at retail prices ranging from $1 to $100 each, with many obtainable for less than $10 apiece.

Popular stock "topics" are mining companies (especially of western states like Arizona, California, Colorado, Idaho, and Nevada), railroads, automobiles, banks, cities, and famous financier signatures on certificates (like Henry Wells and William G. Fargo).

Stock Dealers

Stocks and other fiscal paper are advertised in dealer ads in *Bank Note Reporter*. A well-known stock and bond dealer is R.M. Smythe & Company; send $2 for their latest stock and bond catalog (which recently featured a *Sunflower Mining Company* [of Cripple Creek, Colorado] 1897 share for $350 retail, and an 1870s American Express Company share signed by William G. Fargo for $425):

R.M. Smythe & Company, Inc
26 Broadway, Suite 271
New York, NY 10004
(212) 943-1880

Another stock and bond dealer is Scott J. Winslow Associates, whose retail and mail bid catalogs are spectacular and well-illustrated, and include historical backgrounds to many of the items. A recent 884-lot mail auction catalog of theirs included 18th century *Spanish Royal Trading Companies* stock certificates, 23 U.S. lottery tickets circa 1800, John D. Rockefeller's personal shares in the *Missouri, Kansas & Texas Railway Co.*, a stock certificate signed by Thomas Edison, and letters signed by Napoleon Bonaparte and Andrew Carnegie. Winslow has something for every collecting budget. For information on their next catalogs, or for stocks and bonds in your collecting specialty, contact:

Scott J. Winslow Associates, Inc.
P.O. Box 6033
Nashua, NH 03063
(603) 881-4071

BONDS

A *Bond* is an interest-bearing certificate, issued by government or private business, which promises to pay specified interest sums (as per specified rates) on specified dates. The difference between a stock and a bond is: a stock is a share in the ownership of a corporation; a bond is a loan to that corporation or government.

Bonds are collected as readily as stocks by many collectors. Get the book *Scripophily: Collecting Bonds and Share Certificates* by Hollender ($14.95) from R.M. Smythe & Company (address above). And for $2, get the latest stock and bond retail catalog from that company, which always has a huge selection of reasonably-priced (below $50 each) *Confederate Bonds* for sale, and recently offered the "bonds that made Maximillian Emperor of Mexico!" at $30 each, and Panama Canal construction bonds from 1880 at $40 each. For a fee, Smythe & Co. will also research any stocks and bonds to determine their values as securities.

Scott J. Winslow Associates (above) also offers a nice selection of bonds for sale, including Confederates, railroads, and seldom-seen bonds such as those of early California (circa 1850s-1860s).

SCRIP

Scrip are paper certificates issued by governments or private merchants for limited local exchange for money, goods, or services at specified sums. Scrip is usually issued during fiscal emergencies when money is scarce. Examples: the vast number and varieties of 19th century *Texas Treasury Warrants*, Civil War merchant's scrip, and U.S. municipal (town) scrip of the 1930s when the Great Depression made money scarce for everybody, including local governments whose tax receipts dwindled to lean levels. See the excellent book, *Standard Catalog of Depression Scrip of the United States*, by Mitchell and Shafer (Bibliography) for $27.50 current.

BANK HISTORY

Anything related to the development of governmental or private banks (especially those that issued paper money) is sought as "collateral collectibles" by collectors: bank history books, official ledgers, bank employee diaries, billheads (often ornately engraved), drafts and bills of exchange (used to transfer specie or currency to a distant locality; e.g., by private express companies during the California Gold Rush of the 1850s), sight drafts, certificates of deposit, bank photos, legal documents, bank telegrams, bank postal correspondence, and letters of credit.

Letters of Credit

A *Letter of Credit* is a document from a bank, guaranteeing a customer's credit to a specified sum. Letters of credit have been used from ancient times through the 19th century, before electronic communication made "credit verification" instantaneous. Although not negotiable "money" itself, a letter of credit can be used by its bearer to get cash, goods, or services at a remote destination, often reached by traveling.

CREDIT CARDS

A *Credit Card* is a small rectangular piece of cardboard (or plastic, etc., lately) with which the holder (person to whom the card is issued) can buy goods or services on "credit."

"Charge coins" — tokens issued by American department stores in the 1890s for customer charge accounts — were the first "credit pieces" in the United States. Charge coins were followed by metal charge plates in 1927. Paper credit cards were used in America since the early 1900s, but a drawback to them was the fact that the customer's account number had to be copied by hand onto the sales slip. Companies soon learned to laminate their paper credit cards to improve their durability, evolving into the plastic credit card in the late 1950s.

Over 100 million Americans have valid credit cards today, and many of them are starting to collect these cards, both valid and obsolete. Current cards can be obtained for free (if you have good credit), and obsolete cards can be bought.

Because most owners destroyed their credit cards when they received updated replacements, early paper credit cards are scarce. One collector is currently offering to pay $1,500 for a mint condition Diners' Club® credit card from 1950, the first year of that company's cards. The first American Express® cards were issued October 1, 1958 (expiring April 30, 1959), and these cards go for hundreds of dollars each, even in "worn" condition, when they can be found!

The *Credit Card Collector* is a monthly newsletter with information about these cards and ads offering to buy or sell them. Send $2 for a sample copy to:

Credit Card Collector
150 Hohldale
Houston, TX 77022

MONEY ORDERS

A *Money Order* is a document issued for money by a bank, post office, or private currency exchange firm, made payable to a specified person, etc., for a specified sum out of the account of the issuing agency's own funds. A money order differs from a check in that money orders are one-time drafts payable from the issuer's (money order company's) funds, whereas checks are "endlessly" written against the writer's account for the writer's debts (the writer being different from the check-issuing agency, usually a bank). Old and modern money orders, retrieved (hopefully, legally) from official archives, may be collected.

U.S. Postal Money Orders

The first *U.S. Postal Money Orders* were inaugurated for domestic use in 1864, partly to facilitate the safe transfer of cash between Union Civil War soldiers and their relatives back home (paper money was sometimes stolen from the mails, then as now). These first *U.S. Postal Money Orders* had a maximum pay limit of $30. In 1867, *U.S. Postal Money Orders* to international destinations were begun. Today, you can buy a *U.S. Postal Money Order* at your local post office, payable up to $700, for a 75¢ fee (plus the face value).

SOUVENIR CARDS

Souvenir Cards are limited edition, large-format (for example: 8½ x 10½ inches), specially-issued artistic cards, prepared and sold at moderate cost to collectors by government and private engraving companies, specifically the U.S. Bureau of Engraving and Printing and the American Bank Note Company (for currency-related themes).

Souvenir cards are not legal tender, but they often have beautiful engravings of bank notes or vignettes used on fiscal paper (from the archives of the engraving company). Souvenir cards are printed on card stock (instead of currency paper stock) from printing plates prepared from the original dies, which may have been stored for a century or more in the vaults

of the company. The master dies, used to prepare currency printing plates, are made of steel and can be stored indefinitely when coated in grease and wrapped, although sometimes old dies are discovered to be slightly damaged with rust or scratches and have to be touched up before they are used to lift an impression for souvenir printing plate manufacture.

Souvenir cards allow you to own rare bank note designs for about $5 to $15, rather than spending hundreds or thousands of dollars for the original currency. Souvenir cards are uniface, printed on one side, unlike currency, which is usually biface, printed on both sides. Souvenir cards are often issued in conjunction with numismatic shows, such as the International Paper Money Show held annually in Memphis, Tennessee.

Buying Souvenir Cards Directly from the Printers

To get on the mailing lists of the BEP or ABNC, write to them, asking to be placed on their souvenir card information mailing list, and they will send you currently available card information at no obligation:

Mail Order Sales
Room 602-11A
U.S. Bureau of Engraving and Printing
14th and C Streets S.W.
Washington, DC 20228

The Bureau also sells, by mail if you wish, uncut sheets of $1 and $2 paper money (*Federal Reserve Notes*), and they will tell you the prices for such sheets if you ask.

American Bank Note Commemoratives
7 High Street, Suite 412
Huntington, NY 11743

Buying Souvenir Cards on the After-Market

Market prices of souvenir cards may rise or fall a bit after they are removed from sale by the issuing company. Many dealers handle such cards along with their paper money business proper. One dealer who always has a nice selection of reasonably priced souvenir cards for sale, listed by Souvenir Card Collectors Society catalog numbers, is Ken Barr, who buys and sells such cards by mail and at currency shows that he attends. Send a self-addressed stamped No. 10 envelope for his latest price list of souvenir cards for sale:

Ken Barr Numismatics
P.O. Box 32541
San Jose, CA 95152
(408) 272-3247

Souvenir Card Collectors Society (SCCS)

The Souvenir Card Collectors Society exists for collectors of these cards. The Society publishes a quarterly journal printed on quality paper; dealers' and Society members' ads, offering to buy or sell cards, appear in every issue of this journal (see Chapter 23). Send a self-addressed stamped envelope for SCCS membership information to:

SCCS Secretary
P.O. Box 4155
Tulsa, OK 74159

COLLECTIBLE LOTTERY TICKETS

Lottery tickets, both old and new, are interesting collectibles. In the 18th and 19th centuries, many public and private projects were financed in whole or in part through the sale of lottery tickets. The U.S. Congress, in November 1776, attempted to finance some of the cost of the American Revolutionary War with lottery tickets. Schools, bridges, roads, canals, churches, and hospitals were funded with revenues from lottery ticket sales in the United States, circa 1800, much to the horror of people who were opposed to gambling in any form. Many early U.S. lottery tickets are scarce, and sell for $50 to $100 or more when available. Scott J. Winslow Associates (described above under Stock Dealers) recently offered for sale a Rhode Island 1761 *Providence Street Lottery* ticket (for paving the streets), a Kentucky 1811 *Lexington Library Lottery* ticket, and a Delaware 1823 *Delaware State Lottery* ticket for the completion of St. Peter's Church.

EXPOSITION ("WORLD'S FAIR") ADMISSION TICKETS

Admission tickets to historical expositions (world's fairs, etc.) are collected by people who appreciate the vignettes and beauty of these often nicely engraved tickets. Get these tickets in crisp, clean condition, for a handsome collection. Generally, they're not too expensive ($10 to $20 for an average specimen). Here are the most popular United States Expositions whose paper memorabilia (including admission tickets) is admired by specialists:

POPULARLY COLLECTED U.S. EXPOSITION ADMISSION TICKETS (If you can find them)		
EXPOSITION NAME	EXPOSITION CITY	EXPOSITION YEAR
Centennial Exposition	Philadelphia	1876
World's Columbian Exposition	Chicago	1893
Trans-Mississippi Exposition	Omaha	1898
Pan-American Exposition	Buffalo	1901
Louisiana Purchase Exposition	St. Louis	1904
Lewis and Clark Exposition	Portland, Oregon	1905
Jamestown Exposition	Hampton Roads, Virginia	1907
Alaska-Yukon-Pacific Exposition	Seattle	1909
Hudson-Fulton Celebration	New York City	1909
Panama-Pacific Exposition	San Francisco	1915
Sesquicentennial Exposition	Philadelphia	1926
Century of Progress International Exposition	Chicago	1933
Golden Gate International Exposition	San Francisco	1939
New York World's Fair	New York City	1939

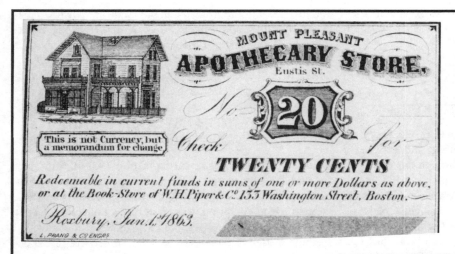

111.   Merchant's scrip of the *Mount Pleasant Apothecary Store* of Roxbury, Massachusetts, 1863. Issued for use as small change redeemable at this store, during the severe coin shortage induced by coin hoarding during the Civil War. Unsigned and unnumbered. Margin cut into design at lower right.

112.   1893 *Columbian Exposition* admission ticket, for the world's fair held in Chicago that year. Made by the American Bank Note Company of New York City. Beware of cheaper later reprints.

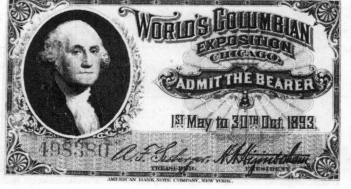

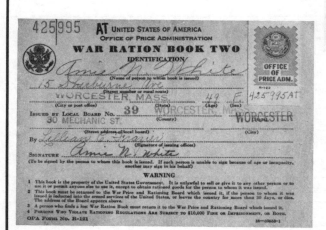

113.   United States "Ration Book" of World War II, with original ration "coupons" (or "stamps") inside. Financial history collateral.

114.   So-called *Baby Bond* — issued in the late 19th century by the State of Louisiana for public indebtedness. Notice the interest coupons at right. Printed by Western Bank Note Company of Chicago.

115. 1938 *Irish Hospitals' Sweepstake* ticket. Engraved and watermarked. Reverse side includes warning: "MOST IMITATION WATERMARKS DISAPPEAR AFTER IMMERSION FOR 20 MINUTES IN BOILING SOLUTION OF ONE PART HOUSEHOLD WASHING SODA TO THREE PARTS WATER." The author advises against this test, however!

116. SPECIMEN of *DM Travellers Cheque*, first issued by West German banks in 1975 — this one for 500 *Deutsche Mark*. Traveler's checks are internationally accepted for currency transfers, with the bearer's original signature (to whom issued) being repeated as a countersignature at the time of "cashing."

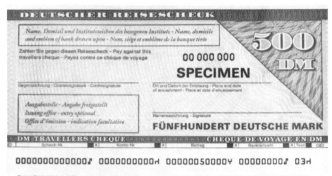

117. Check drawn on *The First National Gold Bank* of San Francisco, dated June 6th, 1882, at Sacramento, California. Payable for $4,500 in "gold/silver" — with U.S. revenue stamp at upper left.

118. 1852 *Second of Exchange* draft drawn for $3,331 on Adams & Company of San Francisco, a bullion exchange firm for California Gold Rush miners.

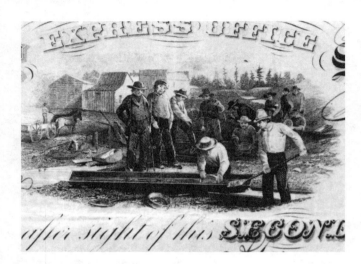

119. Detail of vignette from 1852 Adams & Co. *Second of Exchange* draft in Photo 118, showing California Gold Rush prospectors using a "long tom" for extracting gold dust from the ground.

120. Detail of vignette of allegorical females and anchor on the 1852 Adams & Co. draft in Photo 118. Also used on various 19th century local bank notes.

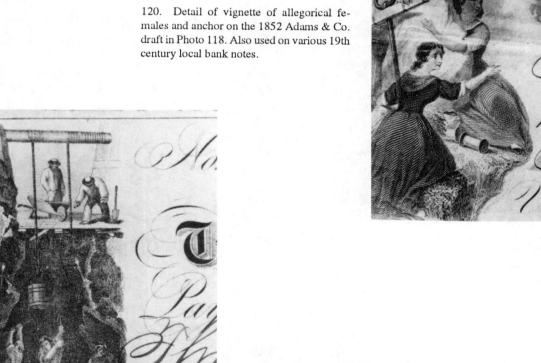

121. Detail of underground hard rock mining vignette on an 1858 company check of the Tuolumne County Water Co. of Columbia, California. Water was necessary to many mining operations during the California Gold Rush of the late 1840s and 1850s, and "water companies" sold water at exorbitant rates.

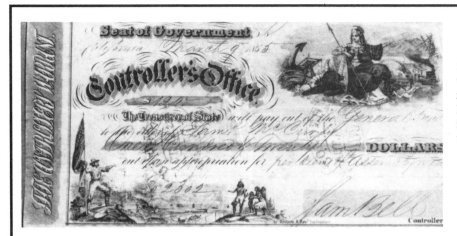

122. 1855 California State Controller's warrant for $120 for "per diem of Assembly men." Prospector and Indians at lower left. Elements of the California State Seal, including the goddess Minerva and grizzly bear, at upper right.

123. The San Francisco office of Adams & Company, where California prospectors brought gold dust to be refined and coined into slugs for more convenient use in commerce. Drafts and other financial services were offered here to currency-starved customers.

124. California mining stock certificate of 1898, with three U.S. revenue stamps affixed, "500 shares."

125. Detail of the proposed, but never issued, *Large Size* U.S. $10 *Silver Certificate*, "Series 1897," which was intended to "complete" the *Educational Notes*. The vignette is entitled, "Agriculture and Forestry," and was engraved by Charles Schlecht from a design by Walter Shirlaw.

126. $5 U.S. Department of Agriculture "Food Coupon" (commonly called "Food Stamp"), Series 1990A. This design has been issued since 1975. Illegal to own unless your household qualifies for the U.S. federal Food Coupon program, which provides these coupons at a discount to low-income citizens.

127. $1,000 *Confederate Bond*, issued 1863, with portrait of Thomas J. "Stonewall" Jackson — the brilliant Confederate General who was accidentally shot by "friendly fire" at the Battle of Chancellorsville, Virginia, on May 2, 1863, dying of pneumonia on May 10. $35 (7% simple interest) paid every six months, as per coupons attached at bottom (not visible in photograph). The Jan. 1, 1865 coupon is missing, but the July 1, 1865 coupon is still attached, and was not redeemed, because the Confederacy collapsed in the spring of 1865.

7

"All beauteous things for which we live
by laws of time and space decay."
William J. Cory (1823-1892)

Handling and Preserving Notes

Paper ages from the instant it is made. Quality "high rag content" bank note papers may age slower than cheap wood-pulp, high sulfurous content papers (like newspaper stock), but all paper ages with more or less irreversible effects.

The average life span of paper varies from about one to eight centuries, depending on its type. It is sad but true that every paper money collection now in existence will someday be dust, if not in a thousand years, then certainly in a million!

This chapter discusses how to handle and preserve your bank notes for your lifetime (which, after all, is the most important time span to you, anyway). Unless you have access to the conservation laboratories and storage vaults of professional archivists, you need to do the best you can with the materials you can afford. Handling techniques, paper money holders, and common repairs await your attention on the next few pages.

THE PHYSICAL ENEMIES OF PAPER MONEY

Many pre-20th century bank notes are delicate because of thin paper, inferior quality paper, chemically destructive inks, aging over a century, and/or wear endured. It is easy to tear or crease such notes, so handle all paper money with care.

Notes can be damaged by:

1. Mechanical pressure and stretching. Don't pull hard on your notes. Don't put heavy weights on your notes (store your currency albums upright). Be gentle when passing a note to the hands of another person. Don't force a note into a soft plastic holder.

2. Fire. Much paper money has been accidentally burned over the years! Store money away from fireplaces, away from heaters, and in fire-resistant containers.

3. Moisture. Besides heat, humidity is a prime attacker of paper. Store notes away from high humidity sources (out of kitchens, bathrooms, and basements; away from open windows in humid climates, rain, and swimming pools). Moisture warps paper and may even cause mold.

4. Mold. Assorted molds attack paper, eventually crumbling it to dust. The Earth isn't covered with a solid layer of millions of years of dead trees because of heat, moisture, and mold. Air out your collection once in a while, and keep notes away from damp, dirty areas where mold spores can germinate. Mold stains on paper are called *foxing*.

5. Heat. Like fire itself, any moderate heat source can desiccate and age paper very rapidly. Heat also speeds up the rate of mold growth. Don't let your bank notes bake in the sunlight streaming through your window onto your desk. Store notes away from ovens and room heaters.

6. Light. Keep direct sunlight away from notes. The colors of paper and inks will fade from prolonged exposure to any strong light source. Don't frame a prized bank note and keep it on your wall for years.

7. Vermin. The animal kingdom will eat up your money faster than inflation will! Protect notes from insects (including termites and silverfish, both of which love dark environments), mice, and bookworms. Do you keep your notes in cabinets or drawers that are open to invasion by vermin?

8.   Dirt. It is amazing how much dirt accumulates in the average room. It blows in through the doorways and windows, it is dragged in by shoes and on clothes, and it will contaminate your notes, little by little, if you give it a chance.

Store paper money above the floor, away from dust-blowing ventilators, away from window openings (did you ever look at a window sill that hasn't been washed in months?), and not on top of a bookcase or cabinet where dust has been settling all day long.

And when your currency albums or note boxes get dusty, wipe them off before opening them and wafting the dust onto your notes. Wash your hands before handling rare notes!

9.   Air pollution. Tobacco smoke, factory fumes, cooking smoke from inside stoves or outside barbecues, paint fumes from your newly-painted hallway, automobile exhaust fumes blowing in the window from the driveway — all kinds of chemicals in the air can assault your currency collection!

Without moving to Antarctica or the moon, we can protect our currency from air contaminants by using common sense. Don't smoke around notes; keep paint, floor cleaners, etc., away from your currency; if you live in a big city, shut the windows on days of heavy air pollution; and think about which direction fans are blowing and what they're blowing besides air!

10.   Hands. The natural skin oils and salts, plus cosmetics, skin lotions, and the day's dirt and assorted adhering chemicals, all get on a bank note when we touch it with bare hands without washing our hands first. Of course, paper money was meant to be handled, but when we collect it, we want to protect it, not "circulate" it.

Sometimes months after touching a piece of paper, you will notice a faint fingerprint beginning to develop, evidence of skin contaminants on the day it was touched. Also, clumsy fingers can irreversibly damage notes by folding, tearing, etc. HANDLE YOUR PAPER MONEY COLLECTION WITH CARE.

BAD WAYS TO STORE BANK NOTE COLLECTIONS

Don't use these items and techniques if you want to protect your notes:

1.   In photo albums — meaning those made expressly for photograph storage. These albums may have harmful chemicals that migrate into your bank notes. Particularly dangerous are the "self-stick" photo albums.

2.   In glassine envelopes — the semi-transparent, light green-tinted envelopes that stamp collectors sometimes use for temporary storage of stamps. Glassine looks like waxed paper without the wax. Glassine usually has high sulfur content that can damage paper items in long-term storage.

3.   With photo-mounting corners. Many old-timers still mount their bank notes in albums, using those little black or white (and, now, transparent) photo-mounting corners for sale at any photography shop. The danger rests not so much from chemical contamination from the corners' paper or gum as it does from: (a) too much chance of bending a note's corner, or of tearing a note, when inserting or removing it from stuck-down corners; (b) a note may work itself free of its restraining corners and fall off the page or get crumpled when you turn the album pages; and (c) notes themselves may get partially stuck down due to leakage from the corner adhesive.

4.   With stamp hinges on pages. The little glassine stamp hinges used by philatelists always leave a small adhesive residue on paper items mounted with them. Most currency collectors don't like hinge marks on their notes!

5.   On any highly acidic or sulfurous papers (which is what many kinds of "notebook" papers are).

6.   In many of the commonly sold soft plastic transparent sheets from stationery stores. These plastics may be of volatile chemical composition, which degrade your notes stored in them.

7.   Piled indiscriminately in a cigar box. Another sure way for your notes to get bent.

8.   Stuffed into one envelope. A sure way for your notes to get bent.

9.   In boxes made from wood with volatile resins. You don't need sap-stained notes!

10.   In "odd-shaped" containers, such as round jars, which could impart a "curve" to the note's paper!

11. In a fireproof safe that is designed to spray its contents with water when the wall of the safe reaches a certain high temperature. When buying a safe, ask a lot of questions: Is it waterproof? Burglar-proof? Carry-proof? And remember: a safe doesn't know what's stored in it. You must get private insurance for anything stored in home or bank safes, with coverage for fire, flood, or theft loss. The ANA offers its members low-cost numismatic insurance (see Chapter 23).

12.   "Sealed" within most envelopes or plastic sleeves. Like people, bank notes must "breathe," and your collection should be aired out every so often to hinder stagnant mold growth, among other things.

13.   In high humidity. The perfect environment for acquiring "foxing" or "ripple effect."

14.   In strong light. Even low intensity light will fade ink or paper color over a long exposure time (months, years).

15.   In temperature extremes. Too hot is worse than too cold, but neither is desirable for paper storage. Hot temperatures can desiccate (dry out) a note and make it brittle, subject to paper cracking and tearing, and/or ink changes.

16.   In rapid temperature fluctuations. A quick rise or drop

of 45 thermometer degrees may cause amusing weather conversation but can hurt your bank notes, due to too rapid expansion or contraction, or accompanied humidification or dehydration.

17. Where dust and dirt accumulate. In general, a "medium elevation" is safest for notes in a room — avoid storing on the floor or against the ceiling on a shelf. A too frequently opened drawer or cabinet may give lots of ventilation to your notes and lots of airborne dust and mold spores as well.

18. Where smoke may accumulate, including cigarette, barbecue, fireplace, automotive, and industrial "smoke."

19. Where volatile chemicals may accumulate paper-damaging concentrations in the air (such as in kitchens, workshops, garages, many basements, some attics, storage sheds, bathrooms, barns). Paper has a "memory" — it never "forgets" an exposure, no matter how small in chemical concentration, no matter how short in time, of any contact with an airborne chemical. Five minutes of auto exhaust fumes (assaulting currency that might be "stored" in or near a garage) once a day for year is equivalent to almost thirty hours of accumulated exposure!

20. Too close to windows or doorways. Drafts, rain, dust, and burglars can sneak through a window, open or closed.

21. Within reach of inquisitive children, pets, or vermin (insects, mice, etc.). Your pet dog or cat may be cute, but it won't be when it is chomping away on your 18th century Bank of England notes!

WHERE TO STORE CURRENCY

It is fun to have our paper money collection at home within quick reach when we want to look at our bank notes. Burglars know this, and the more efficient ones will find your hidden treasures. The first places a burglar looks are drawers, bookshelves, and cabinets. Professional burglars search under beds, in closets, behind pictures, and in boxes or containers that may hide valuables.

Don't keep your whole currency collection in one location in your home. Paper money is easy to hide, but if you keep high-priced notes at home, either insure them or consider buying a safe.

Safes

Burglar-proof safes are different from fireproof safes. If the safe is rated as burglar-resistant, it should have thick steel walls impervious to simple drills and hammers, have a tough combination lock, and be either bolted to the floor or so heavy that it can't be moved without special equipment. A burglar-resistant safe will render your currency untouchable to the casual burglar.

A fireproof safe may not be burglar-proof. Some fireproof safes have walls that are heat resistant; others have water or a chemical that sprays the safe's contents (maybe ruining paper items) when the inside temperature reaches a point near the ignition point of paper. It is wise to avoid storing currency in a fireproof safe, despite what the safe salesman may tell you. A burglar-resistant (no safe is totally burglar-PROOF) safe with its contents fully insured makes sense to most currency collectors.

Bank Storage

There is nothing like the peace of mind that comes from knowing your notes are in a bank safe deposit vault. Many vaults these days have controlled constant temperature and humidity and are usually better than the best possible home storage facility.

Rent a safe deposit box that fits your collection. Store your most expensive notes in it, ideally with the notes positioned upright; i.e., in soft protective plastic holders and "standing" on their bottom long edges. And get insurance: safe deposit box contents are rarely insured by the bank, because banks can't be liable for a fortune in losses from flood, earthquake, fire, or vault burglary. The ANA has cheap insurance (see Chapter 23).

CURRENCY HOLDERS

Always keep your paper collectibles stored in protective plastic holders (soft or hard plastic, individual or album page style). I had a choice *Confederate Bond* that I forgot about, lying face up on a shelf near my front door, and when I came home with my umbrella during the monstrous Los Angeles rainstorm of February 1992, I inadvertently let the umbrella's tip drip rain water all over the *Bond*, which I suddenly noticed, then quickly wiped off because it was completely protected in a heavy soft plastic document sleeve. If the *Bond* had been naked, it would have been water-stained, perhaps forever.

Soft Plastic Holders

Individual soft plastic currency holders are for sale at 20¢ to 40¢ each. Mylar® is the safest plastic, the kind that is used by government archivists. Soft plastic currency holders are sealed on three sides and open along one length. They come in different sizes to fit the common currency sizes. Any currency dealer can help you get some, or order directly from numismatic supply company ads in the numismatic periodicals (see Chapter 22).

Currency albums exist, as well as currency pages that fit normal three-ring binders. Shop around for an album or a page that you like. Some of these pages tend to warp and get permanently bent, along with any notes that might be housed therein, however.

Hard Plastic Holders

For your prized notes, you may want to buy a few hard plastic currency holders of the type made of Plexiglas® acrylic hard plastic, such as the ones for sale by Capital Plastics, Inc. These holders consist of two clear panels fastened to each other with plastic screws, so that both sides of the note are visible. These holders can be displayed and handled without fear of immediate damage to the notes in them (keep away from bright light, of course). These hard plastic holders aren't cheap, costing about $10, depending on the size, but they're the ultimate currency holder. They do present a storage problem, though, because they have "bulk," whereas soft plastic holders are rather flat. Any currency dealer can help you get a hard plastic holder, or order directly from numismatic supply company ads in the numismatic periodicals (see Chapter 22).

For $2, the company that makes these hard plastic currency holders (as well as coin holders, etc.), will send you their catalog:

CAPITAL PLASTICS, INC.
628 North Erie Street P.O. Box 543
Massillon, OH 44648 (216) 832-4287

Inserting or Removing Notes from Soft Plastic Holders

Because soft plastic holders are the standard storage mechanism for currency collections, dealers' stocks, etc., you must become skillful in inserting or removing notes from these holders. Being fragile, paper notes can be damaged by even the most careful person. These are the guidelines that I use for handling my notes. I don't guarantee they will work for you, so practice a bit on cheap currency or money from circulation.

1. Wash your hands first.

2. Always handle notes carefully, slowly, gently, and deliberately. When in doubt, stop, and be more gentle. A torn note is torn forever.

3. Handle only one note at a time.

4. Use both hands to slide a note gently into its plastic holder. Insert to the "strongest" corner first, for worn notes.

5. Always handle notes on a clean, flat surface.

6. When removing a note from a soft plastic holder, use the fingers of both hands to slide it out gently. Don't pull or push vigorously, or the note may buckle, fold, crease, or tear.

7. When the note is entirely within the holder, adjust its position to center it; i.e., the note should not touch the seams of the holder or the open slit.

8. Use fresh, clean holders. These cost about 20¢ to 40¢ each. How much do your valuable notes cost?

9. Store your plastic holdered collection in a protective box made of inert material (such as Plexiglas® if you can find and afford it). No cheap cardboard boxes that can emit dust and detrimental chemicals onto your notes.

10. Store your holdered notes vertically — "standing up" in their holders, with the open sides up — to prevent the weight pressure of a stack of notes from grinding dust and dirt into your notes; to allow notes to "breathe" (expand and contract with normal fluctuations in temperature and humidity); and so it is easy to sort through your notes to look at them and to find a particular one. Store notes in clean boxes and drawers. Some desk drawers and filing cabinets tend to attract too much dust.

Reasons to Remove Notes from Holders

There are three main reasons to take a note out of its protective plastic holder: to study its details, unhindered by any plastic cover; to transfer the note to another holder (or to another owner who doesn't want or need your holder); and to photograph it. Otherwise, all your paper money collection, even the cheap notes, should be constantly in some kind of protective plastic holder.

DISPLAY OF PAPER MONEY

When housed in the proper plastic and glass holders and display cases at currency shows, it is all right to display paper money for a short period of time. I recommend that you don't display your currency at home, framed on your desk or hung on the wall, because:

1. Frames attract dust, which can enter the frame and contaminate your notes.

2. Exposure to light (even low intensity, for long time periods) can fade a note's paper and/or ink color.

3. Displayed notes are subject to all the temperature and humidity fluctuations in the room.

4. Displayed notes invite theft (of the notes on display, and serve to reveal to a burglar that you have currency at home, maybe more somewhere else).

5. Framed notes in a room can be attacked by vermin (insects, etc.).

6. Framed notes may be scratched, torn, stained, or bent — by the frame itself, by the process of putting the note in or taking it out, by sliding around inside the frame, etc. Imagine if your prized *1-Piastre Khartoum Siege Note*, proudly framed on your wall, suddenly fell to the floor, with the frame's glass front shattering and slicing the note into half a dozen fragments!

PHOTOGRAPHING A NOTE

Photographs may show a note to be better or worse than it actually is, because of: (a) lighting angles and intensity; (b) the characteristic of some note defects (such as closed tears, minor thins, maybe lightly colored stains) to hide themselves from a camera's primitive mechanical inquisitiveness; and (c) shabby photo print quality. Don't assume that a note will look exactly like its photograph or photocopied likeness in dealers' catalogs.

Most notes should be photographed on black backgrounds for contrast and to show the note's edges clearly. Most people use a copy stand to stabilize the camera while shooting paper money. Some kind of enlarging apparatus, such as extension tubes, close-up lenses, or teleconverters, is needed for blown-up detail.

Lighting should show the note's details, so two or more copy stand lights, or their equivalent, are usually used. Experiment a little when photographing your collection to see what works with your specific equipment. Any photo shop will give you advice on photographing paper objects. WARNING: It is illegal to print a color photograph of currently legal tender U.S. or foreign paper money, or to print a black-and-white photograph of current U.S. paper money *in its natural size* (see Chapter 21). Another WARNING: Hot lights can curl a note, and any intense light can contribute to its fading over time.

HOW TO LOOK AT PAPER MONEY

Although you may spread out a dozen notes in front of you, always handle only one note at a time outside of its protective holder, and use this procedure:

1. Wash your hands first — handle the note with clean hands.

2. Handle the note over a clean, flat surface (such as a desk, table, or dealer's glass-topped display case). Keep food, drinks, ash trays, and other potential contaminants away from your examination area to avoid inadvertent spilling on the note.

3. Carefully remove the note from its protective plastic holder (asking permission to do so from its owner if the note isn't yours).

4. Use strong front and back lighting (but not sunlight, so your eyes aren't damaged), ideally from a nearby white-frosted incandescent light bulb of 100 watts or greater (the type you're likely to have in your "reading lamp" at home). Fluorescent lighting and natural "skylight" (outside window light, without direct sun's rays) are not good enough for thorough examination.

5. Scan the entire note's obverse and reverse sides with front and back light, holding the note vertically (perpendicular to your line of sight). This technique should show you the most obvious folds, watermarks, and defects (if any).

6. Slowly tilt the back-lighted note so that you can see its surfaces from various angles, including looking down the plane of the note's surface until the note is parallel with your line of sight ("edge-on" view). This technique will often reveal faint folds, surface abrasions, and "ripple effect" (normal and otherwise) in the paper. Consciously search for watermarks (including those that are small or hidden by the printed design), defective paper thins, and signs of repair (glued tears, starch-fillings, erasures, re-inked design detail, etc). Support the note gently with your fingertips so that it doesn't fall far to

the table if you drop it (or flutter down to the dirty floor, much to the panic of its owner if it is a 14th century Ming rarity!).

7. Examine all edges and margins carefully. Look for evidence of cosmetic trimming, replaced corners, and sealed edge tears. Does the edge condition match the general condition of the rest of the note — are perfect edges on a worn note?

8. Lay the note flat on the table gently, first on its reverse, then on its obverse. Does it lie flat? If not, why not? Is it "naturally" wavy from printing or humidity or from washing or ironing?

9. If the note belongs to someone else, and you're studying it in his presence, keep up a running conversation with him, preferably about the note you're examining. Pay special attention to anything the owner says about the note, particularly if you mentally disagree with him.

10. If possible, compare the note with others of its kind, arranging them side by side, and deliberately tallying the likenesses and differences among the specimens. One of the first tests for a counterfeit, for instance, is to compare it with a known genuine example.

11. After you've done all of this, do it all over again, on another day (if convenient) when you can bring a fresh perspective (visually and mentally) to the note. The note shouldn't change in a couple of days, but your opinion of it might, especially for an expensive note that you're considering buying from a dealer.

It slightly irritates some dealers, but I like to browse through their currency show/bourse stocks the first day of the show, then return and buy on the second day, after seeing what all the dealers have to offer. I risk losing a choice note to another buyer the first day, but I avoid impulse purchases by sleeping on it before making my final buying decisions. It is important to explain to the dealers what you're doing: quickly looking at all the show dealers' stocks for notes in your collecting specialty, with the intention to return the next day and spend money for the notes that you like the best (for condition, scarcity, price, importance to your collection, etc.), so that the dealers know you're a potential serious buyer, and not just someone taking up chair space at their bourse table.

BANK NOTE CLEANING, REPAIR, AND RESTORATION

As a general rule, DON'T CLEAN YOUR NOTES OR TRY TO REPAIR THEM. You can break this rule when you become an expert. More notes have probably been damaged than have ever been "improved" by cleaning, and overzealous amateurish repairing is worse than no repairs at all. My feeling is that you are usually better off just selling or trading away a dirty or damaged note and letting someone else worry about it.

Whenever you attempt to clean or repair a note, you risk further damage to it. Expert paper restoration is an admirable art and a technical skill not quickly acquired. I present the following information here because cleaning and repair of paper money are widespread, and serious collectors need to know why they are done and how to recognize them. Neither my publisher nor I assume any liability if you damage your paper money by attempting these techniques.

Paper Conservators

Professional paper conservators are people who spend their working lives repairing and conserving documents and artworks made of paper or paper-related materials. Conservators treat paper money, legal documents, maps, prints, photographs, engravings, watercolors on paper, wallpaper (historical), wood objects, etc.

Top art museums and archival libraries have staff conservators on their payrolls. Paper conservators learn their trade on the job and are experts in the scientific cleaning and cosmetic restoration of paper items.

Of course, currency collectors and dealers throughout the 20th century have been attempting to clean and repair their notes, whether they have training or not before they begin their "treatments." Because cheap notes may not be worth repairing, and expensive notes are too valuable to risk detrimental repair results, many collectors, after thinking about it, may decide to pay someone with paper conservatorship skills to clean and repair a prized bank note. When a professional archivist is hired to treat such collectors' notes, an agreement in writing must be made beforehand, delineating exactly what is hoped to be accomplished, any guarantees offered if results are unsatisfactory, and a realistic cost estimate. If your "paper patient" is further injured on the conservator's "operating table," what happens next?

Guidelines for the Cleaning and Repair of Paper Money, as a Professional Paper Conservator Might Attempt

For your information as a paper money collector, here are some guidelines that a professional conservator might follow, in the repair of his/her own currency collection. Again, I don't recommend that you clean or repair your own notes; however, if you were a professional, you would be considering:

Bank note cleaning and repair rules.

1. Don't. Like the first rule of medical treatment, the first rule of bank note cleaning and restoration is: Don't do more damage to the patient! When in doubt, don't.

2. Make your actions "reversible." Top quality paper conservatorship is practiced so that all treatments can be "reversed"; i.e., the note is not permanently changed beyond recall of the original problem.

3. Err toward conservative actions. You can always do more. It may be impossible to undo what you've already done.

4. Practice your cleaning and repair techniques on cheap notes or pocket currency until your results are consistently satisfactory. Then practice some more on a note of the same paper type, time period, etc., as the "important" note that you are considering treating. What works well on modern currency may fail entirely on old notes.

5. Try a mild treatment on only a portion of an expensive note. You can always go back and treat more of the note's surface.

6. Have realistic goals in your note cleaning and repair. In his book, *A Collector's Guide to Paper Money*, Yasha Beresiner (see Bibliography) gives a warning against washing notes: "Never expect perfect results, nor persist in trying to obtain them."

7. Attack the easiest problem first. For example: Gentle erasing of a tiny graphite pencil mark on an unprinted portion of a note should be attempted before contemplating taping a large tear or filling a large hole. If you can't get an easy job done right, why even bother with intricate repairs? Don't feel incompetent and clumsy; nobody can do everything.

8. Get advice and help from more knowledgeable expert paper conservators.

Some Cleaning and "Restoration" Techniques

Because you will hear about these techniques being done, perhaps to notes that you would like to buy, I present this information so that you can understand what the person was trying to accomplish and so that you might be able to recognize such treated notes. I do not recommend that you attempt to clean or restore any note.

Pencil graphite removal. Let's look at a simple cleaning job: the removal of a tiny stray graphite mark (colloquially called "lead") from a pencil — a pencil mark on a note.

A good quality pencil art eraser rated for soft (#1) pencil "lead" can sometimes remove most of a pencil mark, without leaving a trace of evidence (except for a shallow "pressure groove" on the note's surface, where the pencil mark once was). But pencil marks that run across the inked printed design (or, even worse, any handsigned portion) should not be erased, because part of the design may be erased away!

The eraser should be clean to begin with, to avoid implanting a dirt smear from the eraser itself. The eraser's edge shouldn't be too pointed, or it could tear through the paper. Pressure from the eraser could make the paper buckle into a permanent fold (as has happened to every school child when erasing homework on notebook paper). Some erasers leave their own color (pink maybe) on the paper, and many a paper collector has been shocked to see himself "painting" a pink streak across a portion of a precious paper collectible by innocently using a pencil eraser.

And don't use the eraser attached to a pencil. The cylindrical metal fastener may come in contact with your note and scratch a slice through it, ruining it. Also, all erasure motions should be done away from the center of the note, to minimize the chance of buckling the note's paper. Ink erasers may go through a note like a knife through warm butter. I could write many more pages on erasing pencil marks, and erasing is one of the simplest of currency cleaning techniques!

Tape removal. I prefer to sell or trade away a taped note. Tape removal often causes more damage. Never use on bank notes clear Scotch® type transparent adhesive tapes that are intended for office use. Only "archival tapes" made specifically for repair of rare and valuable documents should be used on paper money.

Some authorities try to remove adhesive tapes from notes by gently touching the taped area with damp blotting paper until the tape loosens. Completely immersing a note in pure cold water baths may also loosen tape, but you may end up with the stigma of a "washed note."

Never rip a piece of tape off a note. The ink and paper may adhere to the tape's adhesive, and leave the note's surface. Leave tape removal to an expert.

Tape stains present a special dilemma, and some tape stains may be impossible to remove completely. Be careful that common adhesive tapes don't come into contact with your notes (such as on facing pages in the album where your notes are mounted).

Washing paper money. Washing may succeed in removing surface dirt from a note, along with detrimentally fading the note's natural colors, and/or removing some of the remaining "crispness" of the note so that it now feels more limp. Expert washing may indeed improve a note's appearance. Amateurish washing usually makes a note look "washed" — something that is now hard to sell because informed dealers and collectors don't want to buy tampered notes.

The decision to wash a note is a serious one. Selection of precise washing techniques for a specific note is crucial to achieving reasonably tolerable results.

I don't recommend that you wash notes because such notes often have faded ink color and loss of paper strength. Never wash notes printed with fugitive inks or notes with handwritten signatures; such inks may smear during washing. Most currency washers use cold water, preferably distilled water to minimize mineral deposition, and maybe a little mild soap of neutral pH (neither acidic nor basic). Washing fanatics wash one note at a time, and monitor the evolving "results" all along the way at each step of the process.

After washing, a note should be gently dried a little between clean white blotters. Be careful not to tear the wet paper, which will inevitably be quite weakened while it is still damp. Don't dry a note in the sunlight, or it may buckle (besides absorbing fade-producing radiation).

Some notes that have been through the home "processing mill" of washing, drying, and ironing will age more in one day than they have since they were issued! You're not baking a cake or washing your clothes, you're meddling in the at-tempted partial restoration of valuable paper money. Are you confident of what you're doing? Should you pay someone else to wash your money? Should you wash notes at all?

Be careful when pressing notes between books to remove curls. Use clean white blotters or neutral papers on both sides of the pressing notes (not newsprint, which can transfer ink and other chemicals to your paper); and don't bend or crease a note as you place it in position for pressing.

Remember: A NOTE CAN ALWAYS BE WASHED MORE, BUT IT CAN'T ALWAYS BE "UNWASHED."

Ironing paper money. Ironing is commonly done to "restore" wrinkled notes. Ironing will not remove true creases that have broken the paper fibers. Ironing can be dangerous — the note can be scorched by too long contact with a hot iron, or made to "shine" artificially, or become brittle due to heat desiccation, or be accidentally bent or torn by careless movements of the iron.

Ironing is most commonly done by placing the note between two smooth pieces of cloth or blotting paper. Both sides of the note should be ironed. The hot iron should never directly touch a note (to avoid burns), nor should it remain in one place for any length of time.

An extremely fragile note may be shredded by vigorous ironing. If excess heat is applied to one side, the note may curl ("away" from the heat). If the iron is too cold, it won't work well either, and you'll be mechanically pressing out the note.

Another problem is that many irons don't maintain consistent heat, either over their whole working surface or in localized areas ("hot spots"). The iron may have been the perfect temperature for the last note you pressed but could suddenly climb to a dangerously high temperature by the time you lay out the next note. Paper burns are permanent; nature is very unforgiving when you're conducting thermal experiments with $10,000 U.S. *Gold Certificates*. Don't forget about a note that you've placed in a book for pressing — it may absorb chemicals (including printing ink) from the book's pages. Place notes between unprinted pages.

Edge trimming. Edge trimming is one of the most common types of note repairs. Frayed edges are clipped off with a snip of the scissors. Rounded corners may be trimmed square. The only trouble is, people don't like trimmed currency in their collections, considering trimming a form of semi-larcenous repair.

Trimmed edges can sometimes be detected by: (a) magnification/comparison with unaltered margins of a similar note type; (b) aligning the suspected edge against a ruler or straight-edge to see if the edge is really "straight"; and (c) evaluating whether or not the "perfectly" straight edge belongs to such a note (a POOR condition note with straight edges has been trimmed).

On the other hand, rounded corners on an otherwise immaculate-appearing note may mean that the note has been cleaned. If the note is really AU or UNC, it shouldn't have rounded corners.

Stain removal. Paper money may be stained due to mold (mildew), human tears or blood or perspiration, food spills, cosmetics, insect damage, water damage, cellophane or other tape, glues, motor oil, soap, extraneous ink (not from the original note), medicines, paint, wallet leather, household "chemicals," industrial chemicals, etc.

A professional paper conservator might treat a stained note in six or seven major steps:

1. Dirt removal; then:

2. Tape removal, with different techniques for different types of tape; then:

3. Stain removal — maybe the most delicate, and most easily mishandled, of these steps. First, the conservator must identify the cause of the stain. Then, an appropriate stain removal method is selected and tried; if this method fails, another may be tried, and so on.

The chemical and physical characteristics of the bank note, its age and condition, the type of stain, the stain's location on the note, the penetration of the note's surface by the stain — all of these must be evaluated in selecting a chemical for stain removal and in determining what concentration (strength or dilution) of the stain removal chemical to use. Some conservators will avoid removing a stain that covers any printed part of a rare bank note, for example.

Mold stains might be treated with a mixture of 50% ethyl alcohol/50% hydrogen peroxide or with dilute hydrogen peroxide alone. Acid stains might be treated with ammonia; animal fat stains with benzine; vegetable fat with acetone; ink stains with dilute oxalic acid — being careful not to clean colored paper or colored ink that may bleach out from the treatment fluid.

Conservators will usually "spot test" a tiny portion of their paper "patient" — with stain removal fluid — to see how it is working, preferably with very dilute fluid along the paper's edges. They may even wait a few days after treatment to observe long-term effects of the "test treatment" before proceeding with more concentrated solution. Then:

4. A bath in pure distilled water, to remove all traces of the stain removal chemicals. Then:

5. Perhaps a mild alkaline "deacidifying bath"; and, finally, either:

6. Reconstruction with starch paste (if necessary) and/or:

7. Repair with special archival tape.

Caution: Handwritten Signatures

Handwritten signatures on notes may be adversely af-

fected by any kind of cleaning treatment. Notes with handwritten signatures are, therefore, often not "treated" on or near the handwritten signatures. Such signatures may smear when washed, change color when heated (in ironing, etc.), fade when exposed to light or chemicals, or even darken.

DETECTING BANK NOTE CLEANING AND REPAIRS

Strong "back lighting" (such as a 100+ watt incandescent light bulb) can often make note repairs visible. So can strong front lighting and even ultraviolet light (if available) for certain repairs. A "currency doctor" will leave evidence of his "paper surgery" for those who know what to look for. Back lighting will often reveal: reattached corners, filled pinholes, filled thins, sealed tears, redrawn design lines, stain removal, crease traces (on washed notes), tape "impressions" (evidence of tape removal), graffiti removal, altered dates, altered signatures, altered Serial Numbers, etc.

Comparing a note suspected of being cleaned/repaired with an assumed untampered note may or may not help you to detect the "currency doctor's work." Like the human beings who made and circulated them, every bank note eventually acquires its own specific traits and appearance, due to the variable effects of different "experiences" from the day it was made until its present state.

Cleaned/repaired notes may have one or more of these suspicious characteristics:

1. They look cleaned — like freshly laundered white clothing that has been bleached, washed, rinsed, and spun dried to a processed, antiseptic appearance.

2. One or more characteristics doesn't fit the general overall condition of the note. POOR notes don't have perfect edges. UNCIRCULATED notes don't have crease traces.

3. The note looks "too good to be true."

4. The note looks "too bad for its overall grade."

5. Certain areas of the paper or design don't match other areas. Why is one Serial Number bright, while another is faded?

6. The note feels limp and lifeless, when it shouldn't, based on its brightness, lack of creases, etc.

7. The note feels greasy or otherwise "strange."

8. Surface "dirt" or repair tape may be hiding defects and repairs.

128. Gentle handling of this miniature 5 *Centavos* note of Revolutionary Mexico, issued by GOBIERNO PROVISIONAL DE MEXICO (Mexican Provisional Government), no date (but probably 1914). Crudely printed on orange pasteboard. (Pick # S697)

129. Mylar® is a safe soft plastic holder material for long-term storage of paper money, according to today's archival authorities. These holders allow you to "handle" notes without actually touching them, and simplify storage of your prized collection. *Large Size* U.S. $10 *Gold Certificate*, Series 1922.

130. *Large Size* U.S. $5 *Silver Certificate*, Series 1899, in its protective soft plastic holder. Reflections from overhead room lights, and dust and scratches, are on the holder, *not* on the note! Author's photo, from the stock of Americana Stamp and Coin Company, Inc. of Tarzana, California.

131. Hard plastic currency display holder, complete with base for standing upright (on your desk perhaps?). But will prolonged exposure to light fade this note's colors?

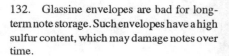

132. Glassine envelopes are bad for long-term note storage. Such envelopes have a high sulfur content, which may damage notes over time.

133. Scratches are on the protective soft plastic holder, not on this 10¢ U.S. *Fractional Currency*, Third Issue (1864-1869), with portrait of George Washington. In the dealer's holder, photographed by the author from the stock of Americana Stamp and Coin Company, Inc. of Tarzana, California.

"RAGS make paper, PAPER makes money, MONEY makes banks, BANKS make loans, LOANS make beggars, BEGGARS make rags."

18th century jingle

8

Condition and Grading

To the beginner in paper money collecting, any condition may be OK, provided that the note excites the unsophisticated curiosity of the neophyte hobbyist. To the serious collector, the problem of condition becomes a vital concern and (usually) a limiting factor in just which notes are purchased.

If you insist on CRISP UNCIRCULATED (CU) condition exclusively, you'll never obtain certain scarce notes, and you'd better have a deep wallet for those you do find. At the opposite extreme, if grossly damaged and ragged notes are all you collect, your collection may never amount to any substantial monetary value (depending on the notes, of course), and it will always have a "beat up" appearance. Almost as atrocious-looking is a "collection" with the full range of conditions displayed side-by-side: GEM CRISP UNCIRCULATED to POOR, intermixed with no discernible logic.

There is something to be said for a currency album with notes of uniform appearance, with all notes relatively clean and attractive, regardless of actual technical grades. Scarce, desirable notes in EXTREMELY FINE (EF or XF) to ABOUT UNCIRCULATED (AU) will always find buyers because there is nothing wrong with a complete collection of high grade circulated notes.(In fact, the owner of such doesn't have to worry about "breathing" on his notes, for fear of reducing their value 50%, as can occur when you change a GEM CU note into a mere UNC one by giving it a slight blemish.)

This chapter discusses condition and grading of paper money, as viewed by collectors and dealers in late 20th century America.

NORMAL WEAR AND AGING OF PAPER MONEY

From the instant that currency is printed, it begins to "age" in its inevitable journey to dust, a cumulative progression of mechanical (physical changes) and chemical (molecular changes) events that can destroy a piece of paper in days or many centuries. We justifiably regret the gradual disintegration of precious pieces of historical paper, much as we rightly mourn the passing of our friends and relatives from the world of the living. But from the obvious recycling and perpetual regeneration of the realities of the universe, we console ourselves with optimistic observations, such as "hope springs eternal" and "life goes on."

Paper ages because of external and internal assault on its molecular integrity. Many papers are self-destructive, manufactured with a high acidic or sulfur content, which attacks the paper fibers and breaks down their strength over time. Paper is made from plant matter, which tends to absorb and retain environmental chemicals that come in contact with it. Bank Note paper, although of very high quality and durability, absorbs humidity like a sponge, and most notes also readily soak up organic compounds such as oils and starch, to the everlasting alteration of their appearance.

"Normal wear" of paper money occurs as it is handled and used for the reasons it was created — to serve as a convenient concentration of universally recognized wealth, and to act as a financial medium of exchange in the daily business affairs of human beings. Normal wear of currency consists of folds, dirt, fading, and tears.

FOLDS

A fold is a mild paper bend. A distinction is made between folds and creases in paper money collecting: a fold is a mild bend in the paper, without breaking the paper fibers or imprinted ink lines. A crease breaks the paper fibers (without cutting all the way through the paper). A fold appears as an angular change in the surface (flat plane) of the note as you look at the note from the correct angle. Some folds are obvious, some aren't. A fold may be through the center of a note, or at a diagonal, or vertically or horizontally off-center.

The first significant fold that a bank note receives is usually a vertical center fold, because the note's owner folds it in half for insertion into a pocket, wallet, or purse.

The next folds that a note receives are often two quarter folds—one on either side of, and parallel to, the vertical center fold. The quarter folds are usually lighter than the vertical center fold because they were done less often than the vertical center fold, and they had to go through a double thickness of paper (whereas the vertical center fold only goes through one thickness of paper). Vertical quarter folds are done to conceal the note and/or to make it fit into a small space.

A central horizontal fold is often the next fold that a note receives in normal circulation, and it intersects the three vertical folds at approximately their midlines. This horizontal fold is usually lighter than the vertical center fold because most wallets aren't thin and long.

A crease breaks the paper fibers and the ink lines of the note. A crease appears as a "white line" on the note, accentuated and outlined by accumulated dirt along the crease's edge in worn notes. Where a fold starts to become a crease is where a note starts to change from ABOUT UNCIRCULATED (AU) to EXTREMELY FINE (EF or XF) condition.

DIRT

Paper money picks up dirt as it circulates, just as children pick up dirt when they play outdoors. If you look at a piece of paper under a laboratory microscope, you will see what seems to be a randomly tangled mass of pressed-together fibers, appearing much like a laundry room floor would if huge bales of clothing were spread out and trampled by a herd of elephants. Little wonder, then, that paper has numerous microscopic depressions and holes in its surface, endless irregularities in which dirt particles get trapped and imprisoned.

Paper creases attract dirt like magnets attract steel. The central groove of the crease tends to be "white" because the mechanical action of repetitive folding pushes dirt towards the "edges" of the crease.

The central intersection is where the vertical center fold and the major horizontal fold meet—a point of great stress on

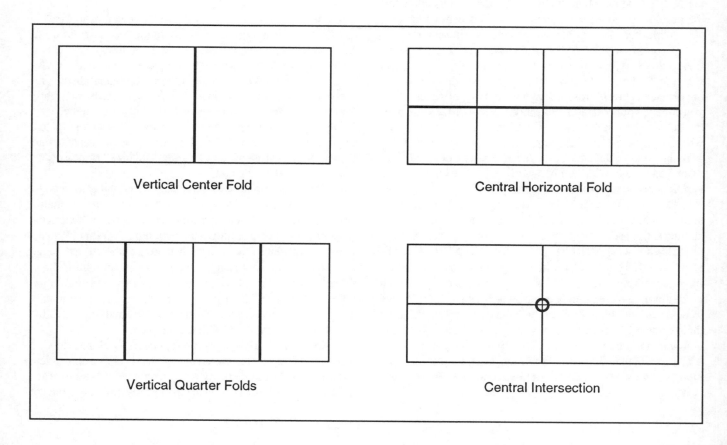

Vertical Center Fold

Central Horizontal Fold

Vertical Quarter Folds

Central Intersection

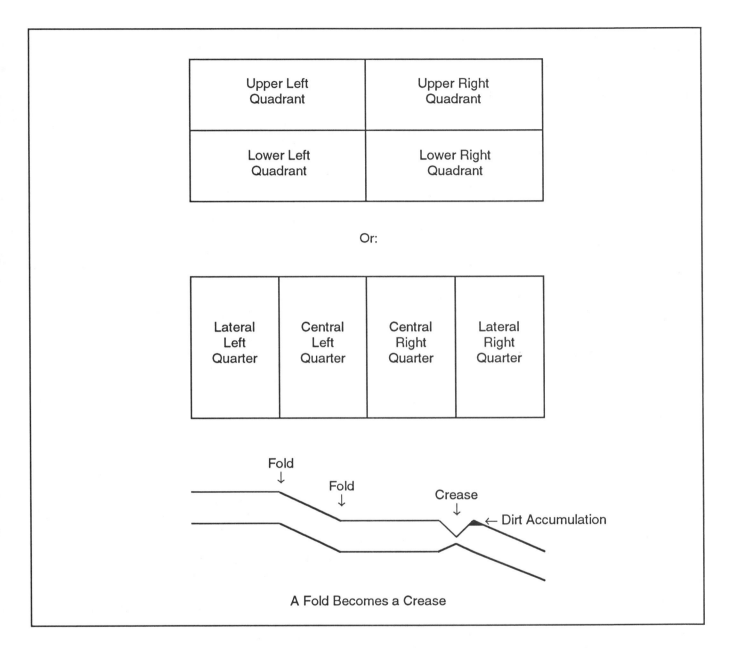

A Fold Becomes a Crease

the paper and much wear on the note's surface, often eroding the design and forcing a hole through the note over time. A hole caused by wear in the central intersection is characteristic of a low grade note in "bad" condition.

And, although it gets a little pedantic and pretentious, you can even label the "regions" of a note based on the natural divisions caused by the primary folds, as shown above.

And then, of course, you have to specify whether you are looking at the face or back of the note.

CREASES

A crease is a deep groove that breaks the paper fibers without slicing all the way through the note (a crease is not a cut). The terms fold and crease are sometimes used interchangeably by dealers and collectors, but, technically, a crease is deeper and more apparent than a fold. A fold becomes a crease if it is done often enough or strongly enough (see above).

Washing the note will get rid of the dirt, but the note will then have an unnaturally "clean but worn" appearance, which is despised by bank note connoisseurs. A washed 80-year-old note sometimes looks a lot like a washed 80-year-old person: very clean, but still 80 years old. A basic rule of paper money collecting is: DO NOT WASH YOUR NOTES. This is why we keep our currency collections housed in protective plastic holders. Let the dirt fall on the plastic, not on your prized notes!

Washed notes tend to be duller, limper, and more faded than their unwashed counterparts in any given grade. Washed notes inevitably lose some of their original brightness. Suspicious traces of white lines may still exist where folds and creases once were more evident, when a note is washed and ironed. A question in the potential buyer's head is: "If they've washed this note, what else have they done to tamper with it?"

FADING

Fading is a loss in color intensity (saturation — the lightness or darkness of the same shade of color) and/or a loss in color hue (shade or tint — i.e., the specific wavelength of the visible light spectrum) of an object.

Both the paper and the ink of a bank note can fade. Fading is caused by chemical changes in the molecules in the surface of an object (bank note), such that the atomic particles vibrate at a different wavelength, producing a shift in the visible light emitted from that object. Fading is caused by washing, exposure to strong light, contact with contaminating chemicals, and/or internal "self-destructive" chemical changes from the bank note's own substance.

The papers used to make currency vary in color from snow white to every imaginable shade of ivory, buff, cream, light yellow, light tan, eggshell, amber, etc. Many countries, including the United States at present, deliberately employ an "off-white" color paper stock for their currency printing as an anti-counterfeiting measure.

All paper money fades over time, and it fades faster the more it is abused in handling, washing, exposure to airborne contaminants, and exposure to light (especially sunlight). We often find pre-20th century bank notes with annoying fading dichotomies; e.g., bright paper and printing ink but badly faded handwritten signatures, or intense printed colors but faded paper color.

The more faded a note is, the less desirable it is to collectors. Fading will lower a note's grade and its market value. The best way to estimate how much a note has faded is to compare it with genuine "unfaded" (very brilliant and well-preserved color) notes of the same type.

Fading cannot be reversed with present technology. Once a note is faded, it is faded. Under no circumstances should a note be soaked in bleach to "brighten" its color or to cover up its dirt. It would make about as much sense to bleach the *Mona Lisa* to sharpen up its appearance!

TEARS

As a bank note circulates, its edges get pulled and twisted by many hands, wallets, cash register trays, note change machines, note counting machines (these days), and other mechanical/physical stresses. Tears shouldn't exist in an UNCIRCULATED note, but they become more likely as we go down the grading scale. Small edge tears are normal in notes graded VERY GOOD, and disastrous tears are expected in POOR condition notes. If a tear fits the grade, it is considered

normal wear for that note; if a distracting tear rips through 10 millimeters of an otherwise purportedly AU note, for example, it is called a defect.

It is customary in the paper money business to describe tears that are defective traits of a note when offering the note for sale. This includes mentioning repairs of tears by saying something such as: "5mm closed tear at upper right corner" or "20mm taped tear, not affecting vignettes."

Sometimes tears are "sealed" by brushing a thin transparent glue on both sides of the tear line, then pressing the note between sheets of waxed paper under heavy weights (like books) until the glue is dried. The less glue used, the less stiffening of the surrounding paper area adjacent to the tear line, and the more natural the final appearance of the tear repair, but the note will still be classified as torn; and gluing, no matter how expertly done, should fool nobody who understands the value of undamaged notes.

RIPPLE EFFECT

A quick word about ripple effect — the gentle wavy appearance of a piece of paper, due to moisture absorption, poor storage, and/or mutative raw materials used in the paper's manufacture. Ripple effect cannot be corrected in a note. Some collectors consider it part of normal aging of paper; others call it a defect. The ethical seller will always mention ripple effect in a note if its presence is dramatic. Ripple effect is not a fold and is not caused by circulation wear.

DEFECTS IN PAPER MONEY

In this book, defects in paper money are acquired flaws due to mishandling (deliberate or accidental) after the notes have entered circulation. It depends on how you define your terms, but post-production acquired defects should not be confused with either natural aging and wear (see foregoing part of this chapter) or production errors (created before the notes circulated; see Chapter 20).

Wear and aging are expected as currency circulates. Error notes are unexpected production "freaks"; i.e., mistakes that should never have gotten into circulation. Defects are abnormal imperfections, faults that notes in a given condition should not necessarily have (the defect helps to lower the note's condition grade), caused by mishandling trauma beyond simple folding and other normal wear.

Defect Detection

Because defects lower the market value of a note, they must be discovered during note transactions. A magnifying lens of about 5 power is good for searching for many defects, while 10+ power may be needed for verifying counterfeits, deceptive repairs, or expert "alterations" (such as strengthening printing lines with a pen). A strong back light (100 watts or greater) is also essential.

Some Common Defects in Paper Money

Common paper money defects acquired from mishandling include: pinholes, large holes, damage thins, damage cuts, surface abrasions, stains, "rubber stamps," graffiti, tape repairs, adhesions, missing pieces, washing, and edge trimming. An argument could be made that all these defects can be "normal wear" if they are acquired in daily use of the money. I'm classifying them as unnecessary and undesirable defects because no note, no matter how old, has to have them, and because I try to avoid them, as a rule, in my paper money collection.

Pinholes. These have got to be the most irritating thing, for their size, of all paper money defects. Some authorities say that an UNCIRCULATED note can have a small pinhole; others say it can't, and must be called "ABOUT UNCIRCULATED" or "defective" or "UNC with pinhole."

Many merchants and banks in the 19th century customarily used spindles and pins to keep bank notes together, so pinholes are common on many old notes. I look at pinholes as defects, and I like to have them pointed out to me by a dealer when I am buying a note with pinholes in it.

As a rule, pinholes should not be repaired, and careful examination with a strong back light should reveal most pinholes, both "open" and "filled."

Location and size determine a pinhole's degree of deleterious effect on the beauty and value of a note. You never want a pinhole through the central portrait's engraved eyeball, or through the "Star" asterisk of the Serial Number of a replacement note. A tiny pinhole through an unprinted area away from the note's center may not be the end of the world (but don't call it GEM CU, either).

Large holes. The bigger the hole, and the more important the part of the design that it obliterates, the worse it is. If pinholes bother you (as they bother me), then larger holes are reason enough not to acquire a note for your collection, except for sentimental or souvenir value (such as a bullet hole through a note carried by a combat soldier). A hole always exists, even when it is repaired, and should be included in the note's condition description.

Damaging thins. Enough paper may be scraped away that you begin to see a "thin" forming on the body of a note. The size (area on the note's surface), location on the design, and depth (how much paper has been scraped away) of the thin combine to characterize its severity in devaluing a note. Some rare notes may be unobtainable without thins, but, in general, pass up a note that is thinned.

Don't confuse damaging thins (acquired defects) with watermarks ("normal" thins deliberately impressed into the paper at the time of manufacture).

Damaging cuts. A cut is a straight slice through the paper, made with a sharp instrument. No paper is removed in a true cut. Cancellation cuts, redemption cuts, and counterfeit-designating cuts may be "normal" notaphilic history to some collectors and defects to other collectors.

Cuts generally reduce the market value of a note, but some notes (like 1861 *Confederates*) are commonly found with such cuts, so their value is not totally destroyed.

My feeling is: if you can afford to buy an uncut note, why tolerate one with cuts (except for historical reasons of government cancellation, etc.)?

Edge trimming. This is perhaps the most common "repair" of worn notes. Trimming is really a type of cutting, and is considered semi-ethical in the paper money business. Obviously, a trimmed note will look better than if you left its edges ragged, but trimming reduces more of the remaining margin, and the note may "look trimmed"; i.e., tampered with and therefore possibly suspect in other respects. If a seller won't hesitate to wash and trim a note, what else will he do to it?

A note that is heavily worn, with deep creases, faded colors, and "perfectly" straight edges looks trimmed, as indeed it may have been. Many dealers and collectors look down on trimmed notes, and call them defective and repaired. Think about that the next time you are tempted to take a pair of scissors and give sharp, 90 degree perfect corners to your limp, worn notes.

Surface abrasions. These are scrapes across the note's front or back sides, with the eroding force applied almost parallel with the note's surface. Ink and paper may both be carried away, leaving an ugly "white spot" in the note's printed design, and maybe even a distracting thin in the paper.

A tiny surface abrasion on a GOOD condition *California National Gold Bank Note* is one thing. A massive vignette abrasion taking away half the design on a modern, easily-replaced cheap note is something else.

Stains. Paper, being highly absorbent organic matter, tends to acquire stains from oil, ink, food, paint and varnish, even water (for smears of handwritten signatures, for a frightening instance). Stains, even small ones, render a note uncollectible in the eyes of fastidious collectors.

Stains acquired after manufacture are defects. The least objectionable stains are small ones, of the same shade as the note's color, which are either "hidden" within the design or are on an unimportant blank area of the note. The worst stains are large "new" colors (different from the paper and printing inks) that penetrate the paper all the way through, all over a major vignette or Serial Number or signature, especially if they obliterate such from recognition.

The romance of a blood-stained note from the military currency stash of wounded soldier has a certain collector value if it can be proven that the stain was made on the battlefield. Or a water-stained counterfeit £5 British note from the Nazi Operation Bernhard, retrieved by scavengers from its intended watery grave at Lake Toplitz! As a rule, though, stains hurt a note's collector value.

Foxing (also called tropical stain) is a mold blemish on paper. Foxing appears as a yellow or brown discoloration, often circular, often with multiple little "spots" where each mold spore landed and grew. Foxing is common on pre-20th century paper items of all types, and common on paper stored in humid climates. Foxing can be prevented, but is difficult to "cure." Don't let foxed papers come in contact with unfoxed ones, and don't cross-contaminate via shared currency holders, etc. Consider foxing a paper disease.

Rust stains are sometimes confused with, or used synonymously for, foxing. Rust stains come from iron oxides flaking off iron-based metal alloys. Office paper clips should never come in contact with bank notes or the envelopes/holders that house collectible notes. Be careful if you store your notes in metal cash boxes — is the metal migrating onto your prized notes?

"Rubber stamps." Notes are often "rubber stamped" with an inked impression from a rubber stamp. Such notes may or may not be true defects. Rubber stamps may surcharge or legally invalidate a note, or they may be banking or merchant counting and routing marks, or they may be stray blemishes from who knows where with no discernible purpose or message.

Handsome rubber stamps that I don't consider note defects are: Wells, Fargo Express Company handstamps on any piece of paper of any kind; revalidation stamps on notes so used; and Counterfeit stamps on contemporary counterfeits. Rubber stamps that are decipherable and of historical interest often add to a note's appeal. Meaningless stray rubber stamp marks usually degrade a note.

Graffiti. The same advice applies to graffiti — the unofficial handwriting on a note, most often seen on notes that have heavily circulated. Graffiti is usually called a defect, but a desirable graffiti would be a cheap $1 U.S. *Silver Certificate* from World War II, with all the signatures of the crew members of an Army Air Corps bomber, properly dated and endorsed by their commanding officer in Italy; or would you rather just have a worn ungraffitied version of this note?

Graffiti may have been done in pencil, fugitive ink (water-soluble), indelible ink (permanent, water-insoluble), crayon, chalk, artist's paints, etc. Steady nerves and some knowledge of how to do it are required for semi-successful graffiti removal. After all, simple pencil graphite marks can be erased with a soft pencil rubber eraser, leaving no trace that pencil marks were ever there — or can they?

Because graffiti is usually detrimental to a note's market value, and because it is difficult to remove most graffiti without damaging the note in another way, most bank note collectors avoid most graffitied notes.

Tape repairs. Tape on a note is a defect, plain and simple. It may be necessary to keep the note from falling apart, but it will always be an irritation to purists who prefer untaped currency. Never use Scotch® type clear adhesive office supply tapes on bank notes, as such tapes cannot be removed without damaging the notes, and their continued adherence on a note will damage it likewise. Special clear archival tapes are used to repair bank notes, but my advice is to leave that job to somebody else, and try to collect notes that are untaped.

Adhesions. These are pieces of foreign matter that are stuck on a note. Tape remnants and glue streaks are adhesions. So are starch fillers that are blended into a note's texture during repairs. A whole note may be given a starch bath to increase its paper "stiffness" and thereby mimic the crispness of a note in better condition; such treatments may leave telltale residues of starch built up in places on the note.

Strong back light will often show starch treatment and glue repairs as darker than the rest of the note.

Natural inclusions. Natural paper inclusions are small visible impurities impressed into paper during its manufacture. There are many types of natural paper inclusions; they may be discolored fibers, unbleached dust particles, a tiny paint chip from a paper mill machine, etc. Natural inclusions may appear to be acquired defects, such as repairs, stains, or artificial adhesions, but they are not. Natural inclusions should not greatly reduce the value of an otherwise nice note, and some note series are notorious for having inclusions.

Missing pieces. Of the most serious defects, few can match the damage done to a note that has missing pieces. Many collectors will avoid buying any note with any missing piece, no matter how small. Remember that whenever you are offered a "missing piece" note at a bargain price!

The size and location of the missing piece are important. An unprinted corner area that is missing is much better than an equivalent area of the portrait cut out. Reattached corners (and synthesized corners) are detectable with strong back lighting or ultraviolet examination.

Should you buy a note with a missing piece? Should you buy a car with a missing piece?

Washed notes. Washing paper money is epidemic for old notes, and due to the stigma associated with it, my advice is to avoid washed notes, if you can detect such! There are plenty of unwashed notes to fill your collecting ambitions.

GRADING PAPER MONEY

No universally accepted Grading Standard (condition criteria) exists for paper money collecting, because: (1) grading is an art, not a science; (2) different note types and different nations have grading variations by custom and logic; and (3) grading standards change.

It can be said that no two people will grade currency exactly alike, and different dealers use different grading standards. Many dealers don't define their grades at all (partly for peace of mind, maybe even for legal safety); instead, they state on their price lists and auction catalogs something to this effect:

Grading is an art, and, like all arts, debatable. I grade my notes based on my 85 years in this business. If you disagree with my grade for a particular note, just return it for a cheerful refund.

There are "trends" in grading theory, however, and conclusions can be drawn from analyzing the "grading standards" of prominent paper money dealers and hobby writers at any given point in time. To prepare the following Grade Definitions, I studied the standard catalogs for U.S. and foreign currency, as used in the United States; a couple of dozen recently published (since 1980) paper money books in the English language; the retail price lists and auction catalogs of over 100 currency dealers from the United States and foreign countries; and my observations that I recorded from conversations with collectors and dealers whom I've met recently at currency shows.

I have combined this information to arrive at the following "composite" descriptions of currency grades, as they are roughly understood by currency collectors and dealers in the late 20th century, with emphasis on the United States market.

THE MEANING OF PAPER MONEY GRADES

1. GEM CRISP UNCIRCULATED (GEM CU) — As nice as the day it was printed. A virtually flawless note, "perfectly" centered with balanced margins (opposite margins of equal width). Large margins, never trimmed. No evidence of handling. No surface marks acquired after printing, which means no smudges or counting marks. No folds. Bright, vivid color of paper and ink. Superb impression. No pinholes, no stains, no ripple effect, no bent corners.

2. CHOICE CRISP UNCIRCULATED (CH CU) — Not quite "perfect." May be slightly off-center, but still has nice margins. May have tiny foxing, faint counting smudges ("teller handling marks"), or a tiny pinhole seen only with back lighting (although some authorities say that all pinholes are defects). Original color. No folds, no major stains, no ripple effect, no bent corners.

3. UNCIRCULATED (UNC) or CRISP UNCIRCULATED (CU) — May have: counting smudges, pinholes, small stains, small ripple effect, corners bent only in the blank (unprinted) areas, evidence of paper aging (yellowing, small foxing). No folds into the design. No corners bent into the design. May be very off-center, with "lousy" margins. Paper is still very clean and crisp, no serious discoloration. Right angle (90 degree) corners. May have original color shade and intensity, or may be slightly faded.

"Plain" UNCIRCULATED (UNC) may be the highest grade given by foreign dealers or given to foreign currency by American dealers. Also called "NEW" by some dealers, especially older and conservative ones. In the first issue of the *Currency Dealer newsletter* (September 1980), U.S. currency price quotes were given for five grades: Gem New, Choice New, New, XF (Extremely Fine), and Average Circulated. As in our sister hobby of coin collecting, the proliferation of more grading categories has occurred in paper currency over the last quarter century.

UNCIRCULATED does not refer to whether or not the note has ever actually entered circulation, as most notes have entered circulation or we wouldn't have them. And UNCIRCULATED doesn't mean never been touched, as virtually all notes in your collection have been touched by human hands. UNCIRCULATED means not folded; showing no evidence of mishandling as would occur if it were used as money.

4. ABOUT UNCIRCULATED (AU) — Also called: ALMOST UNCIRCULATED. One light fold through the center of the note or several light corner folds that pass through the design (printed area). No creases (breaks in paper fibers). Corners not rounded. May or may not have: pinholes, small stains, counting smudges, ripple effect.

AU notes may, at first glance, appear to be UNC, but close inspection by gazing across the planes of the back-lighted surfaces will reveal a faint fold through the main body of the note. Many AU notes have been sold as UNC, either intentionally or accidentally — probably the most common "business error" that dealers make. If a note has a permanent fold or crease, it will never be UNC again. AU is called EF-UNC by some European graders, and some old-fashioned graders don't recognize AU, preferring to go directly from UNC to EF in grading.

A superbly centered AU note of exquisite color, but having a faint center fold, may actually be more desirable (and justly priced higher) than a mediocre UNC note — a fact not always appreciated by beginning collectors.

5. EXTREMELY FINE (EF or XF) — Three light folds through the main body of the note or one major crease. The folds or crease of an EF note are immediately visible with front lighting. Still crisp and clean, with bright colors. No major stains, no tears, no fading. Corners and edges are sharp.

6. VERY FINE (VF) — Three major creases or one major crease and several minor creases (a deep center fold crease and two fainter vertical creases). Or one major vertical crease and one major horizontal crease. Some dirt on paper. Some loss of crispness. Corners show slight rounding. Edge wear, but no tears into border design. Color is slightly faded.

Many experts advise that notes not be collected in grades below VF, but cost and rarity may force lower grades into your albums. Some U.S. *National Bank Notes* may be unobtainable in higher grades. Notes graded below VF, however, have serous aesthetic liabilities to the discriminating collector.

7. FINE (F) — Many folds and creases. Some authorities say: four prominent creases (often three vertical creases, one horizontal crease). Tiny edge tears not into printed designs. Halfway between crisp and completely limp and lifeless. Tiny surface abrasions, often where creases intersect, but no center hole due to folding. May have staple holes. Color slightly faded, but not excessively dirty. No serious tears, stains, or holes. No missing corners. Some wear along major creases.

The average condition of paper money in your wallet is probably FINE to VERY FINE.

8. VERY GOOD (VG) — Showing much wear, with faded color, bad soiling, rounded corners, small edge tears (but only slightly into design), some staining, pinholes, or staple holes. No missing pieces. Limp, folded many times, wrinkled, and dirty. All crispness gone. Design worn off along major creases. May have tiny corner torn off, but not into design.

9. GOOD (G) — Very limp, tiny holes at crease intersections, extremely heavy creases, very dirty. Tiny pieces missing. Missing corners may slightly enter the printed design. Prominent stains. May have graffiti. Frayed margins. Small surface abrasions along creases. Holes can be larger than pinholes. Rounded, dog-eared corners. Margin tears into designs. No large missing pieces. Signatures and Serial Numbers may be unreadable. May have tape or glue repairs.

"GOOD" in paper money talk doesn't mean "good" as used in everyday speech. A GOOD condition bank note is actually not nice-looking.

10. FAIR — Large pieces missing. Prominent holes from wear. Edge tears deep into design. Heavy wear along creases. Very dirty and completely limp. Signatures and Serial Numbers unreadable. Many defects, but still attributable to variety.

11. POOR — Severely damaged with large pieces missing, excessive surface wear, large holes, disfiguring stains, trimmed edges, disfiguring graffiti. May be completely torn in half and taped together. Unpleasant to look at. Would be instantly withdrawn by a bank for destruction/replacement. Design difficult to decipher. Attributable to type, but not to variety.

Except for the utmost rarities or notes of sentimental value (received on a trip, found in a "ghost town," etc.), POOR condition notes have no place in your collection.

THE BRAMWELL GRADING SYSTEM

Douglas Bramwell, a London paper money dealer, advanced his personal note grading system in 1969, based on a table of standardized "damage numbers," which are added up by category to arrive at an overall "numerical" grade. Five to twenty points are assigned to each of these categories: Body, Cleanliness, Edges, Folding, Surface. Notes are then classified according to total number of grading points as follows: UNC (100 total points); EF (about 90); VF (75); F (55); Fair (30).

Although the Bramwell System gives numerical accuracy to grading, it hasn't caught on much in the United States, in my opinion due to: (a) the desire of American collectors for verbal descriptions of notes; (b) long-established custom of "letter grades" UNC, AU, EF, etc.; and (c) the chance that a numerical grade could be misleading; e.g., a note grading 80 in the Bramwell System might be "perfect" in all respects except having a huge hole through its center!

SPLIT GRADES

A note may appear to be between two grades. For example: F-VF means that the whole note grades between FINE and VERY FINE. When one side grades higher than the other side, the front is stated first and is separated by a diagonal line from the reverse side grade: VF/F means the face of the note grades VERY FINE, but the reverse of the note is FINE. But many dealers don't make a distinction between F-VF or F/VF, for example. Many dealers don't use Split Grades. For those who do use split grades, AU-UNC is an impossible grade, as a note is either AU or UNC, not in between.

UPGRADING

A collector is constantly upgrading a collection; i.e., replacing lower grade notes with higher grade ones of the same type. A space filler or filler is a note of atrocious quality, often damaged, grading FAIR or POOR, and used to fill a space in a collection until the collector can find (and afford!) a better specimen.

NOTE GRADES

People who grade notes can be categorized: liberal vs. conservative, knowledgeable vs. uninformed, honest vs. larcenous, "groupers" vs. "dividers" (few grades, many grades). Take a piece of paper money out of your wallet and grade it right now!

134.   1 *Riyal*, so-called *Pilgrim's Receipt*, of Saudi Arabia — used by religious pilgrims traveling to Mecca, after exchanging their native currencies for these notes. Engraving shows entrance to the Royal Palace at Jedda. Can you find the vertical folds and corner folds on this note? (Pick # 2)

135.   25¢ *Dominion of Canada* fractional note ("shinplaster") of 1900 — in the soft plastic holder as purchased by the author for $1 (U.S.) at a currency show. What grade would you give this note? (Pick # 9b)

136.   French *Assignat* of 50 *Sols*, dated 23 May, 1793, with watermark and official embossed "seals." Despite warning at left, LA LOI PUNIT DE MORT LE CONTRE-FACTEUR ("The law punishes with death the counterfeiter"), *assignats* were extensively counterfeited. Notice prominent "worm" hole at right — often seen on old paper items. (Pick # A72)

137. CRISP UNCIRCULATED condition. No folds or other signs of wear. Nice even margins. Good color, sharp impression, no problems. *Small Size* $20 *Federal Reserve Note*, Series 1988A.

138. EXTREMELY FINE condition. Several light folds, the "vertical center fold" being almost a crease. *Small Size* $20 *Federal Reserve Note*, Series 1988A.

139. VERY FINE condition. Several prominent creases and folds. Corners show slight rounding. *Small Size* $20 *Federal Reserve Bank Note*, Series 1929.

140.   FINE condition (at best). Many folds and creases. Some surface abrasion. Color slightly faded. Wear along "vertical center fold." Rounded corners. Banker's handstamped "graffiti" may lower the grade even more, in the opinion of some collectors. *Small Size* $20 *Gold Certif*icate, Series 1928.

141.   VERY GOOD condition (at best). Much wear. Soiling, pinholes, limp, repeatedly folded and creased, wrinkled. Face is badly faded (this note got caught in the laundry!). No missing pieces, however. *Small Size* $20 *Federal Reserve Note*, Series date obliterated. When the author deposited this note at his bank, the teller grabbed the note and asked him: "Is this real?"

142.   FAIR condition (at best). The surface itself actually looks better than FAIR, but the large missing piece and the deep edge tear force this note into FAIR condition (at best). *Small Size* $20 *Federal Reserve Note*, Series 1985. Banks will immediately remove a note such as this from circulation and send it to the Federal Reserve System for replacement.

9

Popular U.S. Notes

A collection of U.S. paper money can be started from your wallet, with $1 or $2 notes at face value, collected for signatures, special Serial Numbers, "old" Series dates, or (if you're lucky) even errors. But if you wish to collect obsolete (non-circulating) American notes, you will have to get them from dealers or other collectors, and your cost will be based on three factors: rarity, condition, and demand.

Collector demand for a note, U.S. or otherwise, has an intellectual and emotional foundation in real and abstract qualities such as: the beauty of the design; the "uniqueness" of the design (is it a "one type" note?); historical associations (Was it issued by Benjamin Franklin? Circulated during the Civil War?); collector obsession with "completeness" (do you need it for a "complete" collection of 20th century *Gold Certificates*?); antiquarian charm (*Fractional Currency, "Broken Bank" Notes*, "odd" denominations—$1.75, $3, etc.); and tradition (if the top collectors and dealers always want it, it must be good!).

Defined broadly, "United States" paper money can include notes issued in localities that are now part of the U.S.A. As such, we might consider about a half dozen major "American currency" collecting areas: (1) *Colonial* and *Continental Currency*, (2) *Broken Bank Notes*, (3) *Confederate* and *Southern States* Civil War notes, (4) U.S. federal *Fractional Currency*, (5) *Large Size Notes*, and (6) *Small Size Notes*. Let's list a few popular notes in each of these categories, notes that are in demand by U.S. currency specialists who can afford them, or wish they could afford them. I'll leave the great rarities to the next chapter.

COLONIAL AND CONTINENTAL CURRENCY

Benjamin Franklin printed *Colonial Currency* for Pennsylvania from 1756 to 1764. Most of these can be obtained for several hundred dollars in VG to VF condition, but are rare in UNC. Paul Revere personally engraved and printed notes in Massachusetts and New Hampshire in 1775. These are a bit more expensive to buy than the Pennsylvania notes of Franklin, and all are rare in UNC condition.

Many *Colonial* and *Continental Currency* notes can be bought for $100 or less in circulated state. Counterfeits are common and are collected also, but try to find out if you're buying genuine or counterfeit! Contemporary counterfeits, made when the genuine notes were circulating, are the desirable ones.

Some states are rarer than others: all Vermont *Colonial Currency* is rare and expensive. Connecticut notes of Revolutionary War vintage are common but are scarce before 1771. Many collectors collect notes of their home state, such as New York or Virginia. Of special interest are notes signed by signers of the Declaration of Independence.

Condition Considerations

Colonial and *Continental Currency* is worth a premium for bright, flawless notes with broad margins. Common damages seen in these notes are: pinholes, tape repairs, split edges, trimmed edges (to "repair" frayed edges), fading of ink, foxing (tropical stains), reattached corners, punch cancels (thought defective by some collectors), soft corners, and "reinforcement" with stamp hinges (which in itself may not be detrimental).

BROKEN BANK NOTES

Also known as Obsolete Currency, Wildcat Bank Notes, State and Local Currency, or Private Bank Notes, the 19th century U.S. so-called Broken Bank Notes are avidly collected by state, city, bank, denomination, time period, vignette design, and "issued" (signed and numbered) vs. "unissued" (unsigned and unnumbered). The tendency today is to call these notes Obsolete Bank Notes, but old-timers will often say Broken Bank Notes because most of these banks went insolvent, many during national economic panics and depressions (such as that of the late 1830s).

First issued in the late 1770s, these private and state-issued bank notes often have beautifully engraved vignettes. Many collectors specialize in the *Obsolete Notes* of their own state, and the Society of Paper Money Collectors (see Chapter 23) has published reference books, some still for sale by the Society, on the notes of individual states, such as: *Indiana Obsolete Notes and Scrip* by Wolka, or *Maine Obsolete Paper Money & Scrip* by Wait.

Criswell's *North American Currency* book has long been used for the catalog numbers of U.S. obsolete currency, but Haxby's monumental four-volume *Standard Catalog of United States Obsolete Bank Notes, 1782-1866* is exhaustive in its coverage (see Bibliography). Some currency dealers will sell you an individual Haxby volume, containing just the alphabetized states for the notes that you collect, so that you don't have to buy the whole set of books.

Although some are rare and seldom seen, many U.S. *Broken Bank Notes* are cheap to buy in EF-UNC condition ($20 or less, often less than the note's face value). Because none of these notes is redeemable anymore, their value is entirely due to collector support.

CONFEDERATE AND SOUTHERN STATES CURRENCY

Of course, the first thing you need is a copy (even an old edition will do) of Criswell's *Confederate and Southern States Currency* book (see Bibliography) — the "bible" for collectors of Confederate and Civil War era paper money of the Southern States. Criswell's book has the standard catalog numbers that collectors and dealers use when referring to *Confederate Currency* and *Obsolete Southern States Currency*. Criswell's price quotes can be scanned for an idea of relative worth of the notes, but up-to-date prices must be learned from dealer price lists (Chapter 3), auction realizations (Chapter 17), and currency shows (Chapter 18).

You can collect these notes by state, denomination, vignette, etc. The Society of Paper Money Collectors (Chapter 23) has published, and offers for sale, reference books on the obsolete currency of certain southern states, such as: *Alabama Obsolete Notes & Scrip* by Rosene or *Arkansas Obsolete Notes & Scrip* by Rothert. Criswell's book, *Confederate and Southern States Currency*, includes notes issued only by state governments, not by private and city banks (as are also included in his *North American Currency* book — see Bibliography). See Chapter 3 for inspiration on collecting *Confederate States of America Currency*.

U.S. FRACTIONAL CURRENCY

By custom, when we say *Fractional Currency* without any additional qualifiers, it is understood that we are referring to United States federal *Fractional Currency* notes issued from 1862 to 1876. Instituted during the Civil War, when coinage disappeared from circulation due to hoarding by a nervous public, *Fractional Currency* is collected by denomination, design types, and issue (date series). GEM UNC notes with large, even margins and bright color are scarce for some *Fractional Currency* types. The fact that U.S. *Fractional Currency* is often found worn and ragged is evidence that it did indeed circulate. *Proofs* and *Specimens* exist for *Fractional Currency* (unlike their unavailability for most federal U.S. notes). Clean, UNC *Fractional Currency* with wide margins commands substantial premiums when sold.

For collectors with deep wallets, the *Fractional Currency Shields*, produced by the Treasury Department in 1866-1867 for sale to banks for use in comparing these genuine uniface designs with suspected counterfeit notes, occasionally appear on the market for strong four-figure prices. The gray background shield is most common, while the pink and green backgrounds are rare. Shields that are damaged, repaired, and refinished are worth less than undamaged ones.

LARGE SIZE U.S. CURRENCY

By definition and custom, U.S. *Large Size Notes* refer to the federal issues from 1861 to 1929. Nicknamed "horse blankets" because of their greater size than, say, the *Small Size Notes* that replaced them in 1929, these *Large Size Notes* measured about 7.42 inches by 3.13 inches (with few exceptions, such as the *Refunding Certificates* of 1879 of approximately 6.75 inches by 3.61 inches). Because *Large Size Notes* no longer circulate, they are sometimes called *Obsolete Currency*, which is confusing, since *Broken Bank Notes* are better known by the name *Obsolete Currency*, and *Broken Bank Notes* are often of a "large size" anyway. *Large Size Notes* of federal issue are usually collected by design type, sometimes by town or state for the *Nationals*, rarely by signatures or Serial Numbers (now that the *Large Size Notes* are getting more expensive). Here are the main types of *Large Size Notes*:

1.   *Demand Notes* — of 1861, the first issue of U.S. paper

UNITED STATES FRACTIONAL CURRENCY — Issue Data				
"ISSUE"	AUTHORIZATION DATES (per Act of U.S. Congress)	CIRCULATION RELEASE DATES	DENOMINATIONS	TOTAL FACE VALUE
First Issue	July 17, 1862	August 21, 1862 to May 27, 1863	5¢, 10¢, 25¢, 50¢ (the "Postage" Currency)	$20 million+
Second Issue	March 3, 1863	October 10, 1863 to February 23, 1867	5¢, 10¢, 25¢, 50¢	$23 million
Third Issue	June 30, 1864	December 5, 1864 to August 16, 1869	3¢, 5¢, 10¢, 25¢, 50¢	$86 million+
Fourth Issue	(As per 1863-1864 Acts)	July 14, 1869 to February 16, 1875	10¢, 15¢, 25¢, 50¢	$166 million+
Fifth Issue	(As per 1863-1864 Acts)	February 26, 1874 to February 15, 1876	10¢, 25¢, 50¢	almost $63 million

money "as we now understand it" (as these notes are sometime defined). Notes in $5, $10, and $20 denominations, all scarce, none cheap, rarely seen in high grades (EF or better). Also called *Greenbacks*. Issued to finance the U.S. government at the beginning of the Civil War.

2.   *Legal Tender Notes* (also called *United States Notes*) — $1 to $10,000 denominations, although the $5,000 and $10,000 issues have all been redeemed. Depending on the type, issued from the Civil War into the 20th century. Many varieties of denominations below $100 are common in worn grades (VG or worse!), but get into four-figure prices in UNC condition. Most collectors like a *Legal Tender Note* of each denomination; the three most popular types are probably: $1 (1869-1917) — with the head of George Washington and vignette "Columbus in Sight of Land"; the $5 (1869-1907) Andrew Jackson and "Pioneer Family" (nicknamed the *Woodchopper Note*); and the $10 Lewis and Clark and Bison note of 1901 (called the *Bison Note*).

3.   *Compound Interest Treasury Notes* — of 1864-1865, $10 through $1,000, rare in any grades.

4.   *Interest Bearing Notes* — of 1861-1865, all rare, issued in $10 to $5,000 denominations. Only the $10 and $20 are available to collectors at perhaps $2,000 or more each, for a circulated example.

5.   *Refunding Certificates* — of 1879, $10 denomination, two types, scarce to rare.

6.   *Silver Certificates* — issued 1878 into the 1920s, depending on the denomination. Issued $1 to $1,000, with the lower denominations being extremely popular and in constant demand by collectors and dealers, especially: the $1, $2, and $5 *Educational Notes* of 1896; the $1 *Black Eagle* of 1899 and the $5 *Indian Chief* note (*Running Antelope* of the Onepapa

tribe of Sioux Indians) of 1899. Besides being beautifully engraved and of American themes, these notes can be found in any grade, making them "starter" notes for collectors on a tight budget or "blue chip" investments for those with deep wallets ($1,000 and up per note, in better condition). Another famous *Silver Certificate* is the so-called *Tombstone Note* — the $10 issue of 1886-1908, showing Thomas A. Hendricks (U.S. Vice President in 1885; dying in office) framed by a tablet that is tombstone-shaped. Be patient when buying *Large Size Silver Certificates* — many dealers have them, so get nice-looking notes for your money, such as the $1 *"Martha" Silver Certificate* (portraying Martha Washington) of 1886-1891 — purchasable for less than $100 if well worn, $1,000 for GEM CU.

7.   *Treasury Notes* (also called *Coin Notes*) — issues of 1890-1891, in $1 to $1,000 denominations. Were redeemable in either gold or silver coin. Collected in all grades.

8.   *National Bank Notes* — issued 1863 to 1929 by National Banks under U.S. charter. Collected by type (for the most dramatic vignettes ever to grace U.S. currency), charter period, state, city, or bank. One of the most avidly sought *Large Size Note* collecting fields. Collected in low grade if the note is scarce. Of special interest and popularity with collectors is the so-called *Lazy Deuce Note*, the $2 *National Bank Note* of the First Charter Period, with an elongated horizontal numeral "2" on the face. According to Hickman, about 350,000 *National Bank Notes* may still exist.

National Bank Notes are summarized in Friedberg's and Krause's catalogs, but are listed in detail in the impressive *Standard Catalog of National Bank Notes* by Oakes and Hickman (see Bibliography for all three books).

9.   *Federal Reserve Bank Notes* — issued 1915 and 1918, in $1, $2, $5, $10, $20, and $50 denominations. The *Eagle and Flag* $1 note and the $2 *Battleship* note (with a 1914 U.S.

battleship pictured on the back) are sought by collectors for their type sets and are not as expensive as the high denominations. Not to be confused with *Large Size Federal Reserve Notes* (below).

10.   *Federal Reserve Notes* — issued from $5 to $100 notes as *Series* 1914; and $500 to $10,000 notes as *Series* 1918. Not to be confused with *Federal Reserve Bank Notes* or with *Small Size Federal Reserve Notes*. A neglected collecting area in the past, many of these *Large Size Federal Reserve Notes* are reasonably priced, at least in the lower denominations.

11.   *National Gold Bank Notes* — all are scarce to rare, and seldom seen in high grades (EF or better). Popular but costly ($1,000 up for a decent-looking worn example).

12.   *Gold Certificates* — The Fourth Issue of these notes is *Series* 1882, and this issue was the earliest made for general circulation. Once redeemable in gold, now they are still legal tender, and collected for their own sake. Popular issues are the $10 *Gold Certificates* of 1907 and 1922; the $20 *Series* 1905, 1906, and 1922 (with the 1905 $20 *Gold Certificate* nicknamed the *Technicolor* note for its handsome coloring; and priced much more steeply than its 1906/1922 cousins); and, for those who can afford them (perhaps heavily circulated), the $50, $100, and $500 *Large Size Gold Certificates*.

All U.S. government paper money of regular issue (not military currency, etc.) from 1861 to date is still worth face value (if at least half of it remains), so its price can never be less than that.

SMALL SIZE U.S. CURRENCY

From 1929 to date, the United States has issued *Small Size Notes* for its regular currency. These notes measure about 6.14 inches by 2.61 inches. About 1,200 major varieties of *Large Size*, and about 1,200 major varieties of *Small Size Notes* exist, so unless you're rich, you're not going to get all of them for your collection. But specialization is possible, and many collectors start (and stay?) with U.S. *Small Size Notes* because they're often cheaper and more readily available than comparable *Large Size Note* categories. Here are the *Small Size Notes*, listed by *Series* dates, as they are commonly collected and studied:

1.   *Legal Tender Notes* (also called *United States Notes*) — $1 (1928), $2 (1928, 1953, 1963 — the "Red Seals"), $5 (1928, 1953, 1963), and $100 (1966). Certain *Series* with suffix letters, such as the *Small Size* 1928-B "Star" (Replacement) $2 *Legal Tender Notes*, are rare and expensive, but just how expensive will require you to look them up in a standard catalog, such as the Krause or Friedberg books (Bibliography).

2.   *Silver Certificates* — $1 (1928, 1935, 1957), $5 (1934, 1953), and $10 (1934, 1953). The *Star (Replacement) Notes*, especially for some signature combinations, are worth ten times or more the price of a normal note. Common *Small Size Silver Certificates* are not scarce, as they are offered for sale by dealers everywhere, sometimes in CU "packs" of 100 notes at a time. *Silver Certificates* have Blue Seals. Collected for varieties.

3.   *National Bank Notes* — This very active *Small Size Note* category of U.S. currency has many collector specialists seeking both *Large Size* and *Small Size* examples of *Nationals* in their "geographical" specialty. Western states' *Nationals* tend to be scarce, with many seldom-seen issues from Alaska, Arizona, Hawaii, Idaho, Montana, Nevada, New Mexico, Utah, and Wyoming. At any currency show/bourse (Chapter 18), you can browse through dealer stocks of *National Currency*, often bundled by state. *National Bank Notes* of *Small Size* format are all *Series* 1929, with Brown Seals.

4.   *Federal Reserve Bank Notes* — scarcer, in general, than the straight *Federal Reserve Notes* (see below). The *Federal Reserve Bank Notes* in *Small Size* format are of *Series* 1929, with Brown Seals. Look up the cost of San Francisco District $5 *Federal Reserve Bank Notes* in *Small Size*.

5.   *Federal Reserve Notes* — issued in many series, 1928 to date, these are the only kind of paper money commonly found in circulation in the United States today, having replaced all others. "Star" (Replacement) Notes, Bureau production errors (Chapter 20), and unusual Serial Numbers are the three most popular areas in *Federal Reserve Note, Small Size* collecting at the present time, all with Green Seals.

"Fancy" Serial Numbers

Collectors and dealers pay a premium for unusual or "fancy" Serial Numbers on *Federal Reserve* and other notes. Here are examples of such numbers:

Low Number: A00000004A

Stutter Number: F38383838B

Radar Number (the digit sequence reads the same from either direction): J12344321C

Repeater (with four 2-digit or two 4-digit repeating groups): G45894589D

Ladder Number: B73747576E or D12345678B or B98765432A (also called Sequential Number)

50/50 Number: H44448888C

Same Digit Repeater: A66666666B

Mismatched Numbers (actually, a printing error of the "Third Print" stage of printing — the two sets of Serial Numbers on the same note have one or more digits different): C38275975B and C38275976B

People also collect consecutive numbered notes, i.e., several notes with their Serial Numbers in sequence, as you get them first from the bank's newly printed money supply.

6. *World War II Emergency Notes — Small Size* U.S. notes overprinted front and back with the word "HAWAII" for use there after the Japanese attack on Pearl Harbor: $1 *Silver Certificates* (1935-A); $5 and $20 *Federal Reserve Notes* (1934 and 1934-A each); and $10 *Federal Reserve Notes* (1934-A only); and all of these are found in "Star" (Replacement) Note versions at substantial premium over normal. Then there are the $1, $5, and $10 *Silver Certificates* with Yellow Seals made for use by U.S. military in Europe and North Africa.

7. *Gold Certificates* — $10, $20, $50, $100, $500, $1,000, $5,000, $10,000, and $100,000 *Small Size Notes,* various *Series* 1928, 1928-A, 1934, depending on the issue. All have Gold Seals. The $10 and $20 *Small Size Gold Certificates* are very popular among collectors of *Small Size Notes.* Called in by President Roosevelt as per the Gold Reserve Act of 1933, all U.S. *Gold Certificates* (both *Large* and *Small Size*) that have survived to today were held illegally (intentionally, or more probably, accidentally in cash hoards). On April 24, 1964, the Secretary of the Treasury, C. Douglas Dillon, made the ownership of *Gold Certificates* legal once again, although they are "just" legal tender, no longer redeemable in gold.

8. *Military Payment Certificates (MPCs)* — special notes used by American military personnel from 1946 to 1973. A popular collecting specialty lately (see Chapter 13). U.S. issues are nicely summarized in the *Standard Catalog of U.S. Paper Money* by Krause and Lemke; and explained in detail in *Military Payment Certificates* by Schwan (see Bibliography).

143. "General Francis Marion's Sweet Potato Dinner" vignette from the $5 *State of South Carolina* note of 1872, printed by the American Bank Note Company of New York City. Also used on a $10 *Confederate Note* of 1861. Marion, nicknamed the "Swamp Fox," was an American General in the Revolutionary War.

144. *Large Size* U.S. $5 *Legal Tender Note* of 1862. Statue of "Columbia" (on top of U.S. Capitol in Washington, DC) at left, Alexander Hamilton (the first U.S. Secretary of the Treasury, 1789-1795) at right. Author's photo, from the stock of Americana Stamp and Coin Company, Inc. of Tarzana, California.

145. *Large Size* U.S. *$2 Legal Tender Note*, Series 1880. Jefferson at left, U.S. Capitol building at center. Author's photo, from the stock of Americana Stamp and Coin Company, Inc. of Tarzana, California.

146. $5 *Confederate Note*, "Sixth Issue" (April 6, 1863), but overprinted with month of actual issue (FEBRUARY, 1864) at right. State Capitol building at Richmond, Virginia at center; C.G. Memminger, Confederate cabinet member, at lower right. Author's photo, from the stock of Americana Stamp and Coin Company, Inc. of Tarzana, California.

147. *Large Size* $5 U.S. *Silver Certificate*, Series 1886, Large Seal. Author's photo, from the stock of Americana Stamp and Coin Company, Inc. of Tarzana, California.

148. Reverse of $5 U.S. *Silver Certificate*, Series 1886 (from Photo 147), showing five contemporary U.S. *Silver Dollar* coins. Author's photo, from the stock of Americana Stamp and Coin Company, Inc. of Tarzana, California.

149. "History Instructing Youth" — detail from *Large Size* U.S. $1 *Silver Certificate*, Series 1896 (the $1 *Educational Note*), souvenir card impression. Designed by Will H. Low, engraved by Charles Schlecht.

150. "Science Presenting Steam and Electricity to Commerce and Manufacture." *Large Size* U.S. $2 *Silver Certificate*, Series 1896 (the $2 *Educational Note*), souvenir card impression.

151. *Large Size* U.S. $5 *Silver Certificate*, Series 1899, souvenir card impression. Portrait of the Sioux "Running Antelope," also called the "Indian Chief" or "Onepapa" or "Oncpapa" note.

152. The celebrated *Bison Note* — *Large Size* U.S. $10 *United States Note* (*Legal Tender Note*), Series 1901, souvenir card impression. American bison at center, explorers Meriwether Lewis (at left) and William Clark (at right).

153. *Large Size* U.S. $20 *Gold Certificate*, Series 1906. Author's photo, from the stock of Americana Stamp and Coin Company, Inc. of Tarzana, California.

154. *Large Size* U.S. $10 *Federal Reserve Note*, Series 1914. Portrait of Andrew Jackson. Author's photo, from the stock of Americana Stamp and Coin Company, Inc. of Tarzana, California.

155.   Reverse of U.S. $10 *Federal Reserve Note*, Series 1914, from Photo 154. Author's photo, from the stock of Americana Stamp and Coin Company, Inc. of Tarzana, California.

156.   Reverse of *Large Size* U.S. $2 *Federal Reserve Bank Note*, Series 1918, picturing the battleship *New York*, from souvenir card impression.

157.   *Small Size* U.S. $5 *Silver Certificate*, Series 1934D. This is a *Replacement Note*, whereby a "Star" replaces the Serial Number prefix letter. Lincoln's portrait on this and current $5 notes was engraved in 1869, and the original master die can still be used to prepare printing plates.

10

> "Riches that come to us with wings fly away on the slightest provocation. Our appreciation of the value of money is in proportion to the difficulty we experience in getting it."
>
> Colonel James J. Ayers
> California Gold Rush participant in 1849

Rare U.S. Notes

The above statement was written in 1896 by Ayers in his book, *Gold and Sunshine: Reminiscences of Early California*. Ayers came to California in 1849 and was a participant and eyewitness to much Gold Rush history. His "easy come, easy go" observations on the personal financial habits of people were as true in 1849 as they were in 1896, as indeed they still are today.

As a rule, rare paper money will always be rare, and may even get rarer, due to: (1) accidental loss to fire, flood, mold, vermin, etc.; (2) unrecovered theft; (3) attrition from natural aging and decay; (4) mishandling; and, in a social sense, (5) competition from other paper money collectors, museums, etc., to obtain, and possibly permanently keep, rare paper money specimens off the collecting market. Hoards of scarce notes are sometimes discovered, and the occasional rare note, long buried and forgotten in someone's collection, will unexpectedly surface and delight the collecting community (both those who can afford to buy the note, and those who can't afford to ignore startling new finds in the lore of paper money rarities, for scholarship value, if nothing else).

This chapter discusses some rare United States currency, of all eras, from Colonial times to the present. Or, perhaps we should title this chapter, "What I Would Buy if I Had Unlimited Money."

OLD AUCTION REALIZATIONS

Because widespread serious U.S. paper money collecting and investing has only been done since, say, the year 1960 or 1970 (depending on when we "old-time" collectors jumped in), it is astonishing to look at the auction prices that exceedingly scarce U.S. notes were bringing a few years before that.

The Grinnell Collection

The Albert A. Grinnell Collection of U.S. Paper Money (see the Anton book in Bibliography) was sold by Barney Bluestone of Syracuse, New York, in a series of auctions from November 25, 1944 through November 30, 1946.

Lot No. 23 of the November 25, 1944 sale was an UNCIRCULATED $500 1862 *Legal Tender Note* (signed by Chittenden and Spinner). It sold for only $680, not much over face value, against a pre-auction estimate of $750! This note is listed as Extremely Rare and is unpriced in any grade in the standard U.S. currency catalogs. And yet, here we have an UNCIRCULATED example of a very high denomination Civil War federal note, selling for only 36% above face value! If this note could be found today, it would sell for a strong five figure price.

Thirty-five lots of *National Gold Bank Notes of California* opened the second Grinnell sale on March 10, 1945, and most of these sold for less than $100 each! It is hard to find a decent-looking *National Gold Bank Note* today for less than $1,000, and AU examples bring hefty four-figure prices (or more). Several "CRISP UNCIRCULATED" $5 Silver Certificates of 1896 (the celebrated $5 *Educational Note*) sold in this same March 10, 1945 sale for $19.25, $31.50, and $30.00!

What we conclude, of course, is that paper money rarity was poorly appreciated a half century ago (or that "hobby" money was hard to come by at the end of World War II). Inflation since 1945 is partly involved, also.

TYPES OF RARITY

As Friedberg points out in *Paper Money of the United States* (see Bibliography), rarity is due either to condition or to design. A note may be common in worn condition, but a rarity in AU-UNC. A note may be of a rarely seen design, hence rare in any condition. Some collectors consider that "condition rarity" is a bit artificial, i.e., based on collector obsession with unusually nice condition for notes that are actually easily obtained in a slightly worn state. Nobody can deny that rarity of design is always desirable, if that design is necessary to complete a "type set." What would you rather have for the same amount of money invested — a dozen SUPERB GEM CRISP UNCIRCULATED notes of common designs, or a few VERY GOOD-FINE *California National Gold Bank Notes*? And when a note is rare both in design and in high grade condition, and in great demand as well, its market price is astronomical.

RARE AMERICAN COLONIAL NOTES

I wouldn't call any of the *Continental Currency* notes of the American Revolution extremely rare, but such cannot be said for many *Colonial* (individual state-issued) notes. All Connecticut notes before 1755 are rare. So are Delaware notes from 1729 to 1739, Georgia currency before 1755, Maryland before 1756, Massachusetts of 1750 or earlier, New Hampshire of 1763 or earlier, New Jersey 1709-1737, New York before 1758, North Carolina 1712-1735, Pennsylvania 1723-1749, Rhode Island 1766 or earlier (and some later ones), South Carolina 1762 or earlier, Vermont of 1781, and Virginia 1755-1771. Therefore, any of these rare dated *Colonial Currency* items must be immediately suspected of being a counterfeit to fool collectors. Buy rare *Colonial Currency* only from the most reputable sources, and, if it is truly rare, a note in GOOD condition or worse may be the only one that you'll ever see, so don't pass it up because it is worn. Price is another matter. For infrequently traded *Colonial Currency*, you must consult several experts (dealers and collectors) to know what a fair market price might be for a given note, as these extremely rare notes are unpriced in the standard catalogs. Is that torn, worn, taped-up scrap of thin 1726 cardboard really worth $20,000, just because somebody says it is? Get Newman's *The Early Paper Money of America* before buying any *Colonial Currency*, rare or otherwise. Then review the actual selling prices of rare *Colonial Currency* dealers (Chapter 17).

OBSOLETE CURRENCY
(U.S. BROKEN BANK NOTES)

While much of it is plentiful, there are many exceedingly rare genuine 19th century *Obsolete Notes* of private banks, state

banks, etc., but these tend to sell for less than federal issues of similar scarcity and condition. See Haxby's reference (Bibliography) before putting serious money into rare *Broken Bank Notes*, and check the retail and auction prices of these notes.

RARE LARGE SIZE U.S. CURRENCY

It seems sometimes every dealer will tell you that almost every note they have is "rare," but truly rare notes are those that you never, or hardly ever, see anywhere, even in museum displays. Here are some *Large Size Note* rarities of 1861-1929 federal issues, most with less than a few dozen examples extant:

1. *Demand Notes* of 1861 — none is common, and most of the $10 and $20 denominations are extremely rare.

2. *Legal Tender Notes* — anything $500 or up is quite rare.

3. *Compound Interest Treasury Notes* of 1864-1865 — all are rare, and the $50 and $100 denominations have been widely counterfeited.

4. *Interest Bearing Notes* of the Civil War — all are rare because most were redeemed for their accrued interest. If you want a challenge, try to find these notes with their interest coupons still attached — in or out of museums. Less than 20 known examples of most types.

5. *Refunding Certificates* of 1879 — only a couple of notes are known with the vertical format written reverse.

6. *Silver Certificates* — All the notes of *Series* 1878 and 1880 are rare, which is one reason all the collector and dealer attention gets focused on the later issues (another reason is that their vignettes are beautiful).

7. *Treasury Notes ("Coin" Notes)* — many are scarce, but of special interest are the so-called *Watermelon* $100 and $1,000 notes of 1890, named after the large green zeros on their backs. The *Watermelon* notes sell for strong five-figure prices in circulated condition; the $1,000 *Watermelon*, in AU, sold for $121,000 in a February 1989 Stack's auction in New York City.

8. *National Bank Notes* — many specific banks are rare or impossible to get, but you have to know which ones, and that means starting with Oakes and Hickman's reference, *Standard Catalog of National Bank Notes* (Bibliography), then closely watching dealer price lists and auction catalogs. If you never see it offered for sale, it could be very rare (or it could also be hoarded in quantity by fanatical hometown collectors!).

9. *National Gold Bank Notes of California* — all are scarce, and all are rare in high grade (EF or better) because they circulated heavily in California, and most were eventually redeemed for gold coin.

10. *Gold Certificates* — *Large Size* 19th century high denominations ($500 or above) are scarce to unknown.

U.S. FRACTIONAL CURRENCY

Certain printing varieties and signature combinations are rare, worth several thousand dollars per note and up, even circulated. Check the standard catalogs. UNCIRCULATED *Fractionals* sell at a substantial premium; don't overpay.

RARE SMALL SIZE U.S. CURRENCY

Considering that it was all issued since and including 1929, it may surprise collectors that any *Small Size* U.S. notes are rare, but rarities do exist (besides the natural scarcity of the large denominations [$500 and up] due to attrition and redemption).

A $10 *Yellow Seal Silver Certificate*, Series 1934, issued for U.S. troops in Europe and North Africa in World War II, is scarce enough in the "normal" Serial Numbers, but is a real rarity if a *Star (Replacement) Note*. Beware of altered Serial Numbers, or of an eradicated letter "A" from the relatively common *1934-A Series* note, Yellow Seal.

Many *Small Size* format of *National Bank Notes* are seldom, if ever, seen from certain small-town banks. Oakes and Hickman's book (see Bibliography) is the best reference on these. It is fun to visit a currency dealer at a shop or bourse, and browse through bundles of *Small Size Nationals*, searching for your favorite banks! Of course, other collectors have seen the same bundles, which means that you're not likely to find a major *National Bank Note* rarity priced at 25% over face! Many *National Bank Notes* from small banks are so rare that they command huge prices, even in ragged condition, because collectors know that they many never see such again.

"RARE" U.S. MILITARY PAYMENT CERTIFICATES

Replacement Notes are the real rarities in the various *Series* of U.S. *Military Payment Certificates (MPCs)*. Replacement *MPC Serial Numbers* have no suffix letter at the end of the string of numerals, and all are worth substantial premiums over the "normal" Serial Numbers (see Schwan's book and the *MPC* section of the Krause/Lemke catalog in the Bibliography). Beware of the suffix letter fraudulently removed to "create" an instant replacement *MPC*.

19TH CENTURY HAWAIIAN BANK NOTES

"Discovered" first by the Polynesians, then by British Captain James Cook in 1778 (who was killed by the natives), the Hawaiian Islands were an independent kingdom from 1795 to 1893, then a brief provisional government, then a republic until 1898 when the islands ceded themselves to the United States. Hawaii was a U.S. Territory from 1900 to U.S. statehood in 1959.

Although these islands were not yet U.S. property, the rare late 19th century bank notes of Hawaii can be considered by romantics to be monetary forerunners of American currency on these islands. All these notes were issued in English, printed by the American Bank Note Company of New York City, and denominated in dollars.

"Hawaiian Islands" Notes

The first issue of Hawaiian notes was the *Hawaiian Islands Certificates of Deposit* series of 1879 (undated, however). These are also known as the Hawaiian *Monarchy Notes* because they were authorized by the Kingdom. They circulated from 1879 to 1895, were redeemable in silver, and are all rare today. Issued in $10, $20, $50, $100 (and $500) designs (but the $500 note is unique, known only as a *proof*), these notes sell for about $4,000 to $6,000 each in circulated condition (as they're usually found), but about $1,500 to $2,000 each if "cut cancelled" or "punch cancelled." *Hawaiian Islands* notes are all "Series A."

Republic of Hawaii Notes

All dated 1895, these *Republic of Hawaii Gold Certificates of Deposit* ("Series B") appeared in $5, $10, $20, $50, and $100 denominations, and were redeemable in gold coin. All are rare and seldom seen.

Also dated 1895, the *Republic of Hawaii Silver Certificates of Deposit* ("Series C") were issued in $5, $10, $20, $50, and $100 values, and were redeemable in silver coin. The $5 and $10 notes sometimes are offered for sale at around $6,000 apiece, circulated, while the higher denominations are quite rare.

158. Souvenir card impression of *Bank of the State of Kansas* $3 note, circa 1861. Original genuine notes are very rare, printed by Danforth, Wright & Company of New York City, absorbed by the American Bank Note Company, which printed this card impression for a 1980 "joint issue" with *Bank Note Reporter* periodical.

159. Scarce *Large Size* $50 *Legal Tender Note* in pristine condition. From a recent auction catalog of Lyn F. Knight, Inc. of Overland Park, Kansas. Reproduced with company permission. ("Lot 1289. Fr. 152. $50. 1874. Only seven recorded CU. An incredible note. At least equal to the finest known. Even though this type occasionally shows up in circulated grade, ones like this are truly rare. It's my sincere pleasure to offer such a true rarity in such marvelous condition. Gem CU (20,000 - 25,000).")

CALIFORNIA

NATIONAL

GOLD BANK NOTES

Lot 125   San Jose Gold Bank, F
#2158. Fr. 1156 $20 GBN A
$20 Gold Bank Note and one of
bank. F/VF (5,000-7,500).

Lot 123   San Francisco Gold Bank, First NB,
#1741. Fr. 1136 $5 GBN An exceptional note
with bold detailed coins on the reverse and exceptional
color. VF/XF (3,500-4,500).

160. *California National Gold Bank Notes* offered for sale in a recent auction catalog of Lyn F. Knight, Inc. of Overland Park, Kansas. Reproduced with company permission.

Lot 126   Oakland Gold Bank, F
Fr. 1158 $20 GBN Original se
$20's are of the best you could a
great opportunity to get a great n
(6,000-8,000).

Lot 124   San Francisco Gold Bank, First NB,
#1741. Fr. 1136 $5 GBN An extraordinary
example of this ever popular type. All of the coins
on the reverse are super sharp. XF/AU
(6,000-9,000).

161.   Scarce *Large Size* $50 *Gold Certificate* in a recent auction catalog of Lyn F. Knight, Inc. of Overland Park, Kansas. Reproduced with company permission. ("Lot 1518. Fr. 1190. $50. 1882. A fantastic example of this very rare type. Jewels like this are what makes a collection shine. Certainly one of the finest known of this type. XF/AU (14,000 - 18,000).")

162.   U.S. $10 *Refunding Certificate* of 1879. Scarce in any condition. Author's photo, from the stock of Americana Stamp and Coin Company, Inc. of Tarzana, California.

163.   So-called *Watermelon Note* from the green color and round shape of the large zeros. The reverse of the *Large Size* $100 U.S. *Treasury Note* (also called *Coin Note*), Series 1890, souvenir card impression. Similar large zeros are on the $1000 *Treasury Note* of 1890.

164.   "Washington Resigning His Commission" — an engraved adaptation of John Trumbull's painting by the same name, on the reverse of *Large Size* $5000 U.S. *Federal Reserve Note*, Series 1918, souvenir card impression. Treasury Department records list thirteen of the original notes still outstanding.

165.   Souvenir card impression of *Republic of Hawaii* $20 *Silver Certificate of Deposit*, issued in 1896 per Act of 1895. Printed by the American Bank Note Company of New York City, the original note is rare and valuable.

166. U.S. *Fractional Currency Shield* (with gray background). Produced by the Treasury Department in 1866-1867 for sale to banks to use in comparing these genuine uniface designs with suspected counterfeits. From the collection of, and photo courtesy of, the Atwater Kent Museum, Philadelphia.

11

"Money speaks in a language all nations understand."
Aphra Behn (1640-1689)
Female English writer

Popular Foreign Notes

The first thing you need if you want to collect foreign notes (especially of several countries) is access to Albert Pick's *Standard Catalog of World Paper Money*, Volumes 1 and/or 2 (see Bibliography). It is available in most public libraries and for sale by any currency dealer. Dealers buy and sell foreign paper money by their "Pick" numbers. If you specialize in one country, you'll also need to know about specialized single country catalogs, for a rough idea of the relative scarcities and market values of notes, and for knowing the catalog numbers of major note types as they are commonly collected. Beginning collectors often say, "Why should I buy a book? I would rather buy notes." The answer, of course, is that by informing yourself about what types of notes are in existence and their approximate market values, you can plan a sensible collection and know if you are overpaying or getting a bargain.

Pick's Volume 2 is what most collectors of worldwide bank notes use in their hobby. Volume 2 lists "general issues" of world notes, i.e., those issued by central governments, the kinds of notes that are in general circulation today, the "mainstream" note designs of at least the 19th and 20th centuries of the world's note-issuing governments. Get Volume 2 if you're a beginner.

Pick's Volume 1 lists "specialized issues" of world paper money; for example: private banks, spurious and expired banks, foreign banks in a country, provincial issues, city issues, some emergency money, revolutionary issues, and a sampling of U.S. *Continental* and *State Currency*. Buy Volume 1 only after you've examined it to be sure that you will be collecting the notes listed in it. And remember, no currency catalog is necessarily complete or the last word on its listed notes. Pick's books are a good summary of worldwide currency; not all notes are listed in Pick!

WAYS TO COLLECT FOREIGN CURRENCY

Here are some popular ways to collect foreign paper money:

1. By country. Single country collection.

2. By region. Groups of countries, such as the British Isles, Central America, Southeast Asia.

3. By political persuasion. Examples: Communist notes, notes issued by democracies, kingdoms, etc.

4. Chronologically. Collecting by time periods. Examples: World War II notes, 19th century.

5. By ruler. Notes issued during the reign or incumbency of specific rulers or leaders, famous or infamous: Queen Elizabeth II, Adolf Hitler, Franklin Roosevelt.

6. Topically. Notes with pictured themes, such as castles, animals, boats. Called *thematic* collecting in Europe.

7. By signatories. Collecting notes by specific signers; usually done for a single country and "issue."

8. Obsolete and invalidated. Notes no longer legal tender.

9. Legal tender. Notes that are still used as money in the country of issue.

10. "Specimens." Notes overprinted or perforated cancelled with the word SPECIMEN or its equivalent, done for making note "samples" for non-monetary distribution.

11. Special use. For example: inflationary notes (Chapter 12), military currency and prison notes (Chapter 13), error notes (Chapter 20), etc., or any combination of the above categories.

THE AVAILABILITY OF FOREIGN CURRENCY

Current legal tender issues can be obtained from currency exchange businesses, from dealers, or directly from the countries themselves if you (or a friend) travel abroad. Obsolete (non-circulating) notes will usually be bought from dealers (see Chapters 15, 17, and 18). As governments rise and fall, older notes often are devalued and declared obsolete, making many of them cheap to buy for collectors. No country today backs its currency with gold or silver; so all paper money that you will ever get is completely worthless — except for its legal tender and/or collector value!

SOME POPULAR FOREIGN NOTES

Let's look at some foreign notes that are in demand by collectors. I haven't mentioned all of them. Neither does Pick!

AUSTRALIA — Any of the *Pounds/Shillings* notes of pre-1966 issue (when Australia converted to *Dollars/Cents*), especially in higher grade (EF or better). George VI issues in UNC.

AUSTRIA — Any scarce pre-World War II note in UNC condition.

BAHAMAS — Any *Pounds/Shillings* notes (pre-decimalization); i.e., before the 1966 conversion to *Dollars/Cents*. U.S. and Bahamas notes circulate interchangeably in the Bahamas.

BELGIAN CONGO — All Belgian Congo notes are in demand, especially in higher grades (EF or better). But don't overpay for one: research the market.

BELGIUM — Anything worth over $50 retail is a worthwhile Belgian note. High denominations (e.g., 500 or 1,000 *Francs* or more) are especially desirable for older (non-circulating) issues.

BRAZIL — Most Brazilian notes issued before the year 1943 and in higher grades (EF or better) are in demand. Many 19th century issues are unobtainable due to rarity, but some, such as the *American Bank Note Company* issues (printed in the U.S.A.) of the 1870s and 1880s, are of great beauty and reasonably priced in circulated grades. Of interest to specialists are the hand-signed notes (across the whole note's face) of the mid-20th century.

(BRITISH) EAST AFRICAN CURRENCY BOARD (EACB) — Provided a common currency from 1920 (1905, if we include the "Protectorate" notes) to 1964 in Aden, British Somaliland, Kenya, Tanganyika, Uganda, and Zanzibar until respective independence. EACB notes have a portrait of the British monarch, and pre-World War II notes are desirable in any grade.

BRITISH EAST CARIBBEAN TERRITORIES (BECT) — This was a "currency board" (common-currency issuing Colonial authority) started in 1950 to provide uniform currency for such places as Barbados, British Guiana, Trinidad, and Tobago. It changed its name to the East Caribbean Currency Authority (ECCA) in 1965, then to the East Caribbean Central Bank (ECCB) in 1985. The notes of George VI (series 1950-1951) and certain Elizabeth II notes are scarce in UNC.

BRITISH NORTH BORNEO COMPANY (BNBC) — Issued notes in North Borneo from 1895 to 1940. Anything, any condition.

BRITISH WEST AFRICA (WEST AFRICAN CURRENCY BOARD [WACB]) — Provided a common currency from 1907 (first paper notes dated 1916) to 1958 for: Gambia, Gold Coast (now Ghana), Nigeria, and Sierra Leone. After independence, these countries issued their own currencies. These WACB notes, picturing a palm tree, are desirable in any grade.

BURMA — Rangoon and "Provisional" notes before World War II, FINE or better condition.

CAMEROON — French (1922), German (1914), and Republic issues (1960s). EF or better.

CANADA — Anything with a large premium over face value. Get the Charlton reference catalogs on Canadian notes (see Bibliography). Popular collecting areas are: 19th century *private banks, Provincial* issues, *Dominion* notes 1870-1925 (all of which are still redeemable at face value), and certain *Bank of Canada* issues, 1935 on. Collectors of Queen Elizabeth II notes seek errors, replacement notes, and "hidden meaning" varieties (such as the "Devil's Face" issues of 1954, with a supposed face of the Devil enmeshed in Elizabeth's hair; these notes were withdrawn and redesigned due to public protest). All 1935 *Bank of Canada* notes in UNC are in demand, if you can afford them.

CHINA — With over 10,000 basic design types known, the rational collecting of Chinese notes requires some selectivity. The turbulent history of 20th century China is recorded in her paper money, issued by the Empire (to 1911), the Republic (1912-1949), and Nationalist and Communist governments (1949 to present, circulating in their respective "countries"). Four different governments issued notes in China from 1908 to 1949 (this, of course, doesn't count notes from private Chinese banks and foreign banks); Pick's *Standard Catalog of World Paper Money*, both volumes combined, devotes over 250 pages to the paper money of China. More specialized references exist for serious collectors of this country. (*Hell Notes*, by the way, are faked bank notes produced in China for traditional burning at a funeral to provide the deceased's soul with "money" in the afterlife. These notes are of no great value, since they aren't real money.)

COLUMBIA, ECUADOR, and other Latin American Countries — 19th century private/local bank notes are often beautifully engraved (by American Bank Note Company, etc.); they come in all price ranges and conditions. Get them AU-UNC if possible.

CUBA — 19th century issues (those under Spanish Colonial administration) are the most desirable, in higher grades (EF or better), or any grade for rare notes. The large Cuban ex-patriate population of Miami, Florida, as well as better-paid inhabitants on the island itself (as Cuba's economy improves), should provide a little demand for early Cuban notes as time goes on.

EGYPT — An ancient land with a recent paper money history (mostly since 1898). All *National Bank of Egypt* notes, 1898-1952, are in strong demand in higher grades (AU-UNC for "common" types, VF or better for scarce types).

ETHIOPIA — The *Bank of Abyssinia* notes (1915-1935) and the *Bank of Ethiopia* notes (1932-1935) are prime Ethiopian paper money, with their native animals and "exotic" look; any condition.

FALKLAND ISLANDS — Anything before Queen Elizabeth's reign; any condition.

FIJI — Anything before World War II, any condition. The same applies to many other former British island possessions.

FRANCE — The *Banque de France* has issued paper money since 1800, and any scarce obsolete note of it is in demand. I especially find attractive all French notes of the first half of the 20th century, with their casual portraits of peasants, allegorical personages, etc. The word *Franc* comes from *Francorum rex* (French King), an inscription on French coins in 1360 during the reign of John II. *Franc* is a monetary unit of Belgium, France, Luxembourg, Switzerland, and former possessions of Belgium and France (African colonies). To this day, nervous French citizens hoard gold, from centuries of disastrous experiences with paper money and war.

FRENCH POSSESSIONS — A popular collecting field. All scarce notes in high grade of former French possessions are sought, especially French Equatorial Africa, French Guiana, French Indo-China (Vietnam, Cambodia, and Laos), and French West Africa (including *Monetary Union* notes from 1955 for: Dahomey, Ivory Coast, Mali, Niger, Republic of Upper Volta, Senegal, and Togo). French Indo-Chinese notes circulated heavily, and types that are easy to find worn are much more expensive in UNC condition. The *Banque de l'Indochine* (Bank of Indo-China) was also a "currency board" of France and issued notes for French Somaliland, New Caledonia, New Hebrides, and Tahiti.

GERMANY — Empire issues began in 1874, and many regional bank notes circulated during the 19th and early 20th centuries — all avidly collected. Post-World War I *notgeld* is cheap and fun to collect. The word *Mark*, monetary unit of the German Empire, is derived from Middle English *marke*, from Old English *marc*, from Old Norse *mork* (a half pound of silver). Nazi Germany had the *Reichsmark*, and modern Germany (since 1948) has the *Deutsche Mark*. Communist East Germans issued their *Ost-Deutsche Marks* starting in 1948. Today, with national reunification, the West German *Deutsche Mark* is the sole national currency unit. Twentieth century German notes range from near worthless to very expensive in cost.

GERMAN POSSESSIONS — Of special interest are the early 20th century notes of German East Africa and German South West Africa, colonies lost at the end of World War I. Any scarce note in high grade is desirable, particularly the East African notes portraying Kaiser Wilhelm II in his military uniform.

GREAT BRITAIN — The older it is, and the better condition it is, the heavier the collector demand. All *Bank of England* notes, from the first ones in 1694, are still legal tender, so none is worth less than face value (with most of the note remaining). Twentieth century notes are often collected by Chief Cashier's signature (Signatories), for example, Kenneth Oswald Peppiatt was Chief Cashier from 1934 to 1949, so any notes bearing his printed signature must date from that time period. Some collectors find pre-Elizabeth II notes of the *Bank of England* boring because of their lack of dramatic vignettes. Other collectors appreciate the conservative and precise look of these notes, a reflection of the British heritage. The word *Pound* comes from the Latin *libra pondo* (a pound in weight) and has been used for the monetary units of Britain, Ireland, Scotland, Israel, etc., and all British possessions (including America, although Parliament would never give us our own coins and paper money). And, of course, don't forget the quaint World War I British *Treasury Notes* in better condition, if you can find and afford them.

GREECE — Many interesting 19th and 20th century notes, the most impressive-appearing being the *American Bank Note Company* larger denomination printings of 1863-1922, in any condition, portraying Georgios Stavros (the first governor of the *National Bank of Greece*) and wonderful allegorical and mythological personages.

GREENLAND — Anything, any condition; many moderately priced ($20 to $100 per note).

HONG KONG — Always in demand by collectors in Asia. Anything obsolete (not circulating), scarce, and higher grade (AU-UNC).

HUNGARY — Many notes, 1914 to date, have dreamy photograph-like portraits of people, real and allegorical — worth collecting for their appearance; in all price ranges, but try to get them VF or better. Mostly cheap, but nice-looking, are the *Hungarian Fund* patriotic notes issued in the United States by Lajos Kossuth to finance his Hungarian Revolution; all issued in 1852.

INDIA — Most popular are the British Colonial issues, 19th century to 1947 (the year of independence), high grade (EF to UNC).

IRAN — Anything scarce is in demand, preferably higher grade (EF to UNC). My favorites are the *Imperial Bank of Persia* notes (1890-1932), any condition; and, for their proletarian vignettes on their reverse sides, the Islamic Republic issues of the 1980s.

IRAQ — The first Iraqi notes were issued in 1931; the second group dated 1947 — all of these are prime Iraqi notes, in EF or better condition.

IRELAND — All of interest to collectors. First Irish notes were issued in the late 18th century. A number of private bank issues appeared in the 19th century. Irish (Republic) notes have been issued 1928 to date; Northern Ireland notes, 1929 to date, but some earlier bank overlap.

ISRAEL — Anything from 1955 and earlier is prime Israeli paper money, preferably UNC. Before 1927, the notes of Egypt and the Ottoman Empire circulated in Palestine. The Palestine Currency Board issued notes dated 1927 to 1945, and every one is in demand, any condition, still redeemable at face value in London, but of greater collector value. Palestine was proclaimed the State of Israel on May 14, 1948 and has issued Israeli government notes since — easily obtainable very worn; get them UNC if you can afford such.

ITALY — Pre-World War II Italian currency looks as classic as a statue in Rome. Where else would you expect to see paper money with a watermark of Leonardo da Vinci's head? My favorite Italian money is unfortunately also the most expensive: 19th century Italian States' notes with handsome portrait engravings (such as the *Banco di Napoli* issues). The word *Lira* (the monetary unit of Italy and Turkey) comes from the Latin *libra* (pound).

ITALIAN POSSESSIONS — If you can find them, the notes of Italian East Africa (1938-1939) and Italian Somaliland (1920-1951) are nice to have in any condition.

JAPAN — Unlike China's seemingly endless types, Japan has a much simpler paper money history. The elongated *Hansatsu* notes of the Japanese Finance Ministry, circa 1872, are reasonably priced for many issues; they were brought back as souvenir bookmarks by European visitors in the last century. My favorite Japanese notes of all time are the *Dai Nippon Teikoku Tsuyo Shihei* (Japanese Imperial Government-Paper Currency) of 1873, printed by the *Continental Bank Note Company* of the United States, with their intricately engraved vignettes (e.g., the 1 *Yen* note's reverse depicts a Japanese warrior scene). This issue isn't cheap, but then, beauty often has a price. All 20th century notes are collected by specialists, with something for every budget; try to get your notes UNC if possible. Japanese note designs tend to be subtle and understated, like the brushmarks on an old rice paper scroll; but scenes of Mount Fujiyama, pagodas, and shrines give this country's currency its distinctive charm. The word *Yen* (the Japanese monetary unit) is derived from the Chinese *yuan* (round — the shape of coins).

KOREA — Basically a 20th century paper money country, Korea was separated into a Communist North and a Republican South in August 1948, with separate currency emissions since then. Many Korean notes are cheap when circulated, but try to get them UNC for better value and collection appearance. Pre-World War II notes can get expensive.

LUXEMBOURG — As a small, stable country, nestled between the borders of Belgium, France, and Germany, the notes of early 20th century Luxembourg are popular with European collectors.

MEXICO — Popular collecting areas include: (1) the many *provincial bank issues*, often nicely engraved, of the 19th and early 20th centuries; (2) the *revolutionary issues* of 1910-1917 (many of which are cheap to buy today); and (3) *modern government issues*. Inflation and invalidation have reduced the spending power of much Mexican currency. When I was a little boy in the 1950s, the Mexican *Peso* was worth 12¢ U.S. Today you can get over 3,000 *Pesos* for a U.S. *Dollar* at currency exchange rates. This means that, for obsolete (non-circulating) Mexican notes, their only value is based on collector demand; you can't buy anything for one *Peso* anymore in Mexico. The word *Peso* comes from the Latin *pensum* (something weighed), and has been used as the monetary unit of Argentina, Colombia, Cuba, the Dominican Republic, Mexico, the Philippines, and Uruguay.

NETHERLANDS — Nineteenth century Dutch notes are rare, so, for practical purposes, all collectors seek only 20th century issues of the Netherlands. The portraits of people on Dutch notes have a self-absorbed, confident appearance, like the characters in a Rembrandt painting, as indeed one of them is (10 *Gulden* note of 1943-1944). All Netherlands notes are popularly collected, in all grades.

NETHERLANDS POSSESSIONS — Popularly collected notes, which can get expensive in higher grades (AU-UNC), are those of Netherlands Antilles, Netherlands Indies, and Netherlands New Guinea. Collect them within your budget, ideally VF or better condition.

NEW ZEALAND — The *Reverse Bank of New Zealand* has issued notes since 1934, and these are possible to assemble in a complete set, in lower circulated grades (e.g., VG-F), if necessary, for collectors on a tight budget. If you collect these notes by signatories, as some collectors do, it gets considerably more expensive, without putting new note "designs" into your collection. For those with deep wallets and classic tastes, the specialized bank issues of New Zealand of the late 19th and early 20th centuries are magnificent (see Pick's *Specialized Catalog* [Volume 1] in Bibliography). Present-day New Zealand banks have no security (such as bars or armed guards); and the regular police there don't carry guns.

NORWAY — One of the first countries to issue paper money (in 1695), 19th century Norwegian notes are expensive, so most collectors concentrate on 20th century issues, circulated and UNC.

PARAGUAY — Many interesting notes, 19th and 20th century, most are reasonably priced.

PERU — Lovely engravings on late 19th century notes (such as "Funeral of Atahualpa" and "Men Loading Llamas"), including the specialized bank issues. Peruvian notes are often encountered in inferior condition, due to circulation and (as Beresiner points out) the climate. Be patient and selective, and try for VF or better condition.

PHILIPPINES — Of special interest are the notes issued under United States administration, dated 1904 to 1944, because they look somewhat like U.S. paper money. The *Japanese Occupation* issues of World War II are mostly cheap and without collector demand. The many issues of *World War II Emergency* and *Guerrilla Currency* are of interest to specialists, and most are not expensive.

POLAND — Poland's currency is of two basic types: (1) war-related and (2) peace-time issues. The Kosciuszko *Treasury Notes* of 1794 have historical romance. Some collectors specialize in *German Occupation* issues of World War I or II. The "between the wars" Republic notes of 1919-1939 have many desirable types, for every collecting budget, but aim for higher grades (VF or better) if you can.

PORTUGAL — Many handsome late 19th and 20th century notes, with portraits of historical and allegorical personages. My favorite Portuguese notes are the circa 1900-1910 issues showing historical scenes (such as "Arrival of Cabral at Lisbon, 1500"). They are rather expensive, though.

PORTUGUESE POSSESSIONS — Popular notes are those of former Portuguese possessions, such as Portuguese Guinea, Portuguese India, and Angola under Portuguese administration.

PUERTO RICO — Mostly rare, circa 1900 notes, hard to find in high grades (EF or better). Buy them if you can afford them. Puerto Rico has used U.S. currency from 1922 to date. Presently a Commonwealth of the U.S., the inhabitants of the island are roughly divided into three stalemated groups: those seeking: (1) U.S. statehood, (2) national independence, or (3) to remain a U.S. Commonwealth without Congressional votes, etc.

RUSSIA — Czarist Empire notes are available, but most are rather expensive; the issues from 1898 through World War I are much cheaper. A lot of regional notes appeared in the 1918-1923 period (North Russia, Ukraine, Transcaucasia, Siberia, and Urals) and are collected by specialists. Union of Soviet Socialist Republics (U.S.S.R.) notes date from 1923; but some collectors still refer to U.S:S.R. issues as "Russian" money, although Russia was just one (but the most powerful) of the Soviet Republics. Of special interest are the *Transport Certificates* of 1924, denominated in gold rubles; the *State Bank Notes* of 1924-1932; and any notes with Lenin's portrait or bust (these latter being cheap). With the breakup of the U.S.S.R. as a political entity in 1991-1992, former U.S.S.R. republics (such as Latvia, Lithuania, Estonia, Ukraine, etc.) all made arrangements to start issuing their own indigenous currency (as many of them once did in the past) to replace the Soviet rubles.

SAUDI ARABIA — Before 1953, only foreign paper money (U.S., India, and neighboring Middle Eastern currencies) circulated in Saudi Arabia. My favorite Saudi notes are the *Saudi Arabian Monetary Agency's Pilgrim Receipts* (dated 1953-1956 Western calendar), issued in 1, 5, and 10 *Riyals* denominations, to facilitate pilgrims traveling to Mecca. These so-called *Pilgrim Receipts* were so well accepted by the local Saudi inhabitants that the government decided to issue its own general circulating currency, the first official Saudi Arabian paper money, which appeared in 1961 (Western calendar).

SCOTLAND — 19th century notes are great, if you can afford them, but most collectors concentrate on 20th century issues of the *Bank of Scotland, Royal Bank of Scotland*, and other banks. Collected in all grades.

SOUTH AFRICA — Anything scarce is in demand, in any condition.

SOUTHERN RHODESIA — Popular with specialists in African notes and/or former possessions of European countries. The same applies to Southwest Africa (look in "Pick" at the price quotes), Cape Verde, etc.

SPAIN — Since 1874, the *Banco de España* has enjoyed the sole note-issuing privilege in Spain (but private bank bonds around 1900 sometimes passed as money). For those with deep wallets, the 1874-1907 notes are choice material. I like the inexpensive *Banco de España* notes of the 1920s and 1930s, with their "pageant" engravings on the reverses ("St. Xavier baptizing Indians," "The Death of Lucretia," "Cortez burning his ships"). The Spanish Civil War issues of the 1930s are of historical interest.

SWEDEN — Anything, any condition, particularly if obsolete.

SWITZERLAND — The Congress of Vienna in 1815 guaranteed Switzerland's neutrality, a trait kept since then. In the last half of the 19th century, many private banks issued notes (including the *Concordat* issues), but these are virtually unobtainable. The *Schwizerische Nationalbank* (Swiss National Bank) opened its doors in 1905 and began issuing notes in 1907. The trilingual (French, German, Italian) Swiss notes are as charming as their prices are sobering; but then, what do we expect from the most stable country in Europe?

THAILAND — Something for every collecting budget; many note varieties for the specialist. Pre-1920 notes of the Siam government get expensive.

TIBET — Issued notes from 1912 to 1950, when the Chinese Communists seized control of the country. The *Srang* denominated notes of the 1940s are curious in that they were made by pasting two single-sided printings together (with a printed security legend on the back before pasting).

VIETNAM — Derived from French Indo-China, Vietnam issued notes starting in 1946 under Ho Chi Minh's Communist government. The French-installed puppet state from 1949 to 1954 was overthrown by Communist guerrillas, and the Geneva agreement of July 21, 1954 partitioned the country into North and South at the 17th parallel. Both North and South Vietnam have issued notes, many inexpensive for the collector and student of Vietnamese history. South Vietnam surrendered to the Communists on April 30, 1975, and since then there has been only Communist currency printed for the country.

WESTERN SAMOA — Considering their recent dates (1920-1961) and low-moderate denominations (10 *Shillings* to 5 *Pounds*), all *Territory of Western Samoa* notes (1920-1961) are scarce and costly in high grades (EF or better), which means, of course, that they are very desirable.

YUGOSLAVIA — My favorites are the notes with the beautiful vignettes, 1920s and 1930s (such as the unissued 1,000 *Dinara* note of September 6, 1939 with "Group of six people, three horses, and a lion").

MRI BANKERS' GUIDE TO FOREIGN CURRENCY

The *MRI Bankers' Guide to Foreign Currency* is a softbound guide to the world's current notes in circulation, along with "outmoded and redeemable notes." It has many black-and-white illustrations of notes — a recent issue had 182 pages. A new issue is published every quarter, and in it all current notes of all countries are listed and described. Of special interest to travelers and people doing business overseas are the "Currency import-export restrictions" listed for each country.

The *MRI Bankers' Guide to Foreign Currency* is used by: (1) banks and exchange bureaus to know which notes are valid, (2) travel agents to inform their customers, (3) central banks to know what the competition is doing, and (4) numismatists/currency collectors because of note descriptions and information about world monetary history.

The current issue of the *MRI Bankers' Guide* is available for $50, and yearly subscriptions are $200. However, for members of numismatic clubs (see Chapter 23), the cost is $40 for a single copy, and $120 for a yearly subscription.

MONETARY RESEARCH INTERNATIONAL
P.O. Box 3174
Houston, TX 77253
(713) 654-1900

CURRENCY IMPORT AND EXPORT RESTRICTIONS

While traveling overseas (for example), a currency collector or currency dealer may wish to buy, sell, exchange, and/or sort through small or large quantities of current foreign paper monies and bring collectible examples back into the United States. The *MRI Bankers' Guide to Foreign Currency* (see above) lists the latest currency import-export restrictions for every nation — very useful if you're planning a "currency-collecting" trip through several countries.

Mr. Arnoldo Efron, the Director of Monetary Research International in Houston, Texas (see above), has given me permission to reprint in this book a portion of the front matter section entitled, "Currency Import and Export Restrictions," which appears in his company's publication, *MRI Bankers' Guide to Foreign Currency*:

> *Many countries have rules and regulations about the amounts and kinds of local or foreign currency that travelers are allowed to take in or out. The rules published here [under each nation's listing in the MRI Bankers' Guide] are those which apply to foreign non-resident visitors ... Consulting Consulates, Embassies and Government Tourist Offices does not always produce reliable answers. The information given in this publication is obtained from sources considered to be reliable ...*
>
> *Common sense indicates that anyone travelling to a foreign country with a reasonable amount of cash should not have any problems, while carrying a large amount of currency may raise suspicions of drug dealing or tax evasion. A prudent traveller will not visit Iraq carrying Israeli currency, or vice versa.*

Some countries have peculiar laws, as making it illegal to bring in some currencies and not others ... Other countries require visitors to exchange a fixed amount of hard currency on arrival. Others yet make it illegal to hold any foreign currency at all. When you arrive you must exchange all of it into local money, when you leave you reconvert. If the bank is closed when you leave, you cannot reconvert, and since it is illegal to export their currency, you may as well give it away.

Do not think of tearing it up. Since money is one of the attributes of sovereignty, to destroy it is considered an insult to the nation.

Regarding "official" versus "parallel" rates of currency exchange (i.e., the legal versus the black market), the *MRI Bankers' Guide* goes on to say:

> *Where there are restrictions for the sale of hard currency, a parallel market develops, and a higher rate may be available. This parallel market may range from open and free to persecuted and dangerous.*

> *It must be stressed that exchanging money in the street entails high risks of being cheated, or getting into trouble with the authorities.*

For example, in the "old" Soviet Union, the KGB secret police used to entrap foreign visitors into black market currency exchanges on the street, then immediately arrest them. "Well, in our country," said Alice, still panting a little, "you'd generally get to somewhere else — if you ran very fast for a long time as we've been doing."

167.   10 *Kronen* note of Austria, 1915. "Boy" vignette. Issued by the *Oesterreichisch-Ungarische Bank* (Austro-Hungarian Bank). (Pick # 19)

168.   Cuban 5 *Pesos* note of *El Banco Español de la Isla de Cuba* (the Spanish Bank of the Island of Cuba), issued at Havana, 15 May, 1896. (Pick # 48b)

169.   Reverse of 5 *Pesos* Cuban note of 1896 (from Photo 168), overprinted with PLATA ("SILVER") in red. Printed by the American Bank Note Company of New York City. (Pick # 48b)

170.   Israeli 5 *Pounds* note of 1968. With engraving of physicist Albert Einstein at right, watermark of his head at left. (Pick # 34a)

171.   1 *Pound* note of Egypt, issued 1952-1960. Sculpture of the Pharaoh Tutankhamen at right, "Sphinx" watermark in circle at left. (Pick # 13)

172.   Reverse of 1 *Piastre* note of French Indochina, no date (but 1949, as per Lao text type). Indochina — comprising Cambodia (Kampuchea), Laos, and Vietnam — was a French colony from the late 19th century until 1954.

173.   100 *Dong* note of the Republic of Vietnam ("South" Vietnam), no date, but issued 1970 (five years before surrender to the Communist forces). (Pick # 26)

174.   Reverse of *Bank of England* £1 note, no date (but type issued 1978-1984). Replaced by £1 coin for circulation. Featuring Sir Isaac Newton, physical science genius. (Pick # 137b)

175.   Detail of reverse of Great Britain £1 note, type of 1978-1984 (from Photo 174) — backlighted to reveal watermark of Newton himself! (Pick # 137b)

176.   100 *Pesetas* note of Spain, dated 1965 (actually issued 1970). Portrait of Gustavo Adolfo Becquer, 19th century Spanish author and poet. (Pick # 150)

177.   Detail of "Imaginary Woman" on reverse of 100 *Pesetas* note of Spain (from Photo 176). (Pick # 150)

178.   *Central Bank of China* 20 *Customs Gold Units* (CGU) note — Shanghai, 1930 issue. To fool an inflation-weary public into believing that their money wasn't recently made, notes with the 1930 date were printed even into the 1940s. (Pick # 328)

179.   Netherlands 10 *Gulden* note of 1944, featuring "Man with Hat" by Rembrandt. Fountain pen graffiti on this note's reverse can be seen bleeding through the large numeral "0" at left. (Pick # 60)

180.   A base metal $1 coin has replaced the circulating $1 note in Canada — and soon, perhaps, in the United States as well? This note is the "modified" hair variety of the 1954 issued note. (Pick # 66B)

181.   Pair of 50 *Rubles* U.S.S.R. *State Bank Notes*. Profile of Lenin at left, watermark of Lenin at right. Top note issued in 1961, bottom note (with color changes) in 1991, during the last year of the Soviet Communist government.

12

"A slow sort of country!" said the Queen. "Now, *here*, you see,
it takes all the running *you* can do, to keep in the same place."
Lewis Carroll (1832-1898)
Through the Looking Glass

Foreign Inflationary Notes

Paper money owes its financial legitimacy to human trust. The real value of paper currency is based on public faith in its market exchange value as an acceptable form of circulating money.

More than anything else in our lives, paper money has recognized wealth only because many people have agreed to accept it "for all debts, public and private." When the citizens' trust in it evaporates, paper money quickly becomes worthless, fit only to stoke a fireplace or to insulate a wall against the winter cold or to grace the albums of paper money collectors who appreciate all paper currency, even notes that were born in a state of fiscal folly and governmental desperation.

This chapter discusses and illustrates some of the various *Inflationary Notes* (abnormally high denomination paper money, issued during times of hyperinflation in a country), with emphasis on foreign 20th century examples. Such notes are often inexpensive for collectors to buy today, as the circumstances that created them also made them in great quantities; and many have been invalidated (declared worthless by their issuing governments), and had little purchasing power when they were legal tender, anyway.

CHARACTERISTICS OF INFLATION

Inflation is the abnormal increase in the supply of circulating money, accompanied by rapid depreciation in that money's purchasing power and steep constant increases in wages and in the prices of goods and services. Inflation is also defined as: "too much money chasing too few goods."

During inflation, the currency in circulation increases faster than the rate of increase in goods and services, with an accompanied disorderly rise in prices, relative to a smaller rise in wages (the nation's wages are often "out of synchronization" with frequent price increases).

"Inflation Mentality"

Among the citizens who are living in an inflationary society, an "inflation mentality" develops — the universal expectation that the country's circulating money will continue to depreciate excessively in short time periods. When people believe that their money will be worth much less in "purchasing power" tomorrow than it is today, "everybody" spends their money as fast as they get it to take advantage of today's cheaper prices. Merchants raise prices to offset their constantly rising cost, including wages that are forced up higher and higher by labor unions and worker unrest.

Governments have expenses, too, and the skyrocketing escalation in the cost of government wages and purchases pressures the money-issuing authorities (usually the government itself) to print paper currency (in modern times) in ever larger quantities in anticipation of still greater increases in the prices of goods and services. Once this "inflation mentality" thoroughly infects the daily affairs of the inhabitants of a country, it is very difficult to stop. Nobody wants to be the first to restrain himself, for fear of losing ground to the more greedy members of the society, so everyone demands more and more money for whatever job they do, and the government prints it as its most expedient option.

INFLATION — AN ANCIENT PLAGUE

The Roman Emperor Nero (who ruled 54-68 A.D.) debased (lowered the "fineness," i.e., the percentage purity of) his silver coinage and reduced the weight of both gold and silver coins — a practice that was repeated by his successors. This deflated the circulating currency, which, when it was inevitably discovered by the public, generated a "corrective" kind of inflation to compensate for the less valuable money.

The world's first paper money, in China, was periodically overissued, causing serious inflation. The Mongols printed currency when they needed it, and paper money production was stopped about the year 1450 in the Ming Dynasty. The disastrous inflationary experiences of the Chinese people so discouraged them that the loss of public confidence in paper money resulted in no Chinese notes being issued for 400 years, from the mid-15th century to the middle of the 19th century. This explains the date gap from the Ming Dynasty note to the Ch'ing Dynasty notes (in 1853) in the Chinese Empire notes listed in Pick's *Catalog*, Volume 2.

Inflationary production of paper money characterized both the American Revolution in the late 1770s (with the *Continental Currency* notes worth 2¹/₂¢ on the dollar by 1780 — see Chapter 2), and the French Revolution of the early 1790s (with *assignats* [land-backed notes] manufactured recklessly until over 50 billion were produced by 1796).

HYPERINFLATION

Hyperinflation is runaway inflation with extreme monetary effects on the society, such as:

1.   Prices and wages increasing at triple-digit annual rates, or greater (going up 100% to 1,000% or more in one year).

2.   Frequent revaluations of paper money (removing zeros at the end of high denominations).

3.   Invalidations of currency (officially declaring "old" money worthless; i.e., replacing high denomination inflated currency with "new" low denomination units).

4.   Bizarre necessities in daily life, such as carrying a whole crate of paper money to buy a loaf of bread.

Hyperinflation in the Past

When precious metallic (gold and silver) coins still circulated along with paper money, the typical pattern of hyperinflationary paper money production was:

1.   War-induced economic stress causes:

2.   Panicking populations to remove all silver and gold coinage from circulation, which causes:

3.   Extreme circulating money shortage, making:

4.   Commerce stagnate because customers aren't spending, inducing:

5.   Governments to print tons of paper currency to finance their war effort or post-war reconstruction, which means:

6.   Hyperinflation: dizzying rises in prices due to pent-up consumer demand, ridiculously large and frequent salary increases, which causes:

7.   Ever more currency printing by the government. Governments printed paper money to finance their wars, with the intention of redeeming this money for gold and silver coin after the war was over. In effect, the war-beleaguered governments learned to finance their huge wartime expenses with paper money, then actually pay for the war costs at leisure by the orderly redemption of war-produced paper money with post-war acquired specie (gold and silver coin), provided, of course, that they won the war, and the paper currency-issuing government was still in existence.

Hyperinflationary Expediencies in Daily Life

Countries with hyperinflationary economies have "built-in" escalator clauses in legal contracts and financial documents. For example, loans are made at astronomical rates of interest, with written provisions for continuing the loan in "new" currency should the government revalue or invalidate the currency in which the loan was made. Because local currency may be so unpredictable, money agreements are sometimes denominated in a more stable foreign "hard" currency (such as U.S. *dollars* or Swiss *francs*), and converted to the equivalent local currency on the day that the money has to be transferred.

Inflation is the opposite of deflation (falling prices, falling wages, increasing purchasing power of the nation's standard monetary unit — even sometimes coincident with an associated general business slump like a recession or depression).

Hyperinflation can be cured, of course, with drastic compulsory measures, but there is always the risk that wage and price freezes, for instance, will only drive the economy "underground" where wages and prices still rise as people, desperate for necessities and luxuries, pay more to get more. In the end, inflation dies as it starts — with changes in public confidence and trust in the real value of their paper money.

SOME 20TH CENTURY HYPERINFLATIONARY CASES

If "history repeats itself," it does so dramatically in the financial lives of nations, in recurring episodes of paper money hyperinflation. The rest of this chapter explores 20th century hyperinflationary time periods in several countries that were textbook examples of the problem.

Germany: 1919-1924

When we think of disastrous inflation, we think of Germany during the years immediately after World War I. As one of the so-called Central Powers (Germany, Austria-Hungary, Bulgaria, and Turkey), Germany was on the losing side of the "war to end all wars." But when the Armistice was signed in November 1918 (the "stab in the back" according to Hitler's Nazi mythology), Germany's monetary battle was just beginning. True, the War had been expensive for Germany (although not as ruinous as World War II was for her); the "peace" was expensive also, because the most horrifying paper money inflation in Germany's history was starting.

Before World War I, the German *Mark* had an exchange rate of about 4.2 *Marks* = 1 U.S. *Dollar*. During 1919, a year after the War ended, 75 *Marks* equaled $1 U.S.; and by November 1923, a frightening total of 10 billion (10,000,000,000) *Marks* were worth $1 U.S.!

At the height of Germany's post-war hyperinflation, 30,000 employees worked in over 80 printing companies to make the country's paper money avalanche.

In September 1923, German stores closed for several hours every afternoon to re-price all their merchandise with newly inflated values! Some businesses found it more economical to sell paper money as waste paper to paper mills for recycling than to use it as money! The story was told of a tourist visiting a German cafe for a cup of coffee; when the waiter brought the customer the "bill," it was double the price of the coffee on the menu. In the time it took the man to drink his coffee, the restaurant's prices had risen 100%.

German factory workers were paid with crates of money on a daily basis, so rapidly was the *Mark* depreciating. People spent their money as fast as they could because prices were absolutely certain to rise the next day. Life savings were wiped out in days and weeks, and the German middle class was financially destroyed, paving the way psychologically for the demagogue Adolf Hitler, who, after some struggle (legal and illegal), was appointed Reich Chancellor by aging Weimar Republic President Paul von Hindenburg on January 30, 1933. Among other things, Chancellor Hitler promised to create a stable German currency that would be worth working for (and, eventually, dying for).

German *Notgeld*

Notgeld literally means "money of necessity" from the German roots *not* (necessity) and *geld* (money).

Notgeld, also sometimes defined as "emergency town money," was produced by almost 3,500 German towns and cities, to the tune of almost 50,000 different note types from 1914 to 1922. *Notgeld* were colorful little notes, often with designs picturing buildings, street scenes, cartoons, and historical people. German *notgeld* was eventually issued for sale to tourists and paper money collectors. Most *notgeld* notes were cheaply "surface-printed" (rather than engraved), and vast quantities are available today in CU condition at a few cents (current U.S. money) per note. Most German *notgeld* were issued in small denominations, of 1 *Mark* or less (25 *Pfennig*, 50 *Pfennig*, etc.).

A slightly inaccurate definition of *notgeld* is "German and Austrian emergency inflationary town money of the post-World War I years." *Notgeld* was issued to serve as small change because the people hoarded coins after the War; and, as such, it is not strictly inflationary money. Also, over 70 countries have issued *notgeld* in the 20th century, as listed in Coffing's *A Guide and Checklist of World Notgeld 1914-1947* (see Bibliography).

German Inflationary Notes

German Reichsbanknoten (Imperial Bank Notes, although issued at this time by the Weimar Republic's "democratic" government) up to 100 *Mark* denomination were issued in 1920; up to 50,000 *Mark* in 1922; and up to 100 Trillion *Mark* in 1923 and 1924. *Surcharges* (overprint changing the denomination) were sometimes placed on notes, rather than making entirely new notes of higher denominations. Most German inflationary paper money of this period is cheap to buy today (many less than $1 per note) because it still exits in large quantities. The highest denomination notes of 1923 and 1924 can get expensive, with hefty three- or four-figure prices (in current U.S. dollars) for CU examples.

Russia: 1918-1924

Russia, at the end of and after World War I, issued large quantities of paper *Rubles* to finance the war-caused expenses and post-war economic chaos. Paper money printed by foreign printers was put into circulation as fast as it arrived in Russia, without signatures, without serial numbers or dates, and (in some cases) without even cutting it. Workers were paid with slabs of sheets of uncut, unsigned, unnumbered notes!

Soviet notes, issued by Moscow, appeared in 1918, from 1 *Ruble* to 1,000,000 *Rubles* in denomination, many of them back-dated so that they would seem to have been issued in earlier years. The "Currency Reform" of 1921 made 1 "new" *Ruble* equal to 10,000 "old" *Rubles*.

In 1923, the Union of Soviet Socialist Republics (U.S.S.R.) was formally created, and issued inflationary notes up to 25,000 *Rubles* (dated 1923 but issued in 1924).

The Russian "Currency Reform" of 1923 made 1 "new" *Ruble* equal to 1,000,000 "old" *Rubles*! This is a common technique used by governments determined to appear to be combatting national inflation (whether or not they actually are): just exchange the old currency for new currency with fewer zeros at the end of the values.

The "Currency Reform" of 1924 made 1 Gold *Ruble* equal to 5,000 ("regular") *Rubles*, somewhat stabilizing the currency, if anything in post-1914 Russia can ever be honestly called "stable." Much Soviet paper money is cheap for collectors to buy, due to periodic devaluations and official invalidations; some notes bring three-figure prices, however (in current U.S. $).

Russian refugees fled to western democracies with their life savings in currency, only to learn the shocking truth when they arrived in their new homelands: that their inflationary money-stuffed suitcases contained worthless pieces of paper.

China: 1942-1949

Chinese Bank Notes in *Customs Gold Units* dated 1930 were issued to pay customs fees and were originally backed 60% with gold. This 1930 issue was printed into the 1940s, however, but backdated 1930 to make the notes seem as though they were issued then. So much paper money was printed in China in the 1930s and 1940s that many of these notes can be purchased today for less than $1 (U.S.) each from currency dealers.

Pre-World War II notes in denominations up to 250 *Customs Gold Units (CGU)* were issued. Notes dated 1947 range from 100 *CGU* to 10,000 *CGU*. In 1948, when notes valued at 250,000 *CGU* appeared, a currency reform introduced the *Gold Yuan* unit at the rate of 1 *Gold Yuan* equivalent to $3,000,000 in old notes (!), and these 1948 *Gold Yuan* notes were backdated 1945. In 1948, China issued a note for 180,000,000 *Yuan*, just before the Nationalist government fell to the Communists and had to abandon the capital. *Silver Yuan* notes denominated in dollars and cents, from 1 *Cent* to 10 *Dollars*, were issued in 1949, but the Communist victory on the mainland made the legitimacy of these notes moot.

Greece: 1941-1944

Greece was attacked by the World War II Axis powers of Italy (on October 27, 1940) and Germany (on April 6, 1941), precipitating a hyperinflation until Greece was liberated by the British late in 1944. The highest regularly issued Greek note before the war was 5,000 *Drachmai*. A note of 100,000 *Drachmai* appeared by January 1944; a 1,000,000 *Drachmai* note in June; 500,000,000 *Drachmai* in October; and a note of 100 billion *Drachmai* during the first week of November, just before liberation! The German occupation had destroyed the country, which was rebuilt with Allied assistance after the war. The Greek World War II regularly issued inflation notes are all cheap to buy because they are not scarce!

Hungary: 1945-1946

Hungary experienced heavy inflation during World War II, with the total currency in circulation quadrupling from 500 million *Pengo* in 1942 to 2 billion *Pengo* in 1944. The highest denomination pre-war note was 1,000 *Pengo*. A note for 10,000,000 *Pengo* appeared in November 1945. In March 1946, a new currency unit, the *Milpengo* (equal to 1,000,000 "old" *Pengo*), replaced the *Pengo*, but by June 1946, notes of 1 billion *Milpengo* (1 quadrillion "old" *Pengo*) were circulating — leading the government to created the *B.-Pengo* monetary unit (equal to 1 billion "old" *Pengo*) — but with a note of 1 billion *B.-Pengo* (a billion billion "old" *Pengo*, i.e., 1 quintillion "old" *Pengo*, or, if we write it out with zeros: 1,000,000,000,000,000,000 "old" *Pengo*!). Hungarian merchants used mechanical calculators to refigure prices, which were rising 100% to 1000% per day! The average citizen couldn't comprehend a piece of paper money with a denomination so big he couldn't pronounce it.

RECENT INFLATION: SINCE 1960

While almost every country has experienced some degree of inflation since 1960, many countries have fared worse than the average. (Artificially manipulated economies, such as the Communist regimes, may superficially seem noninflationary, when, in reality, their oppressive governments' wage/price controls merely push much domestic commerce "underground" — with illegal payments routinely made for goods and services unobtainable at state-fixed prices.) Any nation at war or in revolution is a prime candidate for currency inflation. Israel, much of Latin America, and recently independent (since 1950) ex-Colonial "third world" nations have had their share of high double digit, or even triple digit, annual inflation rates. Such unhealthy currency expansions have been common during the last half of the 20th century, and are more easily temporarily disguised than permanently solved by self-serving politicians who institute pseudo-beneficial "currency modifications." The inhabitants of countries like the United States or Switzerland, with less than 10% annual inflation rates, are lucky people.

182.   German inflationary 50 million *Mark* 1923 *Reichsbanknote*. (Pick # 98) A note for 100 trillion *Mark* was issued shortly after this one!

183.   Hungarian inflationary note dated June 3, 1946 — for the amount of 1 Milliárd *Milpengo* (i.e., a billion million *Pengo* = 1 quadrillion "old" *Pengo*!). (Pick # 137)

184.   500,000 *Gold Yuan* note of the *Central Bank of China*, 1949. (Pick # 423)

185.   Reverse of Chinese inflationary note from Photo 184. Denominations in the millions of *Yuan* were circulating at this time (1949) in China. (Pick # 423)

186.   500,000 *Pesos* note of Argentina, no date (but actually 1980). Vignette entitled, "Founding of Buenos Aires." (Pick # 309)

187.   The effects of hyperinflation are seen on this reverse side of this Bolivian 50,000 *Pesos Bolivianos* note of 1984, which has been revalued by black surcharge at right, to 5 *Centavos de Boliviano*! No date on the surcharge, but 1987. When the *Boliviano* unit was introduced, 1 *Boliviano* equaled 1 million "old" *Pesos Bolivianos*, and 1 *Centavo de Boliviano* therefore equaled 10,000 "old" *Pesos Bolivianos*! (Pick # 196) It is as though $10,000 American currency was suddenly equal to 1 American cent, by fiscal analogy.

13

"Can anybody remember when the times were not hard and
money not scarce?"
Ralph Waldo Emerson (1803-1882)

War Notes, "Distress" Notes, and Money of Necessity

Wars and other times of great adversity and civil strife paradoxically bring out the best and the worst traits of human nature. The 20th century alone, if we choose not to go back further, has provided us with numerous embarrassing examples of deliberately inflicted mass suffering and atrocities, of which we have ample evidence even in our paper money collections. But people, being resilient and innovative in the most stressful situations, manage to survive and carry out their daily tasks under seemingly intolerable circumstances, including such mundane endeavors as making and using emergency currencies.

This chapter discusses military currency, including siege notes, invasion and occupation money, canteen money, partisan and propaganda notes, and prisoner-of-war notes. Concentration camp notes, revolutionary government notes, and civilian prison notes are mentioned, as well as non-war civilian issues such as *notgeld*, bisected notes, and black market currency dealings. Perhaps we should subtitle this chapter, "And You Think You've Got Problems!"

SIEGE NOTES

Siege notes are emergency paper money issued by either the defenders (usually) or the attackers of a town and/or military garrison that has been isolated from material contact with the rest of the country. The collector appeal of siege notes is based on their (1) primitive manufacture, (2) historical associations, (3) simple, clean designs, (4) scarcity, and (5) romance.

Because siege notes circulated within a very small localized population, and did not last very long due to the lifting of the siege, some authorities question whether we should consider them true examples of paper money proper — or merely "paper coins" or "local scrip." I like to classify siege notes as paper money, because they looked like money and functioned as money and were authorized by the only available "government" at the time.

Siege notes were supposedly used at the sieges of Alhambra (1483) and Grenada (1490), but none exist today. *Mainz (Germany) Siege Notes* were issued in 1793 by French invaders who were themselves besieged by the Prussians. *Mainz Siege Notes* are denominated in French *Sous* and *Livres*, and for $100 or $200 you can buy a presentable circulated example. *Lyons* (France) *Siege Notes* of 1793 (undated, however) were issued by Royalists who were besieged by the Republicans for 60 days; all are uniface notes, and are of four main types, by denomination; $200 should buy you a worn and creased specimen.

Colburg, Prussia *Siege Notes* of 1807 are somewhat cheaper to buy today ($100 or so will buy you an intact note). Colburg was a Prussian fortress that fell under siege by Napoleon's troops and naval blockade. *Colburg Siege Notes* were handwritten on cardboard, in *Groschen* units. Collectors with liberal definitions of "siege" sometimes say that the *assignats* of French-occupied Spain are siege notes. France ruled Spain from 1808 to 1814, during which some *Assignado Imperial* notes were issued in *Pesetas*.

In Italy, *Mantova Siege Notes* were issued in 1796 when the Austrians were besieged by the French! The Italian towns of Zara (in 1813) and Palmanova (1814) both issued siege notes for their French forces besieged by Austrians. And in 1848, the Italians at Osoppo and Palmanova issued siege notes when they were attacked by the Austrians. You will need $200 or more to get a nice-looking Italian siege note, although ragged condition costs less.

Khartoum (Sudan) Siege Notes

The *Khartoum Siege Notes* are popular with collectors. Issued in 1884 by General Charles George Gordon, whose British forces were besieged by the revolting Mahdi at Khartoum in the Sudan, these notes were denominated in monetary units of 1 to 5,000 *Piastres*, and one note type of 50 Egyptian *Pounds*. Gordon himself hand-signed many of these notes, but most bore his hectographic (printed) signature. Khartoum captured the patriotic fancy of Britons at home, and the city was cut off for almost a year before the Mahdi successfully overran it and killed Gordon on January 26, 1885. Most of the *Khartoum Siege Notes* were destroyed, but those that survive can be purchased for strong three-figure prices and up, depending on the scarcity and condition of the specific note type. Beware of counterfeits.

Mafeking Siege Notes

During the Boer War, the Boers laid siege to Mafeking in South Africa late in 1899. The British garrison at Mafeking was commanded by Col. Robert S.S. Baden-Powell (who later founded the Boy Scouts and Girl Guides). From January to March 1900, Baden-Powell issued *Mafeking Siege Notes*, in several designs, in 1 *Shilling* through 1 *Pound* values. Some of these notes have an embossed Bechuanaland Protectorate revenue "stamp." The 1, 2, and 3 *Shillings* notes are printed on notebook paper, and $100 or so will buy you a worn specimen today. Baden-Powell personally designed the £1 note, which will cost you a stiff three-figure price today, if you can find one in nice circulated condition. I think that the 10 *Shillings Mafeking Siege Notes* are the most charming, with their "woodcut-appearing" vignettes of a man with a cannon and a man with firearms; priced at $100 and up for a presentable note. Beware of counterfeits.

RUSSIAN POSTAGE STAMP CURRENCY

So-called *Postage Stamp Currency* (not to be confused with U.S. *Postage Currency Fractional Notes*, for example) was issued in small denominations (*Kopeks*) by the Russian Czarist government in 1915-1917, and by the Provisional Government in 1917, consisting of Russian postage stamps printed on thin cardboard for use as currency to alleviate small change shortages in World War I. Some of this *Postage Stamp Currency*, printed in sheets of 36 "subjects" (individual notes), presumably circulated intact as an entire sheet worth the aggregate face value, as a number of these sheets, folded and soiled, have survived.

The celebrated French Canadian *Playing Card Money* was created in 1685 by Jacques de Meulles for his troops at Québec, because the government in Paris didn't send him coins to pay his troops. Fearing impending mutiny, de Meulles improvised by handwriting dates, denominations, and his signature on the blank reverses of playing cards. No extant examples of this first issue of French Canadian *Playing Card Money* exist, since they were destroyed (per order of the King of France) as they were redeemed. Later issues of this *Playing Card Money* have survived, but all are very rare, and most are in museums. This "money" was actually a form of emergency military currency, and was issued from 1685 to 1719, as needed. This *Playing Card Money*, the most classical of Canadian paper money, was replaced by official cardboard notes (scarce items themselves) in 1729.

MEXICAN REVOLUTIONARY NOTES (1913-1917)

When Father Miguel Hidalgo led his march on Mexico City on September 16, 1810, he started a "Revolution" that basically continued over a century, until 1917 when a stable constitution and congress were established. The Revolution of 1910-1917 was financed by printing prolific amounts of *Constitutionalist Paper Money* (the so-called *Mexican Revolutionary Notes*) from 1913-1917, which, according to Gresham's Law, drove the more trusted Mexican bank notes out of circulation (to be hoarded or redeemed). Many counterfeits of the often crudely printed *Revolutionary Currency* appeared, which contributed to the public's nervousness with the new money from upstart authorities. Pick's Volume 1 ("Specialized Issues") and *Mexican Paper Money* by Douglas et al. (Bibliography) list the Mexican Revolutionary issues, including the following.

"Villa's Bed Sheets" (1913)

The *Tesoreria General del Estado* (General State Treasury) notes of Chihuahua, dated 10 December, 1913, were created by General Francisco "Pancho" Villa to pay his Mexican Revolutionary troops. These simply designed notes are known as *Sábanas de Villa (Villa's Bed Sheets)*, and, while there are some scarce varieties, many are inexpensive (less than $10) to buy today in UNC condition. Rich with overprints and historical significance in the fiscal turmoil of Revolutionary Mexico, *Villa's Bed Sheets* are enjoyed by specialists today. "Pancho" Villa, the top Revolutionary Commander in northern Mexico, unintentionally contributed to the inflation of the time by placing large quantities of his notes into circulation.

SPANISH CIVIL WAR NOTES (1936-1937)

Over a million people died in the Spanish Civil War of 1936-1939, fought between the liberal Republican Loyalists and the conservative Nationalists. Both sides issued paper money during the Civil War, and many of these notes are reasonably priced today. Francisco Franco, the Fascist winner of the Civil War, was supported by Hitler and Mussolini. Franco came to power in the spring of 1939, less than six months before Hitler's shock troops smashed into Poland and officially started World War II (on September 1, 1939).

GERMAN AND AUSTRIAN NOTGELD (1919-1923)

Notgeld literally means "money of necessity" in German, and usually (in collector talk) refers to the German and Austrian emergency town money of 1919-1923. *Notgeld* was originally issued during World War I by German cities to serve as small change when coinage disappeared from circulation.

Soon, cities were issuing *notgeld* for sale to paper money collectors, some notes being printed on leather, linen, and silk, as well as on paper and cardboard. *Notgeld* depreciated in value, along with federal government currency, in Germany and Austria in the early 1920s. There are scarce *notgeld* types from this period, but many are cheap to buy today, with dealers often advertising bulk lots of "all different *notgeld*" notes for sale (per 50, per 100 different, etc.). German *notgeld* is in *Mark* and *Pfennig* units; Austrian *notgeld* is in *Heller* units.

BISECTED NOTES

There are two "types" (purposes) of *Bisected Notes* — so-called *Halved Notes* and *Cut Notes*.

Halved Notes

Halved Notes are paper money that was cut in half (usually a central vertical cut), with each half then transported separately between banks, to guard against loss. The second half, bearing the same Serial Number, of course, as the first half, was shipped upon receiving word that the first half had safely arrived. If either half was lost in transit, the entire note, identifiable by the same Serial Numbers on each half, was declared invalid, with no loss to anybody. These *Halved Notes* were commonly sent in the 19th century, before paper and electronic transfer of funds became more reliable.

A *Halved Note* is a type of *Bisected Note* and should not be confused with *Cut Note*.

Cut Notes

Cut Notes are officially bisected (or quartered, etc.) notes, with each piece used fractionally, often with surcharges (value change overprints) declaring their new denominations, and issued during times of currency or coin shortage. *Cut Notes* were issued, for example, in the Ottoman Empire in World War I, Greece in the 1920s, Colombia in 1944, and Finland in 1946.

A *Cut Note* is a type of *Bisected Note*, and should not be confused with a *Halved Note* (see above). However, all three terms are sometimes used synonymously.

MILITARY CURRENCY

Military currency proper includes:

1. *Invasion Notes* — for use by troops alone.

2. *Occupation Notes* — "liberation money" for use by all the people of an occupied country.

3. *Partisan Notes* — used by resistance forces fighting the invaders of their country.

4. *Propaganda Notes* — issued not for money but for political influence in demoralizing the enemy.

5. *Armed Forces Notes* — for use by troops in peacetime as well as war.

Sometimes an invading country's army brings in its own regular national currency; for example, German currency was used in Austria after the *Anschluss* of 1938.

Military Currency "Overprints"

Overprints often distinguish military currency from its civilian counterpart. For example, the *Gallipoli Overprints* used in Turkey during World War I are British *Treasury Notes* of 10 *Shillings* and £1 with "Piastres silver 60" and "Piastres silver 120" (in translation) overprinted on those two notes, respectively (the high value is scarce). These *Gallipoli Overprints* are also called the *Dardanelles Campaign Overprints* and were overprinted on May 21, 1915 and sent for use of the British Military Expeditionary Forces.

Puppet Banks

Sometimes an occupying military force will set up its own banks, but with "dummy" indigenous appearances, so that these banks seem to have the support of the native occupied peoples. Such is the case with the so-called "Japanese Puppet Banks," which issued notes in China after the Japanese occupation of 1938. The two best known of these Japanese Puppet Banks were the Federal Reserve Bank of China (established 1938) and the Central Reserve Bank of China (established 1941).

Military Currency "Collecting Periods"

Collectors recognize four major collecting periods of worldwide military currency:

1. Pre-World War I — Boer War notes, Russo-Japanese War notes, etc.

2. World War I — French and German issues are the most popular.

3. World War II — various Allied and Axis notes.

4. Post-World War II — the vast amounts of military currencies since 1945, issued by the many nations that maintain large standing armies.

WORLD WAR II OCCUPATION NOTES

Occupation notes, for use in occupied territories, were issued by the principals in World War II: Great Britain, France,

Germany, Italy, Japan, the U.S.A., and the U.S.S.R. For example, Germany issued *Occupation Notes* for Poland, Rumania, and Russia.

Japanese Invasion Money (JIM), of World War II, was issued by the Japanese invaders in their occupied countries of Burma, Malaya, Oceania, the Philippines, and Sumatra. The United States counterfeited some of this *Japanese Invasion Money* to disrupt the local economies of Japanese occupied lands. *Japanese Invasion Money* was prepared for the invasion of Hawaii and the United States, but it was never used because the invasion never commenced. The endless quantities of *Japanese Invasion Money* for use in the Philippines is still so common today, half a century after the war, that it is often given away free as a promotion by currency dealers.

"ARMED FORCES NOTES" OF WORLD WAR II

"Armed Forces Notes" of World War II include the following, issued for use by the troops themselves:

1. Britain — British Armed Forces Special Vouchers.

2. Germany — Auxiliary Payment Certificates and Reckoning Notes. The Auxiliary Payment Certificates were a military currency used by German forces at their canteens. The *Verrechnungsschein*, special Wehrmacht notes dated 15 September, 1944 but released in January 1945, were issued to German soldiers, who exchanged them for local money when they arrived on duty in occupied territories.

3. Italy — the scarcest and most expensive to buy today, of the Axis military currencies.

4. Japan — the so-called Bird and Dragon Notes. Japan has the cheapest of the Axis military currencies for collectors to buy today.

5. United States — Allied Military Currency (AMC Notes), issued for each country occupied by U.S. troops.

U.S. WORLD WAR II EMERGENCY NOTES

After the Japanese attack on the U.S. Naval Fleet at Pearl Harbor, Hawaii on December 7, 1941, it was feared that Japan might invade and occupy the islands, and confiscate millions of dollars in U.S. currency to finance the Japanese war effort by "use" overseas (because U.S. currency was accepted around the world).

So, in the summer of 1942, all normal U.S. paper money that could be located in Hawaii was exchanged for special $1, $5, $10, and $20 U.S. *Small Size Notes* with brown Treasury Seals, brown Serial Numbers, and black *Overprints* of the word HAWAII on the front and back of each note. These *Hawaiian Overprints* were the only legal tender paper money in Hawaii until restrictions were lifted in October 1944, and these overprinted notes released into general circulation. If

Japan had occupied the islands, all the Hawaiian overprinted currency would have been declared invalid by the U.S. government in Washington, DC, rendering it worthless in world commerce.

Similarly, a group of $1, $5, and $10 U.S. *Silver Certificates* was made with yellow Treasury Seals, for use by U.S. troops in the invasion of North Africa and Sicily. If large amounts of this currency were captured by the Germans, it would have been invalidated.

PHILIPPINE VICTORY OVERPRINTS

The *Victory overprints* on Philippine notes, at the end of World War II, are sometimes collected in World War II currency collections. Issued in 1 to 500 *Pesos*, these notes are a bit scarce in UNC condition for the higher denominations.

NAZI COUNTERFEITS OF BRITISH NOTES

High priority, in serious warfare between nations, is disruption of the enemy country's economy. In many wars of the last couple of centuries, counterfeits have been authorized for manufacture and distribution in enemy countries — in hopes of both inflating the currency supply and undermining public confidence in their currency (when people find out that much of it is counterfeit).

In World War II, under the code name "Operation Bernhard," the Nazis coerced concentration camp inmates who were skilled engravers to produce counterfeit *Bank of England* £5, £10, £20, and £50 notes, but they were never distributed in England where they were intended for economic disruption. Often called the *Nazi Forgeries*, these notes are illegal to possess today in Britain, where the Bank of England confiscates any that turn up. These counterfeits are very well done but not quite "perfect."

INTERNMENT CAMP NOTES

There are four main types of Internment Camp Notes:

1. Military prisoner-of-war camps — for enemy prisoners.

2. Concentration camps — for political prisoners and persecuted minority ethnic groups.

3. Labor camps — for forced labor workers.

4. Displaced persons camps — for refugees.

Reasons for Collecting "Camp Notes"

Why do we collect the paper money used in places of great human tragedy? For the same reasons that museums collect weapons of war or that scholars scrutinize the archives of dictators and the actions of police states (in which these camps are often located) — because those who refuse to learn from history are condemned to repeat it.

We do not collect Internment Camp Notes to honor the people who created them. We collect these notes because they are a part of human and paper money history. And, like all paper money, Camp Notes teach us about the people and history that produced them. Internment Camp Notes are preserved and studied for much the same purposes that mementoes and souvenirs from traumatic events in our personal lives are kept and occasionally reexamined — not to chain us mentally to tragic times long gone, but to remind us sometimes of where we once were ... and of how easily, with a few changes, we could be there again.

Prisoner-of-War Camp Notes

Military prisoners taken during warfare are often confined to prisoner-of-war (POW) camps, either near the theater of conflict, or somewhere in the "capturing" nation. Such camps may sell incidentals (cigarettes, toothpaste, etc.) to these prisoners, who need "money" to purchase them from the camp canteen. Hence, the issuance of Prisoner-of-War Camp Notes, which are worthless outside of the camp in case a prisoner escapes with them. POW Camp Money replaces the need for barter at the camp canteen, and is mandated by the Geneva Conventions of 1929 and 1949 (which include guidelines for POW inmate pay scales).

POW Camp Money is often credited to a prisoner's personal "account" in the camp finance office, from which can be drawn spendable sums in amounts specified by camp regulations. In some camps, prisoners have been forced to pay for their own food and other necessities with their POW Camp Money, and, as this money is often given as a reward for good behavior, the prisoner has an economic incentive to obey camp rules.

Currency historians have recorded POW Camp Notes from the Seven Years' War of 1756-1763 (Austrian and Prussian issues), Napoleonic Wars, American Civil War, Franco-Prussian War of 1870-1871, Boer War of 1899-1902 (*not* the *Siege Notes*), World War I (including Belgium, Britain, France, Italy, Netherlands, and U.S.A.), and World War II (including Britain, Germany, and U.S.A.). Some of these notes are cheap, some expensive.

Concentration Camp Notes

A concentration camp is a prison camp for political prisoners (prisoners of conscience) and persecuted minority ethnic groups. POWs and actual criminal prisoners may also be confined to a concentration camp, but that is not the primary purpose of the camp. While people have been incarcerated and tortured for centuries, Nazi Germany, during the 1930s, created the horrors that we now associate with the term concentration camp — a prison for the systematic abuse and destruction of human beings.

There were two kinds of concentration camps in Nazi Germany: extermination camps and work camps. Inmate currency is scarcer from extermination camps because most inmates died before they had a chance to use much money. Auschwitz, in occupied Poland, was such an extermination camp, and inmate notes from there are scarce, despite the fact that about 3 million people were killed there.

German Concentration Camp Money was of two general categories: Inmate Money and Guards' Money:

1.   Inmate Money was given to camp internees upon arrival, in exchange for their German (or other) currency, which was confiscated by the Nazi authorities. Examples of Inmate Money are the notes used in the Jewish ghettos of *Theresienstadt* (in Czechoslovakia) and *Litzmanstadt* (in Poland). The *Theresienstadt* notes are the cheaper ones, and the complete set of seven different colored denominations pictures "Moses with the Ten Commandments."

This "Ghetto Scrip" was not well accepted by the Ghetto inhabitants, due to its trivial purchasing power, and it eventually was reduced to use as "currency" in gambling games.

Inmate Notes used in German concentration camps such as Dachau (in a Munich suburb), or Ravensbruck (a concentration camp for women), often have the words *Konzentrationslager* (concentration camp) and *Prämienschein* (premium notes) in the legend, along with the camp name. *Prämienschein* were issued under "Service Regulations for the Granting of Favors to Inmates," per the May 15, 1943 authorization by the concentration camp SS officials in Berlin. *Prämienschein* were given to inmates for good behavior, for use in the camp canteens. These notes sell for several hundred dollars each today, depending on the camp and the condition.

2.   Guards' Money was used by Nazi SS (*Schutzstaffel* — the "protective rank," the special police of the Nazi party) guards stationed at the concentration camps, for buying items in the camp canteen. For example, the *Camp Guards' Notes* of Buchenwald (where over 50,000 people died), in Central Germany, were imprinted: *SS-Standort-Kantine-Buchenwald* (SS Garrison Canteen-Buchenwald) and are available to collectors today in "circulated" condition for $50 or less.

Criminal Prison Money

Criminal prisons are for the internment of civilian prisoners. While such prisoners have tended to be paid in small amounts of their prison's national currency, if they've been paid at all, some civilian criminal prisons have issued special "prison currency" to their inmates, including prisons in the United States and England.

Collecting Internment Camp Money

While some can be purchased for only a few dollars, other Internment Camp Notes cost hundreds of dollars each, even worn, if they can be found at all. These notes tend to have simple designs and primitive printing quality, and are therefore easy to counterfeit for the collector trade. Inmates, of course, were not expected to attempt counterfeiting or forgery, as such offenses, if discovered, would have meant immediate execution in many of these camps.

I advise you to buy a few of the cheaper notes, talk with dealers who handle these notes, and read whatever applicable material you can find if you decide to collect Internment Camp Notes. Beware of counterfeits and forgeries. An excellent book, which raises as many questions as it answers because so little is known about many of these notes, is Lance K. Campbell's *Prisoner-of-War and Concentration Camp Money of the Twentieth Century*, published in 1989, $25 hardbound, $17.50 softbound (see Bibliography).

WAR PROPAGANDA NOTES

Propaganda "Counterfeit" Notes of enemy nations' currency have been dropped from aircraft to demoralize the population and to stimulate desertion of enemy soldiers (also called Safe Conduct Pass notes or Deserter Identification notes). These notes usually consist of a fairly convincing counterfeit front of an enemy country's bank note, but a propaganda message printed over a blank back.

In World War II, the Germans dropped facsimiles of British £1 notes over Egypt, with an Arabic message on the reverse sides: "This note was worth 20 shillings but now not even a beggar would stoop to pick it up." The British dropped counterfeit *Japanese Occupation Notes* over Malaya in 1944, with this message imprinted: "Japanese money and Japan will be finished soon." In the Korean War of the early 1950s, United Nations forces dropped facsimile notes as "Safe Conduct Passes" encouraging desertion — on North Korean Communist troops.

Sixty million counterfeit North Vietnamese notes were dropped on Vietnam by the U.S. Air Force from 1965 to 1972; these notes had an "extension" of the note's margin (often clipped off by the recipients, so the note could be "spent") on which was printed this message in Vietnamese:

> *Here is a resemblance of your money. Everyone knows it is losing purchasing power. This inflation is put on the people because of the war policy of your government. If the war goes on, your money will purchase less and less.*

U.S. MILITARY PAYMENT CERTIFICATES

After World War II, the U.S. Armed Forces had a major peace-keeping role in the world, first to monitor the "democratic"

government establishment in the former war enemies, Germany, Italy, and Japan; later to keep the Soviet Union from overrunning Western Europe and to "contain" the spread of Communism.

An internal-use Military Currency was needed for U.S. military personnel stationed overseas, so it was decided to issue special U.S. *Military Payment Certificates* (MPCs) as this paper money for our Armed Forces. Thirteen different *Series* were used, from 1946 to 1973. On "Conversion Day" between each *MPC Series* (the last day of the old *Series* and the first day of the new *Series*), all U.S. military quartermaster stores, post offices, etc., closed while soldiers converted their "old" *MPCs* into the "new" *MPC Series*. Surprise was essential to the success of Conversion Day, which was announced at the last moment to discourage currency speculators from turning in vast hoards of the "old" *Series*, soon to be obsolete and invalid.

MPCs were issued to U.S. military personnel and some civilians at overseas bases for internal currency control, especially to thwart soldiers' dabbling in black market currency deals.

U.S. *MPCs*' popularity has risen dramatically among collectors since these notes were officially discontinued in 1973. Low denominations tend to be cheap to buy today, but the high denominations often bring three figure prices in high grade (AU-UNC), as few were saved by soldiers who needed to buy things on their moderate salaries.

It is possible to assemble a "type set" of the 90 major designs of the U.S. *MPCs* of the last six *Series*, at modest cost if you're willing to accept lower grade circulated notes. Some can even be purchased at less than face value because none is valid as currency anymore.

My favorite *MPC Series* are the last two: *Series* 681 and 692 (both used only by U.S. forces in Vietnam) for their interesting vignettes of military personnel, Indian Chiefs, animals, etc. Two *MPC Series* (691 and 701) have been printed but not issued yet, remaining in storage for possible use in the future. U.S. *MPCs* were not used in Operation Desert Storm against Iraq in 1991. U.S. *MPC* "Replacement Notes" are missing a suffix letter at the end of Serial Number digits, and are scarce, in demand, and costly compared to their "normal" counterparts. Beware of fraudulently removed suffix letters!

For price quotes for notes, and other data on U.S. *MPCs*, see Krause and Lemke's catalog listings, and Fred Schwan's *Military Payment Certificates* book (Bibliography).

	UNITED STATES MILITARY PAYMENT CERTIFICATES		
	(In use from 1946 to 1973)		
SERIES NUMBER	DATE ISSUED	DATE WITHDRAWN	DENOMINATIONS
461	September 16, 1946	March 10, 1947	5¢ to $10
471	March 10, 1947	March 22, 1948	5¢ to $10
472	March 22, 1948	June 20, 1951	5¢ to $10
481	June 20, 1951	May 25, 1954	5¢ to $10
521	May 25, 1954	May 27, 1958	5¢ to $10
541	May 27, 1958	May 26, 1961	5¢ to $10
591	May 26, 1961	January 6, 1964 in the Pacific; January 13, 1964 in Europe	5¢ to $10
611	January 6, 1964 used in Cyprus, Japan, Korea, Libya	April 28, 1969 used in Cyprus, Japan, Korea, Libya	5¢ to $10
641	August 31, 1965 Vietnam only	October 21, 1968 Vietnam only	5¢ to $10
651	April 28, 1969 used in Japan, Korea, Libya	May 19, 1969 Japan only; June 11, 1969 Libya only; November 19, 1973 Korea only	5¢ to $10
661	October 21, 1968 Vietnam only	August 11, 1969 Vietnam only	5¢ to $20
681	August 11, 1969 Vietnam only	October 7, 1970 Vietnam only	5¢ to $20
692	October 7, 1970 Vietnam only	June 1, 1971	5¢ to 50¢;
		March 15, 1973	$1 to $20

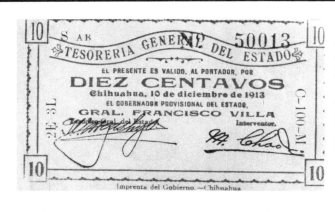

188. "Pancho Villa's" Mexican Revolutionary 10 *Centavos* note of 10 December, 1913, entitled TESORERIA GENERAL DEL ESTADO (General State Treasury), printed at the Chihuahua State Print shop. Also called *Sábanas de Villa* (*Villa's Bed Sheets*), notes such as these were issued in inflationary quantities by General Francisco Villa to pay his Revolutionary troops. (Pick # S550)

189.   World War I French emergency money, issued for use as small change due to a shortage of circulating coins. Dated 31 October, 1915.

190.   Austria-Hungary Prisoner-of-War *Lagergeld* (Camp Money) of World War I. 10 *Heller* note of the camp at Alchach A.D. (listed in Campbell's reference).

191.   The great fire of Neustadt on the night of September 28-29, 1817, featured on a 75 *Pfennig* German *notgeld*. Inscribed: *Gutschein von Neustadt i. holstein* (Credit Note of Neustadt in Holstein) — in northern Germany. GÜLTIG BIS 31. JULI 1921 (Valid until 31 July, 1921).

192.   *Japanese Military Issue* of 5 *Yen,* used in occupied China, no date (but 1938). (Pick # M25)

193.   *Japanese Occupation Note* for the Philippines during World War II, 10 *Pesos.* (Pick # 111)

194.   *Wertschein* ("Money Certificate") of the German winter relief organization, worth 5 *Reichsmark*, valid until January 31, 1940. Nazi Party members made a big deal out of going from house to house, collecting donations for the poor, as embodied in these vouchers convertible into food, clothing, or fuel.

195.   Reverse of German *Wertschein* ("Money Certificate") from Photo 194. Official handstamps in purple at the bottom. Notice that "clothes" and "fuel" have been crossed out with pencil, leaving "food" (*Lebensmittel*) as the choice for which this certificate could be exchanged.

196.   *Small Size* U.S. $20 *Federal Reserve Note*, Series 1934A, overprinted "HAWAII" —emergency issue for use in Hawaii after the Japanese attack on Pearl Harbor there.

197.   German occupation note for *Bohemia and Moravia Protectorate*, World War II. 20 *Korun* note of 1944, perforated SPECIMEN at top center. When Germany lost the war in 1945, Bohemia and Moravia provinces reverted to their original country of Czechoslovakia. (Pick # 9s)

198.   *Allied Military Currency* (AMC) used by World War II Allied occupation forces in France (left and center notes) and Germany (right note), Series 1944. 2 *Francs* note at left has "contemporary" graffiti: "Souvenir from Ray" ... "Oct 10, 1944 To Mary from Ray," etc. (Pick #s 49, 50, M43a)

199.   £5 *Special Voucher* of *British Armed Forces*, "Second Series," no date (but 1950). Issued to British troops for use in their canteens. Invalid today. (Pick # M23)

200.   5 *Kronen* note from the Nazi-instigated Jewish ghetto of *Theresienstadt* in German-occupied Czechoslovakia. Introduced in May 1943, these notes were "rejected" by the ghetto inhabitants, who used them for card games. Moses holds tablets of the Ten Commandments, with his hand hiding the Commandment "Thou Shalt Not Kill."

201. $5 U.S. *Military Payment Certificate* (MPC), Series "681" used only in Vietnam, from August 11, 1969 to October 7, 1970. Used by American military personnel for purchases at their canteens. Invalid today.

202.   *Propaganda Leaflet* dropped by U.S. aircraft over Iraqi troops during Operation Desert Storm in 1991. This side has an imitation 25 *Dinar* Iraqi note, picturing Iraqi leader Saddam Hussein.

203.   Reverse of *Propaganda Leaflet* from Photo 202, revealing it to be a "SAFE CONDUCT PASS" with an Arabic message reading, in part: "You do not have to die. You can be safe and return to your family and loved ones if you cease resistance ..."

14

"'Impossible' is a word only to be found
in the dictionary of fools."
Napoleon Bonaparte (1769-1821)

Rare Foreign Notes

This chapter discusses some paper money that is famous for its extreme rarity, as well as for its intriguing historical lore. Many of these notes can be found only in museums, if they can be found at all. Most collectors will never enjoy the ownership of these notes, but, like all paper monies, these rarities belong to humanity, to the story of human monetary progress, to the pageant of times past as recorded in paper currency reflecting pressing problems and innovative solutions.

ARGENTINA — Many early 19th century notes are of the utmost rarity, including those listed in Pick's *Standard Catalog of World Paper Money*, Volume 1 (Specialized Issues) as "Reported, not confirmed." Examples of Argentine rarities include many *Banco de Buenos Ayres* notes, 1822-1829.

AUSTRALIA — No pre-World War I Australian note can be called "common," but the blue chip gems of Australian paper currency are the seldom seen issues of 19th century private banks (such as the *Bank of Newcastle* of 1828-1829, and the *Bank of Tasmania*, 1853-1885). G.W. Tomlinson's *Australian Bank Notes 1817-1963* was the first reference book in this specialty.

BRAZIL — Of rarity and romance are the provincial issues of 1808-1857, such as the *Bahia* notes of 1828, issued to redeem copper coins; or the *Minas Geraes* 1808-1809 notes, exchangeable for prospectors' gold.

CANADA — French-Canadian *Playing Card Money* of 1685-1728 is very rare, issued due to coin shortage, and almost all redeemed by money-hungry soldiers. Issued by writing on the backs of playing cards by Jacques de Meulles (the Intendant of New France), all these notes were recalled for redemption every year to help combat counterfeiting, and the death penalty was declared for anyone caught with "obsolete" playing card notes — hence their extreme rarity today (most are in museums).

CHINA — Any pre-Ming Dynasty notes (before 1368) are of immense interest, as they were the first paper monies issued in the world. Mostly in museums.

FRANCE — My favorite French rarities are the 19th century local bank issues, such as the notes of the *Banque de Bordeaux* (in operation 1818-1848) or the *Banque de Toulouse* (1838-1848). These notes have a classically naive simplistic look to them, perhaps almost like reincarnated (but with more elaborate border work) French Revolutionary *assignats*, so beware of counterfeits.

GREAT BRITAIN — Most pre-19th century *Bank of England* notes are from scarce to rare, and many 19th century issues are rare also. This is because all damaged and heavily worn notes are destroyed as soon as they are redeemed by the Bank; but all old *Bank of England* notes have collector premium value, no matter what condition, and none are turned in anymore by anyone knowing this. For information on old English notes, see *English Paper Money* by Vincent Duggleby (Bibliography).

GREECE — Some of my favorite rare Greek notes are certain issues of 19th century regional banks, such as the *Privileged Bank of Epirus and Thessaly* (founded 1882; absorbed in 1899 by the *National Bank of Greece*) or the *Ionian Bank* (founded 1839, became the *Ionian Bank*

Limited in 1883). Vignettes on these early Greek notes include "Woman holding torch, with angel below" and "Winged Cupids."

HUNGARY — The first exclusive Hungarian money since the year 1526 was the 1847-1849 Lajos Kossuth notes issued to finance his Revolution. While some of these are common, others are quite rare.

INDIA — My favorite rare Indian notes are certain British-Indian 19th century bank notes, such as the rare types of the *Bank of Bombay* (1850s) or the *Calcutta Bank* (1820s).

IRELAND — About 100 private banks issued notes in Ireland in the early 19th century, and the ones you never see are the ones that are choice and rare. I like them with vignettes of allegories or sailing ships.

JERSEY — Pick's *Standard Catalog of World Paper Money*, Volume 1, devotes 7¹/₂ pages to illustrated £1 notes of Jersey banks; most are rare, but a few are actually affordable. The Bailiwick of Jersey is a British Crown dependency in the English Channel and was annexed by England in 1206. Some of my favorite 19th century Jersey bank notes are those of *Hand-In-Hand Bank* (with a vignette of clasped human hands) and *St. John's Wind-Mill* (with a windmill and an allegorical female "Agriculture").

NETHERLANDS — Most pre-20th century Netherlands notes are rare, as befits a land with a rich history. Their often simple designs, and primitive bank note printing technology of the time, lend themselves to counterfeiting.

PERU — My favorite rare Peruvian notes are many issues of 19th century local banks, printed by bank note companies in the United States. These notes have wonderful vignettes, such as "Indian woman with sword and flag" on the 1 *Sol* 1870-1875 note of the *Banco de Lima*; or the "Boys and mule train" and "Girl holding dog" on the 25

Sols 1871 note of the *Banco de Londres Mexico y Sud America*.

RUSSIA — No Russian note can be as appealing as the sealskin money of the early 19th century, if you can find some.

SARAWAK — If your notaphilic tastes run to the exotic and the unpretentious, perhaps the rare 1858-1863 uniface *Treasury Notes* of Sarawak inspire your imagination: handwritten numbers, most with printed denominations such as "Five Cents." — and with signatures, dated government seal, and inscriptions such as "*Treasury. Pay Bearer.*" Sarawak, now part of Malaysia, forms the northern coast of Borneo, and has used Malaysian money since 1963.

SCOTLAND — The Bank of Scotland has issued paper money from 1695 to date. The pre-19th century uniface notes tend to be rare, choice examples of Scottish monetary heritage. The stereotypical myth of Scottish people being misers, is, of course, false, as much Scottish money is very worn, proving it has circulated heavily.

SOUTH AFRICA — My favorite rare South African notes are many issues of 19th century local banks, such as the *Commercial Bank of Port Elizabeth* (operated 1853-1863) or the *Colonial Bank of Natal* (1862-1868).

URUGUAY AND VENEZUELA — The rarest notes of the 19th century private banks of these and other Latin American countries (especially those printed by U.S. bank note companies) have an undeniable charm due to their well-designed vignettes. Then, too, for sheer nostalgia value, the rare 1811 uniface, black ink on heavy white paper, *Independence Issue* notes of the upstart Estados Unidos de Venezuela (because Spain didn't recognize Venezuela's independence until 1845) deserve our attention also.

15

Buying Notes

I waited until this chapter to discuss buying paper money because I wanted you to read the first fourteen chapters of this book before you run out and start buying notes for your collection. If you haven't read them, take the time to read the previous chapters before your next visit to a currency dealer or currency show. Once you know what types of notes are available, including their conditions and price ranges, then you might want to alter your collecting goals a bit.

The easiest way to get notes is, of course, directly from circulation, either your own country's currency or that of other nations that you visit. Presently circulating currency is quite limiting, however, and most collectors feel impelled to buy obsolete notes from the awesome array of beautiful and historical examples that have been issued in past ages. As for foreign notes, it would not be cost-effective to travel to other countries for the sole purpose of gathering some modern note samples, so virtually all collectors must buy notes.

This chapter explains the ways to buy notes from retail dealers (fixed price lists, store stock, currency shows), from currency auctions, by mail, and directly from fellow collectors. See the end of Chapter 17 for a list and description of currency dealer organizations that help to monitor the business ethics of established currency dealers in the U.S. and elsewhere.

BUYING FROM RETAIL CURRENCY DEALERS

Retail dealers are the source of most paper money for collectors. There are several thousand retail coin dealers in the United States, including those with walk-in stores, mail order, and show circuit business. Many of these dealers stock paper money as well as coins. Some dealers are part-time, especially those who hit the local shows on weekends; some are quite specialized (only U.S. *Large Size Notes*, only cheaper foreign money, etc.); and some handle collecting supplies like currency albums and holders. But the purpose of a retail dealer is to buy a note at wholesale price (usually from a collector or an investor) and sell it at a retail price.

Although paper money collecting tends to be less hectic than our sister numismatic hobby of coin collecting, the selection of a paper money dealer from whom to buy some notes should be done intelligently. Ask yourself these questions: How long has the dealer been in business? Is he a member of any paper money societies (see Chapter 23)? Is he a member of any currency dealers' societies (see Chapter 17)? Is there a permanent address where you can always write or phone? Does the dealer openly state buy/sell prices or is everything "negotiable" depending on how rich the customer looks? Does the dealer offer free and sensible advice? Does the dealer buy back what he sells? Are the notes guaranteed genuine forever (can they be returned if later proven to be counterfeit, although sold as genuine)? Is there a prompt refund policy? What do other dealers and collectors think of the dealer whose business you are considering?

Buying from Fixed Currency Price Lists

Many retail dealers sell from fixed price lists. These are printed lists of currency arranged by country, condition, selling price, and standard catalog number (Pick's reference for foreign paper, Friedberg's numbers for U.S. currency). These lists are frequently updated, rendering older lists obsolete due to changes in prices and stock. Fixed price lists may be illustrated with note photos, or merely long lists of notes and their selling prices. To get new customers, fixed price lists are often printed in part or entirely as display advertisements in the national currency periodicals (see Chapter 22) or in society journals (see Chapter 23).

Advantages to buying from fixed price lists:

(1) You can leisurely select notes for your collection without feeling pressured to "buy now"; (2) you can "comparison shop" with price lists for similar notes from different dealers (especially useful for cheaper UNC foreign notes, virtually all of which are identical in centering, brightness, etc.); (3) you know exactly what the notes will cost; and (4) you know what kinds of notes a particular dealer habitually carries in stock, so you can plan ahead — if you don't buy the note this month, you are sure this dealer will have another one in stock next month or the month after that.

Disadvantages of buying from fixed price lists:

(1) You can't always see the note before you buy it (since most price lists aren't illustrated, and those that are may show just one side of the note); (2) price-listed notes may be mis-described (called CU when they are actually AU; GEM when they are off-center; tiny edge tears or faint blemishes not mentioned); (3) a dealer may have more than one note in stock that fits a particular description on the list, but if you're not one of that dealer's best customers, you may be sent the "worst" specimen of the lot; and (4) it is usually hard to bargain for a lower price because the dealer may want to wait and see if anybody is willing to pay full list price first.

Buying from Currency Store Stock

The economics of the business dictate that few if any dealers can operate a walk-in store with only paper money for sale. This means that you will be going into a coin shop, or at least a shop that handles other items besides paper currency. Most coin shops deal mostly in coins, so you'll have to hunt for the ones that spread a nice selection of U.S. or foreign paper in their display cases. As they are rather large and space-consuming to display individually, bank notes are often kept behind the counter or stored in the shop safe, so always ask the sales clerks if they have the notes that you want. For example, I was pleasantly surprised to be handed a bundle of gorgeous U.S. *Large Sized Notes* (some of which I photographed on the premises for illustrations in this book) when I recently walked into Americana Stamp and Coin Company's showroom in Tarzana, California. Jay Tell, Americana's proprietor, told me, as he placed the notes in my hands, that he just bought these from an estate. I already knew that Americana has long been known for quality stamps in the Los Angeles area, but I quickly learned that they handle U.S. paper money as well.

Coin/currency shops are so much fun to visit that if you live near one whose proprietor is friendly, you're going to spend more time and money there than might be good for you! Most currency store owners are eager to offer free advice and help to a customer, but courtesy demands that you should try to make some kind of purchase (or sale) every time you go in the store so you don't waste the dealer's time and patience. Buying a few plastic currency sleeves (holders) is an adequate purchase for a store visit.

Advantages of buying paper money in a store:

(1) The dealer gets to know you and may save special items that he knows you want; (2) you see every note close up before you purchase it; (3) you can examine a lot of notes (sometimes!) before you decide which one to buy; (4) you can sell your surplus notes or even a whole collection to the same store dealer when you need quick cash; and (5) you can chat with the dealer and other customers in the store, thereby acquiring, over time, valuable numismatic knowledge from other people's experience.

Disadvantages to shopping in a currency store:

(1) The shop may have little or nothing that you need in your collecting specialty (especially if the store emphasizes coins instead of paper money); (2) you might buy a note on impulse just because you see it and the dealer talks you into purchasing it; (3) the store may be out of the way or hard to get to, or have expensive parking, etc.; (4) the lighting may be bad, so when you get a store-bought fluorescently lighted bank note home, you might start to hate its appearance (particularly the faint folds that weren't "visible" at the store) when viewed under your bright incandescent desk lamp; and (5) by the very nature of currency store shopping etiquette, it is a little more embarrassing to drag a note back to the store for a refund than it is to send it back through the mail to a mail order company, because it is often assumed that once you examine a note (in a store or elsewhere), your decision to buy or not to buy is more or less permanent. Of course, most dealers will refund a store-bought note but will definitely get annoyed if you make a habit of returning items. For one thing, while you have the note in your possession, the dealer can't sell it to anyone else, thus losing another potential sale and maybe even a customer as well!

Buying at Currency Shows

Almost every coin bourse (sales area at a coin show) I've ever seen has some dealers who also offer paper money for sale. Although they may call it a "coin show," rest assured that dealers who specialize either partly or entirely in paper currency will also have tables there for serious paper money business. At giant numismatic shows, this is always true, but you can also attend shows where paper money dealing predominates (see Chapter 18 for both kinds).

Advantages of buying at currency shows from retail dealers:

(1) At a show, you can compare the stock and prices of many dealers all at once, and go back several times, if necessary, to the same dealers to reexamine a note that will cost you a lot of money for your budget; (2) you benefit from the opinions and advice of many professional dealers all on the same day, so you can weigh the relative logic and market analysis that one dealer makes against that of other dealers; (3) a currency show, even a small one, will expose you to an enormous quantity of paper money stocks that you can see up close, thereby getting something of a refresher course in your notaphilic education from the sheer volume of material seen on the bourse floor; and (4) you may meet new dealers at shows, see stock you've never seen before, and make new dealer and collector contacts that prove useful in the future.

Disadvantages to buying at shows:

There aren't many disadvantages to buying at shows besides the debatable ones: (1) you might feel "poor" or intimidated if you're a novice currency collector on a small budget and suddenly are overwhelmed with a million dollars' worth of rare paper money in front of you (as exists on the bourse floor of a major show); (2) you may overspend at a currency show from the intense excitement and enormity of it, in much the same way that a casino visitor might bet recklessly when gambling in a lavish "money means nothing" atmosphere; and (3) you run the risk of spending money on "sidelines" and note specialties that you don't already collect — to the detriment of your long-established collecting goals, just because if you're at all human, you're going to find a lot of interesting things at a currency show that you'll wish you owned in spite of your dwindling collecting budget due to show purchases! See Chapter 18 for major currency show locations.

Good visiting strategy at a currency show is to make a quick circuit of the bourse floor to get a general idea of what is available, then spend some time with your favorite dealers and those who seem to offer what you want to buy, then make your final buying decisions during your last hour or so at the show (although one-of-a-kind items may sell before you get around to buying them if you wait too long). And if you're going to sell as well as buy, you may decide to sell your material first to generate spending money for purchases of your own.

IMPORTANT SHOW ADVICE: There will always be other shows in the future. Spendable money is nice to have, too! Don't feel as though you lost something if you walk out of a currency show without spending all the money you brought. Be selective and condition-conscious: if the notes that you want are overpriced or in lousy condition, pass them up and take your money home.

BUYING FROM CURRENCY AUCTIONS

A currency auction company offers great potential treasures for your growing collection. Retail and auction dealers are both listed in Chapter 17, but here are some quick tips on auction buying in general.

Auction buying advantages:

(1) Scarce notes (such as high grade early Confederates or obscure rare foreign pieces) that are seldom seen will periodically come up for sale at auction; (2) the better notes tend to be sold at auction (as opposed to retail price lists, for example), so you are more certain of getting quality merchandise; (3) "prices realized" tend to be an honest reflection of the present-day currency market, hence "fair" purchasing prices; (4) paper money in an auction often comes with "pedigrees" from famous collections, helping to guarantee its authenticity and value; and (5) when you go to resell a note bought at auction, you can say it came from, e.g., "ex-the collection of somebody famous," which provenance will enhance its resale value.

Disadvantages to buying currency at auction:

(1) You might overpay for a note when swept up in feverish, foolish bidding during a hot floor auction battle; (2) most auctions won't allow you to return a note that you've examined on the floor, or that you've bid on by mail and later decide that you don't like for reasons beyond auction catalog misdescriptions; and (3) you might pay more for a note at auction because of the prestige of the auction company with a huge mailing list of wealthy bidders. You don't always get things cheaply at auction, although for frequently-offered material the hammer price tends to be somewhere between normal wholesale and normal retail prices because collectors, as well as dealers, participate in auctions, looking for "bargains." Learn the current retail price of a note (for comparable grade and quality) before you start bidding on it at auction. Why pay more than it would cost you in a high class coin store or at a currency bourse?

Public Auction Bidding Strategies

You can bid by mail or telephone in many floor auction sales, but a phone bid requires written confirmation as soon as possible. On the day of the scheduled auction, you can also, of course, bid in person in the hotel conference room or company gallery where it is held.

Rules vary from company to company, but in general a public floor currency auction will sell a group of collectible items to the highest bidder at a slight (and predetermined) advance over the second highest bid. For example, if the highest mail bidder has sent in a bid of $75 for lot number 374, a group of miscellaneous foreign CU 20th century bank notes, and you are the only floor bidder present who wants to bid on this lot in person, you can have it for maybe $80 if bidding increments in the $50 to $100 lot price range increase at $5.

Here are some tips for successful currency auction buying, based on my 20 years of buying at auctions:

1.   Start small and work your way up in auction buying. Don't spend your life savings in the first auction you can find.

2.   Try to bid the "limit level" before a higher increment is required in the bidding rules. For example, bid $200 instead of $190 for a lot if the next increase over $200 would be $25 more, for a total bid of $225, plus 10% auction commission for a cost of $247.50 (plus shipping and insurance if going to a mail bidder), which is enough to discourage some bidders from topping your $200 bid if they calculate what the next increment will cost them.

3.   Time your mail bids to arrive at an advantageous day. If earlier tie bids get preference over those received later, and you plan to bid high, then send in your bid immediately. If you suspect the company (especially mail sale firms where no live floor bidders are allowed) tells other bidders what their highest book bids (mail bids) are so far, then mail in your bids at the last moment, say three days before the auction date, so the company can't reveal your bids early.

4.   Add all charges when mentally calculating your bids: include the auctioneer's commission (usually 10% each to the buyer and seller-consignor, now that the 20% "American" rate — to the purchaser — is nearly obsolete), state sales tax, and shipping/insurance fees. The total price is not $100 if you bid $100 on a lot. Add $10 commission, maybe 6% sales tax for another $6, and perhaps $5 or more for registered or insured mail if you're having your lots sent to your address, making a grand total of $121 (plus any check or money order fees and the stamps and stationery and phone calls you used to correspond with the company).

5.   Never submit a "Buy" bid (i.e., you'll pay any price to top another bidder). Always put a specified amount of money in the bid sheet boxes, and for firms that offer it, enter a limit on the total amount of your bids so you don't exceed your budget in that sale.

6.   Do your homework before the auction. Research the rare and/or expensive items so you'll be an informed bidder. Don't take the catalog descriptions for granted; although it's less of a problem than with coin auctions, some paper money auction companies may overgrade notes, including both pictured and unillustrated lots, and rarity and numismatic significance may be misstated, even by mistake. "Superb" and "Choice" are mental concepts, not indelible qualities of a note.

7.   Study the catalog auction rules to familiarize yourself with the company's sales terms. What abbreviations are used in catalog descriptions? What currency catalog edition is being quoted? What do the printed lot prices mean — current catalog value, retail value, estimated cash value (ECV), owner's estimated value, wholesale value?

8.   If bidding in person, try to view the lots before the sale date so you can study them leisurely, away from the pressure and noise of last minute crowds in the auction gallery. Always ask permission to touch a note before you remove it from its protective plastic sleeve.

You can also preview lots from certain auction companies by mail, paying insurance and shipping both ways, but I don't recommend this because it is risking getting a lot damaged or lost, to the annoyance of the company and potential bidders, in spite of the fact that the note is insured. Some collectors visit the auction company to preview lots, then submit mail bids.

9.   Request photocopies for lots that are not illustrated in the catalog. Enclose a business-sized (No. 10) self-addressed stamped envelope (SASE), plus another mint stamp or two when requesting a photocopy, and be sure to say which side (or both sides) of the note you want photocopied. Be advised that some photocopy machines make terrible copies of bank notes, and (although it is often done) natural-sized photocopies of valid U.S. paper money are against Secret Service regulations, as per U.S. law.

10.   Control your emotions when bidding. Electricity is in the air — three other floor bidders are determined to duel it out with you for the "junk lot" of limp and damaged U.S. *Nationals*. You get excited and stay in the bidding battle until the auctioneer announces: "Sold to the customer with the hysterical facial expression. Six hundred dollars please, for a lot estimated at a hundred!"

Decide on your absolute top bids and write those amounts next to the lot numbers in the auction catalog, before live bidding frenzy distorts your better judgment (a reason some collectors prefer to send mail bids or use an auction agent). Ego wars and being a flashy spender on the auction floor may momentarily impress some of the spectators as you bask in your glory in the notaphilic spotlight, but they're not the ones who will be paying the hammer prices of the lots that you win. You're not in a movie script, you're at a currency auction where your hard-earned money is at stake.

11.   Bid conservatively. Bid what you think is reasonable for your budget.

12.   Don't be intimidated by an impressive auction gallery, the demeanor of the auctioneer, the other bidders in their fancy clothes, or the high estimated cash value (ECV) of a lot you are considering. A lot knocked down at a bargain price makes more sense than a lot sold for double its normal retail worth.

13.   Pay auction bills promptly (within a month, preferably on receipt) to maintain good credit ratings and a good reputation. Auction companies understand collector whims and cash flow problems, but don't bid if you can't afford to pay.

14.   Study the "prices realized" when they arrive (usually on a printed sheet, if the company gives them at all) to evaluate how closely your bidding levels compare with actual hammer

prices if you were a mail bidder. Should you increase or decrease your bids for similar material in the next sale? What is the general price trend for items in your collecting specialty, in auctions over the past couple of years?

15.   Save important auction catalogs as reference works for your personal notaphilic library. Famous numismatic dealer Q. David Bowers, who has been in business since 1953, says that his numismatic reference library is worth its weight in gold.

16.   Return lots if you honestly believe them to have been seriously misdescribed in the auction catalog. But don't make a pest of yourself by returning lot after lot to a company if you want to stay on their mailing list. Return disappointing lots with a short explanation of your reasons, and most auction companies will honor your sincerity and do their best to resolve your complaints.

17.   It is OK to lose an auction lot. Don't be afraid to walk away from a floor auction empty-handed, without winning any lots. There are currency auctions every month. Why bid in this sale if the material isn't up to your standards or within your collecting budget? Spendable cash has value too — walk out the door with it instead of throwing it away for notes that you'll hate when you get them home.

MAIL BID SALES

Don't confuse public auctions with mail sales. A true auction will have floor action — live bidders present during the "crying" of the sale by the auctioneer (who, by the way, speaks in plain language, not the gibberish of commodities auctioneers you've seen in the movies). A mail bid sale is just that: a catalog, sometimes with illustrations, sometimes without, that lists the lots to be sold to the highest mail bidder, with no actual floor auction to take place.

Some companies conduct only auctions, some only mail sales, others (like the prestigious R.M. Smythe & Company of New York City) do both. Mail sales tend to offer cheaper notes than floor auctions do, but this depends on the company.

Mail bid sales have different rules, so it is smart to get the company's catalog and read the terms of sale before bidding. Often they will say that you cannot return a lot because of centering if it is pictured in the catalog's illustrations. And many mail sales sell lots to the highest bidder (not to the highest bidder at one advance over the second highest bid as in floor auctions).

So you see that mail sales can be more expensive than a floor auction if you bid extravagantly. Also, some mail bid sales have been known to misdescribe or overgrade their notes, but most mail bid companies are honest and ethical, recognizing that repeat business is the only business worth having.

My advice is to send in a small sample bid and see if you like the service and the notes that you happen to win at either auction or mail sale. If you are satisfied with the company, send in larger bids for more expensive lots.

BUYING CURRENCY BY MAIL

While the collectible paper money business is generally not as cold-blooded as the coin business can be, special precautions are necessary for beginning collectors (and even some advanced ones) when buying currency by mail from dealers.

1.   Don't order the first time you see a dealer's advertisement. If the company is successful, legitimate, and in business for the long haul rather than the short pull, you will see more of their ads as the months and years pass. I feel comfortable doing business with a company whose ads I've seen for a long time.

2.   Be extra cautious when sending money to post office boxes. While some of the most reliable humans on earth use post office boxes as their business mailing addresses, so do fly-by-night crooks who open a box to hide their identities and true residence, then take your money and skip town without sending anything in return.

Because paper money inventories are valuable and highly liquid, many currency dealers use post office box mailing addresses and keep their currency stocks in bank safe deposit boxes. So don't be afraid to do business with a PO box dealer, just make sure the dealer has been around for a while.

3.   Check with somebody if you have doubts about a currency company's ad. The publication in which the ad appears, the Better Business Bureau in the town where the company is located, and other currency dealers and numismatic societies should know something about this company. Anybody can buy and sell currency, but a business reputation has to be earned in ways that go beyond mere dollars and cents!

4.   Send a small order first to become acquainted with a mail order dealer's honesty and quality of service. If your trial order is satisfactory, wait a few months and try a larger order.

5.   Type or hand-print your order clearly. This includes your name and mailing address. Make catalog numbers, currency dates/series, and conditions crystal clear on your order sheet so that the dealer knows exactly what you want. I've been ordering paper money by mail for over 30 years, and I believe that anybody who reads English can understand any order that I've ever sent. I use the dealer's order blank or type or hand-print my own neat columns on a piece of paper. Here is an actual order, just as I recently sent it to a mail order dealer as part of my research for this book:

6.   Phone ahead for confirmation on one-of-a-kind items, or list substitutes on your order form if you want to avoid discouragement due to sold-out material. And if you're writing for information before placing an order, always enclose a No. 10 self-addressed stamped envelope, so that the dealer's

---

A Sample Paper Money "Order"

Please send me the following notes from your price list #96. Please refund for anything out of stock:

Country	Pick Catalog Number	Condition	Price
Argentina	P 309	UNC	$2.00
Cambodia	P 32	UNC	2.75
Great Britain	PM 23	UNC	5.00
Honduras	P 49B	UNC	3.50
Iceland	P 46	UNC	5.00
Yugoslavia	P 97	UNC	3.50
		Total	21.75
		postage	2.50
		money order enclosed:	$24.25

---

stationery and price lists/note photos don't have to be squeezed into a tiny envelope.

7.   Send a bank or postal money order for faster service when ordering by mail. Dealers are rightly suspicious of personal checks because sometimes they bounce. Expect your order to be delayed an extra two weeks while the dealer is waiting for your check to clear. Some currency dealers accept credit card payments, which usually allow your order to be processed more quickly, often the same day it is received.

8.   Wait a month after sending an order for currency before inquiring about what happened to it. The company may be waiting for your check to clear. They may be temporarily out of stock of your note but are expecting more any day. It takes time for mail to go both ways between you and a dealer. Registered mail (which is how most expensive currency is sent between people in distant cities) can be particularly slow. I've waited five days to a full week for a registered first class parcel to make its trip in the U.S. mail. And maybe your order was lost in transit. Don't assume that the dealer is a crook just because it takes a month to get a currency order. The company may be a small family or "one-man" operation, or the owner may be on vacation or traveling to currency shows when your order arrives.

9.   Don't hesitate to return currency for a refund if you honestly don't like the quality relative to the price you paid. If a note is advertised as UNCIRCULATED, it had better not have a prominent fold through its middle, because if it does, then it is not UNCIRCULATED. An EXTREMELY FINE note should not have an ugly tear into its design, or stains or missing pieces that weren't mentioned in the advertisement description. Although some dealers may disagree, I think that all pinholes should be mentioned in note descriptions.

Know, however, that if you continually return currency to a company, you will be dropped from their mailing list as a pest and an impossible-to-please "condition crank," whether or not you have valid reasons for disputing the company's currency descriptions. Of course, price has something to do with it also. A currency dealer expects a customer to be fussy about an expensive note (in any condition) and will tolerate normal returns for such material due to the high price tag under negotiation. When you start returning and complaining about notes that retail for only a dollar or two each, you're history as far as that company is concerned.

10.   If it looks too good to be true, it probably is — permanent advice from the U.S. Postal Inspection Service, which forever fights, it seems to me, a losing battle against mail fraud. A first-time advertisement from an unknown dealer who offers for sale currency that is much cheaper (for the grade) than the currency market price for such material may or may not be legitimate. Greedy collectors looking for bargains are prime prey of coin companies, for example, run by outright criminals or those who, in the advertisement description, practice questionable ethics like overgrading and not mentioning that a coin has been cleaned or damaged. My experience with companies that deal solely in paper money is that they are overwhelmingly legitimate, but be wary of fly-by-night coin companies that suddenly stick a few pieces of paper money in their ads; if they habitually overgrade coins, chances are they overgrade paper too. Truly UNCIRCULATED U.S. *Educational Notes* (1896 *Silver Certificates*) can't be bought for a couple of hundred dollars each.

BUYING FROM CURRENCY "APPROVALS"

Some dealers will mail some currency to you "on approval" — to be examined by you, then paid for if you wish to keep any of the notes sent. "Approvals" are a great way to buy from a dealer at a distance, in the comfort of your home, with plenty of time to make your decisions to buy or reject notes, and without feeling obligated to buy anything. Courtesy and custom dictate that you pay postage and insurance costs both ways if you don't buy anything from a given approval shipment. Of course, if you never buy anything from several successive shipments, the "approval dealer" may drop you from his mailing list. Dealers will request that you submit business references (bank account data, or where you've done currency business before), or ask for a cash deposit from first-time customers, before sending valuable currency through the mail to you.

BUYING CURRENCY PER "WANT LISTS"

A want list is an itemized listing of notes that you are seeking, along with grading desired and other personal "needs." Many currency dealers, from the smallest to the biggest, service want lists. It is considered annoying and only quasi-ethical, however, to send your want list to many different dealers without telling them that you are simultaneously doing this. Dealers do not enjoy spending time and money tracking down a note for you only to be told, "Sorry, I just bought it from somebody else."

BUYING CURRENCY FROM OTHER COLLECTORS

Direct purchases of currency from fellow collectors can be advantageous:
(1) You make new currency collecting friends; (2) the prices may be cheaper than if you bought from a dealer; (3) a private collector may agree to a small dollar-value transaction and discuss it with you in more detail than a busy dealer could afford to do; (4) a fellow collector may also buy something that you want to sell; (5) a collector may agree to a note trade more easily than a dealer would (most dealers see no real advantage to trading notes of comparable value and demand, except for keeping their best customer loyal to them); and (6) you can share notaphilic knowledge with a collector who may have a different point of view than your favorite dealer does.

Disadvantages to buying currency from other collectors:
(1) They may not guarantee what they sell or give you a refund if you have second thoughts about the deal; (2) their knowledge may be more limited than a dealer's, to your subsequent detriment (an uninformed collector may inno-

cently misattribute or overprice a note, or sell a counterfeit unknowingly); (3) a collector (like a dealer) may overgrade or overprice a note out of greed; and (4) a collector-merchant who is not personally known to you may be an outright fraud. Be especially careful when sending money to another "collector" who places a "first-time" classified ad. You may never see anything for your money. Establish trust by correspondence, exchanging phone numbers or bank references, or by waiting a month or two before sending money through the mail to a new collector acquaintance (time for a post office box crook, for instance, to fleece a few gullible sheep and skip town).

Local numismatic clubs will introduce you to other collectors who are known to the membership. If the officers of the club tell you that a collector is honest, he probably is. Don't be overly paranoid about doing business with fellow collectors, but always remember that as the cash value of a transaction increases, so does the temptation for larceny in the minds of people who care more about money than about reputation.

PAPER MONEY DEALER ORGANIZATIONS

See Chapter 17 for a list and description of paper money dealer organizations that help to police the business ethics of established currency dealers in the U.S. and elsewhere. Membership in a dealers' organization doesn't guarantee the dealer will be fair and honest, and lack of membership doesn't automatically mean that the dealer is a crook. Maybe he disagrees with something about the organization, or prefers to be a "loner" in the currency business, or is a small-time dealer who thinks that buying a yearly membership for hundreds of dollars (for some dealer organizations) is a waste of money. If a currency dealer has ever been expelled from a numismatic organization (dealer-oriented or otherwise), it would be helpful to know why. The corresponding secretary of an organization will be happy to tell you whether or not a currency dealer is a "member in good standing" of that organization. There are a lot of currency dealers in the world. Why deal with one who has a questionable reputation?

PAPER MONEY AUTHENTICATION

As a service to its members, the American Numismatic Association's Authentication Bureau will issue a photo certificate on genuine paper money, for a fee of $23, plus postage and insurance, for specimens valued up to $4,999; $40 for specimens valued at $5,000 or more.

AUTHENTICATION BUREAU AMERICAN
   NUMISMATIC ASSOCIATION
818 North Cascade Avenue
Colorado Springs, CO 80903
(719) 632-2646

204. £1 note of St. Helena, no date (but actually 1982). Britain's Queen Elizabeth II, and view of this Atlantic Ocean island. (Pick # 9)

205. 20 *Shillings* note of Uganda, no date (but 1973). Watermarked bird's head at right. At left, in Ugandan Army uniform, is Idi Amin Dada, the brutal dictator of Uganda from 1971 to 1979 (when he fled the country). He was responsible for the deaths of thousands of Ugandans who opposed him. (Pick # 7b)

206. 5000 *Cordobas* "Provisional Issue" of the leftist Sandinista government of Nicaragua. The Sandinistas ruled from 1979 to 1990, and surrendered power by election. (Pick # 141)

207.   *Banque de France* (Bank of France) 100 *Francs* note, dated 24 March, 1928. Allegorical personages. Watermark in top center circle. Can you find the four major folds in this note (*not* the corner folds)? (Pick # 25b)

208.   100 *Zaires* note of Zaire, issued 30 June, 1985. Featuring leopard and Mobutu Sese Seko (President of Zaire since 1965). Formerly the Belgian Congo, Zaire achieved independence in 1960, and was called Congo until 1971. (Pick # 29b)

209.   1000 *Dinara* note of Yugoslavia, 1981. "Woman with Fruit" and harvesting scene at left. (Pick # 92)

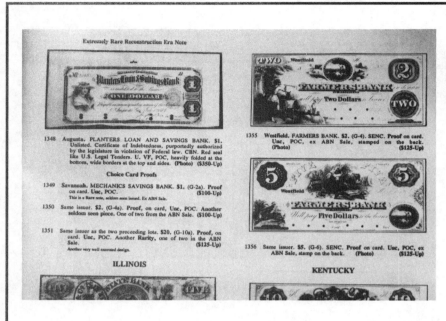

210. A selection of U.S. *Obsolete Currency* from a recent auction catalog of R.M. Smythe & Company, Inc. of New York City. Reproduced with company permission.

211. *Large Size* U.S. $10 *Treasury Note* (also called *Coin Note*), Series 1891. Union General Philip H. Sheridan. Author's photo, from the stock of Americana Stamp and Coin Company, Inc. of Tarzana, California.

212. Reverse of U.S. $10 *Treasury Note*, Series 1891, from Photo 211. Notice the two bands of silk fibers embedded to inhibit counterfeiting. Author's photo, from the stock of Americana Stamp and Coin Company, Inc. of Tarzana, California.

"A fool and his money are soon parted."
Old English proverb

16

Selling Notes

That fateful day has arrived when your resistance to selling items from your collection has worn thin, and you are actually considering getting rid of some of your beloved paper money. I've collected things for almost 40 years, since I was a little boy, and I speak with the words of a true collector when I say that every one of my collectibles, no matter how "cheap" or trivial, was in some degree painful to sell.

We collect for deep emotional reasons that extend beyond the mere intellectual attributions of catalog varieties, or petty calculations of current market values. Your collection is part of you, it springs forth from your unique personality and viewpoint, it was patiently assembled with thought and devotion as an important creation in your life, and (if you are a real collector) its eventual and final separation from you always takes, in a poetic sense, a portion of your soul with it.

This chapter explains how to sell your paper money when that vexing moment of mixed emotions arrives. Timing a currency sale, evaluating a collection, selecting the best market (outright sale to a dealer, private treaty, selling at auction, and selling to other collectors), and assorted miscellaneous selling tips from my personal experience are the highlights of the following pages. (See Chapter 15 when you're ready to buy currency again!)

REASONS FOR SELLING YOUR PAPER MONEY

The decision to sell your paper money will be based on one or more of the following factors: (1) you need spendable cash; (2) you want to "weed out" the poorer specimens and replace them

with better ones to upgrade your collection; (3) you have become bored with your currency and want to start a new specialty; (4) as a currency "investor," you want to take profits in a rising market or cut losses in a falling market; (5) you have acquired duplicates or extraneous notes that don't fit your present primary collecting goals; (6) as a notaphilic scholar/researcher, you have studied these notes and they are not needed for further research.

TIMING A SALE

A currency dealer advertises that "Now is the right time to sell," in the effort to convince you to sell your notes (to him, he hopes!). But no human being can foresee the future, and therefore nobody can honestly know whether the currency market will rise, crash, or remain "flat" for any given note for the near or far future.

The paper money market is not as volatile or as quasi-manipulated as is the coin market in our sister numismatic hobby. The long-term price trend for scarce and valuable notes has been up since World War II, but, of course, there have been mild dips in market prices from time to time as note retail values became overheated, often in conjunction with general national economic recessions or with coinciding coin market crashes (charitably called "market corrections"!).

It is sensible to take a profit when you can, if profits are a goal in your currency collection. It is also logical to "ride out" a heavy potential loss during an abruptly falling market and wait until your notes are worth more before selling. On the other hand, seasons and holidays have nothing to do with obtaining the best prices for your paper money. If your collection is worth substantial cash, someone can be found to pay for it any day of the year.

The only way you'll know what the currency market is doing today is to study and compare price trends over the past year or two, by reading the notaphilic press (Chapters 22 and 23), by visiting dealers/shows to take the financial pulse of the market, and by scanning recent retail price lists and auction results. Never take just one person's word, no matter how respectable, for what is happening in the currency market right now. A sales-hungry dealer may even be unconsciously over-enthusiastic about the "investment value" of the notes that he happens to be selling, and his advice may be sincere but wrong.

EVALUATING A PAPER MONEY COLLECTION

The real price of anything is not what you can buy it for, but what you can sell it for. Many currency collectors live in dreamland regarding what they think their collections are worth. Notes are not necessarily worth full Pick or Friedberg catalog value, and are almost never worth what you just paid for them (retail price) if you turn around immediately and try to sell them back to another dealer (wholesale price). Friedberg's *Paper Money of the United States*, and Pick's *Standard Catalog of World Paper Money* (Volumes I and II) provide a rough guide to retail prices, which should then be cut in half to arrive at a tentative estimate of wholesale (dealer buying) prices, which you might receive from a dealer in an on-the-spot cash transaction. These reference books are in most public libraries or for sale at your local currency dealer (see Bibliography), but try to get the latest editions for valid price quotes.

Paper Money Collection Appraisals

Most dealers will do appraisals on currency collections, with the customer paying a pre-determined appraisal fee if the dealer doesn't subsequently get to buy the appraised notes. When you ask for an appraisal, specify the type of appraisal you want.

1. Replacement value appraisals summarize the current retail cost of replacing the notes in today's currency market. This is sometimes called a catalog value appraisal, meaning it is derived from price quotes in the current edition of a standard currency catalog. This type of appraisal is often used for insurance purposes (against theft, disasters, etc.) or for charitable donations of collections to non-profit organizations.

2. Sales value appraisal (or words to that effect) is how much you can sell the notes for in today's market (wholesale, or "dealer's buying" price) or at auction. Also, most dealers will be happy to glance at a currency collection first to decide if it is worth appraising at all. It wouldn't make sense to spend $100 to have a collection worth $25 appraised! A typical dealer appraisal fee is 5% of total net worth, this fee to be

waived if you choose to sell the collection to the appraiser. Well-known notes are easy to appraise; obscure notes, especially some foreign ones, may require time-consuming research by the appraiser, and this work can get expensive and should be discussed up-front as part of the appraisal fee.

PREPARING A PAPER MONEY COLLECTION FOR SALE

To prepare a collection for sale, you must divide your currency groups into several arbitrary price categories, such as: (1) expensive notes, costing over $500 each at retail; (2) medium-priced notes, say from $50 to $500 each; (3) "cheap" notes, between $5 and $50 apiece; and (4) "inexpensive" notes at under $5 per note. As a young collector on a tight budget, you may want to believe that the mixture of foreign notes you bought at 50¢ or $1 each is going to be fought over by every dealer in town when you give them an opportunity to buy your collection, but chances are that such dealers already have these relatively "worthless" notes in stock and don't need any more unless they habitually handle inexpensive foreign notes, either singly or in bulk lots.

SELECTING A MARKET FOR SELLING CURRENCY

Choose carefully where you sell your notes! Fit the note to the dealer. The cheaper stuff should go to dealers who specialize in such material. Expensive notes should go to big-time dealers who can back up their purchases with real cash and who will probably have a ready market for reselling any expensive notes that they buy from you.

Study the currency company ads in the notaphilic/numismatic periodicals (see Chapter 22). "Buy ads" specifically state what a dealer is buying, maybe even down to prices and grades for individual notes. But don't overlook other dealers, especially those who often sell exactly the kind of material you want to get rid of. There are four main ways for a collector to sell currency: directly to a dealer, by private treaty, at auction, and to other collectors.

SELLING CURRENCY TO A DEALER

The advantages of selling paper money directly to a dealer:

(1) Instant cash, as fast as you can walk in and out of a numismatic store, or wait for the mail to go both ways, or sell at a currency show/bourse; (2) dealers keep up-to-date on the market values of notes; (3) you can sell small amounts, even a few dollars worth, of notes, such as a heavily worn common *Confederate*, or a handful of Chinese "junk" notes; and (4) you build up a working relationship with this dealer for future business, especially if this dealer has a neighborhood store.

Disadvantages of direct sale of currency to a dealer:

(1) You may not get the best price because the dealer may be overstocked, undercapitalized, or short of "cash flow," or may be a borderline con artist; (2) you tend to accept almost any cash offer for small transactions, especially by mail, to avoid the hassles of offering your notes elsewhere; (3) if you are unfamiliar with the present currency market, you never know if the price offered for your notes is fair; and (4) the stress of a "forced sale" for desperately needed cash makes you vulnerable to any offer from the dealer. "Distress sales" (for "scared money") are devastating to collector finances!

In general, though, for a collection worth a few hundred dollars, direct sale to a dealer may be the easiest selling method.

SELLING CURRENCY BY PRIVATE TREATY

Private treaty sales are conducted by dealers who take notes from a collector on consignment and offer them to the public at pre-determined prices, with an agreed upon pre-determined dealer's commission (maybe 10% to 20%) to be deducted after the new customer buys the notes. It is a way for a cash-short dealer to do business, or for esoteric and "hard-to-sell" notes to wait around for the right buyer, or for a collector who can afford to wait for money to realize a greater income from a collection.

Local coin/currency shops sometimes favor private treaties or store bid boards for cheaper notes. Big-time dealers who take out large display ads in the numismatic periodicals are, of course, the ones to approach for private treaty business with expensive notes, say $1,000 or more apiece, although such dealers may prefer to buy outright.

Advantages to selling currency at private treaty:

(1) You, as the seller, can set your own price (with the dealer's advice) … so you know in advance exactly how much your notes should bring, and you wait until you get it; (2) you give business to a dealer, thus keeping you in his mind for future transactions; and (3) you can sell unusual items by waiting for an interested buyer to show up.

Disadvantages to selling by private treaty:

(1) You may wait seemingly "forever" for the "sale" to occur; (2) you have no guarantee that you wouldn't have gotten more at auction; and (3) the general risk of selecting the "wrong" dealer for private treaty selling, or of placing prices too high (which means they'll never sell) or too low (which means that, in effect, you will be losing money in the present currency market). Substantial or famous currency collections are sometimes offered for sale by dealer advertising or even with their own exclusive private treaty sales catalogs.

SELLING CURRENCY AT AUCTION

Paper money auctions are the time-honored method for disposing of famous collections or of individual rarities of great cash value.

Advantages of selling currency at auction:

(1) Your notes will tend to bring currency market prices (typically, somewhere between wholesale and retail, with choice rare notes attracting serious bidding action); (2) the auctioneer's commission is only 10% (usually) of the hammer price (i.e., if a note sells for $100 to a bidder, you receive $90, minus the lotting fee, if any), with the buyer, of course, paying another 10% commission, which only indirectly affects the seller collector; and (3) many bidders (including prominent collectors and dealers nationwide if not worldwide) will compete for your notes, thus assuring fair prices. It is a fact that well-advertised public auctions by popular companies usually bring more money to a collector-consignor than outright sales to a dealer would.

Disadvantages of selling currency at auction:

(1) Unless you set a "reserve" price below which you will not let a note be sold, you run the risk of cheap prices realized, to your financial detriment, in an unreserved public auction; (2) auction companies with limited advertising may not attract appropriate bidders; (3) you have to wait, maybe as much as six months, before you see all your money from an auction, although cash advances against prices realized are often given for large collections; and (4) your notes may be unsuitable for auction due to their cheap value per note or inferior condition.

The finest notes tend to be sold at auction, but you can find auction companies handling cheaper material (such as Lyn F. Knight, Inc., who, in their same auction catalog, will list lots [especially stocks and bonds] with estimated hammer prices of $10 to $20 each, along with great rarities that sell for $25,000 or more — see Chapter 17).

SELLING CURRENCY TO OTHER CURRENCY COLLECTORS

If you have cheaper notes or personally know other paper money collectors, you can always consider selling to them. Or you can take out a classified ad in one of the notaphilic/numismatic periodicals (see Chapter 22), offering your notes for sale at reasonable advertising expense. Some local coin clubs and national notaphilic societies sponsor note trading and sales between members.

Advantages to selling currency directly to other collectors:

(1) You can sell cheap notes without feeling embarrassed in offering them to a professional dealer; (2) you build up friendships and acquaintances with fellow collectors who

share your currency collecting interests; and (3) you can set your own selling prices — with a courteous "take it or leave it" attitude.

Disadvantages of selling currency to other collectors, without using a dealer "middleman":

(1) You have to put up with collector whims, such as their asking for a refund later or complaining about the notes; (2) if selling to "unknown" collectors by mail, you may have your notes stolen without payment being rendered; (3) private collectors seldom want everything you have to sell, whereas a dealer might offer a "package price" for your whole collection; and (4) for notes of substantial value you could be victimized by an armed robber when showing a stranger what you have for sale, in your home or at a pre-arranged location elsewhere. Expensive paper money transactions are often conducted between buyer and seller in the safe deposit box examining room at the seller's bank, with payment being deposited immediately into the seller's account; but that doesn't prevent the "buyer" from accosting you in the parking lot or even following you home for a felonious "house-call." It makes sense to declare openly, as many dealers and collectors do, that "all currency stocks and large sums of cash are kept in the bank"; i.e., a robber or burglar can expect little loot from your residence. Exchanging identification data, phone numbers, society memberships, etc., in advance of meetings with strangers, is a reasonable precaution to avoid robbery. It is also good to let somebody know about the meeting, and to have witnesses look at the customer if you are suspicious of selling expensive items to a stranger. While everyone likes a degree of financial privacy, honest people have little to hide or to fear from a prudent seller.

SUMMARY OF CURRENCY SELLING TACTICS

1.   Sell expensive currency at public auction.

2.   Sell cheap notes either directly to a dealer who specializes in such material, or directly to a fellow collector.

3.   Don't be greedy.

4.   Don't resent the economic necessity for a professional currency dealer to buy cheaper than he sells.

5.   Don't expect a profit on every note you sell.

6.   Don't be afraid to reject an offer. Shop around for another dealer's offer if you don't like the first offer. Remember, however, that "time is money" to a busy dealer, so don't strain his or your patience and sanity by endless petty bickering about the selling price. There are other dealers in the world — sell your notes to someone else.

7.   Be realistic about the wholesale or auction value of your collection in today's currency market.

Life is short. Peace of mind should be valued as highly as the monetary worth of your collection. When you decide to sell some of your notes, sell them, then move on to something else. Do you want to do serious business or do you want to play pointless games?

SHIPPING PAPER MONEY BY MAIL

Collectible paper money can be safely shipped by mail, using either First Class Insured Mail or Registered Mail. Send shipments of moderate value (say, about $300 or less) by Insured Mail, to take advantage of the cheaper rates (for example: $3.50 for $300 worth of insurance, plus postage). Send expensive shipments (over $300) by Registered Mail, the biggest advantage being its high insurance coverage indemnities. The U.S. Postal Service will register a parcel worth thousands of dollars, and registry fees for up to $1,000 coverage are only $5.25 plus the postage charge based on weight. When the Hope Diamond had to be transported to the Smithsonian Institution, it was sent by Registered Mail.

Send nothing by fourth class mail (parcel post). It takes forever to get there and doesn't look very nice when it arrives; pay the extra money for first class mail. The USPS provides insurance liability up to $600 for insured first class items. You also must have a receipt, bill of sale, or other evidence of the value of your contents.

Packing Currency for Mailing

Securely packing your notes is the first step in sending them far away. When I send collectible currency by mail, I use these steps:

1.   Place each note in a separate soft plastic holder, ideally a holder a bit bigger than the note size, in case the note shifts around inside the holder, so it doesn't slide out and get bent.

2.   Stack the holdered currency all facing the same direction, with the open sides of the holders on the same side of the stack, to make it easy for the recipient to sort through the notes when they arrive.

3.   Place the holdered currency in a snug envelope, then inside another envelope, slightly larger than the first one. Seal both envelopes.

4.   Place sturdy sheets of cardboard on both sides of the enveloped bundle of currency (from Step 3, above) and then put rubber bands gently around the cardboard stiffeners, in both directions, perpendicular to each other: Be sure that the rubber bands are not too tight or too loose.

5.   Then place the bundle (from Step 4, above) into another snug envelope (slightly larger than the bundle), and seal.

6.   Place the sealed envelope from Step 5 (above) into an outer strong mailing envelope or box, and seal with tape approved by the Postal Service for Insured Mail or Registered

Mail. (Ask your local postal clerk what kind of tape to use; window clerks enforce the "tape" requirements differently.)

7.   The outside of the mailing envelope or mailing box should be carefully printed in capital letters with waterproof ink with this information:

• sender's name, address, and zip code

• recipient's name, address, and zip code

• carrying directions, such as First Class, Do Not Bend Be sure to leave room on the package's face for postage stamps or meter stamp and the insured or registry stamp or sticker.

8.   Take your currency package to the post office for weighing, stamping, and insuring.

9.   Keep a list of individual notes enclosed in the shipment (maybe even photocopies of the valuable ones) and the insurance/registry postal receipt until the recipient verifies that such notes have arrived safely.

10.   If you are a serious currency investor, the costs of mailing your currency investments (to a dealer for liquidation, etc.) are tax deductible, as per the latest U.S. Internal Revenue Service laws.

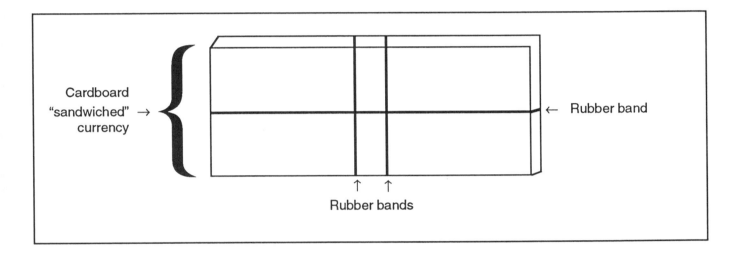

Cardboard "sandwiched" currency → { ← Rubber band

↑   ↑
Rubber bands

213.   100 *Escudos ouro* of Portugal, 1981. (Pick # 88A)

214.   10 *Pesos* note of *El Banco Italiano del Uruguay*, issued at Montevideo, Uruguay, dated 20 September, 1887. Unsigned remainder. Nineteenth century Italian patriots Cavour (at left) and Garibaldi (at right). Allegorical females and flags at center. (Pick # S212b)

215. 50 *Rials* note of Iran, no date (but actually 1971). Engraved portrait of Shah Pahlavi at right, watermark of him as a young man at left. "Pre-Islamic Revolution" currency. (Pick # 90)

216. 10 *Pesos* note of *El Banco del Estado de Chihuahua* (The Bank of the State of Chihuahua), Mexico, 1913, unsigned. "Cowboys Herding Cattle." (Pick # S133)

217. Reverse of *Banque de France* (Bank of France) 100 *Francs* note of 1928. Allegorical personages, common on French and French colonial notes from the first half of the 20th century. (Pick # 25b)

218.   500 *Francs* note of Gabon (formerly part of French Equatorial Africa). Lithographed, dated 1 April, 1978. "Woman Wearing Kerchief" at left, "Logging" at right, antelope watermark in circle. (Pick # 2b)

219.   *Large Size* $20 U.S. *Silver Certificate*, Series 1891. Portrait of Daniel Manning, U.S. Secretary of the Treasury, 1885-1887. Author's photo, from the stock of Americana Stamp and Coin Company, Inc. of Tarzana, California.

220.   Reverse of *Large Size* $20 U.S. *Silver Certificate*, Series 1891. Notice the silk fibers —embedded to inhibit counterfeiting —running in two vertical bands. Author's photo, from the stock of Americana Stamp and Coin Company, Inc. of Tarzana, California.

221.   50 *Shillings* note of Kenya, dated 14 September, 1986. President Daniel T.A. Moi at right. Watermark of a lion's head at left. (Pick # 22)

"A good reputation is more valuable than money."
Publilius Syrus (1st century B.C.)
Roman epigrammatist and compiler

17

Paper Money Dealers

I've chosen to talk about a few paper money dealers in this chapter, but the list includes some of the largest and most famous in the business. I've done business with many of them, but (of course) I have no financial interest in these or any other numismatic companies. Many, many outstanding currency dealers exist, and even though they are not mentioned, their ethics and business practices may very well be on a par with the dealers discussed below. Space limits prohibit praising everybody. Try one of these dealers when buying or selling collectible paper money, or pick another dealer from the ads in the numismatic periodicals (Chapter 22) or the society journal ads (Chapter 23).

And remember: Dealers are human beings — if you don't feel comfortable doing business with one, try another. There are a lot of currency dealers. All of them will not have every note you want to buy or be eager to buy every note you want to sell. And the advice and information that they offer you (usually for free) may be worth more than your currency collection will ever be. Listen to dealers, and ask them questions. Pay for the first phone call to them; enclose a self-addressed stamped envelope (SASE) when requesting information by mail. Always be courteous and up-front about what you need from a dealer. Don't waste his time. Never be shy about politely rejecting a dealer's offer to buy or sell. Just say, "I appreciate your offer and your time. Let me check around a little, and if I can't find a deal that I like with somebody else, I may come back to you for this particular transaction."

WHAT MONEY CAN'T BUY

In Margaret Mitchell's novel, *Gone With the Wind*, Rhett Butler bids "$150 in gold" for a dance with Scarlett O'Hara. While they're dancing, their discussion turns to things that money can or can't buy. Scarlett suggests that money can't buy love or happiness, to which Rhett responds that usually money can buy those things, and that when it *can't*, it can buy "the most remarkable substitutes."

The Roman orator and philosopher, Marcus Tullius Cicero (106-43 B.C.), admits the possibility of people who "can't be bought with money" when he declares: "That man is admired above all men, who is not influenced by money." Benjamin Franklin observed that "he that is of opinion money will do everything may well be suspected of doing everything for money."

My maternal grandmother, Anna Horwath, was the most honest person I've ever met, and when she died a few years ago, the world lost a saint. She worked as a cleaning lady in a bank building and in lawyers' offices in my hometown of Joliet, Illinois. More than once she found sacks of U.S. paper money in the wastebaskets as she made her rounds after business hours and after the other people in the building had gone home. Despite her modest salary, she always returned the money the next day when her bosses arrived for work. When asked why she didn't keep the money for herself, she replied, "It's not my money."

When it comes to doing business with paper money dealers, choose them as much for their integrity, honesty, and numismatic knowledge as for their fancy offices, high annual incomes, or huge merchandise inventories. Paper money, after all, has a very meager value. A good reputation is priceless.

Allen's Coin Shop

ALLEN'S COIN SHOP, INC.
399 South State Street
Westerville, OH 43081
(614) 882-3937

Established in 1960, Allen's deals in currency, coins, stamps, and a lot of other things, both by mail and walk-in trade. (Store hours: Monday, Tuesday, Thursday, and Friday 10:00 A.M. to 6:00 P.M.; Saturday 9:00 A.M. to 5:00 P.M. Closed Wednesday and Sunday.) They have a huge stock of U.S. currency of all types and price ranges, including *Colonials, Confederates, Large Size* and *Small Size Nationals* (listed by state, bank, etc.). Send for their currency price list. Sells currency collecting books.

Americana Stamp & Coin Company

AMERICANA STAMP & COIN COMPANY, INC.
18385 Ventura Boulevard
Tarzana, CA 91356
(818) 705-1100

In business since 1958. Buys and sells all types of U.S. currency, coins, and stamps, and foreign material. Is an aggressive buyer of quality items. Large full-service stamp and coin store with security locking doors, in an upscale Los Angeles shopping center. For illustrations in this book, Jay Tell, the company President, allowed me to photograph some choice U.S. currency that he had recently purchased from an estate. Impressive stock of rare U.S. stamps. No high pressure sales tactics when you visit. Does appraisals and investment planning for collectibles.

Bowers and Merena Galleries

BOWERS AND MERENA GALLERIES, INC.
Box 1224
Wolfeboro, NH 03894
(603) 569-5095

Bowers and Merena Galleries is one of America's leading numismatic firms, having been in business since 1953. Deals mostly with coins, but also handles quality U.S. paper money by retail price list and by auction. A division of this firm, Auctions by Bowers and Merena, Inc., conducts public auctions in New York City and other U.S. metropolitan areas. Their auction catalogs, printed on quality paper and profusely illustrated with lot photographs, become reference works. Does business by mail and at coin/currency shows.

Corbet Cache

CORBET CACHE
P.O. Box 310
Rescue, CA 95672 (916) 677-9034

Buys and sells worldwide bank notes in all price ranges, from $1 up. Issues lovely little retail catalogs, well-organized by country, Pick numbers, etc., including a lot of cheaper and medium-priced notes, great for beginners in world currency collecting.

Terry Cox

TERRY COX
P.O. Box 60
Idaho Springs, CO 80452

Handsome little retail catalogs selling *Obsolete Currency* (U.S. *Broken Bank Notes*, etc.), U.S. currency, *Confederates*, fiscal documents, souvenir cards, etc. A few illustrations, but a lot of informative descriptions and advice written in a conversational, unpretentious style. Buys and sells, including on consignment (which is unusual for small retail currency price lists). His catalog of "Collectible Currency" is extremely entertaining reading; it makes you want to collect what he's selling.

Currency Auctions of America

CURRENCY AUCTIONS OF AMERICA, INC.
Contact any of these principals, who operate this company:
LEONARD GLAZER
P.O. Box 111
Forest Hills, NY 11375
(718) 268-3221

ALLEN MINCHO
P.O. Box 1525
Cedar Park, TX 78613
(512) 250-1475

KEVIN FOLEY
P.O. Box 573
Milwaukee, WI 53201
(414) 282-2388

Currency Auctions of America publishes impressive auction catalogs (a recent one weighed almost two pounds), printed on glossy paper, with photographs and lot descriptions for quality U.S. currency of all types, including *Colonials, Continentals, Obsolete Currency* (listed by state and town), *Large Size* and *Small Size Notes* (including *Nationals* listed by state and town), *Fractionals*, etc. All price ranges, many lots selling for $50 or less, many selling for strong three- or four-figure hammer prices. Call or write for the cost of the next catalog. The principals (listed above) of this company are all serious buyers of quality U.S. currency, and attend the national currency shows. Leonard Glazer is the President, Allen Mincho is the Vice President, and Kevin Foley is Auction Director of Currency Auctions of America, Inc.

Denly's of Boston

DENLY'S OF BOSTON
P.O. Box 1010
75 Federal Street
Boston, MA 02205
(617) 482-8477

Denly's of Boston is operated by Tom Denly. Buys and sells all kinds of U.S. paper money, *Colonials* to date. Publishes full page price list ads in *Bank Note Reporter* (see Chapter 22), listing *National Currency* by state and town, *Large Size* type notes, etc., in all price ranges. Does numismatic/currency shows also. Sells books and supplies for paper money collecting. Send self-addressed stamped envelope (No. 10, business size) and ask for price lists of *Large Size Type Notes* or *National Currency*.

Early American Numismatics

EARLY AMERICAN NUMISMATICS
P.O. Box 2442
La Jolla, CA 92038
(619) 273-3566

Early American Numismatics has one of the largest inventories of Colonial coins and *Colonial Currency* in the United States. Dana Linett is the company president, and his firm stands ready to service want lists for choice *Colonial Currency*, as well as offering periodic fixed price lists and mail bid sales. Mr. Linett's mail bid sale catalogs are handsomely printed, with black-and-white photos, on glossy paper of high quality. He also sells an assortment of reference books on Colonial numismatics.

Early American Numismatics buys and sells all Colonial coins, *Colonial* and *Continental Currency* (400 lots in a recent mail auction), pre-1800 U.S. bonds and fiscal paper, Colonial newspapers and lottery tickets, and encased postage stamps — one piece or entire collections.

Gene Elliott

GENE ELLIOTT
1429 Clairmont Road
Decatur, GA 30033
(404) 329-0811

Specializes in U.S. *Obsolete Bank Notes* and *Confederate Currency*, but a recent retail catalog price list also offered some very reasonably priced *Colonials, Continentals, and Fractionals*. Elliott's catalogs are excellent for beginning and intermediate collectors of these notes. Active buyer of *Confederate Notes, Bonds*, and *Obsolete Bank Notes*. His retail catalog lists many *Obsoletes* by state and bank name.

Steve Eyer

STEVE EYER
P.O. Box 321
Mount Zion, IL 62549
(217) 864-4321

Buys and sells coins and bank notes of the world, by mail and at numismatic/currency shows. Publishes price lists of worldwide paper money for sale, with many moderately priced notes for beginning and intermediate collectors.

Hickman Auctions, Inc.

HICKMAN AUCTIONS, INC.
Drawer 66009
West Des Moines, IA 50265
(515) 225-7070

Conducts wonderful mail bid sales of all types of choice U.S. currency, Colonial to modern. A recent sale had over 350 lots of *Nationals, Obsolete*, and *Scrip*, plus *Colonials* and *Continentals*, 44 lots of *Fractional Currency*, 40 lots of numismatic books, and assorted *Silver Certificates, Legal Tender Notes*, and souvenir cards. Send $5 for Hickman's next auction catalog.

Richard T. Hoober, Jr.

RICHARD T. HOOBER, JR.
P.O. Box 106
Newfoundland, PA 18445
(717) 676-4861

Specializes in U.S. *Obsolete Bank Notes*, scrip, checks, and other paper Americana. Publishes a price list of *Obsolete Notes* (*Broken Bank Notes*, etc.) and other offerings (a recent retail list included four dozen reasonably priced *Colonial* notes).

Lyn F. Knight

LYN F. KNIGHT, INC.
P.O. Box 7364
Overland Park, KS 66207

Wonderful auctions of choice U.S. currency in all price ranges, including *Colonials, Large Size, Small Size, Obsoletes*, stocks, bonds, some foreign notes, etc. A recent Knight auction had seven *California National Gold Bank Notes* from F/VF to XF/AU! Write or call for the catalog price and information on the next auction. Sells at retail also; in business over twenty years.

Gene F. Mack

GENE F. MACK
P.O. Box 60991
Jacksonville, FL 32236
(904) 771-4796

Buys and sells *Confederate Currency* and U.S. *Obsolete Bank Notes* (*Broken Bank Notes*, etc.), as well as *Confederate Bonds* and Confederate documents. A recent retail catalog price list also had old U.S. railroad checks. Mack's price lists are easy to read and understand.

Mid American Currency

MID AMERICAN CURRENCY
P.O. Box 1282
Bartlesville, OK 74005
(918) 335-0847

Buys and sells all U.S. paper money, with emphasis on U.S. federal *Large Size* and *Small Size Notes*. Publishes a nicely illustrated retail price list of U.S. notes, including one of the most comprehensive and detailed listings of U.S. *Small Size Notes* (by Series) available anywhere — good for specialists in *Small Size* types, varieties, special Serial Numbers, etc. Many reasonably priced notes for beginner or intermediate collectors of U.S. notes.

Stanley Morycz

STANLEY MORYCZ
P.O. Box 355
Englewood, OH 45322
(513) 898-0114

Specializes in top quality U.S. federal *Large Size Notes* from 1862 to 1923. Mr. Morycz became interested in U.S. *Large Size Notes* in the late 1950s and started dealing in these notes in the 1960s. He was the first currency dealer to picture every note offered on his price lists. His U.S. currency catalog price lists are the nicest in the business, printed on $8^{1}/_{2}$ by 11 inch quality paper, with each note beautifully photographed, described, and priced. He also offers cheaper notes, including *Small Size* type notes and a few *Confederates*. In a recent personal note to me, Mr. Morycz mentioned that his retail prices are not cheap, but that he tries to offer the best quality merchandise, with Choice to Gem UNCIRCULATED getting priority placing on his price lists. For those who can afford the very best condition.

Old Dominion Paper Collectibles

OLD DOMINION PAPER COLLECTIBLES
P.O. Box 418
Chesterfield, VA 23832
(804) 748-9189

Specializes in *Confederate Currency, Confederate Bonds*, and other Civil War items, such as documents, letters, etc. Publishes an easy-to-read descriptive price list of Confederate paper items for sale. In a recent personal letter to me, Dorsey A. Howard, the company proprietor, said:

After many years of collecting, handling, buying and selling currency, bonds, letters and other documents from [the Civil War] era I still sometimes get chills by holding a piece of paper history that has survived more than 125 years. What a story those bits of paper would tell if they could talk. As a direct descendant of six Confederate States Army veterans, I feel closely connected to that era of American history.

Larry Parker

LARRY PARKER
P.O. Box 1719
Santa Monica, CA 90406
(310) 453-3708

Specializes in *World Replacement Notes*, and publishes a detailed retail price list of such. Also handles German *notgeld* and German *POW notes* of World War I. Buys, sells, trades, and writes about *World Replacement Notes*.

Ponterio & Associates

PONTERIO & ASSOCIATES, INC.
1818 Robinson Avenue
San Diego, CA 92103
(619) 299-0400

Owner and company President: Richard H. Ponterio. Specializes in Mexican numismatics: the paper money, coins, and medals of Mexico. Also handles world paper money, world coins, and ancient coins. Services offered to customers: public auctions, mail bid sales, consignments, and private transactions. Has auctions of elusive Mexican and other foreign paper money at major numismatic/currency shows; had an unrestricted (no "reserves," i.e., no minimum bid) mail bid sale of the John Ford Cowen Collection of Mexican Currency recently. Call or write for catalog prices of the next sales. In business for 19 years.

Hugh Shull

HUGH SHULL
P.O. Box 712
Leesville, SC 29070
(803) 532-6747

Specializes in *Confederate Currency, Confederate Bonds* and other Confederate fiscal paper, *Obsolete Bank Notes* (U.S. *Broken Bank Notes*, etc.) of all states; scrip, checks, and other paper Americana. Publishes a detailed retail catalog (a recent edition had 56 pages) of Confederate paper items, and *Obsolete Bank Notes* listed by state and bank, of all types and varieties, in all price ranges (a recent catalog had all of the rare Montgomery and Richmond issues of the first *Confederate Notes*). *Confederate* and *Obsolete Notes* and prices for everyone from beginners to advanced collectors. Send $2 for latest catalog. In business for 16 years.

R.M. Smythe & Company

R.M. SMYTHE & COMPANY, INC.
26 Broadway, Suite 271
New York, NY 10004
(212) 943-1880

Established in 1880. Auctioneers, appraisers, and dealers in U.S. and foreign paper money, coins, antique stock and bond certificates, autographs, books, etc. Publishes auction and retail catalogs. A recent public auction featured U.S. federal currency, *Confederate Currency* and *Bonds, Obsolete Currency*, international currency, political cartoons of the Jacksonian period, and old stocks and bonds. Handles *Colonial Currency*, vignettes, and bank note proofs and essays. America's oldest "financial history" company. Researches obscure stocks and bonds for a fee. Visit their showroom when you're in New York, or call or write for prices of their next catalogs in your areas of collecting interest.

Stack's

STACK'S COIN GALLERIES
123 West 57th Street
New York, NY 10019
(212) 582-2580

While they're more famous for their rare coin business, Stack's Coin Galleries also handles quality U.S. paper money. A recent Stack's U.S. currency auction featured over 90 uncut sheets of U.S. *National Bank Notes* (the largest such offering since Lester Merkin's sale of February 1971), 30 *National Gold Bank Notes* (including eight of the nine issuing banks), and Spencer M. Clark's personal copy of one of the nine known original "Specimen Presentation Books" of U.S. *Fractional Currency*.

Established in 1858 as a firm that deals in all sorts of collectibles and antiques, Stack's family-run business became an exclusively numismatic firm in 1934. Stack's maintains a small but elegant retail show room at their address (above) in New York City, and has a staff of thirty people, of whom almost half are qualified numismatists; showroom hours are Monday through Friday, 10:00 A.M. to 5:00 P.M., and don't be intimidated by the armed guards or lavish window displays of hundreds of old gold coins. Their auction catalogs are

usually $10 each, but call or write first to be sure their next catalog has material of interest to you. Does retail business also, buying and selling on the premises. Beginning currency collectors on a tight budget might feel more comfortable starting with a smaller dealer than Stack's.

Mel Steinberg & Son

MEL STEINBERG & SON
P.O. Box 752
San Anselmo, CA 94979
(415) 453-9750

Buys and sells world paper money in all price ranges, for beginners to advanced collectors, with most notes in the two- and three-figure price ranges. Publishes a retail price list of world paper money, arranged alphabetically by country and listed by Pick catalog numbers. Services want lists and attends the largest numismatic/currency shows in the U.S. and overseas. Intermediate and advanced collectors of worldwide currency will find many scarce and elusive notes for sale by Mel Steinberg & Son. Call or write for their latest price list.

Superior Stamp & Coin Company

SUPERIOR STAMP & COIN COMPANY, INC.
9478 West Olympic Boulevard
Beverly Hills, CA 90212
(310) 203-9855

While better known for their stamp and coin business, Superior Stamp & Coin Company also buys and sells quality U.S. paper money. Founded in 1930 in downtown Los Angeles, this company holds regular public auctions and has a retail department for mail orders and walk-in trade. Superior's office and showroom hours are: Monday through Friday, 8:30 A.M. to 5:30 P.M. Saturday hours vary; sometimes they're open on Saturdays, sometimes not, so call to verify before a Saturday visit. Their own building in Beverly Hills offers free parking underneath (enter from Olympic Boulevard).

Weymouth National

WEYMOUTH NATIONAL
P.O. Box 540129
Millis, MA 02054

Sells world paper money, old U.S. currency, and some cheaper stocks, bonds, and coins. An outstanding company for beginning collectors, as their price lists have many inexpensive (less than $1 each) foreign notes — listed by country and Pick catalog numbers. Not many companies bother putting foreign notes individually priced at 25¢ each on their printed price lists; this company does. Write and ask for their latest price list of World Currency.

DEALERS OUTSIDE THE U.S.

Jeffrey Hoare Auctions

JEFFREY HOARE AUCTIONS, INC.
362 Talbot Street
London, Ontario N6A 2R6 Canada
(519) 473-5608

Conducts a minimum of three major auctions per year in the Metropolitan Toronto area. Material in these auctions includes: world paper money, Canadian paper money, ancient coins, world coins, medals, and numismatic books. An excellent auction source of scarce Canadian paper money, including *Dominion of Canada, Bank of Canada*, and *Canadian Chartered Bank Notes*, with hammer prices in two- and three-figure ranges. A recent auction also offered many intact collections of Belgian, French, and German *notgeld*. Send $10 in U.S. or Canadian funds for their next auction catalog. In business since 1969; in the auction business since 1986.

Olmstead Currency

OLMSTEAD CURRENCY
P.O. Box 487
St. Stephen, New Brunswick E3L 3A6 Canada
(506) 466-2078 (Day)
(506) 466-2893 (Evening)

Also a United States address:
OLMSTEAD CURRENCY
P.O. Box 135
Calais, ME 04619

Olmstead Currency, operated by Don Olmstead, specializes in buying, selling, and appraising the paper currency and *Silver Dollars* of Canada. Issues periodic retail price lists offering *Dominion of Canada, Bank of Canada*, and *Canadian Chartered Bank Notes*, mostly at reasonable two- and three-figure prices, with many cheaper notes for beginning collectors and those on a low budget. A recent price list even had some note proofs and Newfoundland currency. Also sells the "Charlton" catalogs, and Mylar® currency holders. In business since 1967. Send for their latest price list of "Paper Currency and Silver Dollars of Canada."

InterCol London

INTERCOL LONDON (mailing address)
43 Templars Crescent
London N3 3QR
England
(081) 349-2207

INTERCOL LONDON (gallery address) at
Donay's 35 Camden Passage
London N1 8EA
(071) 354-2599

Operated by Yasha Beresiner, paper money expert, InterCol London sells world paper money, coins, collector playing cards (including pre-20th century antique cards), maps, prints, and numismatic books, by mail or in person at their gallery address. For walk-in business, InterCol's Gallery is open on Wednesdays and Saturdays from 9:30 A.M. to 5:30 P.M., other days by appointment. Publishes retail price lists for the different collectibles. Ask for their paper money price list (minimum total order: £10 or $20 U.S.).

Colin Narbeth and Son

COLIN NARBETH AND SON LTD.
(mailing address)
6 Hall Place Gardens
St. Albans, Herts. AL1 3SP
United Kingdom
(072) 786-8542

COLIN NARBETH AND SON LTD.
(shop address)
20 Cecil Court Leicester Square
London WC2N 4HE
England
(071) 379-6975

Buys and sells paper money of the world, in all price ranges. Operated by bank note expert Colin Narbeth. Publishes a price list of British and foreign bank notes. Does business by mail, or in person at their shop address (above). When in London, visit their shop and browse through their paper money stocks. The shop address is 50 yards from Leicester Square Tube Station, off Charing Cross Road. Shop hours are Tuesday through Friday, from 10:30 A.M. to 5:30 P.M.; and Monday and Saturday, from 10:30 A.M. to 4:00 P.M.; closed Sundays. A good source of 20th century *Bank of England* notes, by Chief Cashier time periods, for specialists in such. Write for their price list of British and world bank notes. Narbeth is the founder and current President of the International Bank Note Society.

Spink & Son

SPINK & SON LTD.
5, 6, & 7 King Street, St. James's
London SW1Y 6QS
England
(071) 930-7888

Spink & Son Ltd. bills itself as the "oldest established coin and medal business in the world." The company evolved from a goldsmith business set up on Lombard Street in London by John Spink in 1666. Since the 1920s, Spink's has been at its present location on King Street.

Besides selling antiques in general, Spink and Son Ltd. has specialist departments including: Banknotes; Bullion; English and Foreign Coins; Numismatic Books; and Orders,

Decorations, and Medals. The numismatic departments are open daily, Monday through Friday, from 9:30 A.M. to 5:30 P.M. London time.

In reply to my request for information about Spink's Banknote Department for inclusion in this book, Mr. Barnaby G. Faull, the Manager of the Banknote Department, sent me a personal letter, in which he states:

> We have a good general stock, specialising in the individual note for collectors, as opposed to the bulk business.

> We hold regular auctions in London, Singapore, and Hong Kong, and you may be aware that we have recently handled the major part of the Amon Carter collection. We also publish books on paper money, including the standard reference work on English paper money by Vincent Duggleby.

Any paper money collector visiting London should visit Spink's. They won't throw you out on the street if you don't buy anything, and you're welcome to come in to browse or chat with the sales clerks. But don't take money in that you can't afford to spend. As for advice to serious collectors, Anthony Spink, one of the current directors of the company, says, "Buy what you can't afford" for the best chances for future value appreciation!

CURRENCY DEALER ORGANIZATIONS

Most currency dealers are members of one or more of the following organizations. While organization membership, or lack of it, isn't the only way to judge a dealer's ethics, it is a fact that outright crooks tend to be expelled from professional organizations. An honest dealer may not be a member of any organization for personal philosophical reasons. But when you are considering doing expensive business with a "new" currency dealer, ask him about his membership affiliations, then check with the organization to verify that the dealer is a member in good standing. Paper money dealers, however, tend to be more ethical, as a group, than many other professions.

American Numismatic Association

AMERICAN NUMISMATIC ASSOCIATION (ANA)
818 North Cascade Avenue
Colorado Springs, CO 80903
(719) 632-2646

While the 30,000+ membership of the ANA consists mostly of coin collectors, many paper money dealers and virtually all big-time dealers in America are also members. If a dealer has been expelled from the ANA, it would be helpful to know why. Write or call the ANA to verify whether a dealer is a member in good standing.

Professional Currency Dealers Association

PROFESSIONAL CURRENCY DEALERS ASSOCIATION (PCDA)
P.O. Box 589
Milwaukee, WI 53201

Members of the Professional Currency Dealers Association often have bourse tables at major coin/currency shows. Others do business by mail and/or from their stores. Write to the PCDA for a list of dealers and auction firms specializing in paper money.

Professional Numismatists Guild

PROFESSIONAL NUMISMATISTS GUILD (PNG)
P.O. Box 430
Van Nuys, CA 91408
(818) 781-1764

The Professional Numismatists Guild is the largest coin dealer organization in the United States, and many PNG members deal in paper money. Potential members are screened for financial and character reliability, and they must agree to a code of ethics by pledging to buy and sell at reasonable prices, to avoid false advertising, to refrain from knowingly dealing in stolen merchandise, to cooperate with governmental authorities in the prosecution of violators of laws involving numismatists, etc.

A free directory of PNG members is available by writing to the above address. Include postage when requesting free information from any organization. The latest PNG Membership Directory is a handsome booklet, weighing $2^1/2$ ounces, and listing close to 500 members. The PNG is non-profit and was incorporated in 1955. There are many currency dealers who aren't members, however.

Canadian Association of Numismatic Dealers

CANADIAN ASSOCIATION OF NUMISMATIC DEALERS (CAND)
2525 Carling Avenue, Suite D4
Ottawa, Ontario K2B 7Z2
Canada
(613) 820-9204

The Canadian Association of Numismatic Dealers is an organization similar to the PNG (above). The CAND members are mostly dealers in Canada, but there are some U.S. dealers also. Many CAND members deal in paper money, especially Canadian currency. For a list of CAND members, contact the Executive Secretary of CAND.

British Numismatic Trade Association

BRITISH NUMISMATIC TRADE ASSOCIATION
  LTD. (BNTA)
P.O. Box 82
Coventry CV1 2SH
England

The British Numismatic Trade Association was founded in 1973. Membership is open to any full-time coin dealer (many of whom also deal in paper money) based in the British Isles and registered for the British "Value Added Tax" (a type of national sales tax that no rational American would ever want to have introduced into the United States' Internal Revenue Service taxing system). The BNTA has grown into a group of nearly 100 numismatic dealers in England, Scotland, Wales, and Ireland.

Not all currency dealers in Great Britain are BNTA members, but many are, and the Secretary of the BNTA (at the association's address above) will be happy to tell you whether or not a British currency dealer is a BNTA member in good standing. The BNTA also distributes a 35-page booklet listing current members.

It is a mark of great courtesy to enclose either the nation's mint stamps or some currency when requesting a reply by mail from an overseas organization. Most local stamp dealers can supply current British postage stamps (send about $1 U.S. in face value). As a last resort, enclose an American dollar bill with your request and gamble that the recipient can convert it to local national currency (or include it in his "inventory" of U.S. currency; so send a CU note!).

Other Organizations for Currency Dealers

Many currency dealers are members of one or more of the currency collectors' societies mentioned in Chapter 23, especially: the Society of Paper Money Collectors (SPMC) and/or the International Bank Note Society (IBNS). Prominent currency dealers often print SPMC or IBNS membership logos in their display advertisements in the society journals themselves or in the numismatic periodicals (Chapter 22). For one reason or another, some currency dealers are just members of collectors' societies, and not members of any formal dealers' organization (saving membership fees, being a part-time dealer, and having paper money as only a small percentage of the business inventory are three reasons).

222. Jay Tell, President of Americana Stamp and Coin Company, Inc., in his Tarzana, California store showroom. When I told Mr. Tell that I was writing this book, he pulled out some bundles of choice U.S. *Large Size Currency*, which he let me photograph for illustrations in this book. Author's photo, printed with permission.

223. The business card of a professional paper money dealer.

224. Currency auction catalogs, such as this one of R.M. Smythe & Company of New York City, become reference works in themselves, useful for information long after the sale has passed. Reproduced with permission of R.M. Smythe & Company, New York City.

225. Bundles of soft plastic holdered choice U.S. *Large Size Currency* in the stock of Americana Stamp and Coin Company, photographed in the store's showroom by the author. Courtesy Americana Stamp and Coin Company, Inc. of Tarzana, California.

226. A selection of *Gold Certificates* in the *Large Size* U.S. currency retail price list catalog of Stanley Morycz of Englewood, Ohio. Reproduced with permission of Mr. Morycz.

227. 100 *Leke* SPECIMEN (overprinted in red) note of Albania of 1976. "Worker and Boy at Dam." (Pick # 46s)

"Money and goods are certainly the best references."
Charles Dickens (1812-1870)
Our Mutual Friend

Paper Money Shows

Just about every large U.S. city has coin shows every year, and in these shows there inevitably are paper money dealers. A couple of shows cater exclusively to paper money and related items. Even small cities may have local bourses.

Technically, a show includes exhibits (competitive or otherwise) as well as dealer tables for buying and selling with visitors. The dealer table section is known as a bourse, a marketplace where buyers and sellers meet to do business. A lot of bourses are called shows, even though there are no exhibits.

One of the priceless advantages to subscribing to a numismatic periodical (see Chapter 22) is that they list in detail the upcoming numismatic shows throughout the United States, and sometimes Canada and other countries, so that you can plan your trips and vacations around the currency show calendars. I like to visit faraway shows that attract different dealers than the ones in Los Angeles (where I live), so I can see new dealers' stocks of paper money and chat with new faces — although you can buy just about anything that's buyable in Los Angeles.

The largest shows, discussed in this chapter, are truly impressive events. Besides having hundreds of dealer tables for you to browse over, the giant shows offer seminars, auctions, lectures and slide shows, and spectacular currency exhibits where you can see in living reality many of the rare pieces that you read about in books (Bibliography), periodicals (Chapter 22), or society journals (Chapter 23). The biggest names in the currency business turn up at the largest shows, and you can say "Hi" to the people you have read about in the numismatic magazines.

CURRENCY SHOW ETIQUETTE

There are some established and unwritten rules to follow when visiting a currency show. Here they are, with my own opinions interjected.

1.   Don't steal. Currency shows have both uniformed and plainclothes security guards walking around, and the inside of the local jail will look a lot more forlorn than the empty spaces in your paper money albums, if you cross the line that separates currency thieves from honest collectors. Don't even look as if you're stealing: keep your hands on the table when you're handling a dealer's stock, keep everything in full view of the dealer, and ask permission to take out some currency of your own to compare with the dealer's — so that there's no question about whose notes are whose. If you find paper money on the floor, turn it in to the desk so you won't be accused of stealing.

2.   Don't let anyone else steal your currency. Keep one eye on your bag of paper money possessions at all times. Place your briefcase (if you bring one) between your feet when you sit in a chair. Protect your wallet from pickpockets.

Patrons have been known to be robbed after they leave a big-time currency show. Don't "advertise" that you're carrying valuables as you walk and ride away, and beware of strangers suddenly approaching you and asking for directions, etc. (They sometimes work in teams, with one person distracting you, while an accomplice steals your bag of currency. A favorite tactic is to slash the tires of your car so that you have a slow leak that forces you to stop a short distance from the show, with the robbers following you. Or they bump into you, causing you to stop long enough to get robbed.)

Don't leave valuables in an unattended car at or away from show premises. If you think you're being followed, go to a public place and call the police. Don't be paranoid, but don't be vulnerable. Collectible currency is valuable loot to a thief.

3.   Plan your currency show activities in advance. Do you want to explore the bourse floor for a few hours first? Will you have enough time to see the exhibits? Do you only have today to spend at the show, or will you be coming back tomorrow? (Warning: It is unfortunately customary for dealers to pack up and leave early on Sunday, the last day of a two- or three-day "weekend" show. If you really want to see the bourse, don't arrive Sunday afternoon!)

Don't spend all your money with the first dealer. I like to look around for a while to compare prices and see what's available before I spend any of my money. And if you go with companions, set a time and place in the show to meet again for lunch, or if you become separated.

4.   Handle the collectible currency (or other merchandise) of others with the utmost care, with more respect than if it was your own:

• Always ask permission before you touch a piece of dealer's paper money, including (and especially) taking it out of its protective holder.

• Handle paper money slowly and gently, with clean hands, and without bending it.

• Handle one note (or other paper collectible) at a time.

• Keep your own notes separated from the notes of others.

• Handle paper money specimens over the table so that if you drop them they won't fall on the floor.

• Keep the dealer's merchandise in full view of the dealer at all times.

5.   Don't lean on glass-topped display cases that might break.

6.   Negotiation is acceptable when buying or selling at a currency show, provided you are courteous and sincere. Don't be embarrassed to ask for a small discount, but don't abuse the dealer's patience with petty bickering over a few cents' difference in price. Shop around when buying or selling items at a currency show. Don't feel obligated to accept the first offer you get (or any offer): just politely say, "Thanks for your offer and your time. I'll think about it, and I may be back." Get away from high-pressure salesmen (who are rare, anyway, in the paper money business) who make you feel as though you are a worthless human being unless you do a million dollars worth of business with them.

7.   Time is money to a busy dealer who has paid for a show table, and maybe traveled a long distance to greet you at this show. Including hotel bills, plane fares, and show table fees, a dealer can easily spend $1,000 or more to see you at this show. It is considered bad manners to chat for an hour with a dealer, taking up chair-space at his table, then do no business with him, while he is losing potential customers who walk away because his table is too crowded with idle visitors. Five or ten minutes is okay; an hour of financially unproductive "visiting" is not.

Small shows, however, are more relaxed and informal than larger shows. I like to go to big shows for serious business, and to small shows to sit and chat with dealers who have more time to do so because they are less busy than they would be at a big show.

8.   Ask questions. If you're curious about something, ask about it: "What's the price of that *Black Eagle* note? Do you have any more British paper money besides the ones in the display case? Is that *Confederate Note* AU or UNC? Why is this note more expensive than that one? Do you have any

stocks or bonds from California or Illinois? What's the story behind that Austrian note? Can I look through your bundle of *Small Size* U.S. notes?"

9.   Currency show food may be tasteless or overpriced (or both). If you don't mind spending $5 to $10 of your collecting budget for a show lunch counter meal of a stale hot dog, a tiny bag of potato chips, a donut, and a heavily iced soft drink, then go ahead. Actually some show chairmen have been working on improving the food quality at their show concession stands, but they know that you're a captive audience (and if you're hungry, you'll eat).

When I go to a currency show, I don't care what I eat because I go for the paper money, not the cuisine. When I go with a companion, we sometimes plan ahead to have lunch or dinner away from the show at a place that serves real food. You can eat anytime, but this show may be only once a year. On the other hand, I can't concentrate on *notgeld* and *Silver Certificates* when I'm really hungry. But I never eat or drink as I'm walking around the show; dealers don't like it when you spill your chili burger all over their CRISP UNCIRCULATED *Ming Dynasty* notes or Montgomery *Confederates*.

10.   Have fun at the show! This is the most important rule, and one that is too often neglected by people who know the price of everything but the value of nothing. If you're not enjoying yourself at a dealer's table, try another one. There are a lot of dealers at a big show!

It's not how much money you spend, or what kind of "bargains" you get, but how much fun you have that makes your currency show visit a success. And don't be afraid to walk away without spending money at a show; if the prices are too high, or if the condition is too low, pass up the offered currency and walk away. There will be other shows, but once your collecting budget is spent, it may be hard to retrieve or replace. Money in your bank account is nice to have, too!

THE BIGGEST CURRENCY SHOWS IN THE U.S.

Two major shows devoted to paper money (and related items) take place each year in the United States: the International Paper Money Show in Memphis, Tennessee in June and the National and World Paper Money Convention in St. Louis, Missouri in October or November.

Four of the biggest national "coin" shows, which also always have substantial paper money dealer presence, are the ANA, the Central States, the FUN, and the Long Beach shows.

People go the these shows to do business with top currency dealers and to take the pulse of the currency market. If you've never been to a big currency show, you're in for a treat because it's a little overwhelming. The first time I stepped onto the bourse floor of the Long Beach show, I stood still in shock for ten minutes while my brain tried to comprehend everything my eyes were seeing. Where else can you see millions of dollars worth of currency up close, and learn a lot about it besides?

International Paper Money Show (Memphis)

The International Paper Money Show (IPMS) has been held every year in Memphis, Tennessee since 1977, and is the largest exclusively paper money show in the United States. Sponsored by the Memphis Coin Club and the Society of Paper Money Collectors, this show attracts over 2,000 visitors and nearly 150 dealers. Tables cost $275 to dealers, and no dealer who has ever been refused membership in or expelled from any numismatic organization may have a bourse table; but tables are available for new dealers to participate.

Affectionately called the "Memphis Show" by collectors and dealers alike, the International Paper Money Show is held in the same place every year: Cook Convention Center at 255 North Main Street. The official hotel of this show is:

Holiday Inn Crowne Plaza
250 North Main Street
Memphis, TN 38103
(901) 527-7300

And a designated backup hotel for the show is:
Brownestone Hotel
300 North Second Street
Memphis, TN 38105
(901) 525-2511

Virtually every kind of paper money is bought and sold on the bourse floor of the Memphis Show, and if you don't see what you want to buy, some dealer there probably knows where to get it for you. Of course, besides paper money proper, large holdings of bank checks, stocks, bonds, scrip, and other fiscal paper (see Chapter 6) are always brought by dealers to this show.

At the last International Paper Money Show in Memphis, there were: (a) the Bureau of Engraving and Printing's Billion Dollar Exhibit, (b) the American Bank Note Commemoratives Exhibit, (c) Commemorative Souvenir Cards issued, (d) a spectacular currency auction by Lyn F. Knight, Inc. (see Chapter 17), (e) fantastic paper money exhibits, (f) numismatic society meetings, and (g) a U.S. Postal Service Temporary Postal Station with commemorative cancels available.

For more information about the International Paper Money Show in Memphis every June, contact Mike Crabb, the show's Bourse Chairman, who can supply hotel room reservation cards, bourse table applications for dealers, airline information, and a flyer announcing the show's dates, phone numbers, etc.:

Michael A. Crabb, Jr.
P.O. Box 17871
Memphis, TN 38187

National and World Paper Money Convention (St. Louis)

The National and World Paper Money Convention (NWPMC) has been held annually since 1986. Affectionately called the "St. Louis Show" by collectors and dealers, the National and World Paper Money Convention is held over a three-day weekend (Friday, Saturday, and Sunday for visitors — Thursday is "Booth Holder Setup Day") in October or November at the Cervantes Convention Center, 801 Convention Plaza, St. Louis, Missouri. The official hotel of this convention is:

Holiday Inn — St. Louis Downtown/Convention Center
811 North 9th Street
St. Louis, MO 63101
(314) 421-4000

Ask for the "Paper Money Convention" room rate when making reservations for the Convention dates.

Sponsored by the Professional Currency Dealers Association (PCDA), this show attracts about 1,500 visitors a year and 100 dealers. It's called a "convention," but it's really everything in paper money, including exhibits, programs, auctions, and a bourse. The bourse tables cost $265 to dealers, and that cost includes three exhibit cases and one light; some tables are usually available to new bourse dealers. The St. Louis Convention is much like the Memphis Show (described above), only a little smaller. The top dealers go to both.

For information on the next National and World Paper Money Convention in St. Louis, contact either:

Professional Currency Dealers Association
P.O. Box 573
Milwaukee, WI 53201

or:

Ron Horstman
Box 6011
St. Louis, MO 63139

ANA Shows

The American Numismatic Association (ANA) numismatic shows (coins and paper money combined) are held twice a year: an Early Spring show and an Anniversary Convention. The ANA has been having regular conventions since 1891. The cities where they are held are determined when a local numismatic club makes a bid; then the ANA Board of Governors votes on the city site proposal.

There are about 450 dealers' tables in the bourse at the Anniversary Convention shows, where the dealer cost per table runs about $900, and visitor attendance averages 10,000 to 15,000. About 200 tables at $500 apiece grace the Early Spring ANA show, where attendance hits 5,000 to 8,000. Although most of the bourse consists of coin dealers, the most prominent paper money dealers in the United States will be at the ANA shows, and you will find plenty of paper money there, in all price ranges. Exhibits, awards, and seminars round out the ANA show schedule.

For information on the next ANA show, contact:

American Numismatic Association
818 North Cascade Avenue
Colorado Springs, CO 80903
(719) 632-2646

Central States Shows

The Central States Numismatic Society (CSNS) shows consist of a spring convention and a fall show every year in the central U.S. Since 1940 the CSNS has been holding annual conventions in different cities each year. The CSNS is a regional organization composed of thirteen states in the upper Midwest. The CSNS shows feature coins and paper money.

The spring convention is larger, with about 375 dealer bourse tables at a cost of $375 per table. There is an auction in conjunction with, but separate from, the CSNS convention, and also educational seminars and competitive exhibits. The number of visitors varies with the location, but runs from 5,000 to 10,000 for the three-day spring convention. For information on the next CSNS show, check the numismatic periodicals' show schedules (see Chapter 22), or write:

Central States Numismatic Society
58 Devonwood Avenue S.W.
Cedar Rapids, IA 52404

FUN Show

The Florida United Numismatists (FUN) show is held early in January each year and is the numismatic show that "kicks off" the New Year season in the numismatic business in the United States. While the bourse may be the main reason most visitors attend, this show is also held expressly for the annual convention of the FUN state numismatic association; always at the Orange County Convention/Civic Center in Orlando, Florida.

Held every year since 1956 in Florida, the FUN show attracts over 500 dealer tables for the bourse and over 20,000 visitors. A regular table costs $600. A corner table costs $900. Many collectors in the South find the FUN show convenient to attend, arriving by either car or airplane. Watch the numismatic periodicals (Chapter 22) for information on next January's show, or write:

Florida United Numismatists
P.O. Box 349
Gainesville, FL 32602

Long Beach Shows

And then there's the Long Beach Numismatic, Philatelic and Baseball Card Exposition (as its evolving title is cur-

rently), held three times a year — in February, June, and October. The show runs for four days for the public: Thursday through Sunday. From my experience at this and other shows, dealers pack up early on Sunday and leave before the official Sunday hours are over, so try to come before Sunday if you want to see the whole bourse.

The Long Beach Expo features 565 dealer tables on the whole bourse floor, and there is a four-year waiting list for renting a table. Table fees run from $300 to $475, but that's irrelevant if you can't get one! The Long Beach Exposition has the highest average attendance of any numismatic show in the world, drawing upwards of 20,000 collectors and dealers. The bourse is open only to dealers on Wednesday, then to the public for the next four days.

Admission is $2, far less than the cost of a movie ticket, for what I think is the most spectacular combined coin and paper money show imaginable. Of course, the Los Angeles freeways are a show in themselves, but if you survive the freeway trip to the Long Beach Convention Center, 300 East Ocean Boulevard, Long Beach, California (where the show is always held), be prepared for a stiff parking lot fee. (The fee is worth paying for the security that it offers, but I prefer to park on a Long Beach side street and walk a few blocks to the Convention Center. The walk may be too long for you, though. The new Southern California Rapid Transit District [RTD] Blue Line passenger train stops two blocks from the Long Beach Convention Center, and is a joy to ride compared to New York City or Chicago subways.)

Although mostly coin dealers occupy the bourse, there are enough paper money dealers to fill up two days of your visiting, including the top paper money dealers in the United States. The paper money dealers are scattered throughout the bourse floor, however, so you have to scout the whole numismatic section so you don't miss any paper money dealers.

Adjacent to the Long Beach Convention Center are two hotels offering special rates to convention participants: the Hyatt Regency Hotel at (310) 491-1234, and the Ramada Renaissance at (310) 437-5900.

Billed as "The Show Often Imitated But Never Equaled!", the Long Beach Expo is run with care and success by Samuel Lopresto and Teresa Darling. The Long Beach Convention Center is a modern facility situated near the oceanfront in downtown Long Beach, and I suggest that you drive or take a taxi to cover the distance to a decent Long Beach restaurant. (Ask the people at the Long Beach Coin Club where they like to eat in town.)

For information on the next show, see their full-page ad in *Coin World* and *Numismatic News* or contact Sam and Teresa at:

Long Beach Exposition
112 East Broadway
Long Beach, CA 90802
(310) 437-0819

228. Bourse floor of the Long Beach Numismatic, Philatelic and Baseball Card Exposition, Inc. at the Long Beach Convention Center, Long Beach, California. Photo courtesy of the Exposition.

229. 200 *Leva* note of Bulgaria, 1951. Communist issue. (Pick # 87)

230. Reverse of 200 *Leva* Bulgarian note of Photo 229. "Tobacco Harvesting." (Pick # 87)

231.   Reverse of 10 *Lirasi* note of Turkey, "dated" per bank law of 1970 on face side. President Ataturk receiving flowers from children. Watermark of Ataturk's bust at right. (Pick # 130)

232.   Reverse of $3 Bahamas note, no date (but per Currency Note Act of 1965). Artist's sketch of Paradise Beach. (Pick # 19)

233.   50 *Francs* note of Belgium, 1966. King Baudouin and Queen Fabiola. (Pick # 69)

19

Currency Investing

Ah, the future: what a fantastic and mysterious place! Sometimes you have to wonder whether it is good or bad that we can't see into the future. There are many reasons to collect currency, and the prospect of financial gain is just one of them. If it were easy to make quick fortunes, we would all be rich. Because the future is uncertain, and because so many factors (including uncontrollable ones) are involved in the market fluctuations of a freely-traded commodity in a supply-and-demand economic system (which is what the paper money business is), investment advice seems a little pretentious. If any so-called "investment advisor" knew for a fact which notes would make big profits in the next year or two, that advisor wouldn't be selling his advice, he'd be taking it himself. Remember that the next time somebody offers you a "get rich quick" deal on currency that will "undoubtedly skyrocket in value in three months!"

Still, it is a challenge to buy currency with an informed eye toward future price appreciation, and that is the purpose of this chapter. Three factors determine a note's market price: rarity, condition, and demand. Some notes are rare but have little collector/investor demand (certain 19th century *Broken Bank* note varieties of the U.S. and Europe). Other notes are rare in UNCIRCULATED condition, but relatively plentiful and cheap when found in a heavily worn state (many *Confederates* of 1861-1862). Still other notes are not rare, but their selling prices are abnormally high because of the permanent tremendous collector demand for them (the $10 U.S. *Legal Tender* "Bison" note of 1901). Then, of course, rarity coupled with demand pushes note prices through the roof (*National Gold Bank Notes* of California in the 1870s, many pre-20th century

Bank of England notes in nice condition, and any *Hawaiian Islands* or *Republic of Hawaii* notes (see Chapter 10).

I suggest that you be a collector first, a notaphilist/numismatist second, and an investor last. In other words, (1) learn how to collect by familiarizing yourself with note characteristics, buying and selling some cheap notes, and training yourself in proper note handling and storage techniques. (2) Then study the notes by reading about them, discussing them with dealers and other collectors, and carefully and repeatedly looking at them for specific traits (paper qualities, printing idiosyncrasies, watermark variations, etc.) — the science of notaphily. (3) Then, if you wish, think a little about investing a small portion of your disposable funds in notes for possible long-term profits. Most experienced paper money dealers agree that a nice meaningful currency collection, built up over a period of years by wise selection of historically important notes in better condition, has a chance of becoming a very profitable investment.

THE DIFFERENCE BETWEEN PAPER MONEY AND COIN "INVESTING"

In its everyday use as a medium of exchange, paper money functions similarly to coins. Indeed, the natural attraction of people to currencies in general results in many "collectors/investors" dabbling in both rare coins and paper money, such that many dealers handle both coinage and paper to accommodate the two major divisions of numismatics as embodied in money. So a casual observer might rashly conclude that the coin and paper money businesses are indistinguishable in basic customs and consequences.

More often than not, the market price movements of collectible paper money more closely mimic those of our sister hobby of philately (stamp collecting) than they do coin collecting because coins have always been more speculative and market-manipulated than paper money has. There are several reasons for this frequently seen discrepancy between the coin and paper money markets: (1) more people collect coins than paper money; (2) coins with precious metal content (like gold or silver) may follow daily bullion spot prices as well as numismatic collecting fads; (3) coins have traditionally been more heavily promoted by "fast-buck artists" as "investments" than paper currency has; (4) the high face value of currently legal tender paper money (of any nation) discourages the spontaneous accumulation of high denomination circulating notes by would-be "investors" who haven't delved into the realm of obsolete currency price history; (5) many issues of paper money are scarcer, and therefore less mass-marketable, than purported "rare" coins that in reality exist in near-limitless quantities (among these are common-date 19th century U.S. *Morgan Silver Dollars*, which every coin dealer in the world has in stock. When was the last time you saw a display ad in a non-numismatic newspaper or magazine, offering to sell 19th century U.S. federal paper currency, per 1/per 10/and per 100 notes?); and (6) paper money collecting tends to attract a more conservative and financially cautious personality than the coin business does.

It is an unusual collectible bank note that doubles or triples in price in one year, once the supply of it is stable and known. It is normal for some coin prices to shoot up or crash virtually overnight, based on coin market rumors and collector/investor crowd psychology. There are both short-term and long-term ups and downs in the paper money market, but paper currency is a more orderly market, in general, than the coin business is.

Collecting fads do come (and go?) with paper money, affecting prices accordingly. *Confederate Notes* received increased collector/investor interest from the recently popular television series on the Civil War that was broadcast in America, and a currency dealer in Los Angeles told me about large quantities of *Confederate Notes* that were bought up and shipped to Japan where the Civil War television series has generated demand for *Confederate Currency* from America. And "special" Serial Number collecting ("radar" notes, low numbers, repeating numbers, etc.) has recently pushed such notes to incredible price heights. Whether they stay there depends on collector/investor whim.

CURRENCY DEALER ORGANIZATIONS

Most big-time paper money dealers in the United States who supply "investment quality" notes are members of one or more of these organizations (write to see if the dealer is a member in good standing; also, see Chapter 17 for descriptions of these organizations):

AMERICAN NUMISMATIC ASSOCIATION (ANA)
818 North Cascade Avenue
Colorado Springs, CO 80903

PROFESSIONAL CURRENCY DEALERS ASSOCIATION (PCDA)
P.O. Box 589
Milwaukee, WI 53201

PROFESSIONAL NUMISMATISTS GUILD (PNG)
P.O. Box 430
Van Nuys, CA 91408

And for a local coin/currency store, check with the local Better Business Bureau or Chamber of Commerce to see how long the company has been in business, and if there are any unresolved complaints against it.

ADVANTAGES OF PAPER MONEY INVESTMENT

Advantages of paper money investment include:

1.   High liquidity — notes with recognized value are easy to sell, although you may have to shop around for the best price.

2.   Small storage space requirements — a fabulous fortune in rare paper money can be hidden between the pages of a book or stored in a bank safe deposit box.

3.   Anonymity — Notes bought or sold for cash amounts under $10,000 per transaction (with exceptions) do not have to be reported to U.S. government authorities. Serious investment profits, however, are taxable income under the U.S. Internal Revenue Service Code (capital gains clause).

4.   Portability — Notes can be transported with ease anywhere in the world. And dealers everywhere recognize the value in paper notes of all countries. National Customs and Border police agents may confiscate paper money being smuggled across international frontiers, but it is possible to escape a country in political-military turmoil with your life savings in rare paper money hidden in your clothing or baggage (but I don't advise folding an original CU currency rarity to get it to fit in a secret compartment in your wristwatch or shoe!).

5.   Moderate durability — Within reason, paper money is durable beyond your lifetime, much of it having been printed on quality paper to begin with, and it can safely be stored for long periods of time without noticeable deterioration (if properly housed in inert soft plastic sleeves, etc.). How durable is a racehorse or fragile oil painting, not to mention its portability and "concealability"? True, paper begins to decay from the moment it is made, but not nearly as fast as a prized rose garden or with as much surprise as a worm-eaten antique chair. If you keep it clean, dark, dry, away from mold and vermin, and in

mild temperatures, paper money should last long enough for you to recover your "investment" in it (or whatever the market will pay).

DISADVANTAGES OF PAPER MONEY INVESTMENT

Realistic people have a balanced view of the world. Before you sink your life savings into rare currency, here are some possible disadvantages of paper money investment:

1.   No regular interest income accrues from currency, as happens punctually with bank savings accounts or "good" stock certificates that pay dividends. All profits from rare currency collections are strictly theoretical and "on paper only" until the notes are actually sold.

2.   Premium quality usually costs premium prices. Such premium quality (PQ, to borrow a term from the coin business) notes are defined as the best examples for their type and grade. But if they're such nice notes, nobody will consciously sell them to you cheaply. So how can you turn a profit if you're paying top dollar whenever you buy notes?

3.   Currency grading disputes and tampering exist. Your prized note may be AU to you but EF to somebody else. A difference in grade can be a big difference in price. And are you sure that the note hasn't been washed, repaired, or fraudulently altered? Can you trust the person who sold it to you?

4.   Some notes are only semi-liquid; i.e., they may take a long time to sell for the best possible price. Examples: damaged notes (some buyers refuse to look at notes with pinholes), esoteric foreign notes, worn rare notes that can be found in high grade, and "pedigreed" common notes whose major value lies in finding a buyer who appreciates the notes' previous owners.

5.   Currency market fluctuations are impossible to predict with perfect accuracy, making note investing a little nerve-racking. Should you buy or sell today? Sounds like the stock market, doesn't it?

QUALITY VS. QUANTITY

Quality is preferable to quantity when contemplating currency investing. Cheap notes in bulk batches have made profits for lucky "investors" who held them until their prices rose significantly. But most dealers want the top quality scarce notes, and what dealers want, smart collectors/investors want also.

Buy one nice note for $100 rather than ten mediocre notes for $10 each. The $100 note should be much easier to dispose of when you decide to sell. Sometimes I've made money, sometimes I've lost money in my paper currency deals, but I've never regretted buying an expensive note of AU or UNC condition.

RESEARCHING THE CURRENCY MARKET

You must research the currency market before spending a dime on paper money "investments." Which notes have the best price track records? Which notes are always in demand? Where are prices today compared to last year? Are these notes as easy to sell as they are to buy? Are they popular with collectors in one country or in many countries? Which conditions are most in demand? Are there dangerous counterfeits known? What are the typical wholesale/retail price spreads of these notes? Are these notes a passing fad or of lasting importance in the serious money market?

You research the currency market by reading: (1) books that discuss the notes that intrigue you (see Bibliography), (2) notaphilic periodicals (Chapter 22), and (3) paper money society journals (Chapter 23). You research the market when you talk with or correspond with currency dealers and study their retail price lists and auction catalogs (Chapter 17). You research the market when you go to paper money shows, if you can get to them, and look and listen until your eyes and ears are tired. And while you're learning, you're also collecting: buying and selling cheaper notes so you can become accustomed to how the currency market operates on a small scale. And after you've done all of this for a year or two, you may be ready to "invest" in your first expensive (for your budget) note.

SPECULATION VS. INVESTING

Speculation is short-term hoping to make a financial "killing" by frequently buying and selling a freely traded commodity. Investing is long-term hoping to make a profit by buying and selling such commodities.

If you buy a bundle of recently devalued foreign notes at a bargain price, and plan to hold them for six months in hopes of a profit upon resale, that's speculation. If you carefully, after long consideration, and over a period of time (say, a year or more), select one choice note every couple of months (to the extent of your investment capital), and gradually build up a note "portfolio" with diversity and individual beauty, and hold these notes for ten years to see what they will be worth, that's investing (or, at least, intelligent collecting).

Collecting history has shown that it is hard to "corner the market" by buying up and hoarding a particular type of note in order to drive up prices. Cornering the market has been attempted many times with varying degrees of success, but in the long run everything "evens out" because everybody knows what notes exist and who owns large quantities of them.

Speculation has temporarily run up the prices of bank notes, but you have to ask yourself this question: is the new price supported by collector demand? Collectors (not speculators, not dealers, not even "investors") are the ultimate consumers of rare currency. If broad masses of collectors aren't pushing the price up for a rapidly increasing currency market price, then it must be due to speculators and dealers buying and selling to each other, a perilous situation financially because when a few of these promoters panic and start dumping their investments on the market, the prices of these notes will crash fast (if not faster than they once rose). Don't confuse artificial scarcity (caused by hoarding and overpromoting) with real scarcity (caused by a minuscule supply of a note when compared with collector demand for it).

The currency investor, on the other hand, doesn't care about daily price fluctuations. The investor is in paper money for the long haul, not the short pull. Most people who call themselves "investors" are really "speculators," and it is speculation that fits the impatient American personality well and helps to line the pockets and wallets of semi-larcenous businessmen (who take advantage of people's obsession with making money) by forever offering to sell overpriced, overpromoted merchandise, a problem much more prevalent in the rare coin business than in the paper money business, but a problem all would-be investors should keep in mind.

CURRENCY MARKET CYCLES

Paper money market cycles are more gentle than the roller coaster boom-and-bust cycles of the rare coin market. Paper money does have its rising markets and its market "dips" (or "corrections" as they are charitably called by optimists). When note prices drop a bit, investors get burned, speculators get discouraged, dealers lose money, and the market stagnates.

Then a fascinating thing happens, as sure as the clockwork of a finely tuned timepiece. Somebody starts to buy again, then more people buy, then the prices of notes rise a little and even more people get interested and buy. And we have the birth of at least a temporary upswing and maybe the ground floor of a new currency boom market.

Bernard Baruch, the Wall Street wizard, had some excellent advice when asked how to make money in the stock market. He replied that his investment philosophy was to buy when others are selling and sell when others are buying. By going against the trend of a changing market ("contrarian" investment strategy), you have a chance to get things at bargain prices and sell them at a nice profit when others are feverishly buying during a boom phase. Unfortunately, it takes nerves of steel to be alone in a crowd!

What will the currency market do during the next twelve months? Nobody knows for sure, which is why all investing involves an element of risk.

WHAT TO BUY

But if we're going to risk our hard-earned money in buying expensive currency, why not choose those notes that have increased in price in the past and are in strong demand today? Let's list some notes that might be worth buying for long-term

investment, say ten years or more. This is provided, of course, that you manage to buy them at a fair market price today, and you'll only know what that is if you shop around, get informed, and find out what these notes are really worth in the legitimate currency market. I don't guarantee you'll make profits, but these are the notes that I would buy if I were a serious and sober note investor, with spendable cash to back up my notaphilic good taste.

1. Any 19th century U.S. federal issue *Large Size* note in AU to CU if obtainable (and affordable!). Don't overpay, however.

2. U.S. *California National Gold Bank Notes* of the 1870s, with price commensurate with grade.

3. Popular U.S. *Large Size* type notes that every dealer and collector wants to buy: the $1/$2/$5 *Educational Silver Certificates* of 1896, the $10 *Legal Tender* "Bison" note of 1901, etc. — AU to CU.

4. Scarce types of U.S. *Fractional Currency*, UNC.

5. Scarce "banks" of U.S. *National Bank Notes, Large* or *Small Size*, especially western states such as Arizona or Nevada where growing economies and increasingly affluent populations may generate indigenous collector demand for such notes — "any grade," with purchase price to match (but avoid tape-stained or otherwise unsightly damaged notes).

6. Expensive U.S. *Military Payment Certificates*, UNC.

7. Any pre-20th century European "Central Bank" (i.e., issued by the main government) "type" notes from countries with present-day strong economies; graded AU or better. Examples: *Bank of England* notes, *Banque de France* notes, German *Reichsbanknoten* (Imperial Bank Notes, with lower grades of these OK due to their extreme rarity in high grade).

8. Notes from former European overseas possessions, any grade (with nice eye appeal), costing $100 or more per note, with handsomely depicted native scenes and/or "topically" oriented. Examples: Belgian Congo (pre-1950), French Indo-China, British India.

9. Expensive ($100 or more) notes from current European overseas possessions, XF to UNC, with "type set" eye appeal so that collectors who specialize in that possession will need the note for their collection to be complete. Examples: Falkland Islands, Hong Kong, St. Pierre & Miquelon.

10. Expensive pre-20th century handsome "type" notes from any Asian country with a prosperous present-day economy. Example: Japanese *Imperial Government* issues of the 1870s and 1880s, in XF or better condition (if you can find them and afford them!).

11. Anything expensive from Canada, issued by the central government (*Province of Canada, Dominion,* or *Bank of Canada* issues), EF or better, with nice eye appeal.

12.   Any expensive pre-1950 beautifully designed "type" note from a well-known country that is poverty-stricken, with a large population, but with a rich romantic history, AU or better. Examples: China, Egypt, India, Mexico.

13.   Expensive "type" notes ($100 or more) from Australia or nearby islands (New Zealand), EF or better.

14.   *Confederate States of America* notes, UNC only, costing $100 or more per note. You may not have a large portfolio of these, but every *Confederate Note* dealer will want to buy them from you if your scarcer notes are truly UNCIRCULATED grade.

15.   Whatever all the currency dealers are forever advertising to buy, year after year, in good times and in bad, in and out of fad collecting areas. If the top dealers continually want it, it must be worth having. They've been in the paper money business longer than you have, and they know what's good!

WHOLESALE/RETAIL PRICE SPREADS

As a very rough rule, dealers pay about half the price at which they sell. It depends on the note, of course — on its collector desirability (demand), condition, and scarcity; whether or not the dealer already has a dozen in stock; and on the cash position (how much he can afford to spend that day) of the dealer. A popular note that is easy to sell may have a tighter wholesale/retail price spread than an esoteric, ugly (by collector consensus), "cheap" note that "nobody" needs to complete a type set collection. But in general, figure on getting about $50 wholesale price from a dealer who will sell you the same note for $100 retail price.

The wholesale/retail price spread is a major reason non-dealer speculators have trouble getting wealthy in their currency deals. If you buy at retail and sell at wholesale, you have to wait for your material to double in value (more or less) just for you to "break even" financially.

Two logical ways around this problem of large gaps between wholesale and retail prices are: (1) try to negotiate prices down when you're buying and up when you're selling if you do business with dealers, and (2) buy and sell notes at auction (auction prices are often somewhere between wholesale and retail prices, but you have to study the current market to know this for any given note).

DON'T OVERPAY FOR NOTES

No matter how breathtaking it is, and no matter how long you've been searching for one, where is the "investment value" in a note that's vastly overpriced in the present market? Pass it up, and buy something else. There is a lot of paper money on Earth, maybe some that's even worth investing in.

Remember: The real value of anything is not what you can buy it for, but what you can sell it for!

STANDARD CATALOG NUMBERS AND PRICES

Good investments tend to be ones that are easily recognized by large numbers of potential buyers, hence the market demand for such items. While "unlisted" varieties can be profitable, too, the smart investment money gravitates toward universally recognized major note types that enjoy prominent catalog number status in the accepted reference book in their field. For "safer" investments, buy notes that are listed as major catalog numbers in these books (see Bibliography): Friedberg's *Paper Money of the United States* (for U.S. currency), and Pick's *Standard Catalog of World Paper Money*, Volumes I and II (for foreign notes).

Catalog values are quoted for average retail prices by condition, and should have been current when the catalog edition was being edited, meaning that the catalog values may not accurately reflect the current market. Also, are you sure that the note's grade is identical to that listed in the catalog for that price? How do you evaluate a note that honestly grades between EF and AU, when catalog values are not given for intergrades? Or for slightly "damaged" notes (one or two pinholes)? Or for faded notes that are "perfect" in other respects?

THE CURRENCY DEALER NEWSLETTER

Published monthly since the first issue in September 1980, the *Currency Dealer newsletter* — also known as the *Greensheet* because of its color — reports the national currency market for U.S. notes from dealer-to-dealer transactions. The *Currency Dealer newsletter* covers "Bid" and "Ask" prices for most commonly collected U.S. note types — listed by Series and Friedberg numbers — for *Large Size, Small Size, Fractional Currency*, and gives periodic updates on specialized areas such as *Colonial* and *Continental Currency* and U.S. *Military Payment Certi*ficates.

The *Currency Dealer newsletter* has an in-depth article each month, written by a paper money expert. Recent articles include: "The American Bank Note Co.," "Grading vs. Authentication," and "Large Size Nationals."

The same company also publishes the *Coin Dealer newsletter* (the *Greysheet*) and the *Certified Coin Dealer newsletter* (the *Bluesheet*), both of which are used by U.S. coin dealers nationwide to monitor the coin market.

Past issues of the *Greensheet* all the way back to the first issue in 1980 are for sale by the company at nominal cost — a valuable opportunity to get in-depth information and past market data.

About the price quotes in the *Currency Dealer newsletter*: "Bid" price is what a dealer is willing to pay for a note; "Ask" price is what a dealer would like to get for a note in dealer-to-dealer "wholesale" transactions.

Subscription rates for the *Currency Dealer newsletter* (the *Greensheet*) are: $44 for 1 year (12 issues), $78 for 2 years. Currency dealers and serious investors who buy and sell U.S. *Large Size* and *Small Size* currency refer to the *Greensheet* for the latest price movements in such currency, and you don't have to be a dealer to subscribe.

Ron Downing, President of the company, has told me that readers of this book may obtain a free sample of the *Greensheet* by mentioning that they read about it in this book and by sending a No. 10 (business-sized) self-addressed stamped envelope to the company's headquarters:

CURRENCY DEALER newsletter
P.O. Box 11099
Torrance, CA 90510

And, in case you're curious, I get no financial reward for sending you to this company or to any other company that I have ever recommended in print.

I have selected three perennially popular U.S. *Large Size Notes*, circa 1900, and listed their "BID-ASK" prices on the accompanying chart — as they appeared in the December 1991 issue of the *Greensheet*. Get the latest copy to see what these notes are worth today.

CONDITION CONSIDERATIONS

No note is a bargain if it vastly overpriced relative to its condition and its demand. Condition "mistakes" become especially costly when trying to distinguish AU from UNC from CU from GEM CU (see Chapter 8). While top quality notes bring the best prices, you have to ask yourself if two or three collections of notes graded UNC to CU are more "worth having" than one collection graded GEM CU — for the same total amount of money. Just be absolutely certain that you are getting GEM CU when you buy GEM CU.

Profits can be made on any notes, even limp "junk" that is sold by the pound (in weight, not by denomination!), but better quality notes tend to be better investments, or at least are easier to sell when you decide to liquidate. Buy your "investment" notes in AU or better condition, if they are available as such.

IRS CASH REPORTING REQUIREMENTS

Under section 6050-I of the United States Revenue Code, form 8300 must be filed for cash transactions of $10,000 or more. "Structured" transactions that attempt to avoid reporting requirements (e.g., a $9,950 deal) may be prosecuted as well by the federal government if it can be proven that you were trying to evade the law. Large cash deals (around $10,000 or more) at currency bourses thus fall in the realm of this law, and expect dealers to obey it.

CUSTOMS SERVICE CASH REPORTING REQUIREMENTS

The U.S. Customs Service of the U.S. Department of the Treasury requires the filing of Customs Form 4790 (entitled "Report of International Transportation of Currency or Monetary Instruments") when currency or other monetary instruments (designated legal tender of the U.S. or any other country) exceeding $10,000 is physically transported, mailed, or shipped from or to the United States.

INVESTMENT HOLDING PERIODS

Plan on holding your currency "investments" for a minimum of five to 10 years. One-year holding is speculation, not investing. Of course, if you got burned by overpaying or getting misrepresented material when you bought it, you may be in for an unpleasant shock 10 years from now when you go to sell your paper money "portfolio."

PAPER MONEY INVESTING TIPS

Here are some tips to make you a better currency investor.

1. Buy the book before the note (see Bibliography, your local currency dealer, and even the public library).

2. Subscribe to and read the notaphilic/numismatic periodicals (Chapter 22).

3. Join some notaphilic societies and read what they send you (Chapter 23).

4. Go to currency shows and find out what notes are really worth (Chapter 18).

5. Start slowly. There are a lot of notes in the world. You don't have to spend your life savings on currency today.

6. Buy quality rather than quantity (one note for $100 rather than ten notes for $10 apiece). If nothing else, you'll be blessed with the chore of finding fewer buyers (maybe) if you have fewer notes to sell when you liquidate.

7. Diversify your "investment." Buy different types of notes to spread your risk.

8. Pay cash or its equivalent when you buy. Avoid credit terms and interest charges. Avoid layaways if possible — discipline yourself to save up for what you want to buy. No "buying on margin" like stock speculating!

9. Take immediate possession of your purchases, and hide them well at home or put them in a bank safe deposit box (see Chapter 7).

10. Keep records of what you bought, date purchased, where purchased, amount paid, note conditions, etc., for your own information and for tax purposes should you declare

capital gains or losses on your "investments." Warning: You have to prove to the Internal Revenue Service that your currency portfolio is an investment rather than a hobby to use your currency transactions for tax purposes; accurate recordkeeping is a good start.

11. Only invest a small portion of your total cash assets, say, about 10% to 20%.

12. Study currency auction prices to keep up-to-date with the market.

13. Review your currency "portfolio" about twice a year to chart your paper profits and losses. You can deduct losses from profits (upon sale) when figuring gross capital gains for the IRS.

14. Separate your currency investments from your idle note collection. It is OK to collect notes at a financial loss; it is not satisfying to invest at a net loss. Of course, the best investment may be a smart collection built up over the course of many years, as the leading currency dealers advise.

15. Get insurance for your collection/portfolio when it grows to present an unacceptable risk for theft, fire, etc. The ANA offers low cost currency insurance for members (see ANA in Chapter 23). Insure notes when sending them by mail or private carrier.

THE DECEMBER 1991 "BID-ASK" PRICES FOR THREE POPULAR LARGE SIZE U.S. NOTES AS REPORTED IN THE *CURRENCY DEALER NEWSLETTER*					
SERIES AND DENOMINATION	FRIEDBERG NUMBERS	CONDITIONS AND PRICES			
U.S. Note (Legal Tender) 1901 $10 ("Bison Note")	114-122	VG Bid $120 Ask $150	FINE Bid $170 Ask $195	VF Bid $225 Ask $290	XF Bid $410 Ask $460
		AU Bid $550 Ask $600	CU Bid $825 Ask $900	CH CU Bid $1100 Ask $1200	GEM CU Bid $1500 Ask $1650
Silver Certificate 1896 $1 ("Educational Note")	224-225	VG Bid $55 Ask $60	FINE Bid $90 Ask $100	VF Bid $140 Ask $160	XF Bid $250 Ask $290
		AU Bid $300 Ask $350	CU Bid $400 Ask $450	CH CU Bid $550 Ask $650	GEM CU Bid $850 Ask $925
Gold Certificate 1905 $20 ("Technicolor Note")	1179-1180	VG Bid $260 Ask $300	FINE Bid $425 Bid $485	VF Bid $835 Ask $935	XF Bid $1900 Ask $2200
		AU Bid $2600 Ask $3100	CU Bid $3600 Ask $4000	CH CU Bid $6100 Ask $6600	GEM CU Bid $8000 Ask $9000
From the *Currency Dealer newsletter*® 1991 by CDN Inc. Used by permission.					

234.   30 *Shillings* Massachusetts *Colonial Currency*, engraved and printed by Paul Revere. From a recent auction catalog of Currency Auctions of America, Inc. Reproduced with company permission. ("Undamaged and with no problems, every word of the text and all of the design is sharp and clear. Issued at the beginning of the Revolutionary War only four months after Paul Revere's famous ride. (2,500 - up).")

235.   *Large Size* U.S. $5 *Legal Tender Note*, Series 1869 (first year of this design). Andrew Jackson at left. "Pioneer Family," also called "Woodchopper," at center. Author's photo, from the stock of Americana Stamp and Coin Company, Inc. of Tarzana, California.

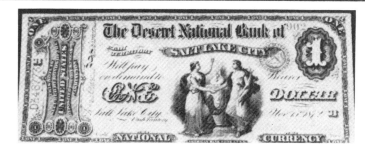

236.   Rare *National Bank Note* of 1872 from a recent auction catalog of Lyn F. Knight, Inc. of Overland Park, Kansas. Reproduced with company permission. ("Lot 576. Salt Lake City, Utah Territory, Deseret NB, #2059. Fr. 382. $1. Original. Super condition for this very rare Utah Territorial. Signed by Brigham Young and rare enough for any collection. XF (4,000 - 5,000).")

237.   *Large Size $2 Lazy Deuce National Bank Note* from a recent auction catalog of Currency Auctions of America, Inc. Reproduced with company permission. ("1908. Boston—$2.00. 1875. Fr. 384. The Continental NB. CH. #524. Possibly ex-Grinnell. Superior color, with a tight bottom margin. Crisp Uncirculated. (1,600 - 2,000).")

238.   *Large Size* $10 U.S. *Silver Certificate*, Series 1886. Commonly called the *Tombstone Note*, with portrait of U.S. Vice President Thomas A. Hendricks, who died in office in 1885. Author's photo, from the stock of Americana Stamp and Coin Company, Inc. of Tarzana, California.

239.   Reverse of *Large Size* U.S. $10 *Silver Certificate*, Series 1886, from Photo 238. Author's photo, from the stock of Americana Stamp and Coin Company, Inc. of Tarzana, California.

240.   *Large Size* U.S. $1000 *Gold Certificate* from a recent auction catalog of Currency Auctions of America, Inc. Reproduced with company permission. ("1619. Fr. 1220. $1,000. 1922. Choice Extra Fine. Appearing Choice Uncirculated at a glance, particularly so from the face, this new number to the census brings the total known up to 21, only 5 of which are near this grade or better. Well margined and perfectly centered on both sides, this gorgeous thousand dollar Gold would be one of the highlights of any collection it entered. (6,000 - up).")

20

Error Notes

Some of the more common errors that occur in the printing of United States paper money are interesting and affordable collectibles.

This chapter is a reprint of my article entitled, "Collecting Paper Money Errors," originally published in the October 1991 issue of *The Numismatist*, and here reprinted courtesy of *The Numismatist*, official publication of the American Numismatic Association, 818 North Cascade Avenue, Colorado Springs, CO 80903. I discuss U.S. *Small Size Note* errors found on modern, currently circulating U.S. paper money, as these are the most commonly collected error notes in the United States, but much of this information is applicable to error notes of other eras and other countries.

Collecting error bank notes is fascinating, yet need not be expensive. The market price of paper money errors increases as: (1) the denomination increases; (2) condition improves; (3) the "obviousness" of the error becomes more striking; and (4) the availability of such errors decreases.

In determining the market price of a paper money error, a collector must consider the note's face value. An error in a $100 note will inevitably cost more than the identical error on a $5 note because the $100 note is worth at least its face value. Some collectors specialize in $1 notes to save money, others limit their error acquisitions to denominations of $20 or less.

Condition helps to determine price almost as much as rarity. A *National Gold Bank* note from California dated in the 1870s will always be desirable in Good or Very Good condition simply because such notes are exceedingly rare in higher grades. And with grading services beginning to encapsulate notes in holders similar to coin slabs, the grading of notes is sure to stir up controversy in the next few years — like the

perpetual coin grading debates of "slabbed" vs. "raw" coins, "MS-this" vs. "MS-that"!

Robert Friedberg's *Paper Money of the United States* (which, by the way, doesn't picture or price error notes) lists nine grades for paper money: Gem UNCIRCULATED, Choice UNCIRCULATED, UNCIRCULATED, About UNCIRCULATED, Extra Fine, Very Fine, Fine, Very Good, and Good. (Instead of "UNCIRCULATED," some dealers call a note "New.")

Notes that are heavily creased, stained, torn or faded, or display pinholes or missing corners are best avoided by the error collector, unless it can be demonstrated that such defects are "part" of the error. Beware of "contrived" errors, that is, notes that have been artificially bleached or otherwise altered to make them appear to be genuine errors. Anyone can purchase sheets of current $1 and $2 Federal Reserve notes from the Bureau of Engraving and Printing, then deliberately miscut the notes to give them the appearance of a trimming error or faulty alignment.

These are some of the common errors found on modern, small-size U.S. currency:

PRE-PRINTING PAPER FOLDS

This type of error (also referred to as "blank creases") occurs when bank note paper is creased or bears a minute fold prior to printing. The result is an even white streak, devoid of printing ink, across a note's face. Such errors are more valuable if they have multiple creases, large creases, or creases through a note's portrait. Retail prices for a minor $1 note crease range from $25 to $35 in About UNCIRCULATED condition.

INK SMEARS

Sometimes called "plate smears," these errors usually are attributed to poorly functioning automatic inking machinery that imparts excess ink to the printing plate, resulting in smeared ink on the face or back. This type of error is easily faked, so don't pay a lot for such specimens. Typical retail for a dramatic AU note ink smear error is $20 or $30.

OFFSET TRANSFERS

When the printing press is started before the paper has been fed through it, a reversed image of all or part of the note's design is created on the other side, such as a back impression on a note's face. The darker and more complete the image (up to 100 percent offset transfer), the more valuable the note. For an UNCIRCULATED note ($1 through $20 in denomination) that shows heavy, complete offset transfer, the retail price usually is less than $100 per note!

MISSING PRINT

If a note lacks one of the three stages of printing, the error is described as "missing a print." U.S. currency is printed first on the back in green ink; this is referred to as the *first print*. The next day, the sheets are printed on the face with black ink; this is the *second print*. The Treasury Seal and note Serial Numbers in green and the Federal Reserve District seal and numbers in black are then added to the sheet as the *third print*.

Notes with a completely blank back are "missing the first print" (that is, no green ink on the back). Retail price for a $10 or $20 note of this type is about $150. Rarer and more valuable are notes "missing the second print" (that is, no black-inked design on the face) — maybe $300 retail for a low-denomination UNCIRCULATED note. Notes "missing the third print" lack either the black or green overprint applied during the third printing state — these usually are the least expensive of the "missing print" errors, retailing for around $130 for an UNCIRCULATED $10 or $20 note. In some instances, all overprints may be missing.

INVERTED THIRD PRINTS

Sometimes the Treasury seal, Serial Numbers, Federal Reserve seal, and district numbers are inverted on the note's face, caused when the sheet is fed into the press upside-down during the third printing. In the lower denominations, such notes can be purchased from dealers for $100 or less in AU to UNCIRCULATED. A small "epidemic" of inverted prints appeared in series 1974 and 1976 notes.

THIRD PRINT ON BACK

This error can be either "normally" readable or offset in a reversed image. Specimens retail for $150 or so for a low-denomination note.

THIRD PRINT SHIFTED

Also called "overprint shifted," these notes show the third printing shifted out of position, either horizontally or vertically (or, very rarely, diagonally, usually as a result of some other production problem, such as a paper fold). These errors are inexpensively priced, generally triple or quadruple the face value for $5, $10, or $20 denominations in AU condition. They are worth a little more if the Federal Reserve seal intersects the central portrait.

UNEVEN PRINTING, UNDERINKING, AND INSUFFICIENT PRESSURE

These printing problems all result in weak or partly missing impressions on a note. Such paper money errors usually are not expensive — about four to five times the face value for AU notes of $5, $10, or $20 denominations. When examining such error notes, be sure that the color hasn't been bleached out or chemically removed.

This brings us to apparent color changelings. Notes that are all blue or all yellow in color instead of "bank note green" on the backs are almost certainly the result of tampering after they left the Bureau. An amateur chemist can fool around with a note until he or she finds a liquid solution that will bleach out one or more pigments in the ink. As a interesting experiment, try placing a dollar bill, back side up, in the sunlight for a couple of months. The green color will fade and change. Notes that have been "doctored" by con artists are worth just face value.

DOUBLE IMPRESSIONS

These errors can exhibit two images of the entire design or just the overprints. Dramatic notes with strong doubling can be worth $150 or more. A complete double impression of the second print in UNCIRCULATED condition can fetch hundreds of dollars over face value. If the automatic numbering machine turned between the two impressions, the two Serial Numbers on double-printed notes may be in sequence rather than identical.

DESIGN PARTIALLY MISSING DUE TO PAPER ADHERENCE

A note with a completely blank portion on either the face or back, usually with a sharp delineation between the blank area and the correctly printed area, is caused when a scrap of paper or other foreign object adheres to the sheet as it is printed. An AU to UNCIRCULATED example with a 1-inch-wide blank streak can retail for $100.

MISMATCHED SERIAL NUMBERS

The lower left and upper right Serial Numbers aren't the same because a cylinder in the automatic numbering machine jammed. These paper money errors usually are valued at $50 to $100 over face value in UNCIRCULATED condition.

INVERTED FACES

The face and back of the note are upside-down in relation to one another. On correctly printed notes the face and back designs are aligned in the same direction. Since the backs are printed first, these notes are called "inverted faces," not "inverted backs." A Choice UNCIRCULATED note can bring $100 or more over its face value. Such a note may circulate for a while without being recognized as an error.

DOUBLE DENOMINATION

Some of the rarest and most valuable bank note errors are those with a double denomination, for example, a $5 face design with a $10 back design! Such errors can retail for several thousand dollars in Choice UNCIRCULATED. Beware of counterfeits, including "paste-ups" of two different denominations that are made by literally gluing together two notes after shaving the designs off one side of each. Double-denomination notes always have the face of one denomination and the back of another denomination — *never* two faces.

Currency dealers can supply specimens of error notes for you to examine — either from stock or on approval from other dealers. Don't be overly impressed by the first error note you see. Many error notes exist or their market values would be much higher. It is better to save your money and buy one note in Choice UNCIRCULATED condition for $100 than two or three error notes in circulated condition for the same amount.

Keep your notes clean and in safe currency holders, available at any coin shop. I like the flexible Mylar® holders because they are inexpensive and easy to store in your home or in a bank safe-deposit box. And, like any paper money in your collection, error notes should be kept away from high humidity (kitchens, bathrooms), direct sunlight, and heat.

The handiest reference for U.S. small-size currency errors is the *Official 1993 Blackbook Price Guide of United States Paper Money* (25th edition), usually available for sale in coin shops for $5.95. Besides including 22 pages of fully illustrated error note information, this 242-page book serves as a price guide and collection checklist for large- and small-size U.S. currency in denominations of $100 or less. I like this book because it is small (4 x 5½ inches) and easy to take along to shows or when you want something worthwhile to read on vacation. Like many catalogs, however, the *Blackbook*'s quoted retail prices tend to go up every year regardless of actual market conditions. As a result, the prices listed are often too high. You can buy error notes for less than *Blackbook* prices, so shop around to get acquainted with real market prices and have some fun collecting United States error notes!

241. "Missing Third Print"; i.e., no *Serial Numbers*, no *Seals*, no *District Numbers* on this Series 1981 U.S. *Federal Reserve Note*. In Plexiglas® acrylic hard plastic holder.

242. *Large Size* "Double Denomination" note in a recent auction catalog of Lyn F. Knight, Inc. of Overland Park, Kansas. Reproduced with company permission. ("Lot 1163. Fr. 765. $2 & $1. 1918. Chicago. Double Denomination. The elusive $3 bill. A beauty and they normally aren't found in this grade. VF/XF (6,000 - 7,000).")

243. "Pre-printing paper fold" on reverse of a modern (*Small Size*) $10 U.S. *Federal Reserve Note*. Author's photo, from the stock of Americana Stamp and Coin Company, Inc. of Tarzana. California.

244. "Plate smear" on reverse of modern (*Small Size*) U.S. $10 *Federal Reserve Note*. Photographed over a white card for contrast. From the stock of Americana Stamp and Coin Company, Inc. of Tarzana, California.

245. Beware of "contrived errors," for example, "freak margins" deliberately cut from easily obtainable recent U.S. currency sheets.

21

"Everything that deceives may be said to enchant."
Plato (circa 428-348 B.C.)

Forgeries, Counterfeits, and Fantasy Notes

Horace (65-8 B.C.), the Roman poet, tells us in his *Epistles*, "Make money, money by fair means if you can, if not, by any means money."

Counterfeiting is the fraudulent replication of money with intent to defraud. The counterfeiter makes realistic appearing currency imitations from scratch, by using raw materials of blank paper, ink, security threads, etc.; and making a printing plate (or, in modern times, photocopying) and actually printing the notes.

Forgery is the criminal falsifying of documents that already exist. Forgers falsify signatures, denominations, payee names, dates, etc., on existing checks, money orders, bonds, stocks, paper money, even on contracts, wills, bills of sale, and other documents, so their larcenous task is considerably easier than the work of counterfeiters, who make the whole document.

To simplify our discussion in this chapter, the words counterfeit and forgery will apply only to paper money, unless otherwise stated. Drivers' licenses, passports, loan applications, business letters, etc., are both counterfeited and forged, but this book is mostly about paper money, so let's limit this chapter to paper currency manipulations.

Fantasy Notes are imitations of paper money that were never intended to fool anybody into thinking that these pieces are real money. Fantasies include bogus notes (either approximate facsimiles of their genuine counterparts, or of a design that is very different from real notes that exist), play money, stage money, school money, movie money, gambling "money," cartoon caricatures of real notes, etc. Of course, there is some overlap in our definitions: e.g., "propaganda counterfeits" may have one side appear to be a genuine note, while the other side bears printed instructions on how to surrender to enemy soldiers. Shall we say that this example is half fantasy, half counterfeit?

This chapter explores this shadow world of paper money, the realm of counterfeits, forgeries, and fantasies of the United States and foreign countries, of the present day and of times past.

THE HISTORY OF COUNTERFEITING

Counterfeiting began not long after the first coins were invented more than twenty-five centuries ago in ancient Lydia in Asia Minor (what is now Turkey). The temptation to "get something for nothing" runs deeply in the souls of people who would rather cheat their neighbors than earn their wealth honestly. The counterfeiter's motivation may be economic, political, or egotistical (or all three). Counterfeiters like to make passable money, to harass their perceived adversaries, and/or to be regarded as clever by the frustrated, defrauded recipients of the faked money. According to the 20th century Royal Canadian Mounted Police, counterfeiting is a crime "never committed by accident, nor by ignorance, nor in the heat of passion ..."

Past Penalties for Counterfeiting

In ancient Rome, coin counterfeiters were burned alive or fed to the animals in the arena. Chinese T'ang Dynasty (618-906 A.D.) paper money bore printed anti-counterfeiting warnings of cutting off the hands of counterfeiters and the transfer of counterfeiters' property to informers. Convicted ancient Chinese counterfeiters were also worked without pay. Paper money counterfeiting at times became so harmful in ancient China that the production of paper currency was periodically suspended. The Ming Dynasty (1368-1644 A.D.) notes were counterfeited in the 19th century to fool collectors.

In 11th century England and 13th century Scotland, counterfeiters had their hands cut off. As the use of paper money was introduced into countries around the world, especially during the 18th century, coin counterfeiters turned with glee toward the somewhat simpler task of counterfeiting the primitively made bank notes of that time. In an age when many people were poor or illiterate, or didn't know what genuine paper money looked like anyway, an 18th century counterfeiter's creations were accepted as readily as genuine notes, and often looked better than the genuine!

French Revolutionary *assignats* of the 1790s were widely counterfeited, which contributed to their quick discredit among the French people, who are always jittery about paper money anyway. The Bank of England made French *assignat* forgeries during the French Revolution to disrupt the French economy. If they could be caught, French counterfeiters risked having their heads cut off.

Between 1797 and 1829, 618 people were convicted of bank note forgery in England, and several hundred of these were hanged, a sentence that fell disproportionately upon the poor, who were often hanged for innocently passing a counterfeit bank note they couldn't even read. In 1817, an estimated 30,000 counterfeit bank notes were circulating in England. Employees of the Bank of England were embarrassed about testifying against poverty-stricken commoners convicted of "raising" (forging a higher denomination on) a genuine note so their families could eat — knowing that the forger was very likely to be hanged for a £5 offense.

More enlightened English citizens of the Society of Arts advocated, in their 1819 publication entitled *Report on the Mode of Preventing the Forgery of Bank Notes*, that paper money should be made of the highest quality workmanship to hinder counterfeiting. Public pressure had its effects, and in 1832, capital punishment for forgery was outlawed in England, with banishment to Australia substituted as the penalty.

While death and dismemberment have generally been outlawed as penalties for counterfeiting in 20th century nations, some harsh vestiges of the past have persisted. Counterfeiters in Nazi Germany or Stalin's Russia were shot or incarcerated in a slave labor camp. In recent years, Russia and Communist China have still had the death penalty for counterfeiting. You might get your hand chopped off for setting up a money-printing operation in modern Saudi Arabia. About $1,000,000 in counterfeit money is made each year by Canadian criminals, and the Criminal Code of Canada has prison sentences of up to 14 years for counterfeiting.

In the 20th century, most countries have prescribed fines and imprisonment for persons convicted of counterfeiting, provided they can catch the perpetrators. Pancho Villa's notes of the early 20th century Mexican Revolution were forged by his own agents who issued them when they couldn't get official approval to issue more, making them guilty of at least two crimes — insurgency and counterfeiting.

Per the Geneva Convention of 1929, thirty-two signatory nations recognize similar anti-counterfeiting laws prohibiting the counterfeiting of their own and foreign currency, and they have agreed to cooperate in apprehending international counterfeiting fugitives, partly via the International Criminal Police Organization (Interpol), which is headquartered in Paris. Suspects can be extradited to return them to the country "scene of the crime" for prosecution.

Counterfeiting in Colonial America

Just one year after the first American paper money, the 1690 *Bills of Credit* of Massachusetts Bay Colony, the ²/₆ (two *shilling*, six *pence*) "notes" were being "raised" to 10 *Shillings* and 20 *Shillings* and passed as the higher denominations by forgers named Robert Fenton and Benjamin Pierce.

From 1715 through 1722, Mrs. Mary Peck Butterworth made over £1,000 worth of counterfeit notes of Connecticut, Massachusetts, and Rhode Island, and was the ring leader of a gang that finished and passed the notes. She counterfeited by hot-ironing a piece of moist muslin over a note to pick up the money's ink. She then ironed the muslin on a piece of blank paper to transfer the image, which was touched up with a quill pen. She immediately burned the cloth in her fireplace, so there was no incriminating copper printing plate (which would guarantee conviction of a Colonial American counterfeiter). She was arrested but not convicted, as there was no plate for evidence!

Counterfeiting was a serious problem in Colonial America, which was cash-starved, semi-literate, and more trusting than its 20th century successor. Many poor people who couldn't read or write were duped with crudely counterfeited "bills" — they had no way of knowing whether the bills were good or bad. Colonial silversmiths, possessing excellent engraving skills, sometimes became counterfeiters of coin and paper money, as did the poor who were down on their luck.

Counterfeiting penalties varied greatly among the American Colonies — with death in New York to six months imprisonment in Connecticut (plus paying for "damages," and possible ear cropping, and standing in the pillory). Death penalties, however, were often pardoned or reduced to imprisonment on appeal (unlike England where counterfeiters were hanged as often as not). Many counterfeiters were convicted in Colonial America when two or more accomplices agreed to testify against their associate by turning Crown's evidence.

Colonial American counterfeiters, like counterfeiters today, seem to have been recidivists, committing their crimes over and over again, between prison terms. Colonial counterfeit gangs worked in teams, with a division of labor, and different gangs shared information with each other. Bail for counterfeiters was often forfeited in lieu of prosecution by money-hungry Colonial local governments. Many Colonial counterfeiters simply escaped from the flimsy jails of the time. Counterfeit American Colonial notes were often made in England or Ireland where nobody could be prosecuted for engraving the plates or even for making American counterfeit money (which wasn't recognized outside America, anyway).

In 1777, the British forces in America encouraged the counterfeiting of *Continental Currency* to undermine the American rebel economy, and this was done extensively.

Counterfeiting in 19th Century America

Paper money counterfeiting was epidemic in 19th century America, especially before the introduction of a uniform federal currency during the Civil War. The 19th century has been called the "Golden Age of Counterfeiting" in the United

States — private Bank Notes were counterfeited as fast as their legitimate versions were issued.

In his address to the Connecticut Legislature in May 1826, Governor Walcott said:

> *With us the currency which is required by the daily exchange between people ... is almost exclusively in Bank notes [and] neither the amount of currency which is issued, nor the amount of that which is suddenly suspended, withdrawn, or annihilated, is subject to any practical limitation ... The effects produced upon the people are, that no man can travel fifty miles in any direction, without receiving paper notes of which he possesses no means of ascertaining the value, or even the authenticity, and this difficulty increases in proportion to the distance of an individual from some one of these Banks ... Many counterfeited and altered notes are so skillfully prepared, as to defy the scrutiny of adepts ...*

So many different types of Bank Notes were circulating in 19th century America that bankers themselves were often confused, referring to frequently updated publications known as "Counterfeit Detectors" and "Bank Note Reporters" to help them identify the latest counterfeits. *Heath's Detector* was the most popular. In 1884, detective Allan Pinkerton observed that U.S. merchants "preferred a good counterfeit on a solid bank to any genuine bill upon a shyster institution."

Counterfeiting in the Confederate States

In January 1862, a young girl in the Confederacy remarked, "Judging from the looks of the paper money, one would be convinced that many people are making their own." In fact, counterfeit *Confederate Notes* began appearing soon after the first genuine ones were made in 1861. So many counterfeit $20, $50, and $100 notes were passing in Charleston in the summer of 1862 that the banks suspended acceptance of these denominations.

Much counterfeit *Confederate Currency* was made outside the Confederacy, usually in the North with its extensive printing facilities. Then the faked notes were smuggled South, where they were often accepted as valid. One of the most famous counterfeit *Confederate Notes* is the *Havana counterfeit* $100 *Lucy Pickens* note of 1864, which was supposedly made in Cuba, then smuggled past the Union Naval blockade and into the Confederacy.

From March 12, 1862 to August 1, 1863, Samuel C. Upham of Philadelphia made over 1½ million facsimile *Confederate Notes* with a value of $15 million, which he sold in the North as "souvenirs" at $5 per hundred notes. While not expressly intended to be "counterfeits," many of Upham's facsimiles had their advertising border trimmed off, were smuggled South, and passed for real money in the Confederacy.

Many people were arrested, but few convicted, and only one executed (for forging signatures onto stolen unsigned *Confederate Notes*) in Confederate counterfeiting. Confederate Treasury officials kept a running battle against counterfeiters, using watermarks, color-tinted papers, and more complex designs to delay counterfeiting technological "improvements." Counterfeiting contributed to currency inflation, depreciation, and economic disintegration of the Confederacy, and made the Southern currency untrustworthy. Some scholars estimate that during the Civil War between ¼ and ⅓ of the circulating currency in the South was counterfeit. See Benner's book, *Fraudulent Finance: Counterfeiting and the Confederate States: 1861-1865*, for a summary (Bibliography).

U.S. SECRET SERVICE

The U.S. Secret Service was born on July 5, 1865 to suppress counterfeiting. Some estimates are that ⅓ of all U.S. circulating paper currency in the North during the Civil War was counterfeit; this includes many private Bank Notes that were being driven out of existence by the new federal currency.

The U.S. Secret Service, operating in the Department of the Treasury, has several techniques in exposing counterfeit paper money:

1. Public education.

2. Undercover infiltration of counterfeiting gangs.

3. Undercover purchasing of counterfeit notes.

4. Action on tips from informers (anonymous or otherwise) that local counterfeiters may be at work.

5. Monitoring the buyers of high grade bond papers (of the types that might be used for Bank Notes).

6. Investigating offset printing shops experiencing financial problems.

COUNTERFEITING IN THE U.S. TODAY

U.S. currency counterfeiting has been attempted more than that of any other country, due to its use and acceptance throughout the world. Even counterfeiters are sensitive to inflation: $1 and $5 notes were the most common counterfeits in the 1930s; $10 notes in the 1940s; $20 notes in the 1960s; and $20, $50, and $100 notes today.

Two to three hundred counterfeiting operations are uncovered by the Secret Service every year in the United States. New York City has long been a big source of U.S.-made counterfeiting operations, because of the well-established printing industry there. Los Angeles makes a lot of counterfeits because of its mobile population and because it has many skilled photographers.

In a personal letter to me, dated December 10, 1991, Robert R. Snow of the U.S. Secret Service included this information, which I requested for this book:

The U.S. Secret Service seized approximately $66.3 million in counterfeit notes during fiscal year 1990. We estimate that approximately one-third of the counterfeit currency passed and/or seized during fiscal year 1990 was actually printed in a foreign country. In terms of methods, today's counterfeiters are more likely to use offset printing as opposed to the engraved printing plate method, which is rarely encountered today.

The $66.3 million was seized before being circulated in 1990; this doesn't include $14 million in counterfeit notes that were passed on the public that year, as per statistics also supplied to me by Mr. Snow. These figures are typical for an "average" year lately; but this doesn't seem excessive, considering that, at any given moment, about $45 billion in genuine U.S. notes are circulating simultaneously with about $1.5 million in counterfeit U.S. notes.

Improvements in photocopying machines have threatened our currency, so several anti-counterfeiting measures have been implemented lately, microprinting around the portrait and insertion of a security thread being the most important. And ever since a 14-year-old boy was caught by the Secret Service in 1967 when he was making $1 bills on a photocopying machine, then exchanging them for coinage at a laundromat money changing machine, such machines have been improved to reject suspicious bills.

Quality counterfeiting is a technical skill. Major problems faced by the counterfeiter are: (1) obtaining good quality rag-content paper; (2) obtaining quality inks; (3) preparing printing plates that can produce a convincing impression; and (4) passing the notes without immediate detection. (Distribution is the biggest obstacle of successful counterfeiting and where most counterfeiters get caught. Counterfeiters often distribute in crowded stores on weekends in towns where banks are closed until Monday morning; or they sell their offset-printed notes at 20% of face value to "wholesalers" who, in turn, sell them at maybe 30% to 40% to "passers" who spend the notes and get real money in change.)

The U.S. Secret Service maintains a Counterfeit Note Index whereby descriptions of newly seen counterfeit notes are given to every U.S. bank. Also, local merchants are warned about new counterfeits being circulated in their localities, including specific note details such as Serial Numbers. The conviction rate for prosecuted counterfeiting cases by the Secret Service in the United States is 99.5%.

U.S. Counterfeiting Laws

The *U.S. Criminal Code* statutes that apply to counterfeiting are in Title 18, Chapter 25, Counterfeiting and Forgery, of the *U.S. Code*. Title 18, Section 471, "Obligations or securities of United States" states:

Whoever, with intent to defraud, falsely makes, forges,

counterfeits, or alters any obligation or other security of the United States, shall be fined not more than $5,000 or imprisoned not more than fifteen years, or both.

Section 472 prescribes the same penalties for passing, selling, or possessing, etc., such "forged, counterfeited, or altered" securities (i.e., paper money, among other things). And Section 474 has the same penalties for making, selling, possessing, etc., the "plates or stones for counterfeiting obligations or securities." Section 478 has a maximum $5,000 fine and five years imprisonment, or both, for counterfeiting or forging "foreign obligations or securities." And Section 479 has a maximum $3,000 fine and three years imprisonment for passing foreign items. Section 480 has a maximum $1,000 fine and one year imprisonment, or both, etc., for possessing counterfeit foreign bank notes, etc.

"Raising a Note"

"Raising a note" is a type of forgery whereby a bank note is made to appear to be of a higher denomination. Raising can be done by artwork on a single note, bleaching out and redrawing denominations, "transplanting," etc. In transplanting, a piece of another note is pasted onto the note to be "raised." Usually a zero is cut off another note to "raise" a denomination of, say, 10 to 100 units. That's one reason most paper money has its denomination printed both in numerals and words, preferably repeated several times on each side. Title 18, Section 484 of the *U.S. Criminal Code* deals specifically with transplanting/raising of paper money:

Whoever so places or connects together different parts of two or more notes, bills, or other genuine instruments issued under the authority of the United States, or by any foreign government, or corporation, as to produce one instrument, with intent to defraud, shall be guilty of forgery in the same manner as if the parts so put together were falsely made or forged, and shall be fined not more than $1,000 or imprisoned not more than five years, or both.

IF YOU RECEIVE A COUNTERFEIT NOTE

The U.S. Secret Service recommends the following procedure if you receive a counterfeit note:

1.   Do not return it to the passer (even if the passer offers to exchange it for a genuine note).

2.   Delay the passer if possible.

3.   Observe the passer's description, as well as that of any companions, and the license numbers of any vehicles used.

4.   Telephone your local police department or the United States Secret Service.

5. Write your initials and the date on a blank portion of the suspect note.

6. Do not handle the note. Carefully place it in a protective covering, such as an envelope.

7. Surrender the note only to a properly identified police officer or U.S. Secret Service agent.

ANTI-COUNTERFEITING SECURITY FEATURES OF U.S. PAPER MONEY

In the United States, these anti-counterfeiting measures are incorporated into the manufacture of paper money:

1. Special bank note paper—high quality cotton and linen rag content bond paper, made exclusively for use by the U.S. Bureau of Engraving and Printing by Crane & Company of Dalton, Massachusetts. The paper is cream-colored and of superior durability.

2. Blue and red silk fibers in the paper.

3. Special inks that are hard to duplicate in shade or performance qualities.

4. Sharp intaglio printing of engraved lines of ink, especially in portraits and background design.

5. Intricate lathework of border designs.

6. Unique Serial Numbers and other control numbers from the printing plate.

7. Inscribed security thread (on notes first distributed in 1991, *Series* 1990 $50 and $100 *Federal Reserve Notes* to start). The clear polyester thread is embedded in the paper and runs vertically to the left of the Federal Reserve Seal. On $20 denominations and lower, as they are phased into circulation, the security thread has USA and the denomination repeated over and over again, such as: "USA TWENTY USA TWENTY" — with the numeral value of the $50 and $100 notes, i.e., "USA 50 USA 50." But $1 notes were not immediately planned for security threading, because they aren't counterfeited much anymore. The security thread can be seen with a backlight, but be sure that it was authorized for the Series and denomination of your particular note.

8. Microprinting. Beginning on the $50 and $100 denomination, *Series* 1990, *Federal Reserve Notes* (first released in 1991), U.S. currency started to bear microprinting on the portrait rim, with the words "THE UNITED STATES OF AMERICA" repeated. This microprinting can only be read using magnification. Neither the new microprinting nor the security thread feature can be accurately reproduced by present day office copying machines.

Some Bank Note Security Measures of Other Countries

In addition to, or instead of, some of the above security measures, other characteristics are placed in various foreign Bank Notes to inhibit counterfeiting:

1. Watermarks. Designs appearing as slightly thinned areas in the paper, impressed at the time of the paper's manufacture. Visible when backlighted. European currency tends to be watermarked by tradition, but the United States and Canada, for example, prefer the stronger, more durable unwatermarked paper. If current federal U.S. or Canadian currency is watermarked, it is counterfeit.

2. Underprint. Background tint of color on a note, placed on the paper before the main printed design, usually of a different color than the main design.

3. Multicolored fronts or backs, or different colors for different denominations. By tradition, since the Civil War, U.S. federal currency has been mostly black on the face, green on the reverse. The green backs were originally used because green couldn't be reproduced photographically in the 1860s.

4. Planchettes are little bits of colored paper put into the pulp during paper-making. Planchettes appear either on the surface or within the body of the note. Genuine planchettes can be picked off the note's surface. Counterfeit planchettes are usually dots of ink that can't be picked off the note. Green planchettes have been used on modern Canadian notes.

5. Latent image printing. Visible on the genuine article but not on lithographic or Xerographic reproductions.

6. Security threads of different appearance than the newly introduced U.S. types. Some foreign security threads are made of metal, or are easily visible with front lighting.

7. Counterfoil. Part of the sheet attached to the note's design during printing, on which identical Serial Numbers and signatures were affixed before the note was detached for circulation to verify the note's legitimacy when it was redeemed. Not done today because it is too time-consuming; used in the 19th century in Latin American countries and others.

HOW TO DETECT COUNTERFEIT U.S. PAPER MONEY

U.S. paper money is made by master craftsmen using steel engraved printing plates and intaglio printing machinery of great sophistication and cost. Most modern counterfeiters use a photo-mechanical or offset method to make a printing plate from a genuine note. Even the old fashioned expert counterfeiters, with acid-etched zinc or copper plates, or good steel ones, usually made counterfeits that were inferior to genuine notes. Even a Bureau master engraver cannot duplicate his own line-engraving work, much less that of another engraver.

You can feel the difference between an engraved intaglio-printed U.S. note and a surface-printed counterfeit. The genuine note has raised lines of ink (except for the surface-printed

Serial Numbers and Federal Reserve Seal and Numbers); surface-printed counterfeits have smooth surfaces all over.

Look for differences, not similarities, when comparing a suspected counterfeit with a known genuine note. The U.S. Secret Service recommends these "tests" for inspecting your notes:

1.   Portrait. The genuine portrait appears lifelike and stands out distinctly from the fine screen-like background. The counterfeit portrait is usually lifeless and flat; details merge into the background, which is often too dark or mottled.

2.   Federal Reserve and Treasury Seals. On a genuine bill, the sawtooth points of the Federal Reserve and Treasury Seals are clear, distinct, and sharp. The counterfeit seals may have uneven, blunt, or broken sawtooth points.

3.   Serial Numbers. Genuine Serial Numbers have a distinctive style and are evenly spaced. They are printed in the same color as the Treasury Seal (green, for modern *Federal Reserve Notes*), but a different shade than the back of the note. On a counterfeit, the Serial Numbers may differ in color or shade of ink from the Treasury Seal, and the numerals may not be uniformly spaced and aligned. No two notes of the same type, denomination, and Series will have identical Serial Numbers (including the prefix and suffix letters). If you have two such notes, at least one of them, and probably both, is counterfeit.

4.   Border. The fine lines in the border of a genuine bill are clear and unbroken. On the counterfeit, the lines in the outer margin and scrollwork may be blurred and indistinct.

5.   Paper. Genuine U.S. paper money has no watermarks, but it does have tiny red and blue fibers scattered and embedded. Often counterfeiters try to simulate these fibers by drawing them in or printing them with ink on their paper. Close inspection reveals, however, that on the counterfeit note the lines are printed on the surface, not embedded in the paper. It is illegal to reproduce the distinctive cream-colored, silk-fibered quality Bank Note cotton-linen rag-content paper that is used in manufacturing currency in the United States.

Sometimes counterfeit money has the wrong "feel": too smooth, too greasy, or slippery. It may not "crackle" or have the strength of genuine currency. Both genuine and counterfeit inks will rub off and smear a little when rubbed on another piece of paper, so rubbing off the ink is not a foolproof method of counterfeit detection.

HOBBY PROTECTION ACT

The U.S. Hobby Protection Act of 1973 states that replicas of numismatic items (including paper money) made for commercial distribution must be labeled COPY. But items made before 1973 and current items made in foreign countries that are beyond U.S. control may bear no such warning.

HAND-DRAWN CURRENCY

If the note looks good enough to pass, it may be declared a counterfeit, even if hand-drawn! Emanuel Ninger made and passed over $40,000 worth of hand-drawn U.S. currency in the 1880s and 1890s! Perhaps the ultimate compliment that an artist-counterfeiter can get is: "We're putting you in prison because your hand-drawn money looks better than our genuine notes!"

Some 19th century artists made such realistic paintings of paper money that the local police were astounded that the notes were not real ones pinned on the canvas!

Anne-Marie Rojas, an French housewife, made hand-drawn counterfeit *Banque de France* 500-Franc notes, and passed them in 1974 at local Bayonne supermarkets. She was caught when *Banque de France* authorities noticed that, in the note's tower clock vignette, the clock's hands were set at 12:05 on her notes, but at 12:00 noon on the genuine. They notified local supermarkets where she was quickly identified by a cashier who recognized her note's discrepancy.

OPERATION BERNHARD

In World War II, the Nazi government of Germany counterfeited $630,000,000 worth of faked British Bank Notes for several purposes: (1) to undermine the British economy by "dumping" the notes in huge quantities in England; (2) to exchange for gold and U.S. currency; and (3) to pay overseas spies. These counterfeiters were superb, perhaps the best ever done on *Bank of England* notes. They were made by inmates who were skilled in Bank Note work at the Mauthausen concentration camp in lower Austria. The camp forgers were ordered executed to shut them up should their camp ever be liberated by Allied invaders, but these inmates were apparently shipped to other camps, and most, if not all, survived. The equipment, records, and many of the original counterfeit *Bank of England* notes from Operation Bernhard were dumped in nearby lakes and rivers, from which some of these notes have been since recovered.

Some of the Operation Bernhard British counterfeits passed successfully in Switzerland by Nazi agents; other notes were stolen by Nazis for their own enrichment. The notes were never air-dropped over Britain, partly because the counterfeits were discovered by the British, partly because the Luftwaffe was short of fuel needed for combat aircraft. The Nazis reportedly were at work to master a $100 U.S. note counterfeit, but the war ended before these were finished.

OTHER COUNTERFEIT LORE

A little-publicized fact is that many countries, including the United States, have stockpiled currency of a different design, color, etc., in bomb-proof underground vaults, to be used if an enemy nation ever floods their country with counterfeit money for economic disruption. Of less concern are the propaganda facsimiles of enemy nations' notes, made to demoralize the local population.

Many counterfeit *Bank of England* £5 notes (*White Fivers*) were made for distribution in England between World Wars I and II. If these or any other British counterfeits, including the Nazi forgeries, are presented to the *Bank of England*, they will confiscate the notes without payment (as will the U.S. Treasury for current counterfeits), after assuring you with a worthless "receipt" that your notes were, indeed, counterfeit!

FORGERIES

Technically, forgery is a fraudulent alteration in an existing genuine document, with intent to deceive. Although the terms are often used interchangeably, even by police and paper money authorities, counterfeiting creates the complete document from scratch (although the blank paper may be stolen instead of handmade, etc.), while forgery is usually a minor (in relative document area, not necessarily in the labor expended or in the seriousness of the crime) illegal change in some aspect of the printed material on a genuine document.

As applicable to paper money, forgery has been often done to fool the public by "raising" the denomination of a note, then passing it at its greater face value. The collector of currency has often been the victim of forgers who do one or more of these things on a genuine note:

1. Change the denomination — usually by adding or subtracting digits, especially zeros. The lettering for denomination has to be changed on most notes, also.

2. Change the signatures — U.S. federal currency and *Bank of England* notes are commonly collected by signature varieties. A different signature sometimes makes an enormous difference in the note's market value.

3. Change the date(s) — Same design but different date *Series* can mean vastly different prices for a note.

4. Change the Serial Numbers — This is most dangerous for *Replacement Notes*, which are popularly collected today. Changing one digit/letter to a "Star" makes an "instant" rarity.

5. Change major design element — such as a vignette, Treasury or Federal Reserve Seal, major legend, etc. Less often done due to the difficulty.

6. Bleaching a note to remove part of the design. Do you really have a "missing Serial Numbers" error, or have the numerals been bleached out?

7. Color alterations — by chemical treatment, which can change the colors of the paper, the ink, or both. Treasury Seals may be changed in color, in conjunction with other design alterations, to make, for example, a *Gold Certificate* out of a *Small Size* U.S. *Federal Reserve Note*. It is easy to make the back ink on current U.S. currency look blue or yellow instead of its normal green. So-called "missing color errors" may, in fact, be contrived. True color changelings (different colors made at the time of manufacture) of radically different shades should be verified by an expert.

8. Transplants — when a piece of another note is attached to the note being "forged." When expertly done, transplants can be dangerously convincing, the more so because every design element is genuine. A date scraped off and substituted with a different date transplanted from another note, then blended into the paper with starch fillers, may need magnification or ultraviolet inspection to detect.

9. Some combination of the above. The smart forger makes the smallest change possible, and doesn't exceed his ability — a tiny "lie" on a bank note goes a long way.

Worn or damaged notes should always be suspected of forgery if they are expensive. Tape repairs, glue marks, stains of any kind, surface dirt, creases, handstamps, blurred design elements, and graffiti may be hiding the "forger's" craftsmanship. Do you really have a rare £5 note in G-VG condition … or is it a £1 note with the "1" changed to look like a "5"?

Check Forgery

Check forgery is done much more often, by more criminals, and for a vastly larger aggregate dollar amount of all the check forgeries combined than all the paper money counterfeiting and forgery operations put together. Check forgery may be both a local and a federal crime, depending on what documents and actions are involved. Unauthorized signatures and/or amounts, and dates, are usually forged onto checks. Check forgery is very different from, and should not be confused with, overdrawing a checking account due to insufficient funds (which, if intentional, may be a crime, also).

FANTASY NOTES

Fantasy Notes are spurious creations that resemble paper money (in some aspects, at least) but were never intended to be used as money or to fool collectors. Fantasy notes are sometimes called bogus notes, and may be similar to real money, or even be passed by people trying to use them as real money. Fantasy notes include play money, business school money, military training money, promotional facsimiles, game money, movie money, gambling money, and enigmatic bogus money. While all of these can also be coins, we'll just define them here as notes.

Play Money

What child hasn't spent Play Money in the course of carefree childhood play? Toy stores sell simply designed pieces of paper, with various denominations marked on, usually in different colors per denomination. Of no value to anyone but a child (to whom such "money" may be precious, indeed).

Game Money

Actually a type of Play Money, the colored bits of simply-designed paper known as Game Money are used in the play of various commercial boxed games. The most famous Game Money in the United States is Monopoly® money, from the 1930s invented board game sold by Parker Brothers. Of little value, unless: (1) you're playing the game, or (2) you are one of the few people who collect Game Money.

Business School Money

In the late 19th and early 20th centuries, it was customary for American business schools, including the business departments of colleges, to use Business School Money, actually a type of Play Money for adults, in teaching how to handle cash in business jobs. To avoid the obvious security and theft problems that real money would tempt, small paper notes, sometimes nicely engraved with amusing vignettes, were counted and passed around by the students in class. Has some collector value; $5-$25 for average pieces, more for rare notes needed by specialists.

Military Training Money

Similar to Business School Money (above), Military Training Money has been used to teach finance clerks how to handle: (1) their country's currency, (2) foreign currencies in occupied countries (including exchanging into different national currencies), and/or (3) military currency proper. Military personnel use national or special military currency at canteens, military postal facilities, and paymasters' offices. The clerks who handle massive amounts of currency every day have to be trained for it.

The U.S. Army Adjutant General School and the Finance School of the Administrative Center at Fort Benjamin Harrison, Indiana have issued and used Military Training Money notes in various denominations.

Movie Money

Paper currency shown on camera in movies is usually fantasy money, even if it appears to be real to the viewer. Movie Money is rented to production companies by prop houses that charge about 50¢ a day for a note, $3.50 for a stack of 100, and 50¢ for each note destroyed (less for quantities). Movie Money usually has "Motion Picture Use Only" printed somewhere on the note. When you see suitcases full of currency in movies, that is almost invariably imitation money. When actor Ray Liotta rifled off a handful of money to give his wife to go shopping, in the movie *Goodfellas*, the currency looked and sounded "too crisp," like a pad of fresh typing paper or a deck of playing cards, not like a stack of U.S. *Federal Reserve Notes*, no matter how "UNCIRCULATED"!

A million dollars in real U.S. currency, in 10,000 new $100 *Federal Reserve Notes* currently circulating, would form a stack about 43 inches high, weigh almost 20½ pounds, and snugly fill up an average size suitcase (not briefcase).

Gambling Money

Gambling Money is of two major types: (1) that used in real casinos and (2) that used in "home" games. Most casinos use a variety of clay chips (called "checks" by casino personnel) for table games, and metal tokens and real coins for slot machines. Casinos have been known to issue paper or thin cardboard Casino Money for use as substitute money in actual gambling play. It has a little collector value, or real face value if still current in the casino of issue. While most friendly home poker tournaments still use the time-honored plastic poker chips or real cash, some die-hard social gamblers add variety to their weekend card games with paper Gambling Money of some sort (even Play Money "borrowed" from a boxed game) to facilitate betting.

Promotional Facsimile Money

Facsimile Money, which looks "almost" like currency that was actually issued, but of different paper, printing technique, slightly different design, etc., has been made for commercial sale as tourist souvenirs and as advertising promotions for private business. Every coin and currency dealer in the country has been approached from time to time by people who have high hopes of selling their "facsimile" money; e.g., some of the endless modern copies made of the 1864 issue of *Confederate Currency*. Facsimile Money may or may not have a disclaimer, such as the word COPY or FACSIMILE, somewhere on the note, usually on the lower margin; such disclaimers and facsimile company imprints may be trimmed off also. Old "contemporary" facsimiles, such as the Upham facsimiles of *Confederate Currency*, have collector value. Modern promotional facsimiles, from a cereal box or a gas station grand opening celebration, are more or less worthless but still collectible.

Bogus Money

Bogus Notes are of designs that were never issued as real money, but may or may not have circulated as money in a poorly informed population. Bogus Money is often used synonymously with Fantasy Money, but I prefer to restrict the definition of Bogus Money to notes that may have been passed as money and seen actual circulation, such as the 1861 *Female Riding Deer* $20 note of the Confederacy.

Propaganda Forgeries

Propaganda forgeries are notes made to expound some political opinion, usually consisting of a realistic appearing front side, but a propaganda statement on the back side (in lieu of a note design, as issued). Often dropped on enemy nations in time of war (see Chapter 13).

COUNTERFEITING OR ALTERING THIS NOTE, OR PASSING ANY COUNTERFEIT OR ALTERATION OF IT, OR HAVING IN POSSESSION ANY FALSE OR COUNTERFEIT PLATE OR IMPRESSION OF IT, OR ANY PAPER MADE IN IMITATION OF THE PAPER ON WHICH IT IS PRINTED, IS FELONY, AND IS PUNISHABLE BY $1,000 FINE OR 15 YEARS IMPRISONMENT AT HARD LABOR OR BOTH.

246.   Anti-counterfeiting clause on reverse of *Large Size* $100 U.S. *National Bank Note*, Series 1882 ("Second Charter Period"), souvenir card impression. The number 150 refers to the Charter Number of the *First National Bank* of Nashville, Tennessee, which was one of the original 179 National Banks chartered in 1863 when President Lincoln signed the National Currency Act.

247.   "Contemporary" counterfeit of $50 *Confederate Note* of September 2, 1861 (Third Issue). Handstamped once on the reverse and twice on the face, with bluish-green inked blocks containing the word COUNTERFEIT — perhaps affixed by observant Confederate Treasury officials?

248. Crude facsimile *Confederate Note*. Notice the word "FAC-SIMILE" at lower left; and with other design alterations from the original genuine note (see Photo 63).

249. Advertising reverse of *Confederate Note* facsimile of Photo 248. When Confederate money was still considered "worthless," such ads were even printed on genuine notes.

250. *Bogus Confederate* note — never officially issued, but nevertheless circulated in the South. Printed signatures and handwritten Serial Numbers. This is the famous "Female Riding Deer" note. Its origins are obscure, apparently produced during the Civil War in the North, then smuggled into the South where it actually passed as currency. The "originals" are on plain paper with blank backs; later varieties and post-war examples often have printed reverses and modified face designs as well.

251. Well-known falsification of the $100 *Imperial Bank of Canada* note of 1917 — perforated twice with the word "VOID" (at bottom); handstamped with pink "COUNTERFEIT" three times on the face, three times on the reverse. Supposedly made by Germany (though never admitted) in World War I, probably to pay overseas spies. This note was cashed in Persia. (Pick # S1141 Type Counterfeit)

252. Crude copy (replica) of the unique (known only as a single genuine unissued Proof) $500 Hawaiian Islands *Silver Certificate of Deposit*. Undated, but original of 1879. Copy made in 1977 (see inscription in lower left margin).

253. A genuine *portrait* appears lifelike, especially in the eyes and facial expressions. The counterfeit portrait is usually lifeless, flat, and with background-merging details. Courtesy U.S. Secret Service.

Genuine

Counterfeit

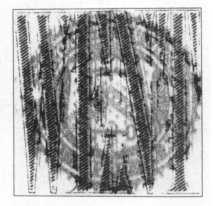

Genuine

Counterfeit

254. On a genuine note, the sawtooth points of the Federal Reserve and Treasury Seals are clear and sharp. Counterfeit Seals may have uneven, blunt, or broken sawtooth points. Courtesy U.S. Secret Service.

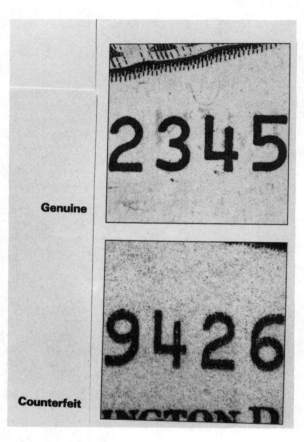

255. Genuine Serial Numbers have a distinctive style and are evenly spaced. Counterfeit numbers may be poorly spaced, misaligned, or indistinct. Courtesy U.S. Secret Service.

256. The fine lines in the scrollwork, etc., are clear and uniform when genuine. On the counterfeit, the lines may be blurred and indistinct. Courtesy U.S. Secret Service.

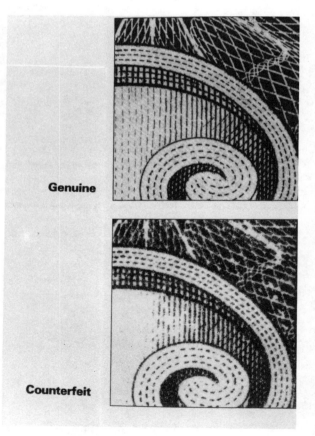

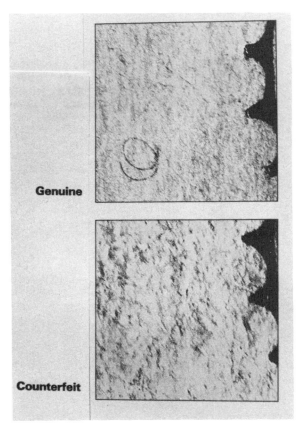

Genuine

Counterfeit

257.   Genuine U.S. currency paper has no watermarks. It has tiny red and blue fibers embedded in it. Counterfeit paper varies in several aspects from the genuine. Courtesy U.S. Secret Service.

258.   A "raised note" is a type of forgery whereby fraudulent alterations are done to increase the apparent denomination. A common method is to glue numerals of a higher denomination onto a note of lower denomination. Courtesy U.S. Secret Service.

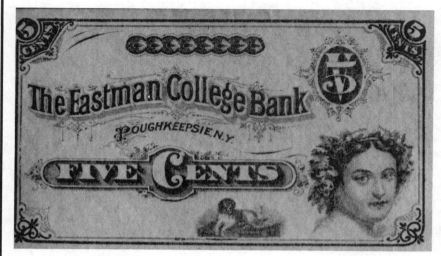

259. Nineteenth century U.S. *College Currency* — also called *Business School Money* — used in business classes as a currency substitute.

260. Anti-war propaganda surface-printed facsimile of a West German 100 *Deutsche Mark* note of 1977 with "overprint" KRIEGSSTEUERBOYCOTT (Boycott war taxes) and added inscriptions at left.

22

"The simple News that Nature told — With tender Majesty."
Emily Dickinson (1830-1886)
American poet; Poem "No. 441"

Currency Periodicals

There is only one commercial (privately-owned, for profit, non-dealer non-society) strictly paper money-oriented periodical in the United States: *Bank Note Reporter* (*BNR*), and it only appears monthly. This lack of paper money magazines and newspapers is because (a) fewer people collect paper money than, say, coins; (b) the paper money market is more orderly (less volatile, fewer speculative market booms and crashes) than the markets for many other collectibles, including coins; (c) paper money collectors tend to be intelligent and not easily "manipulated" with "cheap, sensational, superficial" publications, hence such collectors won't subscribe to anything but quality paper money publications; and (d) many paper money collectors already belong to one or more paper money societies (Chapter 23), and consequently get specialized information about their hobby from their society publications. They are therefore well-informed about paper money and will not support any upstart paper money periodical unless it tells them things that they don't already know or can't learn elsewhere.

What all this means is that paper money collectors read *Bank Note Reporter* every month, for news about both U.S. and foreign paper money, as well as for the dealer ads and information about upcoming paper money shows and auctions. They also read one or more general numismatic periodicals (such as *Coin World*, *Numismatic News*, and *The Numismatist*), both for the paper money articles contained therein, and for "sister hobby" information in case these paper money lovers also happen to collect coins, tokens, or medals, as is often true. There's always the chance, of course, that a vital bit of paper money information will appear in just one of these periodicals and not in the others (such as recently discovered bank note errors or counterfeits, news about dealer bankruptcies, announcements about local coin shows that may have local paper money dealers also present). And because what we learn in one hobby is often transferable to another hobby, it is a fact that serious paper money enthusiasts read widely and deeply. For example, if there's a revolution going on in the Soviet Union (or in its resultant separate entities), the paper money from that country may soon change in design, redeemability, and collector desirability.

I disagree with the observation of English satirist Jonathan Swift (1667-1745), who said, "No man will take counsel, but every man will take money ..." I believe that paper money collectors take both advice and money, and willingly take them both when they're properly offered.

You can survive as a paper money collector without reading any currency periodicals, just as you can survive a trip to a foreign country without knowing much about that country before you go there. But why would you want to?

Bank Note Reporter

Bank Note Reporter (*BNR*)
700 East State Street
Iola, WI 54945
(715) 445-2214

Published monthly by Krause Publications (no relation to this author), also the publisher of *Numismatic News* (below) and many numismatic reference books (including the universally used *Standard Catalog of World Paper Money* by Pick).

Bank Note Reporter subscriptions are $29.95 per year for U.S. addresses; write for foreign subscription prices. *BNR* is an 11¼ x 14½ inch monthly newspaper averaging 40 to 52 pages per issue. Both U.S. and foreign paper money articles appear in every issue, as well as these Departments every month: "Advertisers' index, Bank Note Clinic, Classified ads, Foreign Exchange (in both U.S. dollars per foreign currency unit and number of foreign units per U.S. dollar), Reader Response (Letters to the Editor), Show calendar, World Currency section, and World Update."

Besides the Letters to the Editor and dealer ads, one of my favorite sections of *BNR* is "Bank Note Clinic" — written in question-and-answer format, often with note photos to illustrate one of the questions. Recent questions that were answered in "Bank Note Clinic" were: "What are metameric colors?" and "With all the Silver Certificates that were redeemed back in the 1960s, why haven't the remainder shot up in price?" and "I have a 'Town of Paris' promissory note, which I've been unable to trace. Any help?" (note is illustrated, along with the editor's response) and "My bank note is supposed to have a red seal, but it is actually a bright orange. Was this some bad ink or what?"

A typical issue of *BNR* has over 200 classified ads, listed in the Classified Marketplace section at the end of the newspaper, under several pages of separate categories, such as "National Banknotes," "Worldwide General," and "Bonds and Stock Certificates." The top paper money dealers advertise in *BNR*, sometimes with full-page ads listing individual U.S. or foreign notes for sale.

Send $2.75 for a sample copy of *Bank Note Reporter*.

Coin World

Coin World (CW)
P.O. Box 150
Sidney, OH 45365
(513) 498-2111

Published weekly, $26 per year for U.S. addresses, $66 per year for foreign subscribers. Published by Amos Press.

Coin World is an 11 x 15 inch weekly newspaper with more than 100 pages in a typical issue. Most of the publication is devoted to coins, but there is always some paper money information included, and the information is up-to-date because it is published weekly. Three recent cover story articles on paper money, in three different issues of *CW*, were: "Treasury unveils new notes"; "Paper money collectors prize mistakes"; and "Covert device fights FR note counterfeiting."

CW often has data on recent counterfeit notes and Bureau of Engraving and Printing announcements. With a circulation of about 74,000, *CW* reaches many of the coin/paper currency collectors in the United States. Although mostly coin ads, many of *CW*'s display ads feature paper money for sale, and the classified section also has paper money ads. A currency

dealer who advertises in several periodicals shows a certain amount of stability and, therefore, may deserve your business.

Send $2 for a sample copy of *Coin World*.

Numismatic News

Numismatic News (NN)
700 East State Street
Iola, WI 54990
(715) 445-2214

Published weekly, $27.95 per year for U.S. addresses, $108.95 for foreign subscribers. Published by Krause Publications (no relation to this author), also publishers of *Bank Note Reporter* (above), as well as a variety of numismatic/paper money books.

This 11 x 15 inch weekly newspaper runs about 50 to 80 pages per issue. *Numismatic News* is slightly shorter in number of pages than *Coin World*, but covers similar current numismatic news (including paper money information), show schedules, auction announcements, market fluctuations, etc. *NN* tends to be a little less formal in editorial style and writing than *Coin World*, but both are quality weeklies, and many collectors subscribe to both, some to just one.

Numismatic News is the longest running of all the current commercial numismatic periodicals in the United States, having been first issued on October 13, 1952 as a single page composed on the dining room table of founder Chet Krause (no relation to this author). Krause Publications is a large publishing house of hobby publications, employing 322 people.

Although, like *Coin World*, most of *Numismatic News* concerns coins, much information on paper money appears in *NN* over the course of the year, including occasional special "paper money sections," which feature paper currency and items such as stocks and checks.

Recent paper money articles in *NN* include: "New $100 Federal Reserve notes moving smoothly into circulation" and "Ink vanishes on run of notes" ... and for stock and bond collectors: "Standard Oil certificate brings high bid" — being a report of prices realized in a mail-bid(!) auction by R.M. Smythe and Company (where a Standard Oil Company stock certificate issued to John D. Rockefeller, and with three of his signatures affixed, sold for $12,000, including the 10% buyer's fee).

Numismatic News has a question-and-answer format "Coin Clinic" every week, wherein paper money questions appear from time to time (a recent example: "A friend has a Bank of United States $1,000 note, with serial No. 8894. I've told him it is worthless, but he won't believe me. Would you print something to satisfy him?" followed by *NN* editorial writer Alan Herbert's answer that this note is one of the best known facsimiles of all the notes ever "copied" for promotional and other reasons, and that this "famous" Serial Numbered 8894 note is worthless).

Send $1.50 for a sample copy of *Numismatic News*.

The Numismatist

The Numismatist
818 North Cascade Avenue
Colorado Springs, CO 80903
(719) 632-2646

Published monthly by the American Numismatic Association (ANA), $28 per year ($26 to ANA members) for U.S. addresses, $33 for foreign subscribers ($28 for ANA members).

While officially the journal of the ANA, a nonprofit society (see Chapter 23 for more information), and not a commercial, privately owned periodical like the others I've listed in this chapter, I decided to include *The Numismatist* here because: (1) so many serious paper money collectors are ANA members; (2) information on currency shows, auctions, and new paper money books appears in *The Numismatist* just as in the other periodicals; and (3) many prominent paper money dealers have current ads in *The Numismatist*, including dealers who handle paper money as part of their overall numismatic business.

The Numismatist averages 160 to 174 pages per issue, is about 7³/₈ by 9¹/₄ inches in paper size, and has pages of clean white paper with a slick-surfaced stiffer cover. Copies of *The Numismatist* will stand upright on a book shelf, or they can be bound in hardcover yearly "volumes." I like this magazine's size because it is small and easy to read on an airplane or a bus, and its printing quality lends itself to permanent filing.

The Numismatist features articles of lasting value every month, on U.S. and foreign coins, medals, and paper money, with most emphasis on coins, written by experts and serious students of numismatics, often with illustrative photographs and a list of references at the end of each article.

Departments every month in *The Numismatist* include "Letters" (to the editor) wherein readers' comments and debates are aired; "Membership News" — a calendar of upcoming coin/paper money shows, club activities, and ANA membership data; "Consumer Alert" (one of my favorites) by Kenneth Bressett, who notifies readers of numismatic rip-off schemes, usually from advertisers in non-numismatic media; and a wonderful regular monthly column, "Notes on Paper," written by paper money expert Gene Hessler.

The Numismatist has dealer display ads, usually in understated good taste (ANA members are hard to fool), as well as a small classified ad section at the back of each issue. If all you want to read is paper money ads, then you might be better off just subscribing to *Bank Note Reporter* (mentioned first in this chapter) and getting the journals of the Society of Paper Money Collectors (*Paper Money*) and the International Bank Note Society (*"IBNS" Journal*) — the three of which collectively contain most of the paper money dealers' ads that you will ever see anywhere in the United States.

But ANA membership itself is worth something, too, besides *The Numismatist* every month. A long-held ANA membership number is a prime business reference in the paper money market, because the ANA expels outright crooks whenever possible. And the ANA Resource Center Library has an outstanding selection of paper money books that can be borrowed by members for only the cost of postage and insurance both ways (see ANA information in Chapter 23).

The late Jack Eigen, who was my favorite Chicago radio talk show host when I lived there many years ago, used to say, half humorously, on his late night phone-in talk show, "You only live once, but if you live right, once is enough!"

You may "only" collect bank notes, and nothing else, but if you learn about them from everywhere you can (including periodicals that have "only" one or two articles of interest to you), you'll start to know enough about paper money to really enjoy it, and perhaps get a few other benefits as well.

261. Published monthly, *Bank Note Reporter* (BNR) is the only commercial, exclusively notaphilic, comprehensive periodical in the United States. Front page reproduced courtesy of *Bank Note Reporter*, Krause Publications, Iola, Wisconsin.

"The love of money overcomes us all."
Aristophanes (circa 448-380 B.C.)

23

Paper Money Societies

Membership in a paper money society has benefits that far exceed the annual dues, which average between $15 and $25. A chance to meet other collectors who are also interested in your specialty area, trading privileges, current market analysis (selling prices of notes), and the opportunity to read the latest published research and expert commentary are certainly worth a dollar or two a month! One fact learned from one issue of a society journal can repay your membership fee many times over.

The societies in this chapter are all national non-profit organizations, and each one of them has members from all over the United States (and, in some cases, from many foreign countries also). You can confidently join any of these societies from the comfort and safety of your home; nobody will come to your home or beg for extra donations if you join a national paper money society. Most guard their membership lists with special trust, and you may keep your address confidential if you wish. Membership in currency societies is one mark of a mature and serious collector; a ten-year ANA or SPMC member is looked upon as a dedicated numismatist/notaphilist. Long-term society members are considered responsible people who are somewhat creditworthy, so society membership is good for references.

Here are some of the most important paper money societies in the United States. Send a business size (No. 10) self-addressed stamped envelope for the latest information regarding membership requirements, benefits, annual dues, etc. All these societies welcome beginning collectors — how can you learn unless you start somewhere?

American Numismatic Association

AMERICAN NUMISMATIC ASSOCIATION (ANA)
818 North Cascade Avenue
Colorado Springs, CO 80903
(719) 632-2646

"Everybody" is a member of the ANA, the largest numismatic organization in the United States (32,000 members). Founded in 1891 to advance and promote the study of coins, medals, tokens, and paper money, this society caters mainly to coin collectors, but paper money enthusiasts find many benefits of membership, including the handsome monthly 160 to 174 page journal, *The Numismatist*; access to the world's largest lending library of numismatic references (more than 30,000 items, including many paper money books that can be borrowed by members for the cost of postage and insurance both ways); a *Numismatic Resource Directory*; a fabulous money museum (see Chapter 24); access to research services by ANA staff; and twice-a-year conventions held in changing cities across the country.

You'll find that the ANA journal, *The Numismatist*, mostly concerns coins, but every month there is notaphilic expert Gene Hessler's column, "Notes on Paper," for paper money collectors; and there are other occasional paper money articles (such as mine entitled "Collecting Paper Money Errors," which appeared in the October 1991 issue of *The Numismatist*, reproduced as Chapter 20 of this book).

Annual ANA dues are $26, plus a one-time initiation fee of $6. Senior citizens (age 65 or older) pay $22 per year. Junior members (under age 18) pay $11 per year and receive a quarterly magazine, *First Strike*.

American Society of Check Collectors, Inc.

AMERICAN SOCIETY OF CHECK COLLECTORS, INC. (ASCC)
P.O. Box 71892
Madison Heights, MI 48071

The American Society of Check Collectors, Inc. is an organization of collectors of checks and check-related fiscal documents (including stocks and bonds, but mostly checks). The ASCC serves not only the check collector proper, but also those interested in banking history, vignettes and engravings used on fiscal documents, revenue stamps, types of fiscal documents, and security printers. The Society publishes *The Check Collector*, a quarterly newsletter that is sent to all members. All Society officers are elected and serve without pay. A serious check collector should be a member of this Society.

Annual dues are $10 for residents of the U.S., Canada, or Mexico; $12 for other countries.

Fractional Currency Collectors Board

FRACTIONAL CURRENCY COLLECTORS BOARD (FCCB)
Route 1, Box 331B
Allen, TX 75002

The Fractional Currency Collectors Board was formed in 1983 by a group of U.S. *Fractional Currency* collectors at the Memphis International Paper Money Show. Current membership is about 125 and includes the best known collectors of U.S. *Fractional Currency*. Society newsletters are published on an "as news indicates" basis and include new information/articles on *Fractional Currency* as well as updates to the *Encyclopedia of United States Fractional and Postal Currency* by Milton Friedberg. Each member gets a copy of the *Encyclopedia* upon joining. Society meetings and an educational seminar are held each year in Memphis at the International Paper Money Show.

The FCCB also derives its initials from one of the earliest *Fractional Currency* collectors, F.C.C. Boyd. During the 1930s, he bought many large and impressive collections, such as the Proskey Collection and much of the Brand Collection; Boyd's Collection remains virtually intact today.

Membership dues in the FCCB are $15, which includes a $5 new member charge for the latest update to Freidberg's *Encyclopedia*.

International Bank Note Society

INTERNATIONAL BANK NOTE SOCIETY (IBNS)
P.O. Box 1642
Racine, WI 53401

The International Bank Note Society was founded in 1961, and now has over 1,600 members from over 60 countries. The Society publishes a newsletter and a handsome quarterly journal appropriately titled the *International Bank Note Society Journal*, which has informative articles on worldwide paper money, a Letters to the Editor page, and currency dealer ads. Recent journal articles include: "Dachau Concentration Camp Scrip," "Specimen Notes," "Broken Serial Numbers on Scottish Notes," and "Bank Notes of the Central Reserve Bank of China." The journal articles are well-illustrated with note photos.

The IBNS holds mail bid auctions twice a year, giving members the opportunity to bid by mail on worldwide bank notes. Society Congresses are held annually in Great Britain, the Netherlands, and the U.S. (in Memphis). The Society also has a London, England address: IBNS, 11 Middle Row, North Kensington, London W10 5AT England.

In U.S. dollars, membership dues are $17.50 per year; $9 for Juniors (age 11-17); $22.50 for family memberships. All serious collectors of worldwide paper money should be IBNS members, in my opinion.

Latin American Paper Money Society

LATIN AMERICAN PAPER MONEY SOCIETY (LANSA)
3304 Milford Mill Road
Baltimore, MD 21207

The Latin American Paper Money Society was founded in January 1973 for collectors of Latin American and Iberian (Spain and Portugal) paper money. South America, Central America, Mexico, and Caribbean islands (including former British, Dutch, French, and Spanish possessions there) are included in the currency studied by LANSA.

All new members receive all available bulletins and a free advertisement in each bulletin. Membership benefits include a newsletter, an auction, library access, and a society directory. Much history, geography, and culture can be learned from Society newsletters. Annual membership dues are $8, plus a $1 initiation fee payable by check or money order drawn on a United States bank, or by current U.S. paper money, or by current UNCIRCULATED bank notes of acceptable foreign countries at the official rate of exchange.

Society of Paper Money Collectors, Inc.

SOCIETY OF PAPER MONEY COLLECTORS, INC. (SPMC)
P.O. Box 6011
St. Louis, MO 63139

At the 1960 ANA Convention in Boston, a small group of paper money collectors met informally and agreed that a regular organization would be desirable. During the next year, an organization was formed, comprising collectors of tokens, medals, and obsolete paper money. At the 1961 ANA Convention in Atlanta, it was decided to withdraw the tokens and medals group and organize separately into the Society of Paper Money Collectors. In June 1964, the Society was incorporated as a non-profit organization under the laws of the District of Columbia.

SPMC membership benefits include the handsome bimonthly journal, *Paper Money*, which has informative, illustrated articles that emphasize old U.S. currency. Recent *Paper Money* articles: "America's First Historical Vignettes on Paper Money," "Minnesota State Scrip," and "Moneta and the Confederate Treasury." The journal also has news about the paper money hobby, classified ads from Society members, and display ads of important paper money dealers.

The SPMC co-sponsors the Memphis International Paper Money Show and the Professional Currency Dealers Show (see Chapter 18), the two largest annual gatherings of paper money collectors and dealers in the United States. At each of these shows, as well as at other regional shows, the SPMC holds a general membership meeting, to bring everyone up-to-date on the Society's activities; additionally, the SPMC sponsors educational forums presenting various topics, often with illustrations.

American collectors of general foreign currency tend to be members of the International Bank Note Society (see above). Collectors specializing in old U.S. bank notes tend to be members of the Society of Paper Money Collectors. Many collectors (including me) are members of both of these organizations, the two major paper money societies in the United States.

The SPMC also publishes reference books on obsolete currency for various U.S. states.

Annual dues for the SPMC are $20 for U.S. residents, $25 for Canada and Mexico addresses, and $30 for all other countries, payable in U.S. funds. Members who join the Society prior to October 1 receive the journals already issued in the year they join. Members who join after October 1 will have their dues paid through December of the following year. They will also receive, as a bonus, a copy of the journal issued in November of the year in which they join.

Applicants for SPMC membership must be sponsored by a current SPMC member, or provide suitable bank and numismatic references.

Souvenir Card Collectors Society

SOUVENIR CARD COLLECTORS SOCIETY (SCCS)
P.O. Box 4155
Tulsa, OK 74159

The Souvenir Card Collectors Society is an organization of collectors and dealers of souvenir cards (see Chapter 6). Membership includes a quarterly publication, *The Souvenir Card Journal*, which has articles and news on souvenir cards (especially recent issue information), dealers' and collectors' ads offering to buy or sell cards, and *Journal* editor's comments. Recent *Journal* articles include: "A Thumbnail Sketch of Engraving History," "Two German Souvenir Cards of 1990," and "New Intaglio Printed Cards." Back issues of the *Journal* to 1981 are available for purchase, and from time to time the Society offers souvenir cards for sale.

Annual dues for the SCCS are $20 for North American collectors ($30 for dealers), and $25 for overseas collectors ($35 for dealers). All membership years begin on January 1, and members joining at any time during the year will receive all *Journal* issues for that year. Members get one free ad in each *Journal* issue.

Canadian Paper Money Society

CANADIAN PAPER MONEY SOCIETY (CPMS)
P.O. Box 465
West Hill Post Office
West Hill, Ontario M1E 2P0
Canada

The Canadian Paper Money Society was established in 1964 and incorporated in 1972. The CPMS is a non-profit educational and historical organization, promoting the study and collection of Canadian paper money, the history of Canadian banking, etc. A quarterly publication, *The Canadian Paper Money Journal*, is sent to all members. Annual dues are $22.50 in Canadian dollars to Canadian addresses; $22.50 in U.S. dollars to all other addresses.

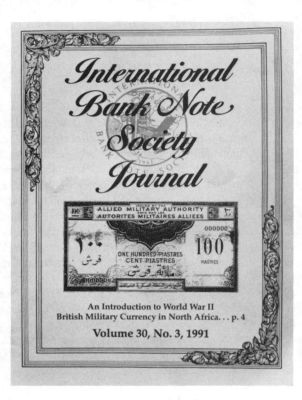

262. The *IBNS Journal*, published quarterly, has articles of lasting value on many aspects of paper money. Front page reproduced courtesy of the International Bank Note Society, Racine, Wisconsin.

263. Published six times a year, *Paper Money* is the informative journal of the Society of Paper Money Collectors. Front page reproduced courtesy of the Society of Paper Money Collectors, St. Louis, Missouri.

24

"What is infamy so long as our money is safe?"
Juvenal (circa 60-140 A.D.)

Museums

Here are some museums that have paper money exhibits on display and currency research collections. Call or write before traveling far to visit them, so you can be sure they will be open when you arrive.

Why go to a museum to see paper money? You'll see a lot more notes at a small currency show (Chapter 18) or even at a well-stocked coin/paper money shop (Chapter 17) than you'll ever see on display at the average museum with currency exhibits. You go to a museum to see currency specimens of historical importance … for the explanatory exhibits and displays of historical artifacts that were fashioned contemporaneously with the currency … and for the "period" atmosphere of museum exhibition halls and galleries, which make mere paper Bank Notes come to life in a way that a simple currency auction catalog or dealer's price list can't hope to accomplish.

The following museums are representative of the many that may have some fascinating paper money on exhibit when you arrive.

California

WELLS FARGO HISTORY MUSEUM
420 Montgomery Street
San Francisco, CA 94104
(415) 396-2619

This museum traces the history and success of the Wells Fargo Express Company from its beginnings in 1852 in San Francisco. Besides handsome exhibits of California Gold Rush era gold coins and gold dust samples, this museum always has some interesting paper monies on display (e.g., *California's Varied Money* exhibit).

In addition to paper money proper, there is always an impressive selection of other fiscal paper "collateral" (Chapter 6) on exhibit at this museum, including bills of exchange, old bank checks, stock and bond certificates, and express company receipts and letters. Be sure to see the gorgeous polished metal gold scale made by Howard & Davis (Boston) and the authentic Concord stagecoach.

The San Francisco Wells Fargo History Museum is open Monday through Friday, 9 A.M. to 5 P.M., with free admission.

Colorado

ANA WORLD MONEY MUSEUM
818 North Cascade Avenue
Colorado Springs, CO 80903
(719) 632-2646

This museum is open 8:30 A.M. to 4:00 P.M., Monday through Friday; and the same hours also on Saturday between Memorial Day and Labor Day. Admission is free to American Numismatic Association (ANA) members (see Chapter 23) and to children under 10; 50¢ to those 10 to 17; $1 for nonmembers 18 and older.

Located on the campus of Colorado College at the foot of Pike's Peak in Colorado Springs, the ANA Museum is one of the largest museums in the world for coins, medals, and paper money — all of which are on display in profusion in eight galleries of exhibits, some permanent, some changing periodically.

Of special importance at the ANA Museum: the Norman H. Liebman Collection of paper money related to Abraham Lincoln; the Robert T. Herdegen Memorial Collection (of

United States *Fractional Currency*, among other things); handsome vignettes and accompanying scarce notes from the J. Roy Pennell, Jr. Collection; and the extraordinary United States Paper Money Collection of Aubrey and Adeline Bebee (of Omaha, Nebraska), the most complete in existence. Choice examples of the Bebee Collection of U.S. Paper Money, assembled over a period of forty years and valued at $2 million, are on prominent display at the Museum.

The ANA World Money Museum is in Colorado Springs, Colorado, about sixty miles south of Denver off U.S. Interstate Highway 25.

Florida

> MUSEUM OF FLORIDA HISTORY
> R.A. Gray Building
> 500 South Bronough Street
> Tallahassee, FL 32399
> (904) 488-1484

The Museum of Florida History's paper money collection includes Florida *Territorial Currency*, Florida *State Currency* from the Civil War period, *Confederate Notes*, and federal *Fractional Currency*. Examples from these collections are on display at three sites: the Museum's Main Gallery in the R.A. Gray Building, the Old Capitol Building exhibits (which include several examples of Florida railroad currency), and the Union Bank exhibits (including *Union Bank* currency and Florida *Territorial* and *State Currency*). All are within walking distance of each other.

Directly across Monroe Street from the Old Capitol, the Union Bank building, built in 1841 territorial Tallahassee, is Florida's oldest surviving bank building. Hours exhibits are open to the public are: R.A. Gray Building and Old Capitol — 9:00 A.M. to 4:30 P.M. Monday through Friday; 10:00 A.M. to 4:30 P.M. Saturday; and 12:00 noon to 4:30 P.M. Sunday. The Union Bank is open 10:00 A.M. to 1:00 P.M. Tuesday through Friday (closed Mondays); and 1:00 P.M. to 4:00 P.M. Saturday and Sunday. All sites are closed Thanksgiving Day and Christmas. Admission is free to these interesting places in Florida's capital city. And, like most museums, collections in storage may be examined by qualified researchers upon prior written request to the Chief Curator of Collections and Research.

Iowa

> HIGGINS MUSEUM
> Sanborn Avenue (Airport Road)
> Okoboji, IA 51355
> (712) 332-5859

One of the few museums in the world devoted solely to paper money. The purpose of this museum is to acquire, preserve, and display the notes and artifacts of the U.S. National Banks (see Chapters 2 and 9). The various types and denominations of notes issued by the National Banks are displayed here, as well as several representative notes from the States, the Territories, the District of Columbia, and Puerto Rico.

Sometimes called the "Higgins National Bank Note Museum and Library," this museum was established from the proceeds of the 1973-1974 auctions of the 7,000+ collection of world crowns (silver dollar-sized coins) of William R. Higgins, Jr., who was mayor of Okoboji from 1960 to 1974. John T. Hickman, a leading cataloger and dealer in *National Bank Notes* (see the Oakes and Hickman *Standard Catalog of National Bank Notes* in Bibliography), has been the Curator since the museum opened.

The museum's exhibits emphasize the *National Bank Notes* of Iowa and two bordering states: Missouri and Minnesota (Okoboji Lake is just a few miles from the Minnesota border via Highway 71, and a few more miles from U.S. Interstate Highway 90 in Minnesota — send a self-addressed stamped envelope for the Museum's brochure, which includes a map).

The two "Iowa Rooms" at this Museum display the most complete state collection of *National Bank Notes* ever assembled from a major state. There are 278 different Iowa towns represented from all 99 Iowa counties. Many of these notes are the only notes known to exist and are of the finest condition available.

The "Missouri Room" has several rare uncut sheets. The most complete collection of the notes issued by the banks of Missouri is arranged alphabetically, by town, around the walls.

The "Minnesota Room" has many rare and interesting notes from Minnesota, including the "number one" $1 note from the *First National Bank of Northfield*, the bank robbed by the James brothers, and the only known note from Sleepy Eye Lake is featured.

Call to be sure the Museum will be open when you want to visit. Opening date: Mid-June. Closing date: Labor Day. Open Tuesday through Sunday, 11:00 A.M. to 5:30 P.M. Closed Mondays. For *National Bank Note* admirers.

Missouri

> MERCANTILE MONEY MUSEUM
> Mercantile Tower
> 7th & Washington
> St. Louis, MO 63101
> (314) 421-1819

"Money makes the world go 'round," so you will enjoy seeing old and new money at the Mercantile Money Museum. On display is the Eric P. Newman Collection of coins and currency, a wealth of U.S. and foreign coins and paper money. Newman founded the museum, which is a cooperative undertaking of the Mercantile Bank and the Eric P. Newman Numismatic Education Society.

In addition to many changing exhibits, representing over 80 countries' numismatic material, the museum features two audiovisual mannequins (perfect for kids visiting the museum) — Benjamin Franklin and a counterfeiter. Franklin expounds on money matters and the world scene, peppering his remarks with many witticisms. The counterfeiter, in prison garb, ruefully explains his predicament and the penalties for counterfeiting. A charming Victorian library houses the Newman Collection of Numismatic Literature and is available by appointment to serious numismatic students and scholars.

In St. Louis for the autumn Paper Money Convention? Then go see the Money Museum! Open 9:00 A.M. to 4:00 P.M. every day of the year. Free admission.

New Jersey

THE NEWARK MUSEUM
49 Washington Street
Newark, NJ 07101
(201) 596-6550

The Numismatic Collection of The Newark Museum was begun in 1909, the year of the museum's founding. Internationally recognized, this is the only public comprehensive numismatic collection active within the state of New Jersey. In storage and on exhibit are coins, tokens, and paper currency, and other objects related to finance, such as lottery tickets, checks, bonds, and bullion. The collection currently numbers more than 28,000 items and continues to grow through gift and purchase.

Highlights of the paper money collection include 350 obsolete New Jersey *State Bank Notes* and *Merchant's Scrip*, including *proof* notes engraved by Asher B. Durand in the 19th century; a *Fractional Currency* Shield; about 1,000 notes from Colonial and Independent African states (from Algeria to Zaire); and over 2,000 pieces of World War I era German *notgeld* (gift of Paul Mausolff, 1934). A visitor to the small but interesting Numismatic Gallery of the Museum will be likely to encounter exhibits of New Jersey paper money and scrip (from Colonial times to the Great Depression) and assorted African notes.

Gallery hours are: Tuesday through Sunday, 12:00 noon to 5:00 P.M. (closed Mondays and major holidays). Free admission but donations are welcome. Parking is available at the adjacent Penny Lane lot on the corner of Central and University Avenues. Have the parking ticket stamped at the museum's Information Desk.

New York

AMERICAN NUMISMATIC SOCIETY MUSEUM
(ANS MUSEUM)
Broadway at 155th Street
New York, NY 10032
(212) 234-3130

The first museum in the world to exhibit only numismatic items. Nearly one million specimens (mostly coins) are in this museum, and it has the world's most comprehensive library of numismatic literature. It is operated under the auspices of the American Numismatic Society (founded in 1858), not to be confused with the ANA Museum (see Colorado listing in this chapter).

The ANS Museum has many important collections, only parts of which can be exhibited at any given time. The museum owns specimens of *Continental Currency* of the American Revolution, 19th century U.S. *Broken Bank Notes*, and various foreign paper currencies (including prisoner-of-war and occupation money). Important donations, such as the 4,431 notes donated by Archer M. Huntington in 1914, have given the museum substantial paper money holdings.

The ANS Museum is more of a "research" museum than a "public entertainment" type of museum; i.e., scholars and researchers ask permission to examine specific items from the museum's collections, for studies on the museum's premises. The ANS Library has almost 100,000 publications.

For information on what is presently on exhibit, call or write the museum. Visiting hours are Tuesday through Saturday from 9:00 A.M. to 4:30 P.M.; and Sunday from 1:00 P.M. to 4:00 P.M. Closed on national holidays. The Library section is closed on Sundays. Free admission. Don't be intimidated by the impressive buildings and antiquarian atmosphere.

South Carolina

SOUTH CAROLINA CONFEDERATE RELIC ROOM
     AND MUSEUM
World War Memorial Building
920 Sumter Street
Columbia, SC 29201
(803) 734-9813

Established in 1895, the South Carolina Confederate Relic Room and Museum focuses on South Carolina military history. This museum is housed in the World War Memorial Building, constructed in 1935 to honor South Carolina veterans of World War I. The building is on the University of South Carolina campus.

This museum maintains a small continuous exhibit of coins, paper money, bonds, loans, stamps, letters, and covers. Specimens recently on exhibit include: *Confederate States of America* $5, $50, and $100 Notes, a 25¢ piece cut in half for circulation during 1861-1865, and state and private bank notes. They also have a few Japanese and German occupation notes.

Located in South Carolina's historic capital city, this museum is open Monday through Friday, 8:30 A.M. to 5:00 P.M. Free admission.

Virginia

MONEY MUSEUM
Federal Reserve Bank of Richmond
701 East Byrd Street
Richmond, VA 23219
(804) 697-8148

About 575 specimens are on display, representing 350 kinds of money — primitive monies, ancient coins, Colonial commodity money, *Colonial* and *Continental* coins and paper money, U.S. coins and paper money, *Confederate Currency*, early paper money of Virginia, and U.S. commemorative coins. On exhibit at this museum are: a Franklin Printing Press, a Production Balance Beam (on which coin blanks and coins were weighed at the third U.S. Mint), a Cannonball Safe (once used by banks and merchants to store money), and barter money (like wampum and tobacco). A lovely museum, with modern exhibiting techniques. Be certain to see the $500, $1,000, $5,000, and $10,000 *Federal Reserve Notes*, and an uncut sheet of twelve $100,000 *Gold Certificates*.

Open Monday through Friday, 9:30 A.M. to 3:30 P.M. Free admission.

Washington, DC

NATIONAL NUMISMATIC COLLECTION
National Museum of American History Smithsonian
   Institution
Constitution Avenue at 14th Street, NW
Washington, DC 20560
(202) 357-1300

The Hall of Monetary History and Medallic Art is on the third floor, and exhibits a breathtaking array of U.S. and foreign coins, tokens, medals, and paper money. Over 900,000 specimens reside in the National Numismatic Collection, and obviously only a small fraction of them can be displayed at any given time. My feeling is that they show too many specimens in too small a space, but what do you expect when you're faced with the problem of exhibiting one of the finest numismatic collections in the world?

The National Numismatic Collection had its origins in the mid-19th century, shortly after the Smithsonian was founded in 1846. Various numismatic collections, including paper money acquisitions, have been added to the museum from time to time.

In response to my request for information about the paper money in the National Numismatic Collection, Elvira Clain-Stefanelli, Executive Director of the National Numismatic Collection, wrote me a personal letter dated January 13, 1992, in which she states: "Yes, we do have a substantial collection of paper money of the U.S. and the world, it constitutes the larger half of our holdings of over 900,000 items." She also sent me information about the collection, which, for the museum's paper money holdings, I summarize here:

Over 100,000 paper notes of the world were donated by Mr. and Mrs. Mortimer Neinken to the National Numismatic Collection in recent years. The late Mr. Neinken was a New York industrialist and philanthropist, and his paper money donations are especially rich in Austrian notes and financial documents from the 18th to the 20th centuries.

The Stack family (of the New York City numismatic company, Stack's) donated a 1666 Swedish note and important American *Colonial Notes*, and Mr. and Mrs. James Leigh donated interesting Chinese, Manchurian, Mongolian, and Russian notes in 1970. Two very rare Russo-American Company "sealskin" notes issued in Alaska in 1816-1817 were acquired by the museum. Mr. Philip Chase in 1963 donated the personal album of *Confederate Currency* researcher Raphael P. Thian entitled, "The Currency of the Confederate States." In 1971, the widow of Mr. Herman K. Crofoot (a collector from Moravia, New York) donated his magnificent collection of over 600 U.S. *Fractional Currency* notes (including a rare "pink" *Fractional Currency* Shield).

In yearly transfers over a period of nine years, the Bureau of Engraving and Printing "donated" over 300,000 certified *Proofs* for the printing of U.S. paper money; and in 1978, the Department of the Treasury "gave" 808 notes to the museum, with a face value of over $500,000, with many rare federal issues of the 1860s. In 1978, the Smithsonian acquired the famous Chase Manhattan Bank Money Museum's collection of coins, medals, tokens, paper currency, and related items (such as the earliest known "check," drawn for £20 in London in 1664; and a group of checks with the names of almost every U.S. President).

Wear comfortable shoes, and allow plenty of time when you go to see the National Numismatic Collection. The museum is open every day of the year except Christmas: 10:00 A.M. to 5:30 P.M. in the winter; 10:00 A.M. to 7:30 P.M. from April to the beginning of September. No admission fee — what a bargain!

Canada

BANK OF CANADA CURRENCY MUSEUM
245 Sparks Street
Ottawa, Ontario K1A 0G9
Canada
(613) 782-8914

The Canadian National Currency Collection of more than 100,000 items is at this museum; about 10% of the collection is on permanent display.

The Currency Museum consists of eight galleries that trace the history of money from barter to modern currency, with emphasis on Canada's monetary history. The museum is in the process of presenting the reference collection of Canadian paper money from the earlier issues of the French regime to the latest note of the *Bank of Canada*. About 550 world bank notes of the 20th century were on display recently. The exhibits in this museum have been assembled to appeal to everyone: the general public, the collector, and the serious numismatist.

The Currency Museum has a 7,500-volume library open to the public during business hours.

Museum hours: Tuesday through Saturday, 10:30 A.M. to 5:00 P.M.; Sunday 1:00 P.M. to 5:00 P.M. Closed Mondays and holidays, but open Mondays from May to Labor Day. Free admission.

Great Britain

THE BRITISH MUSEUM
Great Russell Street
London WC1B 3DG
England
(071) 323 8404 (for Department of Coins and Medals)

The Department of Coins and Medals in the British Museum houses one of the world's finest numismatic collections, containing over 600,000 objects, of which there are some 50,000 items of paper money, contained in the museum's own collection and that of the *Chartered Institute of Bankers*, which is placed here on indefinite loan.

As befits the national collection, British material is strongly represented, with particular emphasis on the private bank issues of paper money of the 18th and 19th centuries. However, both collections contain paper money from all over the world, including historical and modern notes. Many note-issuing authorities regularly provide the museum with specimens of their current notes. In addition to bank notes, the collections include related material, such as cheques, skit notes, proofs, and some artwork for note designs.

The museum's Department of Coins and Medals mounts several temporary exhibitions each year in the Coins and Medals foyer gallery, many of which include paper money. A special Students' Room is available for those who wish to study the collections or consult the Department's library, which contains a wide range of banking histories and paper money catalogs. Admission to the Students' Room is by appointment, and intending visitors must have a letter of recommendation and proof of identity.

Hours: Monday thorough Friday, 10:00 A.M. to 12:30 P.M. (except Wednesday), and 2:00 P.M. to 4:30 P.M.; and Saturday, 10:00 A.M. to 12:30 P.M. Free admission.

264.   Russian 3 *Rubles* note of 1938, with Soviet soldiers at left. (Pick # 214)

265.   Mexican Revolutionary 5 *Pesos* note, state of Oaxaca, March 15, 1916. Two handstamped signatures, national coat-of-arms at left. (Pick # S949a)

266.   5 *Pesos* note of *El Banco Peninsular Mexicano*, issued 1 April, 1914, local Mexican note. Locomotive at left, dock workers at right. (Pick # S465)

267.   £1 note of Biafra, no date (but issued 1968-1969). Palm tree and rising sun. (Pick # 5a) Biafra was a temporary military breakaway region of Nigeria, from May 30, 1967 to January 15, 1970.

268.   1 *Chiao* note of the People's Republic of China (Communist China), 1962, featuring "contented" workers. (Pick # 877c)

269.   50 *Cruzados* note of Brazil, no date (but 1986). (Pick # 210)

"Among themselves all things have order ..."
Dante Alighieri (1265-1321)
The Divine Comedy, Paradise, Canto I

Glossary

This is a glossary of some common paper money terms and their recognized abbreviations, as used in the standard catalogs and reference books, numismatic/notaphilic periodicals, currency society journals, dealer price lists, and auction descriptions, and at currency exhibitions. See Chapter 20 for Currency Error definitions.

Also, to simplify everything, unless otherwise stated, I use the word "note" where a more complete definition might include "checks, stock certificates, bonds, etc."

ABOUT UNCIRCULATED (AU) — One light fold in an otherwise "unworn" note. Also called ALMOST UNCIRCULATED.

ALLIED MILITARY CURRENCY (AMC) — World War II notes used by Allied military personnel (U.S., British, Free French, etc.). Not to be confused with post-war Military Payment Certificates.

ASSIGNATS — Notes of the French Revolution, "backed" by land confiscated from the Church. Also from other nations.

ASTERISK NOTE (*) — "Replacement Note" issued by Canada when the "normal" note is damaged during production. So-called from the "Asterisk" (*) prefix in Serial Numbers, begun in Canada in 1954.

ATTRIBUTION — Identifying a note; i.e., which country it came from, when it was made, who is portrayed on the design, who signed the note, etc.

AUTHENTICATION — Declaring a note genuine. Done by expert currency dealers, collectors, numismatic society authentication services, commercial grading services, museum curators, or bank note company employees.

BACK — Reverse side of a note. Opposite the Front.

BANK — An establishment for financial transactions; e.g., receiving deposits, making loans, sometimes even issuing its own paper money.

BANK NOTE (BN) — Paper money issued by a bank, either private or governmental. But commonly used synonymously for paper money, bank-issued or not. Also written: Banknote.

BILINGUAL — Note with two languages imprinted; e.g., notes of Canada, South Africa, etc.

BILL — Slang term for American or Canadian paper money; derived from early American Bill of Exchange.

BILLETS DE CONFIANCE — Emergency low denomination notes issued during the French Revolution to alleviate small change shortage.

BLUEBACKS — Nickname for *Confederate Currency*, which, in later years, bore blue ink printed reverses.

BOGUS NOTE — A Fantasy Note, never having been issued as real money. Examples: Play Money and Stage Money. Strictly defined as false money, which may have passed in actual monetary circulation.

BOND — An interest-bearing certificate, denoting a loan to a corporation or government.

BORDER — Limiting boundary of a note's design. Often confused with, or used synonymously for, Edge or Margin.

BOURSE — A place where dealers and collectors gather to buy and sell paper money.

"BRADBURY" — English *Treasury Note* of 1914-1927, named after the British Secretary of the Treasury, Sir John Bradbury, who signed the first three *Series* of these notes.

BRAMWELL SYSTEM — Method of paper money grading by point values. Not used in the United States.

BROKEN BANK NOTE (BBN) — Paper money issued by banks that later became insolvent, especially referring to pre-Civil War U.S. private bank issues of the 1830s, etc.; also refers to similar Canadian 19th century banks.

BULLION — Precious metal (like gold or silver), in ingot or coin form, used to "back" or guarantee the value of paper money in the past.

BUREAU OF ENGRAVING AND PRINTING (BEP) — Where U.S. paper money is made (Washington, DC; also, since 1991, Fort Worth, Texas).

CAMP NOTE — Currency made expressly for use in prisoner-of-war camps, concentration camps, civilian internment camps, etc.

CANCELLATION (CANC or CAN) — Invalidation of a note by: handstamp, overprint, manuscript, or mechanical defacement (punch holes, patterned slits, etc.). Often done to withdrawn/redeemed notes. Worth less to collectors than uncancelled notes.

CARD MONEY — Emergency currency issued on playing cards or other card stock in Canada and France during times of coin shortage.

CASH — Synonym for money.

CATALOG VALUE (CAT VAL or CV or C/V) — Note's market price in one of the standard collector catalogs.

CENTER (CTR) — "Middle" of a note. For example, the Center hole.

CENTRAL BANK — National government bank (as opposed to private or commercial banks).

CHERRY PICK — Buying only the best notes at prices often less than what they're really worth, often from an owner who doesn't know the notes' actual value. Derogatory term, implying greed and possible dishonesty. Not as common in the paper money hobby as in some other collectibles.

CHOICE (CH) — A superlative, meaning better than average for the grade. Examples: Choice About UNCIRCULATED = CH AU. Choice Crisp UNCIRCULATED = CH CU.

COIN NOTE (CN) — Synonym for U.S. *Treasury Note* of 1890-1891, once redeemable for gold or silver coin, at the Treasury's choice.

COLLEGE CURRENCY — "Business School Money," used in 19th century business classes.

COLONIAL CURRENCY — Pre-Revolutionary War American paper money.

COMMERCIAL BANK — A private bank (as opposed to a central bank or government bank).

COMPOUND INTEREST NOTE (CIN) — Note paying face value plus stated compound interest upon redemption (e.g., certain Civil War federal U.S. notes). CONDITION — Grade of a note; a measure of the accumulated wear and defects of a piece of currency.

CONFEDERATE CURRENCY (CC) — Paper money of the Confederate States of America, issued 1861-1864 (and used into 1865).

CONTINENTAL CURRENCY — American Revolutionary War notes, issued by the Continental Congress from 1775-1779.

CONVERTIBILITY — Officially redeemable in something valuable — e.g., specie (gold or silver coinage).

COPY — A note reproduction, often made obviously so (e.g., with the word "COPY" imprinted thereon). Not meant to pass as a counterfeit. Also called: Facsimile or Replica.

CORNER (COR) — The corner of a note. (Usage example: Small Corner Crease = "sm. cor. cr." in shorthand.)

COUNTERFEIT (CTF) — A completely faked note, made to look real. Done usually for two reasons: to pass as legal tender currency or to fool collectors. Often used synonymously, and erroneously, for Forgery.

COUNTERFOIL — Part of the sheet from which a note was separated, with identical Serial Numbers and signatures as the note; used as a pre-20th century "record" of issue.

CREASE (CR) — A permanent "line" in a note, caused by deep folding. (Usage example: Central Vertical Crease = cen. vert. cr.)

CRISP UNCIRCULATED (CU) — A note in "New" condition; i.e., no wear, no folds, etc.

CRISWELL NUMBER (CR #) — A note's catalog number, as per one of Criswell's catalog books. Used for *Confederates* and U.S. *Obsoletes*.

CURRENCY (CUR) — Synonymous with paper money (in this book unless stated otherwise).

CURRENT (CUR) — Presently circulating.

CUT CANCEL (CC) — A slit in a note, done for invalidation. Don't confuse with Cut Out Cancel. Cut Cancels remove no paper.

CUT NOTE — Officially bisected (or quartered, etc.) note, done to generate paper fractionals during a coin small change shortage. Don't confuse with Halved Note.

CUT OUT CANCEL (COC) — Paper removed from a note, for invalidation. Don't confuse with Cut Cancel.

DATE (D) — The year (Date) that appears on a note; may be a "Series" date; may or may not be the actual year of printing.

DECIMALIZATION — A monetary unit system based on progression by tens; e.g., 10 cents = 1 dime, 100 cents = 1 dollar, etc.

DEMAND NOTE (DN) — First official federal U.S. currency during the Civil War; also called "Greenback."

DEMONETIZATION (DEMON) — Official declaration that a note is worthless. Also called Invalidation. Used synonymously, but erroneously, for Devaluation.

DENOMINATION (DENOM) — Face value of a note, usually so stated in words and numerals in its design.

DESIGN (DES) — Printed part of a note.

DEVALUATION (DEVAL) — Officially declaring a note to be worth much less than its face value, but still worth something as circulating currency value. Sometimes used synonymously, but erroneously, for Demonetization.

DEVIL'S HEAD NOTE — *Bank of Canada* 1954 note with a "Devil's Head" disguised in the design of Queen Elizabeth's hair — or so some people imagine.

DIAGONALLY (DIAG) — Across a note, from one corner to the opposite corner:

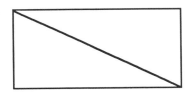

DIE — Flat metal upon which the original note's design was engraved. The Master Die is used to make printing plates.

DOLLAR ($) — Standard monetary unit of the United States, Canada, Australia, Bahamas, New Zealand, etc. Equivalent to 100 cents. Often used to refer to a note of $1 denomination, e.g., a "Dollar Bill."

DOUBLE NOTE — Note printed on the blank back of a Broken Bank Note — done in the South, during the Civil War paper shortage, for example.

EDGE — Limiting boundary of a note's paper.

"EDUCATIONAL NOTES" — Common term for the $1, $2, and $5 U.S. *Silver Certificates* of 1896, due to their design themes.

ENGRAVING (ENGR) — Etching each line in a note's design on a Master Die, then preparing a printing plate for Intaglio (or Recess) printing, the way modern U.S. currency is made.

ERROR — Note production defect that somehow escaped into circulation.

ESSAY — Rejected design for a note.

EXTREMELY FINE (EF or XF) — Condition of a note, usually meaning one major crease, or three light folds.

FACE — Front or Obverse side of a note. Face is term used in the United States.

FACE VALUE — The denomination that is printed on the note.

FADING — Loss of color intensity or hue of a note's ink and/or paper color.

FAIR — Very worn note; large pieces missing.

FANTASY NOTE — Imitation paper money, never intended to pass as real money. Synonymous with Bogus Note in common notaphilic usage.

FEDERAL RESERVE BANK (FRB) — A district or branch bank of the U.S. Federal Reserve System.

FEDERAL RESERVE BANK NOTE (FRBN) — Note issued by actual District Banks of the Federal Reserve System.

FEDERAL RESERVE NOTE (FRN) — Paper money issued by the U.S. Federal Reserve System as a whole. The only paper money presently made in the U.S.

FEDERAL RESERVE SYSTEM (FRS) — Monetary organization that regulates the issuance and use of U.S. paper money; created in 1913.

FIAT MONEY — Money not backed by bullion (or other valuables). Having no intrinsic value. Example: modern U.S. paper money. Synonymous with Fiduciary Money.

FINE (F) — Note condition; having many creases and folds.

"FLYING MONEY" (*fei-ch'ien*) — Ninth century Chinese paper money, so-called because of its easy transportability (as opposed to heavy and bulky coinage).

FOLD — A light bend in a note's paper. Used synonymously, but inaccurately, for Crease.

FORGERY — Technically, a fraudulently altered genuine document, with intent to deceive (e.g., a "raised" note, fraudulent signatures, etc.). Often used synonymously, but erroneously, for Counterfeit.

FOXING — Mold stains on old paper. Also called Tropical Stains.

FRACTIONAL CURRENCY (FRAC CUR or FC) — Notes that are less in face value than a country's standard monetary unit; e.g., U.S. *Fractional Currency* issued from 1868 to 1876, in denominations from 3¢ to 50¢.

FRAME — Border of a note's design.

FRANC (FR) — Monetary unit of France and many French-speaking countries.

FRIEDBERG NUMBER (FR #) — Catalog number for a note, as per Friedberg's book, *Paper Money of the United States*. Standard numbers used by collectors and dealers in U.S. currency.

FRONT — Face or Obverse of a note.

GOLD CERTIFICATE (GC) — Paper money redeemable in gold (or once was); e.g., so designated U.S. notes from 1863 to 1928, etc.

GOOD (G) — A very worn note, with tiny pieces missing.

GRADE (GR) — Condition of a note, which can be debated even by experts.

"GREENBACK" — U.S. *Demand Note* of 1861 and later; so-called because of the green ink used to print the reverse. Slang term to this day for U.S. paper money.

HALVED NOTE (HN) — Paper money officially bisected, with each half transported separately between banks, to prevent loss. Common in the 19th century. Don't confuse with Cut Note.

HANDSIGNED — Manuscript signature; i.e., signed with pen and ink, rather than machine printed.

HANSATSU — Local Japanese currency, in elongated paper shapes, common in the 19th century.

HECTOGRAPHIC (SIGNATURE) — Facsimile signature, reproduced by machine on a note; the way that most paper money is "signed" today. In contradistinction to "Manuscript Signature."

HELL MONEY — Fake bank note produced in China for burning at a funeral to provide the deceased with "money" in the afterlife. Who says you can't take it with you?

HOARD — A secretly hidden bundle of paper money; and/or a deliberately accumulated "collection" of certain note types.

HOLE CANCEL (HC) — Invalidation by means of a large hole (or holes).

HORIZONTAL (HOR) — Across a note's length (for "conventionally" oriented note designs):

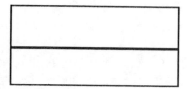

"HORSE BLANKET" — Slang term for pre-1929 U.S. *Large Size Note*.

INFLATION NOTE — Abnormally high denomination note, issued in hyperinflationary times. Examples: Germany of 1923, Greece in the late 1940s, much of Latin America since 1960.

INK CANCEL (IC) — Invalidation by ink.

INSCRIPTION (INSCR) — Lettering on a note. Also called Legend or Text.

INSOLVENCY — A bankrupt bank or other institution.

INTEREST BEARING NOTE (IBN) — Paper money that paid regular rates of interest on the note's principal (face value); e.g., certain *Confederates* and U.S. federal issues of the 19th century.

INVALIDATION — Official declaration that a note is worthless; i.e., no longer legal tender. Also called Demonetization. Used inaccurately for Devaluation.

INVASION MONEY — Currency used by occupying troops, or for occupied nationals.

JAPANESE INVASION MONEY (JIM) — Currency used for Japanese-occupied countries in World War II.

KEY NOTE — Rarest note in a Series, usually the one with the lowest press run.

LARGE SIZE NOTE — U.S. federal currency from 1861 through 1929; with exceptions (such as *Fractionals*).

LEGAL TENDER — Lawful money.

LEGAL TENDER NOTE (LTN) — A type of federal U.S. currency issued 1862 into the 20th century. Also called: *U.S. Note*.

LEGEND — Lettering on a note. Also called Inscription or Text.

LIBERTY — An allegorical female representation on early U.S. notes.

MANUSCRIPT (SIGNATURE) (MS SIG) — Signature that is hand-signed in pen ink. Rarely done in the 20th century. In contradistinction to Hectographic (Signature).

MARGIN (MAR) — Unprinted area outside of a note's design.

MASTER DIE — Engraved metal impression of a note's design (or design parts), from which a printing plate is made.

MILITARY CURRENCY (MC) — Money used by armies and/or in occupied territories. Includes subtypes: invasion notes, occupation notes, liberation notes, partisan notes.

MILITARY PAYMENT CERTIFICATE (MPC) — Military currency, for internal use by military personnel at their canteens. U.S. issues from 1946 to 1973.

MING NOTE — Chinese paper money of the Ming Dynasty (1368-1644 A.D.), printed on mulberry bark paper.

"MONTGOMERY ISSUE" — First *Confederate Currency*, of 1861, issued at the early Confederate capital of Montgomery, Alabama but printed in New York City.

MOTTO — Patriotic and/or religious slogan on a note. Examples: "IN GOD WE TRUST" or "REX DEI GRATIA" ("King by the Grace of God").

MULE — A note whose face doesn't match with its authorized reverse.

MULTILINGUAL NOTE — Currency with more than one language in the legend.

NATIONAL BANK NOTE (NBN) — So designated U.S. currency, issued by chartered banks from 1863 to 1929.

NATIONAL GOLD BANK NOTE (NGBN) — Currency redeemable in gold, issued in the 1870s by National Gold Banks so chartered — nine in California and one in Boston.

NECESSITY MONEY — Emergency money. Also, synonymous with *Notgeld*.

NO DATE (ND or N/D) — Undated note.

NOTAPHILY — The collecting and study of paper money.

NOTE — Piece of paper money.

NOTGELD — Literally: "Money of necessity" in German. "Town-issued money," especially referring to German and Austrian emergency town money of 1919-1923.

NUMISMATICS — The study and collection of paper money, coins, medals, tokens, and related objects. A Numismatist is a student of such.

OBSOLETE NOTE — Currency that no longer circulates. May or may not still be redeemable (legal tender). Commonly used for 18th and 19th century insolvent private and state bank notes, U.S. and foreign.

OBVERSE (OBV) — Front or Face side of a note. Opposite of Reverse. Not used by many American collectors. Used by many European collectors.

OMNIBUS ISSUE — Notes of several countries, with similar design themes (e.g., French Colonial issues).

OVERGRADING — Describing a note as having a better condition than it does. Done deliberately by unscrupulous sellers; done accidentally by ignorant or honestly liberal graders.

OVERPRINT (OVPT) — Official printing done on a note after the initial printing. Done for Serial Number affixing, surcharging, revolutionary currency appropriations, local restricted use, etc.

PAPER MONEY (PM) — Any type of currency printed on paper or paper surrogate. Used synonymously with Bank Note.

PERFORATED CANCEL (PC) — Invalidation of a note with tiny holes (usually) in the configuration of alphabet letters, etc.

PESO ($) — Monetary unit of many Spanish-speaking countries.

PINHOLE — A tiny (in size, not in subjective disfigurement) hole in a note.

PLAIN BACK (PB) — Unprinted back of a note. Synonymous with Uniface.

PLATE LETTER (PL) or PLATE NUMBER (PN) — Tiny control letter (or numeral) on a note, to indicate which printing plate produced that note. Also called: Plate Check Letter, etc.

PLAY MONEY — Crude imitation money, used in children's games and never intended to fool anyone as to its status.

PLAYING CARD MONEY — Notes printed on the backs of playing cards, specifically 17th and 18th century French and Canadian types. POOR — Severely damaged note, with large holes, large missing pieces, etc.

PORTRAIT — "Head/face view" of a person, real or allegorical, in a note's vignette.

POSTAGE CURRENCY (PC) — U.S. *Fractional Currency* with postage stamp designs; issued during the Civil War. Don't confuse with "Stamped Money." Sometimes used for Encased Postage Stamps.

POUND (£) — British monetary unit used in Great Britain and in many former and present overseas possessions. Equivalent to 20 *Shillings* or 240 *Old Pence* or 100 *New Pence* (starting in 1971). Also called: Pound Sterling.

PRISONER-OF-WAR MONEY (POW MONEY) — Currency for specific use only in prisoner-of-war camps.

PRIVATE CURRENCY — Notes issued by non-governmental authorities (e.g., private banks, businesses, associations, etc.).

PROMISSORY NOTE — A document promising to pay a specified sum. In a sense, all paper money issues are Promissory Notes.

PROOF (P or PR or PF) — A trial printing of a note in its design as finally issued, in whole or in part, either in black ink or in issued colors. Usually uniface, and on paper different from bank note paper, and without signatures or Serial Numbers. A Progressive Proof shows only part of the note's design.

PROPAGANDA NOTE — Counterfeit/facsimile note of "enemy" currency design, with a propaganda message on one side.

PROVENANCE — The "collector pedigree" (ownership history) of a note. A listing of auction appearances, private sales, and famous collections in which the note has resided.

PROVISIONAL NOTE — Temporarily issued currency.

PUNCH CANCEL (PC) — Invalidation of a note, with small holes.

"RAISED NOTE" — A type of forgery in which the note's denomination is altered to appear greater.

REDEEMABILITY — Either: (1) the old-fashioned concept whereby notes were convertible (exchangeable) for specie (gold or silver coin), no longer done in any country; or (2) the "honoring" of the note in "lawful money" by its issuing authority (or both).

REFUNDING CERTIFICATE (RC) — A type of U.S. $10 note of 1879, bearing interest.

REMAINDERED NOTE — Unissued note, sold or confiscated for: collecting, study, samples, waste, etc. Usually has no signatures or Serial Numbers. Also called: Unissued Remainder.

REPAIRED (REP) — A damaged note that has been repaired.

REPLACEMENT NOTE — Note issued to replace a note damaged during manufacture. Replacement Notes usually bear distinctive Serial Numbers, such as a "Star" (*) for U.S. notes.

REPLICA — Copy of a note, usually a crude and obvious Facsimile. Often imprinted with the word "REPLICA" or "COPY" or "FACSIMILE," but these words may be clipped off, for fraud.

REVALIDATION — Paper money that becomes legal tender again, after previous invalidation, and generally by receiving some official marking indicating such (e.g., "VERIFICATO" in Italian).

REVALUATION — Overprinting to change a note's face value. Used synonymously for Surcharge.

REVERSE (REV or RV) — Back side of a note. Opposite of Face.

"RICHMOND ISSUE" — Second printing of the First Issue of *Confederate Currency* of 1861, issued at the newly established capital of Richmond, Virginia and printed in New Orleans.

SAFETY PAPER — Security paper used for bank notes, checks, etc., to inhibit forgery and counterfeiting.

SCRIP — Paper money substitute, issued by local governments or merchants — usually convertible to real money or exchangeable for goods and services. Not legal tender in itself. Sometimes spelled Script.

SCRIPOPHILY — Collecting and studying stocks and bonds.

SCROLLWORK — Ornately printed design along the note's border. Also written: Scroll Work.

SEALSKIN MONEY — Russian "currency" of the early 19th century, made on sealskin. Very rare.

SECRET SERVICE — The branch of the U.S. Department of the Treasury that apprehends counterfeiters in the U.S.

SECURITY THREADS — Special filaments of flexible plastic, metal, etc., placed in currency paper to inhibit counterfeiting.

SERIAL NUMBER (SN or S/N) and SERIAL LETTER (SL or S/L) — "Unique" set of digits (and/or letters) on a note, serving as: (1) internal control by issuing authorities, and (2) an inhibition to counterfeiting.

SERIES — Notes of a given type or common design. U.S. notes have imprinted "SERIES" year dates, indicating when a small change is made in the note's design (but not necessarily the same year that the note was printed).

SHILLING ("/" OR "SH") — British monetary unit. Equivalent to 12 *Old Pence* or 5 *New Pence* (starting in 1971) in Great Britain.

"SHINPLASTER" — Slang term for U.S. and Canadian *Fractional Currency*.

SIEGE NOTE — Paper money issued during a military siege. Sometimes called "Obsidional" or "money of necessity."

SIGNATORY — A person who officially "signs" a note.

SIGNATURE — Either: (1) the actual handwritten signature of a person authorized to sign notes, or (2) a facsimile printed signature of such person.

SILK PAPER — Paper with silk threads in it.

SILVER CERTIFICATE (SC) — Currency redeemable in silver (or once was); e.g., designated U.S. notes from the 19th and 20th century.

SLEEPER — An underpriced note, not selling for its higher potential value in the collector market.

SLIDER — A note just below its purported grade. Example: AU note sold as "SLIDER UNC."

SMALL SIZE NOTE — U.S. federal currency, 1929 to date.

SOUVENIR CARD (SC) — Limited edition, large format (for example: 8 1/2 by 10 1/2 inches) engraved artistic card — with currency-related theme, prepared for collectors.

SPECIE — Circulating coinage, especially of gold or silver. Opposite of Fiat Money.

SPECIMEN (S or SP) — An invalidated sample note overprinted or perforated with the word "SPECIMEN," etc. Made for: (1) reference files, (2) authorizing officials, (3) distribution for currency recognition by other governments, etc., and/or (lately) (4) sale to collectors. Also: Collectible Note.

SPLIT GRADE—Note between two stated grades; e.g., "Fine to Very Fine" (F-VF OR F/VF).

STAMPED NOTE — Paper money with postage/revenue adhesive stamps on it to indicate value. Don't confuse with Postage Currency.

"STAR" NOTE (*) — A Replacement Note, in the U.S., etc.

STATE BANK NOTE (SBN)—Currency authorized by state (instead of federal, directly) government.

STOCK CERTIFICATE — A paper document denoting partial ownership of a corporation.

SUBJECT—"One individual note design" on a printing plate or currency sheet.

SURCHARGE — Overprint revaluation on a note.

SUTLER NOTE — Private merchant scrip of the American Civil War.

TEAR — A rip in a note's paper.

THIN — A defective shallow area in a note's paper.

TREASURY NOTE (TN) — Either: (1) a type of British currency, 1914-1927; but *not Bank of England* notes, or (2) a synonym for U.S. *Coin Note* of 1890-1891.

TYPE (T) — A major design of notes, usually given major catalog number status. Examples: The "Bison" $10 *U.S. Note* of 1901, or any piece of paper money in your wallet.

TYPE SET—One note of each type in a series or time period.

UNCIRCULATED (UNC) — A note that shows no evidence of having been in circulation. "New." Must not be folded or creased.

UNCUT SHEET — Unseparated note "subjects" on original sheet as printed, either Full Sheet or Partial Sheet.

UNDERGRADING—Assigning a lower grade to a note than it deserves. May be done deliberately or accidentally.

UNDERPRINT—A color tint or fine pattern printed under the main note design, as an anti-counterfeiting measure.

UNIFACE — Printed only on one side.

UNIQUE—Only one known. Inaccurately used in hyperbolic advertising: e.g., "semi-unique." A note is either unique or it isn't.

UNISSUED REMAINDER — Unissued note in the issued design; i.e, unsigned and without Serial Numbers (usually).

UNITED STATES NOTE (USN) — "Legal Tender Note," a type of federal U.S. currency from the 19th and 20th centuries.

UNLISTED (UNL) — Not in the standard catalogs.

UPGRADING — Replacing notes of inferior condition with higher graded notes to improve the overall quality of the collection.

VARIETY (VAR) — A subtype of a basic catalog numbered type; same basic note design, different distinguishable printings.

VERTICAL (VERT) — "Up and down" across the note's height or width (for conventionally oriented note designs):

VERTICAL FORMAT — Note with design oriented vertically instead of the more conventional horizontal. Example: many Chinese notes.

VERY FINE (VF) — Condition of a note; usually meaning three major creases, or the equivalent.

VERY GOOD (VG) — A well-worn note, but no missing pieces.

VIGNETTE (VIG) — Pictorial part of the note's design; e.g., the engraved portrait on the face of current U.S. notes, the "buildings/scenes" on the backs of current U.S. notes $2 through $100.

"VILLA'S BED SHEETS" — Mexican Revolutionary War notes of "Pancho" Villa, circa 1913.

WATERMARK (WMK)—A slightly thinned area of a note's paper that is impressed on it at the time of manufacture, as a security measure against counterfeiting.

WILDCAT BANK — Bank that issues notes without proper backing in specie. Usually refers to 19th century spurious U.S. and Canadian banks.

WITHDRAWN NOTE — Currency type no longer in legal tender circulation. Usually invalidated, but not always.

> "Ignorance is bold, and knowledge reserved."
> Thucydides (circa 460-400 B.C.)
> Athenian historian

Bibliography

Paper money collecting tends to attract people who are above average in intelligence and who enjoy reading for its own sake. An informed collector is a smart collector, someone who is a pleasure to do business with, someone who appreciates rarity and quality when it is offered for examination or sale. Currency dealers encourage their customers to educate themselves about paper money by reading the references available.

First, read the currency books (if any) in your local public library (filed under "769" call numbers in the Dewey Decimal System). Then visit your local numismatic/currency dealer (probably listed under "Coin Dealers" or "Coins for Collectors" in the telephone book Yellow Pages) to see what kinds of currency books the dealer has to offer. The classified ad sections of the numismatic/currency periodicals (see Chapter 22) have ads offering currency books for sale.

For scarce and out-of-print currency literature, try these dealers who specialize in such (among other topics), at fixed prices or by mail bid sale:

CURRENCY LITERATURE DEALERS

CHARLES DAVIS
P.O. Box 1412
Morristown, NJ 07962
(201) 993-4431

SANFORD J. DURST
29-28 41st Avenue
Long Island City, NY 11101
(718) 706-0303

LAWRENCE FALATER
Box 81
Allen, MI 49227
(517) 869-2541

ORVILLE J. GRADY
6602 Military Avenue
Omaha, NE 68104
(402) 558-6782

GEORGE FREDERICK KOLBE
P.O. Drawer 3100
Crestline, CA 92325
(714) 338-6527

MARLCOURT BOOKS
P.O. Box 956, Station "B"
Willowdale, Ontario M2K 2T6
Canada (416)
490-8659

NUMISMATIC ARTS OF SANTA FE
P.O. Box 9712
Santa Fe, NM 87504
(505) 982-8792

Some currency dealers (Chapter 17) and currency societies (Chapter 23) publish their own currency books; as you become acquainted with the dealer or society, you'll find out what those books are. Most currency dealers either sell a selection of currency books (especially those that relate to their business inventory of notes, etc.) or can direct you to someone who can supply a book that you seek.

BNR PRESS

The BNR Press is a leading publisher of specialized paper money books (including *Military Payment Certificates* by Schwan and *Prisoner of War and Concentration Camp Money* by Campbell — both available in hard or soft cover — see listings by author below). The BNR Press also stocks all of the

Society of Paper Money Collectors books. Send a self-addressed stamped envelope, and ask for their list of paper money books for sale:

BNR PRESS
132 East Second Street
Port Clinton, OH 43452
(419) 734-6683

SELECTED PAPER MONEY BOOKS

Here are a few books on paper money topics, something for the beginner through the specialist, with emphasis on material that I discuss in this book. Most of these books have been written by recognized authorities. Many are still in print, and others can be obtained either from: (1) currency literature dealers or (2) lending libraries (such as the ANA Library — see Chapter 23). I've included some standard handbooks and recognized price guide catalogs also. I have no financial interest in any of these books or in the businesses of the preceding currency literature dealers.

Anton, William T., Jr., and Morey Perlmutter. *The Albert A. Grinnell Collection of United States Paper Money: A Complete Reprint in One Volume of the Seven Sales Which Comprised the Most Complete Collection of United States Paper Money Ever Assembled by any Individual.* Watertown, MA: by the authors, 1971. Auction catalog reprints and prices realized for this collection, which was sold by Barney Bluestone of Syracuse, New York in seven auctions from November 25, 1944 through November 30, 1946. 651 pages, plus end matter, hardbound. Out of print, but in the ANA Library. No illustrations, but astoundingly low prices realized, as I guess they should be, considering the sales occurred half a century ago, before paper money collecting boomed in popularity.

Benner, Judith Ann. *Fraudulent Finance: Counterfeiting and the Confederate States: 1861-1865.* Hillsboro, TX: Hill Junior College (A Hill Junior College Monograph), 1970. 70 hardbound pages, illustrated with black-and-white photos of a few *Confederate Notes* and Civil War celebrities. "Fraudulent Confederate Finance" was Benner's Master's thesis topic at Trinity University, and this book summarizes her research. Fascinating background to contemporary counterfeiting of *Confederate Notes*. Extensive bibliography. In the ANA Library.

Beresiner, Yasha. *A Collector's Guide to Paper Money.* New York: Stein and Day, 1977. Superb summary of world bank note collecting with historical and market comments for each country, arranged alphabetically. 255 hardbound pages. Handsome color photos of world notes. Valuable reading for the beginning collector. Out of print, but in many public libraries and for sale by numismatic literature dealers. Written by a paper money expert, now a dealer in England. Originally sold at $15.95.

Beresiner, Yasha, and Colin Narbeth. *The Story of Paper Money.* New York: Arco Publishing Co., 1973. Excellent short history of world paper money with emphasis on 18th, 19th, and 20th century notes through World War II. Written by two paper money authorities, both now dealers in England. 112 pages, hardbound. Many black-and-white note photos. Out of print, but in some public libraries. Originally sold at $6.95. Narbeth is the founder and current President of the International Bank Note Society.

Bloom, Murray Teigh. *The Brotherhood of Money: The Secret World of Bank Note Printers.* Port Clinton, OH: BNR Press, 1983. 365 hardbound pages of solid print telling many entertaining inside stories behind paper money, U.S. and foreign, legal and counterfeit. Maybe more than a beginning collector wants to know, but absorbing reading for anyone seriously interested in 20th century paper money lore. In ANA Library. $20 current.

Campbell, Lance K., ed. *Paper Money Stories: 30th Anniversary Anthology by the members of the International Bank Note Society, 1961-1991.* International Bank Note Society, 1991. 163 hardbound pages, illustrated in black-and-white. A reprinting, with updated revisions, of 29 of the best articles that appeared in the International Bank Note Society Journal during its first 30 years of existence. Examples of "articles" in this book: "The Currencies of Kuwait," "French Bank Notes of the Nineteenth Century," and "Bank Notes from Ottoman Tunisia." The articles are readable and easy to understand by readers with no specialized paper money knowledge; written, of course, by serious students of these currencies. For those interested in foreign paper money lore. $26.95 current ($22.50 to IBNS members).

Campbell, Lance K. *Prisoner-of-War and Concentration Camp Money of the Twentieth Century* (title page "title"). Port Clinton, OH: BNR Press, 1989. A handsome overview of this subject, with notes listed by country, with retail market values when known. Covers the four main types of camp money: POW, internment, displaced persons, and concentration camps. Absorbing reading for the background stories behind the notes because little is known about many of them. Useful also in the comments on counterfeit and fantasy notes. $25 hardbound, $17.50 softbound, current.

Coffing, Courtney L. *A Guide and Checklist of World Notgeld 1914-1947.* Iola, WI: Krause Publications, 1988. 184 softbound pages, covering 11,865 cities of over 70 countries. An excellent introduction to notgeld (local emergency money) from its beginnings in World War I. $14.95 current.

Criswell, Grover C., Jr., *Colonel Grover Criswell's Compendium, a guide to Confederate Money* (cover title). Brannon

Publishing Co. (printed under license with Criswell's Publications), 1991. Handy 58-page softbound guide to *Confederate Notes* — with notes illustrated and data on each (and "Criswell's numbers," which are the standard catalog numbers for collectors and dealers of Confederate Currency). Price quotes for notes are a bit conservative for retail. $5 current.

———. *Confederate and Southern States Currency: A Descriptive Listing, Including Rarity and Prices* (Criswell's Currency Series, Volume I). Citra, FL: Criswell's & Criswell's Publications, 1976 (first published in 1957, revised in 1964). The "bible" of *Confederate Currency* catalog numbers and varieties. Everyone who collects or deals in *Confederate Notes* refers to Criswell. Useful especially for his listings of relative rarities of "Serial Letters" per note type. 294 hardbound pages. In and out of print over the years. A 1992 revised edition by BNR Press is being produced.

———. *North American Currency.* Citra, FL: Criswell's Publications, 1969 (Second Edition). First published in 1965, this book was the result of twenty years' experience by Criswell in the paper money hobby. Typical examples of 19th century U.S. *Obsolete Currency* are listed alphabetically by state, along with *Colonial, Continental, Confederate*, and federal U.S. *Large Size* and *Small Size* type notes. Used most often for "catalog numbers" of U.S. *Obsolete Currency* (*Broken Bank Notes, State Notes*, etc.). Many black-and-white note photos of notes from Criswell's collection. Retail prices, when known, are quoted for VERY GOOD and UNCIRCULATED conditions (but circa the year of the book edition!). Has been superseded by other books (e.g., Haxby's catalog), but by custom, collectors and dealers still use Criswell's "catalog numbers" for *Obsolete Currency*. 942 pages of glossy paper, hardcover. In some public libraries. Out of print. Available from some currency book dealers.

Cross, W.K. (Publisher). *The Charlton Standard Catalogue of Canadian Government Paper Money.* Toronto, Canada: The Charlton Press, 1992 (5th Edition). This is the book to get if you're a beginning collector of Canadian currency. The recognized collectors' catalog for "central government" paper money of Canada, including Provincial, Municipal, Dominion, and *Bank of Canada* issues. Useful background to the notes, and their retail prices in commonly collected grades. 271 softbound pages. $14.95 current (Canadian or U.S. $).

For Canadian private banks and merchants' notes, see the massive *The Charlton Standard Catalogue of Canadian Bank Notes* by the same publisher — 2nd Edition, 1989; $59.50 softbound or $89.50 hardbound, current. Get the cheaper book (above) if you're a beginner, unless you're determined to start with Canadian private bank notes (which are quite beautiful, and come in all price ranges).

Douglas, Duane D., Claudio Verrey, and Alberto Hidalgo (Edited by Colin R. Bruce II). *The Complete Encyclopedia of Mexican Paper Money* (cover title). Iola, WI: Krause Publications, Inc., 1982. 368 softbound pages, with many black-and-white illustrations of the notes. Written in English. All of the authors are experts in Mexican paper money.

Basically, a catalog of Mexican paper money, with a discussion of the issuing authorities of each bank; incomparable advice on the availability and commonly encountered conditions of notes in each category; and note market prices (circa the edition of the book). With detailed listings for: Bancos (Early Banks), Pre-/Post-/and Revolutionary issues, and *Banco de Mexico* notes. In ANA Library. Douglas is a dealer in Mexican currency and lives in Mexico City.

Duggleby, Vincent. *English Paper Money.* London: Stanley Gibbons Publications Ltd., 1975. 108 hardbound pages, with black-and-white photos. This book is an expansion of the earlier *Collect British Banknotes* (53-page softcover booklet by the same publisher). Discusses and prices (in Pounds, circa the edition) the major types of British *Treasury Notes* and *Bank of England Notes.* The *BofE* notes are listed by "Chief Cashier" — as they are usually collected — from 1782 to date. The recognized collector catalog of these notes. In the ANA Library. Now published by Spink & Son Ltd.

Felix, Ervin J. *The Bank Note Collector's Guide & Companion.* Boston: H.E. Harris & Co., 1976. 144 pages, softbound, size $5^{1}/_{4}$ by $8^{1}/_{4}$ inches. Good for its 41-page section entitled, "World-Wide Bank Note Identifier," with translations of foreign words commonly found on notes. $1.50 original price.

Friedberg, Robert. *Paper Money of the United States.* Clifton, NJ: The Coin and Currency Institute, 1989 (12th Edition). The "bible" of U.S. currency catalog numbers, which are used by all collectors and dealers. Lists all major varieties of *Large Size* and *Small Size* federal U.S. notes, and *Fractional Currency*, some *Colonial* and *Continental Currency.* First published in 1953, this book is often out of print because each new edition sells out. Priced a bit over $20 when available. In every public library (or should be). Notes are cataloged by signatures. 284 hardbound pages.

The first time I saw a copy of this book was accidentally — as I was browsing through the public library in my hometown of Joliet, Illinois, on an idle summer afternoon in the 1950s when I was on summer vacation from elementary school. The title looked interesting, so I reached for the book and spent the next two hours in unexpected wonder, sitting in one of the old wooden library chairs, and looking back and forth, again and again, at every page and at every note illustration. Until that day, I never knew that any U.S. paper money existed besides the *Small Size Notes* in modern circulation. If one of the librarians, that day, had walked up and whispered in my ear: "In the far future, you will write a paper money book of your own, and even describe this library visit in it ...", I would probably have smiled in disbelief.

Gouge, Wm. M. *The Curse of Paper-Money and Banking; or A Short History of Banking in the United States of America, with an Account of its Ruinous Effects on Landowners, Farmers, Traders, and on all the Industrious Classes of the Community.* London: Mills, Jowett, and Mills, 1833. Reprint (1968) by Greenwood Press of New York, available on loan from the ANA Library. Amusing diatribe against paper money, circa 1833, with lots of quotes from celebrities of the time.

Guiseppi, John. *The Bank of England: A history from its foundation in 1694.* Chicago: Henry Regnery Co., 1966. 224 pages, hardbound. Not light bedtime reading, but simpler than the more "definitive" works (*The Bank of England from Within* by Wilfrid Marston Acres, 1931, and *The Bank of England: A History* by Sir John Clapham, 1944, both of which Guiseppi assisted in preparing, in his job with the Bank's archives department). $7.50 original price, out of print, but in some public libraries. Bank histories give boundless depth to otherwise two-dimensional bank notes, and enrich our collecting experiences as much as the notes themselves do.

Haxby, James A. *Standard Catalog of United States Obsolete Bank Notes, 1782-1866.* Iola, WI: Krause Publications, 1991. Four volumes, hardbound, 2,784 total pages, covering all private and state bank issues of the turbulent wildcat and broken bank era of the late 1700s through the mid-1860s in the United States. Arranged alphabetically by state: Volume I: Alabama through Maryland; Volume II: Massachusetts through New Jersey; Volume III: New York, North Carolina, Ohio; Volume IV: Pennsylvania through Wisconsin, and the "Banks of the United States" (pre-Civil War).

The set of four volumes is $195 current (but individual volumes can be purchased separately from currency literature dealers, for around $59 each, in case you only need a few states' coverage). More than 77,000 note listings from over 3,100 note-issuing banks, with over 15,000 total illustrations. Market values for three grades. Every state bank note believed to have been issued in this era is listed, including "Surviving Examples Not Confirmed" (SENC). Valuable data on counterfeit, spurious, and altered varieties. Imagine researching this "catalog" from scratch!

Hessler, Gene. *U.S. Essay, Proof and Specimen Notes.* Portage, OH: BNR Press, 1979. 224 hardbound pages, with many black-and-white illustrations of notes, partial note designs, and some Bureau of Engraving and Printing scenes. Background data behind many U.S. *Large Size* notes, written by paper money expert and present editor of *Paper Money* (the Journal of the Society of Paper Money Collectors). $19.50 current. In ANA Library also.

Hollender, Keith. *Scripophily: Collecting Bonds and Share Certificates.* New York: Facts on File, 1983 (published in England in 1982). 144 pages hardbound, well-illustrated with interesting U.S. and foreign stocks and bonds. Has collecting tips and information about stocks and bonds by country and topic (railways, cities, automobiles, signatures, mining, banks, etc.). The "first" word, rather than the "last" word on these collectibles — an entire encyclopedia could be written on U.S. mining stocks, for instance. $14.95 current (from R.M. Smythe & Co. of New York City and other dealers).

Hudgeons, Mark. *The Official Guide to Detecting Altered & Counterfeit U.S. Coins & Currency.* Orlando, FL: The House of Collectibles, 1985 (2nd Edition). Although dealing mostly with coins, there are 59 pages of excellent discussion of genuine versus counterfeit characteristics of current U.S. notes, by denomination $1 through $100, as well as illustrated pages of error notes. 210 softbound pages of closely-spaced print, well worth $7.95 current.

————. *The Official 1993 Blackbook Price Guide of United States Paper Money.* New York: House of Collectibles, 1992 (25th Edition). Handy 242-page softbound checklist and retail price guide to U.S. *Large* and *Small Size Notes*, *Fractional Currency*, and *Confederates*, with a useful section on error and freak notes. Notes are priced in commonly collected grades per specific issues (e.g., GOOD, VERY FINE, and UNCIRCULATED); as well as a dealer's wholesale "Average Buying Price" (A.B.P.) — the approximate sum paid by currency dealers for the lowest grade listed for a given note. This book measures about 4 by 5³⁄₈ inches, perfect for carrying with you to a currency show, or for reading on a bus, plane, etc. $6 current.

Kemp, Brian. *British Empire and Commonwealth Banknotes* (Stanley Gibbons Guides). London: Stanley Gibbons Publications Ltd., 1977. 32 softbound pages in booklet format, summarizing the types of notes produced by the various members of the British Commonwealth (e.g., Australia, British West Indies, Canada, India, South Africa, etc.). Collecting tips and scarcity information. Black-and-white photos of notes. Not a lot of information, but pleasant reading if you are attracted to old British Commonwealth notes. Out of print.

Kranister, Willibald. *The Moneymakers international.* Cambridge, England: Black Bear Publishing Ltd., 1989. 326 hardbound pages, with 800 handsome color illustrations of foreign currency and bank note printing operations. A superb "coffee table" book, worth buying for the bank note photos alone. Explains how paper money is made, from artist's designs to finished notes; with brief histories of paper money of: Australia, Austria, China, England, Germany, Spain, Sweden, and the United States. Written by the Executive Director of the Austrian National Bank, with cooperation of the above countries' government currency officials. $59.95 current (U.S. price).

Krause, Chester L., and Robert F. Lemke. *Standard Catalog of United States Paper Money*. Iola, WI: Krause Publications, 1991 (10th Edition). Over 5,000 items listed, every major variety of federally issued U.S. paper money from 1812 to the present. 208 hardbound pages, with over 550 original photographs. Listings feature: Series designations, signature combinations, and types of Seal imprints. Market values are given, even for many rare notes. Older editions in many public libraries. Good companion volume to Friedberg's reference; lists some things that Friedberg doesn't. $21.95 current.

Kwart, Herbert J. *United States Paper Money Grading Standard*. Hiawatha, IA: Five Seasons Publishers, 1984. Excellent little 48-page softbound guide to currency grading, with photographs and descriptions of U.S. *Small Size Notes* in 12 grades: Poor through Superb GEM CU. What this booklet lacks in volume, it compensates for with useful grading information, although, like all grading guides, it is somewhat subjective, because: (1) grading is an art, not a science; and (2) there always seem to be differences of opinion about just what constitutes a particular grade's characteristics. $7.95 current.

Lake, Kenneth R. *Investing in Paper Money*. London: Pelham Books, 1972. Plenty of tips on collecting paper money of all kinds, and investment advice. Entertaining to read, written under the pen name of a British philatelic expert, among other qualifications. 158 hardbound pages. In ANA Library.

Mitchell, Ralph, and Neil Shafer. *Standard Catalog of Depression Scrip of the United States*. Iola, WI: Krause Publications, 1961, 1984. The first serious research book and comprehensive collector catalog of these items. Covers over 3,500 issues of scrip used in the United States in the 1930s, with over 2,000 photographs, scrip descriptions, and market prices. Necessary to the specialist collector of *U.S. Depression Scrip* (which circulated as emergency "currency" in the 1930s). 310 softbound pages, $27.50 current.

Muscalus, John A. *Recycled Southern Paper Money: A Reference List of Southern Paper Money Printed on the Backs of Scarce Unused Notes and Documents*. Bridgeport, PA: Dr. John A. Muscalus, 1973. One of dozens of paper money monographs written by Dr. Muscalus, who spe-

cialized in researching useful lists of U.S. *Obsolete Currency* (19th century *Broken Bank Notes*, state currency, etc.) and whose compilations are great for topical collectors and bank note historians. 24 stapled softbound pages, copied from typewriter print, not illustrated. For sale by currency literature dealers, and in ANA Library.

Other titles of Muscalus' voluminous output are: *Famous Paintings Reproduced on Paper Money of State Banks, 1800-1866; Railroad Currency: Bank Notes and Scrip Representative of over One Hundred Railroads, 1830's - 1900's*; and *Paper Money of Early Educational Institutions and Organizations*.

Muszynski, Maurice. *Les Billets de la Banque de France, Les Émissions du Trésor* (The Notes of the Bank of France, Treasury Issues). Paris: Société Numismatique de Paris et sa Région (SNPR), Edition Le Landit, 1975, 1981 (la nouvelle édition). 156 hardbound pages, in French, illustrated with black-and-white photos. Excellent summary of all *Banque de France* (Bank of France) notes, 1800 to date, plus 20th century military issues. It's good to learn some of the language of the country whose notes are your collecting specialty. In the ANA Library.

Newman, Eric P. *The Early Paper Money of America*. Iola, WI: Krause Publications, 1990 (Third Edition). First published in 1967, with "Bicentennial Edition" in 1976. An illustrated, historical, and descriptive compilation of information on "American" paper money from its inception in 1686 to the year 1800. Detailed sections on individual British, French, and Spanish Colonies now part of the United States; the United Colonies and the United States (1775-1777); individual American States (1776-1788); "Incorporated" and "Unincorporated Banks" (1686-1800); and "Individuals, Businesses, Organizations, Cities, and Counties" (1729-1800).

Essential to the collector of American *Colonial Currency*. Almost 900 illustrations. 480 hardbound pages. Get the latest edition for revised data and updated values. $49.95 current.

Nussbaum, Arthur. *A History of the Dollar*. New York: Columbia University Press, 1957. A very readable summary of American monetary history from Colonial times through the post-World War II era, written in that clear, unpretentious writing style characteristic of many American non-fiction books circa 1957. 308 hardbound pages. In the ANA Library and some public libraries.

Oakes, Dean, and John Hickman. *Standard Catalog of National Bank Notes*. Iola, WI: Krause Publications, 1990 (2nd Edition). First published in 1982. A comprehensive study of all known U.S. *National Bank Notes* (both *Large Size* and *Small Size*) issued from 1863 to 1935. More than 117,000 notes are listed from 12,544 note-issuing banks,

Market prices given in three grades: VG, VF, and AU. Rarity ratings, known Serial Numbers, and quantities issued for each note. Essential if you plan to spend serious money on these notes. 1,216 pages, illustrated. $95 current. Not cheap, but how much do your notes cost?

Pick, Albert (edited by Colin R. Bruce II and Neil Shafer). *Standard Catalog of World Paper Money*, Volume I (Specialized Issues). Iola, WI: Krause Publications, 1990 (6th Edition). The most comprehensive reference catalog ever assembled for "specialized" paper money of the entire world (not to be confused with general issues — see Volume II, next listing).

This book, called "Pick's Volume I" by collectors and dealers, deals with 300 years of state, provincial, commercial, revolutionary, and other "limited circulation" currency (such as siege notes) from 365 note-issuing authorities. Listings for 16,700 notes, many with market values (when known) in several grades commonly collected. 7,660 original black-and-white note photos. First published in 1975, each succeeding edition updates the market prices of notes in three grades, and gives new information as note research continues. Notes listed in this book, Volume I, have the prefix letter "S" (for "Specialized") in their catalog numbers. Available everywhere: currency dealers, coin shops, public libraries. 1,008 hardbound pages. $55 current.

————. *Standard Catalog of World Paper Money*, Volume II (General Issues). Iola, WI: Krause Publications, 1990 (6th Edition). This is the book to get if you're starting a general collection of world paper money. The "bible" of nationally circulated government legal tender notes of the world from the last 300 years.

This book, called "Pick's Volume II" by collectors and dealers, is more practical, I think, for a beginning collector, than the "Specialized" Volume I described above, but eventually you'll want to study both. This book, Volume II, has 1,136 hardbound pages, listing more than 21,300 notes from 265 note-issuing authorities, with price quotes in three grades and over 9,750 black-and-white illustrations. Notes are listed alphabetically by country. If the note "isn't listed in Pick" (i.e., in neither Volume I nor Volume II of this catalog), some collectors don't collect it. Available everywhere: currency dealers, coin shops, public libraries. $49 current.

Reinfeld, Fred. *The Story of Civil War Money*. New York: Sterling Publishing Co., 1959. 93 hardbound pages. Easy-to-read story of Union and Confederate Civil War currencies, well illustrated with black-and-white photos. If you collected coins in the 1950s, you probably saw Reinfeld's coin books at coin shops or in your public library (where they may still be). Out of print, and the price quotes are

outdated: you can't buy the 1864 $500 Confederate Note in "crisp New" condition for $20 anymore! In ANA Library, and some public libraries.

Rochette, Edward C. *Making Money*. Frederick, CO: Renaissance House Publishers, 1986. Entertaining and informative stories of actual counterfeiters of coins and paper money, written by the President of the American Numismatic Association. Softbound, 107 pages plus end matter. $9.95 current.

Royal Canadian Mounted Police. *The Counterfeit Detector*. Ottawa, Canada: Roger Duhamel, F.R.S.C., Queen's Printer and Controller of Stationery, 1968. 17-page softbound pamphlet with excellent tips on recognizing counterfeit notes. The centerfold pages show lovely examples of steel-plate engraving and the same designs "surface printed" (as a counterfeit might be), compliments of the British American Bank Note Company Limited; and on page 10 are actual specimens of genuine and "counterfeit" planchettes (color paper inclusions, inserted in the paper during manufacture as an anti-counterfeiting device). Typical Canadian government understated sublimity at its publishing best. In the ANA Library.

Schwan, Fred. *Military Payment Certificates*. Port Clinton, OH: BNR Press, 1981, 1987 (Second Edition). 176 pages, both hard and softbound. Many black-and-white illustrations (of average quality, however). Precious information and essential to the serious collector of these notes. Covers post-World War II U.S., and some foreign, *Military Payment Certificates* (not to be confused with the earlier *Allied Military Currency* of World War II, etc.) in detail; and related items of military finance (ration cards, coupons, training money, etc.). Impressive research on all aspects, from official regulations to printing statistics, presented in unpretentious simple language. $30 hardbound, $20 softbound, current.

Scott, Kenneth. *Counterfeiting in Colonial America*. New York: Oxford University Press, 1957. 283 hardbound pages. Extremely entertaining and fascinating actual counterfeiting stories, with a complimentary Foreword by U.E. Baughman, then the Chief of the U.S. Secret Service. Hunt in libraries for it. The same author wrote monographs on individual American Colonies' counterfeiting, of which this book seems to be a partial summary compilation.

Shafer, Neil. *A Guide Book of Modern United States Currency*. Racine, WI: Whitman Coin Products, Western Publishing Co., 1975 (7th Edition). First published in 1965. A handy little hardbound book, convenient to read on a bus or an airplane. 160 hardbound pages, with book dimensions 5¼ x 7¾ inches. This is a nice summary of *Small*

Size U.S. notes (1929 to "date"), including all issued Series of U.S. Military Payment Certificates and some error notes. Many notes pictured in black-and-white photos on the glossy paper, with retail prices circa 1975. Still in some libraries; for sale by currency literature dealers.

Slabaugh, Arlie R. *Confederate States Paper Money.* Iola, WI: Krause Publications, 1991 (7th Edition). First published in 1958, this latest 112-page softbound edition is a wonderful collector's companion for anyone interested in *Confederate Currency*. Besides being a catalog showing retail prices of notes in six grades (Good to UNC), this little book is a gold mine of information about notes and their historical backgrounds. Over 100 black-and-white note photos. I take this book with me when I look at *Confederate Currency* in dealers' stocks. The only thing I don't like about this softbound book is that the plastic-coated covers tend to curl outward as their inside surfaces absorb humidity. You need to refer to Criswell's books also, because of: (1) his additional information, and (2) the standard acceptance of Criswell catalog numbers for Confederate notes. Get the latest edition of this book, for only $9.95 current. Essential for *Confederate Currency* collectors.

Smith, Ward D., and Brian Matravers. *Chinese Banknotes.* Menlo Park, CA: Shirjieh Publishers, 1970. 225 hardbound pages, in English, in small type, describing more than 5,000 subvarieties of Chinese bank notes, with emphasis on the 20th century. 1,800 black-and-white illustrations of these notes. Excellent for the student of the complex story of 20th century Chinese paper money. In ANA Library.

Sowards, Neil, ed. *The Handbook of Check Collecting.* Copyright Neil Sowards; printed at Fort Wayne, IN: Darrell Kessler, 1975. 97-page softbound introduction to check collecting — being a compilation of various authors, with useful chapters, such as: "Grading and Quality of Checks," "Values of Checks," and "Allegorical Figures and Symbols" [on checks]. Check collectors should know what's in this book. In ANA Library.

Takaki, Masayoshi. *The History of Japanese Paper Currency* (Johns Hopkins University Studies in Historical and Political Science, Series XXI, No. 5). Baltimore: The Johns Hopkins Press, 1903. 60 pages, in English, no illustrations; the ANA Library copy seems to have been privately hardbound. Background information about late 19th century Japanese monetary policy, presented in four chapters: (I) "Genesis of Japanese Paper Currency," (II) "Circulation of the Paper Currency," (III) "Kinds of Paper Currency," and (IV) "Redemption of Paper Currency." Not a collector's price catalog but stories about how this currency came to be. In ANA Library.

Tomlinson, Geoffrey William. *Australian Bank Notes: 1817-1963.* Melbourne, Australia: The Hawthorn Press Pty Ltd., 1963. 143 hardbound glossy pages, with one or more black-and-white note photo for each of the over fifty banks that issued notes in Australia. Not a lot of information; mainly a summary of each bank in several sentences, a list of known notes issued, and a lot of note photos. But you have to start somewhere in a study of these intriguing notes. In ANA Library. As for the notes themselves, good luck in finding them.

U.S. Secret Service (Department of the Treasury). *Know Your Money.* Washington, DC: U.S. Government Printing Office, 1991 edition. Excellent 24-page pamphlet printed on glossy paper, with black-and-white photos of counterfeit and genuine notes. Written by the experts in this field. Obtainable free from the U.S. Secret Service.

U.S. Treasury Department. *History of the Bureau of Engraving and Printing: 1862-1962.* Washington, DC: U.S. Department of the Treasury, 1962 (and reprinted in 1978 by Sanford J. Durst, New York City). 199 hardbound pages, illustrated with historical black-and-white photos of Bureau scenes. Not intended as light bedtime reading, but nevertheless in non-technical language, as this was a book written for the general public. Available from currency literature dealers who stock out-of-print books; in some public libraries; in the ANA Library. The title explains the book's contents. The original edition also has color plates.

Index

A

Alabama Obsolete Notes & Scrip, 114
Allen's Coin Shop, Inc., 174
Allied Military Currency, photo, 151
American Numismatic Association, 161, 179, 185-6, 190, 199, 221, 223-4
American Numismatic Society Museum, 229
American Society of Check Collectors, Inc., 82, 224
Americana Stamp & Coin Company, Inc., 174
ANA shows, 185-6
ANA World Money Museum, 227-8
Appraisals, 166
Arkansas Obsolete Notes & Scrip, 114
"Armed Forces Notes" of World War II, 146
Army Bills (Canada), 13
Aslett, Robert, 15
Assignat, 1793 French, photo, 18
Assignats (France), 16
Auction catalog, photo, 181
Austria-Hungary Prisoner-of-War Lagergeld, photo, 150
Austrian *notgeld*, 145
Authentication, 161
Ayers, James J., *Gold and Sunshine: Reminiscences of Early California*, 121

B

Baby Bond, State of Louisiana, photo, 86
Baden-Powell, Robert S.S., 144
Bank checks, 81-2, 87
    American Society of Check Collectors, 82
    collecting specialties, 81-2
    conditions, 82
    dealers, 82
    The First National Gold Bank, photo, 87
    prices, 82
    variations, 82
Bank history, 83

Bank Note Ledger®, 73
Bank Note Reporter, 83, 219, 221
Bank notes, 12, 17, 91-100
    bad ways to store, 92-3
    bank storage, 93
    cleaning, repair, restoration, 95-8
        caution regarding handwritten signatures, 98
        paper conservators, 96
    currency holders, 93-4
    detecting cleaning and repairs, 98
    display of, 94
    first, 12
    first issues of selected countries, 17
    handling and preserving, 91-100
    photographing, 94-5
    where to store, 93
Bank of Canada Currency Museum, 230-1
Bank of Canada Notes, 13
Bank of England, 13-5
    founding of, 14
    history of, 13-5
    in 18th century, 14
    in 19th century, 14-5
    in 20th century, 15
Bank of England 10 Shillings note, photo, 20
Bank of the State of Kansas $3 note, photo, 124
Bank robbery, 62
Banks, 12, 15, 28
    how they go broke, 28
    central, 12
    commercial, 12
    origins of, 12
    private British, 15
Banque de France 100 Francs note, 1928, photo, 163, 170
Barter, 23
Baruch, Bernard, 192
Beresiner, Yasha, 178
Billets de Confiance (France), 16
Billets de l'Estat (France), 16
Billets de Monoye (France), 16
Bills of Exchange (Canada), 13

Bimetallism, 33
Bisected Notes, 145
    Cut *Notes*, 145
    Halved *Notes*, 145
Bison Note, photo, 119
Bland-Allison Act, 33
Bluestone, Barney, 121
Bogus *Confederate Note*, photo, 214
Bonds, 83
Bowers, Q. David, 159
Bowers and Merena Galleries, Inc., 174
Boyd, F.C.C., 224
Bradbury, John, 15
Bramwell, Douglas, 108
Bramwell Grading System, 108
Bressett, Kenneth, 221
British Museum, The, 231
British Numismatic Trade Association Ltd., 180
British *Treasury Notes*, 15
Broken Bank Notes, 29-30, 114
Bryan, William Jennings, 33
Bureau of Engraving and Printing, 61-2, 69
    early history, 61
    illustration, 69
    paper money printing security, 61
    tours, 61-2
Business school money, 212, 218
    photo, 218
Butterworth, Mary Peck, 206
Buying notes, 155-64
    at currency shows, 156-7
    by mail, 159-60
        sample order, 160
    dealer organizations, 161
    from currency "approvals," 161
    from currency auctions, 157-9
        bidding strategies, 157-9
    from fixed price lists, 155-6
    from other collectors, 161
    from retail currency dealers, 155-6
    from store stock, 156
    mail bid sales, 159
    per want lists, 161

C

Caisse d'Escompte notes (France), 16
California National Gold Bank Notes, photo, 124
California State Controller's warrant, 1855, photo, 89
Canadian Association of Numismatic Dealers, 179
Canadian notes, early, 13
Canadian Paper Money Journal, The, 225
Canadian Paper Money Society, 225
Capital Plastics, Inc., 94
Card Money (Canada), 13
Cash in Circulation in United States, chart, 36
Central Bank of China 20 *Customs Gold Units*, 1930, photo, 136
Central States Numismatic Society, 186
Central States Shows, 186
Certified Coin Dealer newsletter, 193
Chase, Philip, 230
Check Collector, The, 224
Checks, see Bank checks
Chinese notes, 12-3
Cicero, Marcus Tullius, 173
Civil War, 45-6, 30-2
    Confederate currency depreciation-inflation cycle, 46
    Confederate financial problems, 46
    North's advantages, 45
    South's advantages, 45-6
    Union monetary problems, 30
    Union paper currency, 30-2
        Compound Interest Treasury Notes, 31
        Demand Notes, 30
        Fractional Currency, 31-2
        Interest-Bearing Notes, 30-1
        Legal Tender Notes, 31
        National Bank Notes, 31
        value fluctuations, chart, 32
Clain-Stefanelli, Elvira, 230
Clutterbuck, Charles, 14
Cohen, Joshua I., 71
Coin Dealer newsletter, 193
Coin Notes, see *Treasury Notes*
Coin World, 220
Colin Narbeth and Son Ltd., 178
Collateral fiscal paper, 81-90
Collecting specialties, 71-79
    types, 74-5
Collection, 73-4
    completeness, 73-4
    inventory of, 73

Collectors, mistakes of beginning, 72-3
Colonial Currency, 23-5, 27, 37, 113-4
    arguments for and against, 24-5
    Issues of Individual Colonies, chart, 27
    Parliamentary prohibition of, 25
    photo, 37
Columbian Exposition admission ticket, 1893, photo, 86
Concentration camp notes, 147
Condition, 101-6, 110-1
    creases, 103-4
    dirt, 102-3
    fading, 104
    folds, 102
    normal wear and aging, 101-2
    photos, 110-1
    ripple effect, 104
    tears, 104
Confederate and Southern States Currency, 49
Confederate Currency, 114
"Confederate Note, The," 52
Confederate States of America notes, 45-54
    collecting, 48-9
        "matched color set," 48
    condition, 47, 48
    counterfeit, bogus, and facsimile, 49
    dealers, 52
    end of, 48
    printing, 47
        Northern printings, 47
        quality and supply problems, 47
    public acceptance of, 47-8
    Southern state currency, 49
    type set, chart, 50-1
    vignettes, 47
    ways to collect, 48-9
Confederate States Paper Money, 49
Continental Currency, 25-6, 27, 113-4
    inflation and depreciation, 26
    Issues of Continental Congress, chart, 27
Corbet Cache, 174
Counterfeiting, 205-11, 215-7
    hand-drawn currency, 210
    history of, 205-7
    how to detect, 209-10
    if you receive counterfeit note, 208-9
    in Colonial America, 206
    in Confederate States, 207
    in 19th century America, 206-7
    in U.S. today, 207-8

Counterfeiting, cont.
    Operation Bernhard, 210
    past penalties for, 205-6
    photos, 215-7
    "raising a note," 208
    security features of other countries, 209
    security features of U.S. paper money, 209
    U.S. laws, 208
    U.S. Secret Service, 207
Cox, Terry, 174
Crabb, Michael A., Jr., 185
Crane & Company, 58, 209
Creases, 103-4
    illustration, 103
Credit Card Collector, 84
Credit cards, 83-4
Crofoot, Herman K., 230
Currency Auctions of America, Inc., 174-5
Currency Dealer newsletter, 72, 193-4
Currency holders, 93-4, 99, 100
    glassine envelopes, photo, 100
    hard plastic, 93-4, 100
        photo, 100
    Mylar®, photo, 99
    soft plastic, 93, 94
        inserting or removing notes from, 94
Currency import and export restrictions, 132-3
Currency market cycles, 192

D

Darling, Teresa, 186
Davis, Jefferson, 48
Dealers, 173-82
    organizations, 179-80
Defoe, Daniel, 14
Del Mar, Alexander, *A Warning to the People: The Paper Bubble*, 30
Denly's of Boston, 175
Depression, 36
Dillon, C. Douglas, 117
Dirt, 102-3
DM Travellers Cheque, photo, 87
Dominion of Canada Notes, 13
Downing, Ron, 194
Duggleby, Vincent, *English Paper Money*, 153
Durand, Asher B., 229

E

Early American Numismatics, 175

Early Paper Money of America, The, 122

Efron, Arnoldo, 132

Eigen, Jack, 221

Elliott, Gene, 52, 175

English Paper Money, 153

Error notes, 199-203
  contrived errors, photo, 203
  design partially missing due to paper adherence, 200
  double denomination, 201
  double impressions, 200
  ink smears, 200
  inverted faces, 201
  inverted third prints, 200
  mismatched Serial Numbers, 200-1
  missing print, 200, 201
    photo, 201
  offset transfers, 200
  plate smear, photo, 203
  pre-printing paper folds, 199
  third print on back, 200
  third print shifted, 200
  uneven printing, underinking, and insufficient pressure, 200

Exposition admission tickets, 85
  chart, 85

Eyer, Steve, 175

F

Facsimile *Confederate Note,* photos, 214

Fading, 104

Fantasy notes, 211-2
  bogus notes, 212
  business school money, 212
  facsimile money, 212
  gambling money, 212
  game money, 212
  military training money, 212
  movie money, 212
  play money, 211
  propaganda forgeries, 212

Faull, Barnaby G., 179

Federal Bureau of Investigation (FBI), investigation of bank robbery, 62

Federal Reserve Act, 34

Federal Reserve Bank, Los Angeles Branch, 60-1, 69
  photo, 69

Federal Reserve Bank Notes, 34

Federal Reserve Notes, 34

Federal Reserve System, 34-5
  functions, 34
  organization, 35

Fei'-ch'ien, 12

Fenton, Robert, 206

50¢ *Confederate Fractional Currency,* 1864, photo, 54

50¢ *Florida "State" Currency,* 1863, photo, 40

50¢ *Fractional Currency,* "Fourth Issue," photo, 41

50 *Cruzados* note, 1986 Brazil, photo, 232

$50 *Confederate Note,* 1861, counterfeit, photo, 213

$50 note of *Citizens' Bank of Louisiana,* photo, 37

50 *Francs* note, 1966 Belgium, photo, 188

50 *Leke* note, 1976 Albania, photo, 77

50 million *Mark* 1923 *Reichsbanknote,* photo, 141

50 *Pfennig* German *notgeld,* 1921, photo, 20

50 *Rials* note, 1971 Iran, photo, 170

50 *Riels* note, 1979 Kampuchea, photo, 78

50 *Rubles* U.S.S.R. *State Bank Notes,* photos, 136

50 *Shillings* note, 1986 Kenya, photo, 171

50,000 *Pesos Bolivianos* note, 1984, photo, 142

First Strike, 224

(First) Bank of the United States, 27-8

5 *Centavos* note, 1914 Revolutionary Mexico, photo, 99

$5 *Confederate Note,* "Sixth Issue," photo, 118

$5 *Military Payment Certificate,* Series "681," photo, 152

$5 note, 1852 *Columbia Bank,* photo, 38

$5 note, 1978 Bermuda, photo, 78

$5 *State of South Carolina* note, 1872, photos, 41, 117

$500 Hawaiian Islands *Silver Certificate of Deposit,* counterfeit, photo, 215

500 *Francs* note, 1978 Gabon, photo, 171

500,000 *Gold Yuan* note, 1949 *Central Bank of China,* photos, 141, 142

500,000 *Pesos* note, 1980 Argentina, photo, 142

5 *Kronen* note, *Theresienstadt,* photo, 152

5 *Pesos* note, *El Banco de Guerrero,* photos, 76, 77

5 *Pesos* note, *El Banco Español de la Isla de Cuba,* 1896, photos, 133

5 *Pesos* note, *El Banco Peninsular Mexicano,* 1914, photo, 232

5 *Pesos* note, 1916 Mexican Revolutionary, photo, 231

5 *Pesos* note, Paraguay, photo, 18

5 *Pounds* note, 1968 Israel, photo, 134

£5 *Special Voucher* of *British Armed Forces,* 1950, photo, 152

5000 *Cordobas* "Provisional Issue," photo, 162

Florida United Numismatists, 186

Folds, 102
  illustrations, 102

Foley, Kevin, 174, 175

"Food Coupon," photo, 90

Foreign notes, 127-42, 153-4
  inflationary notes, 137-42
  popular, 127-36
    availability of, 128
    ways to collect, 127
  rare, 153-4

Forgeries, 211
  check, 211

4 *Reales* note, 1869 *El Banco Oxandaburu y Garbino,* photo, 19

Fractional Currency, 114

Fractional Currency Collectors Board, 224

Fractional Currency Shield, photo, 126

France, early paper money of, 16

Franklin, Benjamin, 24, 25, 113
  A Modest Inquiry into the Nature and Necessity of Paper Money, 24

Fraudulent Finance: Counterfeiting and the Confederate States: 1861-1865, 207

French bank notes, private, 16

Friedberg, Robert, *Paper Money of the United States,* 199

FUN Show, 186

G

Gambling money, 212

Game money, 212

German *notgeld,* 145, 150
  photo, 150

German occupation note for *Bohemia and Moravia Protectorate,* photo, 151

Glass, Carter, 34

Glazer, Leonard, 174, 175

Gold Certificates, 33, 182
  photo, 182

Gold Reserve Act, 35, 117

Gold Standard Act, 33

Gordon, Charles George, 144

Gouge, William M., *The Curse of Paper-Money and Banking*, 28, 30
Grading, 106-8
    Bramwell Grading System, 108
    split grades, 108
    upgrading, 108
Gresham's Law, 25
Grinnell, Albert A., Collection of U.S. Paper Money, 71, 121
Guest, William, 14
Guide and Checklist of World Notgeld, A, 139

H

Hamilton, Alexander, 26, 27
Heath's Counterfeit Detector, photo, 30, 38, 207
Hell Notes, 128
Herbert, Alan, 220
Hessler, Gene, 221, 223
Hickman Auctions, Inc., 175
Hidalgo, Miguel, 144
Higgins Museum, 228
Hindenburg, Paul von, 139
Hitler, Adolf, 139
Hobby Protection Act, 210
Hoober, Richard T., Jr., 82, 175
Horace, 205
Horstman, Ron, 185
Horwath, Anna, 173
Howard, Dorsey A., 52
Hull, John, 24
Huntington, Archer M., 229
Hyperinflation, 138-40
    China, 1942-1949, 140
    Germany, 1919-1924, 138-9
    Germany, notes, 139
    Greece, 1941-1944, 140
    Hungary, 1945-1946, 140
    Russia, 1918-1924, 139-40

I

India, paper money of, 15-6
Indiana Obsolete Notes and Scrip, 114
Inflation, characteristics of, 137
InterCol London, 178
International Bank Note Collectors, 180
International Bank Note Society, 71, 224
International Bank Note Society Journal, 224, 226
International Paper Money Show, 185
Internment camp notes, 146-8
    collecting, 147-8
Inventory, 73

Investing, 189-97
    advantages, 190-1
    condition considerations, 194
    currency market cycles, 192
    Customs Service cash reporting requirements, 194
    difference between paper money and coin, 189-90
    disadvantages, 191
    don't overpay, 193
    holding periods, 194
    IRS cash reporting requirements, 194
    quality vs. quantity, 191
    researching market, 191
    standard catalog numbers and prices, 193
    tips, 194-5
    vs. speculation, 191-2
    what to buy, 192-3
    wholesale/retail price spreads, 193
Irish Hospitals' Sweepstake ticket, 1938, photo, 87
Irish paper money, 15

J

Jackson, Andrew, 29
Japanese bank notes, 16
Japanese Military Issue, 5 *Yen*, 1938, photo, 150
Japanese Occupation Note, 10 *Pesos*, photo, 150
Jefferson, Thomas, 26
Jeffrey Hoare Auctions, Inc., 178
Jiao Zi, 12
Jonas, S.A., 52

K

Kazanjian, M.S., 82
Ken Barr Numismatics, 84
Knight, Lyn F., 175
Kreditiv-Sedlar, 12
Kublai Khan, 12

L

La Banque Générale (French notes), 16
La Banque Royale (French notes), 16
Lake, Kenneth R., 12, 72
Large Size Notes, 38, 39, 40, 41, 42, 43, 44, 78, 79, 90, 99, 114-6, 117, 118, 119, 120, 124, 125, 164, 171, 196, 197, 213
    Compound Interest Treasury Notes, 115
    Demand Notes, 114-5
    Federal Reserve Bank Notes, 115-6
    Federal Reserve Notes, 116

Large Size Notes, cont.
    $50 *Federal Reserve Note*, Series 1914, photo, 78
    $50 *Gold Certificate*, 1882, photo, 125
    $50 *Gold Certificate*, Series 1922, photo, 44
    $50 *Legal Tender Note*, 1874, photo, 124
    $5 *Legal Tender Note*, 1862, photo, 117
    $5 *Legal Tender Note*, Series 1869, photo, 196
    $5 *Silver Certificate*, Series 1886, photos, 118
    $5 *Silver Certificate*, Series 1896, photos, 43
    $5 *Silver Certificate*, Series 1899, photos, 99, 119
    $500 *Gold Certificate*, Series 1882, photos, 42
    $5000 *Federal Reserve Note*, Series 1918, photo, 125
    Gold Certificates, 116
    Interest Bearing Notes, 115
    Legal Tender Notes, 115
    National Bank Notes, 115
    National Gold Bank Notes, 116
    $1 *Legal Tender Note*, 1862, photos, 39
    $1 *Silver Certificate*, Series 1896, photo, 118
    $100 *National Bank Note*, anti-counterfeiting clause, photo, 213
    $100 *Treasury Note*, Series 1890, photo, 125
    Refunding Certificates, 115
    Silver Certificates, 115
    $10 *Demand Note*, 1861, photos, 38
    $10 *Federal Reserve Note*, Series 1914, photos, 119
    $10 *Gold Certificate*, Series 1922, photo, 99
    $10 *National Currency*, Series 1882, photo, 42
    $10 *Silver Certificate*, Series 1886, photo, 197
    $10 *Silver Certificate*, "Series 1897," 90
    $10 *Treasury Note*, Series 1891 photos, 164
    $10 *United States Note*, Series 1901, photos, 43, 119
    $10,000 *United States Note*, Series 1878, photo, 41
    Treasury Notes, 115

Large Size Notes, cont.
  $20 *Federal Reserve Note*, Series 1914, photo, 44
  $20 *Gold Certificate*, Series 1906, photo, 119
  $20 *Interest Bearing Note*, 1863, photos, 40
  $20 *Legal Tender Note*, 1862, photo, 39
  $20 *Silver Certificate*, Series 1880, photos, 41, 42
  $20 *Silver Certificate*, Series 1891, photos, 171
  $2 *Federal Reserve Bank Note*, Series 1918, photo, 120
  $2 *Lazy Deuce National Bank Note*, photo, 197
  $2 *Legal Tender Note*, Series 1880, photo, 118
  $2 *Silver Certificate*, Series 1896, photos, 79, 119
  $2 *Treasury Note*, photos, Series 1891, 42, 43
Latin American Paper Money Society, 224
Law, John, *Money and Trade Considered with a Proposal for Supplying the Nation with Money*, 16
Leather money, 12
Legal Tender Act, 33
Leigh, James, 230
Letters of credit, 83
Lincoln, Abraham, 45
Linett, Dana, 175
Logan, James, 25
Long Beach Exposition, 186, 187
  photo, 187
Lopresto, Samuel, 186
"Lost Cause, The," 52
Lottery tickets, 85
"Lucy Pickens" $100 *Confederate Note*, 1864, photo, 54
Lyn F. Knight, Inc., 175

M

Mack, Gene F., 52, 176
Maine Obsolete Paper Money & Scrip, 114
McKinley, William, 33
McWhirter, Norris, 71
Mel Steinberg & Son, 177
Mercantile Money Museum, 228-9
Meulles, Jacques de, 144
Mexican Paper Money, 144
Mexican Revolutionary *Notes*, 144
  "Villa's Bed Sheets," 144

Mid American Currency, 176
Military currency, 145
  collecting periods, 145
  "overprints," 145
  puppet banks, 145
Military Payment Certificates, 117, 148, 149
  chart, 149
Military training money, 212
Mincho, Allen, 174, 175
Mioka, Hachiro, 16
Monetary Research International, 132
Money, "missing," 36
Money Museum, 230
Money orders, 84
  U.S. Postal, 84
Morycz, Stanley, 176
Movie money, 212
MRI Bankers' Guide to Foreign Currency, 132, 133
MSL Software, 73
Municipal Issues (Canada), 13
Museum of Florida History, 228
Museums, 227-32

N

Narbeth, Colin, 178
National and World Paper Money Convention, 185
National Bank Note, 1872, photo, 197
National Gold Bank Notes, 33
National Numismatic Collection, 230
Nazi counterfeits of British notes, 146
Neinken, Mortimer, 230
Nero, 138
Newark Museum, The, 229
Ninger, Emanuel, 210
North American Currency, 114
Notgeld (German), 139
Numismatic News, 220
Numismatic Resource Directory, 223
Numismatist, The, 199, 221, 223

O

Obsolete Currency, photo, 164
Official 1993 Blackbook Price Guide of United States Paper Money, 201
Old Dominion Paper Collectibles, 52, 176
Olmstead, Don, 178
Olmstead Currency, 178
1 *Chiao* note, 1962 People's Republic of China, photo, 232
1 *Cruzeiro* note, 1943 Brazil, photo, 76
$1 *Educational Note*, photo, 118

$1 *Hungarian Fund* note, 1852, photos, 19
$1 municipal note of *Baton Rouge*, 1866, photo, 41
$1 note, 1983 Guyana, photo, 77
$1.75 note of *Bank of the Commonwealth*, 1862, photo, 39
100 *Deutsche Mark* facsimile, photo, 218
$100 *Imperial Bank of Canada* note, 1917, counterfeit, photo, 214
$100 interest-bearing *Confederate Note*, 1862, photos, 53
$100 note of *Canal & Banking Company*, photo, 37
100 *Dong* note, 1970 Republic of Vietnam, photo, 134
100 *Drachmai* note, 1978 Greece, photo, 77
100 *Escudos ouro*, 1981 Portugal, photo, 169
100 *Francs* note, 1978 Rwanda, photo, 78
100 *Leke* note, 1976 Albania, photo, 182
100 *Mark* note, 1911 *Sächsische Bank*, photo, 20
100 *Pesetas* note, 1965 Spain, photos, 135
100 *Zaires* note, 1985 Zaire, photo, 163
1 Milliárd *B.-Pengo* note, 1946 Hungary, photo, 141
1 *Piastre* note, 1949 French Indochina, photo, 134
£1 *Bank of England* note, photos, 135
£1 note, New Zealand, photo, 21
1 *Pound* note, 1952-1960 Egypt, photo, 134
£1 note, 1965 Gibraltar, photos, 21
£1 note, 1968-1969 Biafra, photo, 232
£1 note, 1983 Ireland, photo, 21
£1 note of St. Helena, 1982, photo, 162
1 *Sol* note, *El Banco de Tacna*, photo, 18
1000 *Dinara* note, 1981 Yugoslavia, photo, 163
$1,000 *Confederate Bond*, 1863, photo, 90
Operation Bernhard, 210
Ordonnances (Canadian *Treasury Notes*), 13

P

Palmstruch, Johan, 12
Panic of 1837, 29
Paper Money, 225, 226

Paper money, 13, 28, 55, 62, 71-2, 91-2, 94, 95, 104-6, 161-2, 168-9
  authentication, 161-2
  characteristics of, 55
  debate over, 28
  defects in, 104-6
  display of, 94
  how to look at, 95
  persistence of, 62
  physical enemies of, 91-2
  replacing coins, 13
  shipping by mail, 168-9
  why collect, 71-2
Paper Money of the United States, 122, 166, 193, 199
Parker, Larry, 176
Peppiatt, Kenneth Oswald, 129
Periodicals, 219-26
Philippine *Victory overprints*, 146
Pick, Albert, *Standard Catalog of World Paper Money*, 127
Pierce, Benjamin, 206
Pinkerton, Allan, 207
Pitt, William (the Younger), 14
Play money, 211
Playing Card Money (Canada), 13
Polo, Marco, 12-3
Ponterio, Richard H., 176
Ponterio & Associates, Inc., 176
Portal, Henry, 14
Prison money, 147
Prisoner-of-war camp notes, 147
Private and *Chartered Bank Notes* (Canada), 13
Professional Currency Dealers Association, 179, 190
Professional Numismatists Guild, 179, 190
Propaganda leaflet, photos, 152
Provincial Issues (Canada), 13

R

"Raised note," photo, 217
Ration book, World War II, photo, 86
Refunding Certificates, 34
Report on the Mode of Preventing the Forgery of Bank Notes, 206
Republic of Hawaii $20 Silver Certificate of Deposit, 1896, photo, 125
Revere, Paul, 113
Ripple effect, 104
R.M. Smythe & Company, Inc., 83, 177
Rojas, Anne-Marie, 210
Roosevelt, Franklin D., 35
Royal Bank of Scotland, 15
Russian *Postage Stamp Currency*, 144

S

Scott J. Winslow Associates, Inc., 83
Scottish bank notes, 15
Scrip, 83, 86
  Mount Pleasant Apothecary Store, 1863, photo, 86
Scripophily: Collecting Bonds and Share Certificates, 83
Second of Exchange draft, 1852, photos, 87, 88
(Second) Bank of the United States, 29
Selling notes, 165-71
  appraisals, 166
  at auction, 167
  by private treaty, 167
  evaluating collection, 166
  preparing for sale, 166
  reasons for, 165
  selecting market, 166
  tactics, 168
  timing a sale, 165-6
  to dealer, 166-7
  to other collectors, 167-8
Shays, Daniel, 26
Shays' Rebellion, 26
Sherman Silver Purchase Act, 33
Shows, 183-7
  etiquette, 183-4
Shull, Hugh, 52, 176-7
Siege notes, 143-4
  Khartoum, 144
  Mafeking, 144
Siege of Lyon notes (France), 16
Silver Certificates, 34
Silver Dollars (U.S.), 33
Small Size Notes, 35-6, 44, 66, 67, 79, 110, 111, 116-7, 120, 151
  "fancy" Serial Numbers, 116
  Federal Reserve Bank Notes, 116
  Federal Reserve Note, Series 1934, photo, 44
  Federal Reserve Notes, 116
  $50 *Federal Reserve Note*, photo, 66
  $5 *Silver Certificate*, Series 1934D, photo, 120
  Gold Certificates, 117
  Legal Tender Notes, 116
  Military Payment Certificates, 117
  National Bank Notes, 116
  $100 *Federal Reserve Note*, photo, 67
  $1000 *Federal Reserve Note*, Series 1934, photo, 44
  Silver Certificates, 116
  $10 *Federal Reserve Note*, photo, 66

Small Size Notes, cont.
  $20 *Federal Reserve Bank Note*, Series 1929, photo, 110
  $20 *Federal Reserve Note*, photo, 111
  $20 *Federal Reserve Note*, Series 1934A, Hawaii overprint, photo, 151
  $20 *Federal Reserve Note*, Series 1985, photo, 111
  $20 *Federal Reserve Note*, Series 1988A, photo, 110
  $20 *Gold Certificate*, Series 1928, photo, 111
  $2 *Federal Reserve Note*, Series 1976, photo, 79
  types, 35-6
    Federal Reserve Bank Notes, 35
    Federal Reserve Notes, 35-6
    Gold Certificates, 35
    Legal Tender Notes, 35
    National Bank Notes, 35
    Silver Certificates, 35
  World War II *Emergency Notes*, 117
Snow, Robert R., 207-8
Societies, 223-5
Society of Paper Money Collectors, Inc., 71, 114, 180, 224-5
South Carolina Confederate Relic Room and Museum, 229
Southern state currency, 49
Southern States Currency, 114
Souvenir Card Collectors Society, 84-5, 225
Souvenir Card Journal, The, 225
Souvenir cards, 84-5
  buying directly from printers, 84
Spanish Civil War Notes, 144
Specialties, see Collecting specialties
"Spider" printing press, photo, 43
Spink & Son, 178-9
Spurious and Expired Banks (Notes) (Canada), 13
Stack's Coin Galleries, 177
Standard Catalog of Depression Scrip of the United States, 83
Standard Catalog of National Bank Notes, 115
Standard Catalog of U.S. Paper Money, 117
Standard Catalog of United States Obsolete Bank Notes, 1782-1866, 114
Standard Catalog of World Paper Money, 153, 154, 166, 193
Stanley Gibbons Currency Ltd., 71
Stock certificates, 82-3, 89
  dealers, 83

Stock certificates, cont.
    1898 California mining, photo, 89
Stockholms Banco, 12
Superior Stamp & Coin Company, Inc.,
    177
Swift, Jonathan, 219

T

Tears, 104
Tell, Jay, 174, 180
    photo, 180
10¢ *Fractional Currency*, Third Issue,
    photo, 100
10¢ *State of North Carolina* fractional
    note, 1863, photo, 40
10 *Centavos* note ("Villa's Bed Sheets"),
    1913 Mexico, photo, 149
$10 *Confederate Note*, 1863, photo, 54
$10 *Confederate Note*, 1864, photo, 54
$10 *Hagerstown Bank* note, photo, 37
$10 *Refunding Certificate*, 1879, photo,
    125
Thian, Raphael P., 230
10 *Gulden* note, 1944 Netherlands,
    photo, 136
10 *Kronen* note, 1915 Austria, photo,
    133
10 *Lirasi* note, Turkey, photo, 188
10 *Pesos* note, *El Banco del Estado de
    Chihuahua*, 1913, photo, 170
10 *Pesos* note, *El Banco Italiano del
    Uruguay*, 1887, photo, 169
30 *Shillings Massachusetts Colonial
    Currency*, photo, 196
$3 Bahamas note, photo, 188
3 *Rubles* note, 1938 Russia, photo, 231
Treasury Notes, 33-4
Treasury Warrant of *State of Texas*,
    photo, 40
Tsai Lun, 11
20 *Cedis* note, 1982 Ghana, photo, 76
$20 *Confederate Note* (counterfeit),
    1861, photo, 53
$20 *Confederate Note*, 1861, photos, 53
$20 *Confederate Note*, 1864, photo, 54
25¢ *Indian Head Bank* note, 1862, photo,
    39

$2 *Educational Note*, photo, 119
$2 note of *Tallahassee Rail Road Com-
    pany*, photo, 38
$2 note of *The West River Bank*, photo,
    37
2 *Pfennig* German *notgeld*, photo, 20
200 *Leva* note, 1951 Bulgaria, photos,
    187

U

U.S. notes, 113-20, 121-6
    popular, 113-20
        Broken Bank Notes, 114
        Colonial and *Continental Cur-
            rency*, 113-4
        Confederate and *Southern States
            Currency*, 114
        Fractional Currency, 114
        Large Size Notes, 114-6
        Small Size Notes, 116-7
    rare, 121-6
        Colonial and *Continental Cur-
            rency*, 122
        Fractional Currency, 123
        Large Size Notes, 122
        Military Payment Certificates,
            123
        19th century Hawaiian bank notes,
            123
        Obsolete Notes, 122
        old auction realizations, 121-2
        Small Size Currency, 123
    types of rarity, 122
U.S. paper money, 23-44, 55-69
    bank note paper, 58
    bank note printing inks, 58
    Bills of Credit, 24
    buying uncut sheets of, 62
    Colonial Currency, 23-5
    engraving plate, photos, 64
    essays, 59
    examining for defects, photo, 65
    history of, 23-44
    how serial numbers determined, 57
    life expectancy, 59
    making modern, 55-69

U.S. paper money, cont.
    mutilated/damaged, photos, 67, 68,
        69
    new notes, photos, 65, 66
    obsolete design elements, 56-7
    overprinting new notes, photo, 65
    parts of printed design, 55-6
    portraits and back designs of current,
        chart, 63
    printing press, photos, 64
    proofs, 59
    redemption of mutilated, 59-60
    redemption of worn-out notes, 59
    security features, illustrations, 63
    stages in bank note production, 57-9
    Star notes, 58
    statistics, 59-60
    worn-out currency processing and
        destruction, 61
U.S. Secret Service, 207
U.S. Treasury building, illustration, 69
U.S. Treasury Seal, 26
U.S. World War II Emergency Notes,
    146
Upham, Samuel C., 49, 207

V

Villa, Francisco, 144
"Villa's Bed Sheets," 144

W

War propaganda notes, 148
Washington, George, 25
Watermelon Note, photo, 125
Watson, John F., *Annals of Philadel-
    phia*, 28
Wells Fargo History Museum, 227
Wertschein, photos, 151
Weymouth National, 177
Wildcat Banks, 30
Willis, H. Parker, 34
Wilson, Woodrow, 34
World War I French emergency money,
    photo, 150
World War II *Occupation Notes*, 145-6